1986

# How to Teach Reading Successfully

# How to Teach Reading Successfully

**John D. McNeil**
University of California, Los Angeles

**Lisbeth Donant**
Atascadero Unified School District, California

**Marvin C. Alkin**
University of California, Los Angeles

**Little, Brown and Company**

Boston
Toronto

Library of Congress Catalog Card No. 79-88441

First Printing

Published simultaneously in Canada
by Little, Brown & Company (Canada) Limited

Printed in the United States of America

# Preface

*How to Teach Reading Successfully* is for elementary school teachers and for those aspiring to be teachers. Throughout, the focus is on helping the teacher acquire methods by which children can learn useful strategies in the perception and understanding of written materials. Theory and research findings have been incorporated in the discussion as they bear on reading instruction.

The text is comprehensive and eclectic. It features topics that both novices and teachers of teachers expect from a methods book. The chapters dealing with motives for reading, diagnosis, meeting special needs, and teaching reading in a multicultural context introduce content previously unavailable in textbooks for the teaching of reading.

The scope of the content is unusual in that it systematically offers methods appropriate for a range of approaches to the teaching of reading — basal, technological (competency-based management systems), language experience, and individualized. In addition, there is extensive description and explanation of the teaching of reading at four levels — readiness, beginning, middle, and upper. Hence, those using the book can acquire more understanding of ways to teach reading to different age groups than is allowed in texts devoted primarily to a given level.

A unique feature of this book is the inclusion of *self-instructional exercises* at the end of each chapter. These exercises aid in developing teaching competency rather than just relating information about some aspect of reading. The exercises both reinforce the content of the chapters and introduce additional methods for successful teaching.

An instructor's manual has been prepared to provide suggestions and activities for teaching with this book, questions for discussion and tests, and additional source references.

Writing this book was a cooperative venture. Each author contributed suggestions to the others. Responsibility for the chapters, however, has been placed: Marvin C. Alkin for Chapters 8 and 11; Lisbeth Donant for Chapters 3, 7, and 9; and John D. McNeil for Chapters 1, 2, 4, 5, 6, and 10.

Appreciation is extended to reviewers of the manuscript: Ruth N. Hartley, California State University, Sacramento; and Hildegard Kuse, University of Wisconsin, Stevens Point. Special thanks is expressed to Professor Dorcas Cavett of the University of Nebraska at Lincoln, who made many valuable suggestions and shared much of her own experience in the teaching of reading. Through the arduous process of converting our manuscript into a book, we were pleased to have the extraordinary assistance of Elizabeth Schaaf, our book editor. We are indebted also to the editor who helped in planning, writing, and publishing the book — Mylan L. Jaixen.

J.D.M.
L.D.
M.C.A.

# Contents

# How to Teach Reading Successfully

# 1

# The Importance of Reading

Teachers give many reasons for teaching reading. Some want children to experience the joy of reading as entertainment; others want pupils to be better informed or have a deeper understanding of the human experience. Leaders in totalitarian societies believe the teaching of reading will help them exercise control. In Revolutionary Cuba, for example, the literacy campaign not only enabled nearly a million former illiterates to read posters, poems, and songs, it achieved the political goal of uniting farmers, workers, and students and built close ties among generational groups and between urban and rural populations.[1] Cynics in our own society have tied the teaching of reading to a desire to create avaricious consumers. (Conspicuous consumption is a characteristic of our culture. Even children's primers have illustrations that feature supermarkets, toy stores, and pet shops and show children stuffing themselves with cones, hot dogs, and other goodies.) Neil Postman, in fact, has said that a minimal reading competence is necessary for people to develop a keen interest in the many products that must be sold. He does not believe the basic purposes of reading instruction are to open the pupils' minds to the wonders and riches of the written word, to give them access to great literature, to permit them to function as informed citizens, or to help them experience the sheer pleasure of reading. Instead, Postman holds that the teaching of reading

---

[1] Jonathan Kozol, *Children of the Revolution: A Yankee Teacher in the Cuban Schools* (New York: Delacorte Press, 1978).

is a sinister political scheme to develop the minimal reading skills people need to follow the instructions of those who govern and to transmit the myths and superstitions of society. By *myths* he means views slanted to show only the nobleness of our history, the justice of our laws, and the strengths of our institutions.[2] Although we do not fully agree with Postman's condemnation of the teaching of reading as a sinister activity, we think he is right in having us ask, "What is reading good for?" and "What are our motives in promoting it?" *before* we consider the techniques of teaching reading.

Without a sense of purpose, teaching is mindless. Thus it is important for teachers to clarify their reasons for teaching reading. If they can see how their teaching of reading serves encompassing and noble purposes and that the acquisition of reading skills is not an isolated and ultimate end in itself, they will make reading instruction worthy of their best efforts. Also, in understanding the goals of reading, teachers are better able to order experiences in the classroom to contribute to these ends.

This chapter will help you examine your reasons for teaching reading by encouraging introspection of your own experiences with reading, by reviewing motives for reading, and by showing how particular national attitudes have influenced the teaching of reading at given times in the United States. Finally, through the self-confirming exercises at the end of the chapter, you will have the opportunity to acquire the competency to relate specific instructional activities in teaching reading to desired objectives and to the larger purposes to which the activities and objectives point.

## Why Read?

Most of us underestimate the very large part reading plays in our lives. Much of our reading we take for granted: reading information on the side of a cereal package; glancing at the newspaper; reading letters or postcards; reading TV guides, timetables, advertisements, menus, street names, and a special magazine. To tease out your arguments for teaching reading, you might ask, "What would my life be like if I couldn't read?" This may remind you of the instrumental uses of reading like helping you solve problems. Has reading also helped you in

---

[2] Neil Postman, "The Politics of Reading," *The First R: Readings on Teaching Reading,* ed. Sam Sebesta and Carl Wallen (Chicago: Science Research Associates, 1972), pp. 28–39.

dealing with vocational needs? With perplexities about health? With relating to others? With orienting yourself to the universe? Has it influenced you to behave in a certain way? What authors and writings have had a significant impact on your life? Has reading provided intellectual inspiration for you or has it caused you to participate vicariously in the experiences of the characters you read about?

A report of how adults perceive reading in their lives appears in a study by Beverly Miller and Frances Pollard: *What Reading Does for People.* Two findings from this study support beliefs about the need for directed teaching of reading in the early years. Those adults who value reading had the reading habit established in early childhood and their initial stimulus to reading came through the efforts of another person rather than as a self-initiated activity.[3]

### Your Role as a Reader

Shirley Fehl has studied the roles persons assume when they are reading and has identified several categories of readers: *observers*, those who externally evaluate what they read; *participators*, those who affiliate or identify with what they read; *synthesizers*, those who create new images of self on the basis of the encouragement and ideas found in reading; and *decision makers*, those whose reading has influenced them to make particular choices of action.[4]

It is doubtful that you have been only an observer or participator while reading, or that you have adopted only one of the four basic roles. Instead you probably have reacted by assuming more than one of these roles depending on the book. For instance, we believe many readers responded as decision makers to *Silent Spring* but as participators to *Roots.* Also whatever responses you now make to what you read may result in part from the way you were taught. Perhaps your teacher asked questions that led you to identify with certain characters and situations, to look at yourself from another's point of view, to weigh consequences of courses of action, or to link decisions and actions. Two important reasons for examining adult experiences with reading are to show the variety of uses to which reading can be put and to lay the groundwork for the argument that methods of teaching affect reading roles in adult life.

---

[3] Frances M. Pollard and Beverly Miller, *What Reading Does for People* (Charleston, Ill.: Eastern Illinois University, 1977).

[4] Shirley L. Fehl, "When Does Reading Make a Difference?" *Reading Between and Beyond the Lines,* Claremont Reading Conference, 37th Yearbook (Claremont, Calif.: Claremont Graduate School, 1973), pp. 93–103.

### Learners' Motives for Reading

No discussion of the importance of reading is complete without considering the personal needs of learners that can be satisfied through reading. Too often teachers accept the teaching of reading solely on the assumption that learning to read is a most important element in learning how to learn, and that without this instruction, pupils are unlikely to fulfill their potentials in school and in society at large. We believe that teachers will be more successful in teaching reading if they attend to the learners' own motives for reading as well as to the reading demands imposed by school and society.

Learners are motivated to read by a variety of needs and desires. Their *motives*, then, are the expected satisfactions that cause them to act — in this case to read. The desire to feel good about oneself and the need for friendship are examples of motives. A prestige motive for reading is seen in pupils' desires to put themselves in the place of those characters in books who do things that win admiration. Children's self-esteem may increase as they envision themselves as the real or unreal heroes of their reading. Other expressions of the prestige motive are seen when pupils seek prestige or anticipate praise because they have read a recommended book.

The need to understand is another motive for reading. The sheer satisfaction of understanding can be rewarding. Using reading to answer one's questions about mechanics, animal life, and human nature is a case in point. The need to understand is often related to a fundamental desire to control. Many specific motives, in fact, are built upon the desire to control one's environment. Hence pupils sometimes want to understand people in order to control them.

About forty years ago, Douglas Waples and others labeled a group of motives *respite motivation*. Respite motives imply a search for writing that will diminish anxiety or boredom by intensifying aesthetic experiences, supplying vicarious adventures, or merely diverting the reader's attention from personal worry. Unlike other motives, the effect of respite reading tends to evaporate as soon as one's eye leaves the page and is almost never followed by overt behavior.[5]

The need for security constitutes another motive for reading. To read pseudoscientific articles on psychology and health, for example, may be seen as stemming from concern about mental and physical security. Pupils with personal problems, such as lack of parental affection, an impending divorce, and overprotective parents, sometimes

---

[5] Douglas Waples et al., *What Reading Does to People* (Chicago: University of Chicago Press, 1940).

find it helpful to read materials that deal with these problems.[6] Teachers who learn about pupils' attitudes toward themselves, parents, and friends often are able to put these pupils in touch with materials that may help satisfy their need for security. Books can be helpful in moments of sadness and tension. As teachers learn what pupils cherish in their attitudes toward themselves and others, they are able to tell what pupils will find in a writing and how they are likely to respond to it.

The following are some of the most important reasons why pupils learn to read. The ordering of items does not imply priority and there is some overlap.

1. To be accepted by parents, teachers, peers, community, employers, and religious and other groups

2. To help others through reading, for example, reading to the blind

3. To participate more fully in the religious experience and to seek spiritual understanding and inspiration through reading

4. To solve problems related to obtaining food, shelter, and other basic needs

5. To engage in intellectual study, hobbies, and other interests

6. To attain a satisfying economic level by holding a job that requires particular reading skills and to improve one's performance through reading

7. To escape psychologically through fairy tales, plays, short stories, and the like

8. To find pleasure through the written word, including an appreciation of fine writing, and to seek knowledge for the pleasure of knowing

9. To expand one's views and satisfy one's curiosity through reading

10. To improve oneself by finding specific information, new opportunities, and new studies in reading

11. To protect one's political and economic interests by understanding through reading the forces that are affecting one's life

---

[6] The basic idea that literature has therapeutic properties is an old one. Guidance in the solution of personal problems through directed reading is termed *bibliotherapy*. Such guidance is practiced by many librarians, educators, psychologists, social workers, and others. A fine collection of articles on bibliotherapy appears in Rhea Joyce Rubin's *Bibliotherapy Source Book* (Phoenix, Ariz.: Oryx Press, 1978).

Now that you have seen some of the reasons students have for learning to read, let us examine the possible reasons that you, as teachers, might give as purposes for teaching reading.

# The Contrast between Purposes and Activities

Some teachers do not like to make choices regarding the uses of reading, especially when doing so involves imposing their values upon children. These teachers say, "I'll teach the basic skills of reading — how to decode words and how to comprehend the printed text; but I'll leave the application of these skills to the learner." In short, these teachers make the teaching of reading skills their end purpose rather than an enabling task.

We prefer that teachers consciously exercise choices at three levels: the goal level, the instructional objective or skill level, and the activity level. Although reading is sometimes regarded as a purely mechanical activity, it is a mistake to think that having learned the mechanics of reading, one can read anything. The goal of reading job-related technical materials, for example, calls for different instructional skills and activities than does the goal of reading novels. Skills such as interpreting schematics and literally following detailed instructions instead of merely recalling information are necessary for the reader of job-related technical materials. However, skills for interpreting the theme and for forming mental pictures from the descriptions of the author are indispensable for the reader of novels.

### Goal Statements

A reading goal is one level of purpose for the guidance of educational activity. Statements of goals imply both values and commitment of instruction for their attainment. Teachers are stating reading goals when they say that reading should be taught in the interests of improving oneself, obtaining a job, or enjoying a good story. Goals are vague statements in that they convey different ideas among individuals. But they are not meaningless. It would be difficult, for example, to mistake the instructional implications of a goal calling for critical reading for those of a goal calling for fluent oral reading.

### Objective or Skill Statements

Another level of choice is the instructional objective or skill level. An instructional objective is a statement of what pupils are supposed to know, be able to do, prefer, or believe as a result of instruction. Hence, a teacher who has critical reading as a goal would probably have a number of specific objectives in mind for pupils, such as the ability to recognize propaganda techniques. For example, given printed advertisements, the learner can label each instance of a propaganda technique or will acquire the habit of asking, "Why is this book or selection made available to me? Who wrote it? What action is expected of me?" Instructional objectives specify what it is intended that the pupil can do, or what skill will be acquired as a result of a given activity, lesson, or program of instruction. The behavior sought must be sufficiently explicit for it to be observed or to be readily elicited by means of a testing instrument. In Chapters 4, 5, and 6 of this book, you can examine the most commonly used instructional objectives (skills) in the initial teaching of reading. In these chapters, the fundamental skills of learning to read are defined and stated as objectives, not goals.

### Activities

Instructional activity is a third level of choices. Activities or learning opportunities include the lessons, reading selections, games, learning centers, discussions, cassettes, films — all of the things and events that children engage in when learning to read. An objective might call for children to recognize propaganda techniques. The teacher, then, could arrange an activity by which pupils (1) learn that the *bandwagon technique* is characterized by an implication that everyone is doing a particular thing so the reader should do the same and (2) are given an opportunity to identify instances of the technique in advertisements or narratives.

# Different Emphases in Reading Goals

You can see the relation of goals to activities by noting how content and learning opportunities vary with changes in goals. In the following paragraphs, note the close association between goals and activities popular at different times and with learners at different levels of maturity.

## Goals for Teaching Reading in the Past

In Nila Banton Smith's classic work treating the teaching of reading in America from 1607 to 1934, she identified five goals, each of which characterized a period of reading instruction.[7] The first goal, which was prevalent during the period 1607–1776, was religious. Children were expected to read the word of God directly and draw their own conclusions so they would not be dependent on others for biblical information. The chief reading textbook of the time was the primer, which gave pupils the opportunity to learn to read letters, syllables, the Lord's Prayer, the Ten Commandments, and other religious selections. Once graduated from the primer, the children read the Bible, responding to questions posed by the teacher and memorizing verses.

A nationalistic goal dominated the teaching of reading in the new nation from 1776 to 1840. Reading was taught to build national strength and unity. Thus teachers emphasized the reading of works written by American rather than English authors. Most of these works were historical material intended to instill patriotism and to develop character. They also included governmental information, such as a federal catechism explaining the Constitution of the United States. Expressive oral reading and elocutionary (oratorical) delivery of patriotic speeches were emphasized on the grounds that such skills would aid participation in the new democratic society. Rules and exercises in correct pronunciation and enunciation were featured in the reading program as a means to overcome the diversity of dialects and to promote American unity.

To teach reading as a means of obtaining information was a third goal. This goal prevailed during the period 1840–1888. The child read much informational and expository material (material that explains), including pieces drawn from science, history, philosophy, economics, and politics. Every beginner read realistic materials, such as stories of nature. Although oral reading continued to be stressed, the goals of acquiring knowledge and improving intellectual powers through reading were added to it. Of course, this emphasis upon enlightenment can be considered an extension of nationalism — from patriotic sentiment to the ideal of an intelligent citizenry.

To awaken a permanent interest in literary material was an overriding goal for teaching reading in the 1880s and until about 1918. Instead of merely teaching the child to read, teachers were advised to cultivate the child's taste for the pure, the elevating, and the instructive. Indeed some worried at the time that learning to read might be dangerous. They feared that reading might be a key to the base and ignoble and that one might read to injury rather than to profit. Therefore, the teacher was to teach the child *what* to read as well as *how*. It

---

[7] Nila Banton Smith, *American Reading Instruction* (New York: Silver, Burdett, 1934).

was the teacher's duty to help the pupils discriminate between good literature and bad. The very young child read fables and fairy tales. Myths that appealed to the child's imagination were given to the pupils who were a little older, and the upper grade pupils read historical and legendary lore in the form of tales and poems.

The value of utility rather than beauty had priority in the period 1918–1925. Teachers justified reading as a utilitarian asset and related it more to the events of daily living than to literature. They gave more opportunities for silent reading than for oral reading. Comprehension was stressed more than literary appreciation. The study of how adults used reading was one basis for deciding what to teach children. As a consequence, pupils were taught to read current events, to follow instructions, and to read for pleasure during leisure hours. The use of reading in other school activities was another basis for determining what to teach. As a result, reading lessons began to call for finding answers to questions, drawing conclusions, and remembering what was read.

By 1934 there were multiple goals for teaching reading. Teachers taught reading to extend the pupils' experiences and interests. They viewed reading as a valuable way for the child to use leisure time in a wholesome manner. They also taught reading to stimulate the thought of the child, particularly with respect to what was going on in the world. Teachers taught the "mechanics of reading"—skills that would generalize to many reading situations. Reading instruction in the primary grades offered more fictional than factual selections, and realistic narratives and informational pieces were more common in the upper grades.

## Goals for Teaching Reading Today

Currently there are two emphases in the teaching of reading. One of these focuses on the development of the intellectual skills involved in reading. Word recognition skills and comprehension skills, such as the ability to identify a statement in a selection that represents the central idea, are taught without specifically considering the purpose for which these skills ultimately will be used. The other emphasis focuses on the specific situation in which the pupil is to apply reading skills: reading signs, labels, want ads, yellow pages, dictionaries, and newspapers. The latter emphasis reflects a concern about pupils who are *functionally illiterate*, those who lack the reading competencies necessary to function successfully in contemporary society.

Legislators in most states are mandating testing in reading either to strengthen high school graduation requirements or to promote what they consider the "real-world reading needs" of graduates and adults. Jeanne S. Chall's survey of this competency testing found two types of tests being used to measure minimal competency in reading: (1) tests that measure a child's ability to read more difficult material at increasingly demanding levels of comprehension and (2) "real-life" tests designed to measure reading tasks thought to be essential for adult participation in society.[8] This emphasis upon minimal competency testing and its implied goals of functional literacy comes from the pressure of parents and economic interests. Complaints about job applicants who cannot read well enough to fill out applications or meet the reading requirements of entry-level positions have generated this political response.

Business interests view reading as a tool for the economic development of the nation. For example, the prestigious Committee for Economic Development has observed that the private sector has to bear the costs of supplementary training or suffer the effects of a less productive work force. The problem, however, of deciding what it is one should be able to read as an adult has not been resolved. Some jobs, such as that of Army cook, demand reading at the sixth- to seventh-grade level; others require reading of instructional manuals written at least at the twelfth-grade level.

Critics charge that our society is using reading as a screening process, as a way to maintain the relative positions of people by placing them according to their reading ability.[9] These critics believe the stress upon learning to read is having bad consequences. They say, for instance, that in our literary-oriented society, a child's emotional stability and security are dependent upon whether the parents are proud of the child's reading ability or ashamed that he or she is having difficulty in reading. Bad self-concepts, conformity, isolation from live interaction with people, and an unjustified belief that something printed must be true are the negative implications of overstressing learning to read. These critics do not argue for eliminating the teaching of reading nor do they want to give up the positive influences that reading has had. They do, however, ask for the removal of exaggerated pressures of literacy by encouraging other forms of communication and other ways of learning, such as long-playing records, films, television, videotapes, and radio, drama, photographic, and stereophonic presentations. Obviously teachers and parents should not convey to children that their worth and acceptance rest upon the ability to read. Further, reading,

---

[8] Jeanne S. Chall, "Minimum Competency in Reading: An Informal Survey of the States," *Phi Delta Kappan* 60, no. 5 (January 1979): 351–353.

[9] James M. Gibson and James C. Hall, Jr., *Damn Reading!* (New York: Vantage Press, 1969).

like other good things, must be placed within a larger frame of values. Our view is that until the values of reading are perceived as important by the learner — until children are willing to see reading as a tool for furthering their own goals — reading will not be the powerful instrument for personal and social fulfillment that it can be. This is one reason we want teachers to have conscious purposes for teaching reading and to be able to demonstrate its values.

## How Reading Purposes Vary with Maturity

Important purposes are not achieved all at once. Learning to use reading for self-improvement and fulfillment, for solving problems and intellectual study, for gaining economic and political benefits, is a lifelong task. As Goethe said on his eightieth birthday: "The dear people do not know how long it takes to learn to read. I have been at it all my life and I cannot say I have reached the goal." Whatever your goals in teaching reading, your specific objectives must be within the range of possibility for the pupils — appropriate to their maturity, attainment, predispositions, and the like.

Edgar Dale illustrates how the teaching of reading differs with the maturity of children. He makes a distinction between the skill of reading what the book "says" and the art of reading that enables us to describe what the article, pamphlet, or book meant to the author and what it means to us now. Teachers give much of their time helping beginners *to read the lines.* This activity is at the simple level — word recognition and decoding — of reproducing what is said in printed words, phrases, and passages and their relation to each other. As soon as children are able to read the lines, the teacher must teach them *to read between the lines.* This aspect of reading calls for discovering what the author meant to say — whether the author has written ironically or sarcastically — and learning to understand metaphors. A third phase of reading is *to read beyond the lines.* In this phase, children learn to draw inferences from what they read and to apply what they have learned. Each learner must learn to ask after reading, "What does this mean to me?" and "How can I make use of it?" [10]

Although these three aspects of reading can occur in the beginning as well as in the most advanced classroom, emphasis upon a given aspect is determined by "where the reader is." The teacher must, therefore, have sufficient information about particular pupils to know what desired objectives are possible for them. An example of the kind

---

[10] Edgar Dale, "The Art of Reading," *The News Letter* 32, no. 3 (December 1966): 1–4.

of data that teachers collect from their pupils for use in making inferences about what objectives to teach appears in Jeanne Fryer's list of
facts obtained from certain learners about their interest in reading and
in the reading instruction they have received. The list also illustrates
how the sequential development of objectives contributes to the important goal of reading enjoyment.

> Stage 1 — four to five year olds — nonreaders. They tell stories but find it
> hard to stick to a story line. They enjoy playing with language but lack ex-
> pectancy of what reading is going to be like.
>
> Stage 2 — five to six year olds. They can recognize many words, know the
> alphabet, and like to read things they know over and over again. They like
> word rhymes and word sound games. They are aware of the nature of alpha-
> betic symbols and are beginning to associate patterns of letters with the
> sounds of speech.
>
> Stage 3 — seven to eight year olds. They enjoy reading new and "hard"
> things and like stories about people similar to themselves. They like to read
> each other's stories and to make up new endings to stories. They are aware
> that they are using a letter-sound approach in recognizing words and specu-
> late on rules governing spelling.[11]

Teachers emphasize certain purposes at particular times. Before
the fourth grade, teachers tend to think of learning to read as acquiring
the reading acquisition skills of word recognition and comprehension.
Reading is chiefly for the purpose of getting the simple sense of what
the writer says. After this grade, teachers view learning to read as
gaining information or learning from the text. They present fewer
activities for learning to read and more activities aimed at teaching
children how to read in order to learn. Only after a reader is a mature
person is he or she likely to be a mature reader.

# Summary

Superior teaching of reading requires having valid purposes as well as
effective teaching methods. What is taught in the name of reading
depends on your view of how it is to be used and your reason for
promoting it. We have argued for comprehensive purposes rather than
narrow ones stemming chiefly from the demands of contemporary
society and from the recognition that reading is a basic tool in school

---

[11] Jeanne Fryer, "No, I Can't Read: What Children Think About Reading," Claremont Reading Conference, 40th Yearbook (Claremont, Calif.: Claremont Graduate
School, 1976).

learning. The pupil's own motives for learning to read constitute a source to use in determining what should be taught. The learner's motives imply the kind of reading instruction that can be offered to satisfy them.

For instructional activities in reading to be useful and show relatedness, it is important for the teacher to know the objectives to be reached through the activities and the broad goals that provide a sense of the larger values that should guide instructional practices. In the final analysis, the teacher who recognizes how a method or reading activity is related to the skills of learning to read and to the goals of self-actualization, intellectual development, or other value is a better teacher — that is, more rational — than one who engages in instructional activity without a sense of its place in a bigger scheme. Not long ago a young teacher was observed using a large paper cutter. When asked what she was doing, she replied, "I can give you three answers. One, I'm cutting paper to make word cards. Two, I'm teaching pupils how to read. Three, I'm making citizens."

# Self-instructional Exercises

One distinguishing feature of a good teacher of reading is the ability to relate the direct activities of a single day to the more important values to which the activity leads. A case in point is the kindergarten teacher who has children engage in an activity involving categorization: "I'm thinking of a word. The word is *chair*. Can you think of another word?" "I'm thinking of two words — *brown* and *blue*. Can you think of another word?" A good teacher justifies this activity not only on the grounds that it is useful in teaching the concepts of furniture and color but on the basis that it is an enabling activity that provides an initial understanding of the term *word*, a prerequisite to subsequent progress in reading. Perhaps, too, the teacher is conscious that the activity may initiate a lifelong intellectual adventure in pursuit of the concept *word*.

In the first exercise, you will learn to distinguish reading activities from instructional objectives and goals for reading. In subsequent exercises, you will learn to relate activities to objectives and to match objectives with goals.

### Exercise 1. Differentiating Goals, Objectives, and Activities

**Goals**  Goal statements are more encompassing than either objectives or activities. A goal statement expresses a value. Critical reading, comprehension, and appreciation of literature are examples of goals that may give general direction to the teacher but are not explicit enough to provide for detailed planning.

**Objectives**    Instructional objectives are specific in that they indicate what a learner will be able to do *after* instruction. Usually they consist of a statement indicating a situation or stimulus (paragraph, type of textbook, newspaper) and the kind of overt *response* (underlining, naming, pronouncing, stating, identifying) to it that the learner should make to show achievement. The following are examples of instructional objectives:

Given words containing silent letters (for example, *knife, gnat*), the child will identify the silent letters.

Given paragraphs, the child will underline the topic sentence in each paragraph.

Given printed directions on worksheets, the child can follow them.

**Activities**    Activities describe what a learner might undergo to achieve an instructional objective. For example, the process of showing a child a number of words where *b* appears after *m* as in *bomb, comb, lamb,* and *thumb*; pronouncing them; and then asking the child to pronounce *limb* and *numb* is an instructional activity.

Put an *A* by each activity; put an *O* by each instructional objective; and put a *G* by each goal statement.

1. _____ The pupil will develop study skills in reading.
2. _____ Given a paragraph written in the passive voice, the pupil will be able to restate the sentence in the active voice.
3. _____ The child has an opportunity to hear literature interpreted through music.
4. _____ The child will read for recreation and personal fulfillment.
5. _____ Given books from which to choose, the child selects those books that are in keeping with present reading ability.
6. _____ The learner will be exposed to a range of literature, such as biography, fantasy, and mythology.

**ANSWERS TO EXERCISE 1**

You should have put an *A* by statements 3 and 6. These statements indicate activities or opportunities without specifying what the child will be able to do as a consequence of the activity.

You should have put an *O* by statements 2 and 5 because they are instructional objectives indicating observable behavior by which one can recognize the pupil's achievements.

Statements 1 and 4 are goals, suggesting important but nonspecified or measurable outcomes.

## Exercise 2. Relating Activities to Objectives and Goals

Activities frequently give pupils the opportunity to practice the same behavior called for in the objective. Instructional objectives, however, seldom tap the rich dimensions of thought and practice implied by a goal. The most we expect from an objective is that its attainment will advance the learner in a direction consistent with the goal.

Read each activity and check the objective with which it is probably associated.

1. Comparing Paul Bunyan stories with stories about today's loggers

   a. _____ Can determine whether a given conclusion is correct when given two or more premises

   b. _____ Can determine sequence of events in stories

   c. _____ Can distinguish fantasy from fact

2. Reading a story and then drawing a picture about it

   a. _____ Can make inferences about what is read

   b. _____ Can use imagery as a memory device for passages read

   c. _____ Can follow instruction

3. Reading a story and then telling it in the same order to others

   a. _____ Can identify metaphors, irony, and other devices

   b. _____ Can read aloud at a suitable pace

   c. _____ Can keep track of sequence

4. Reading a story and then discussing why the main characters did the things they did

   a. _____ Can make inferences about what is read

   b. _____ Can recall events, main ideas, and details from reading

   c. _____ Can verify the accuracy of printed material

**ANSWERS TO EXERCISE 2**

The answers are: 1c, because Paul Bunyan stories are fantasy; 2b, because drawing a picture after reading is creating an image and images are excellent for helping both retention and comprehension; 3c, because telling a story in the correct order of events is an exercise in sequence; and 4a, because attributing motives to actions involves the making of inferences.

## Exercise 3. Matching Activities and Objectives to Goals

Check the goal best served by the activity or instructional objective.

1. The children are considering statements by several authors judging whether some statements are more beautiful than others, some truer than others.

   a. _____ Obtaining information
   b. _____ Elevating literary tastes
   c. _____ Diminishing anxiety

2. The teacher encourages a discussion of humor-producing elements in literature. The humorous use of words and play on words are brought out. The children decide to make a chart listing books to laugh with.

   a. _____ Extending interests
   b. _____ Gaining inspiration
   c. _____ Resolving personal perplexities

3. The children are allowed to select their own reading materials. Some read about brave soldiers and other heroes and vicariously live the lives of their heroes although they themselves show a cowardly spirit in physical activities.

   a. _____ Aiding in making a decision
   b. _____ Identifying with what one reads
   c. _____ Elevating literary tastes

4. The teacher has students read a depressing article about a social problem in their community. As a result, the pupils decide to take some action regarding the problem.

   a. _____ Reading lines
   b. _____ Reading between the lines
   c. _____ Reading beyond the lines

5. Given the words *cat, mate, flap, bake, ran,* and *rain,* the child will be able to identify those words that have a long *a* sound.

    a. _____ Gaining information from the text

    b. _____ Acquiring the decoding tools of reading

    c. _____ Using reading in daily living

6. Illustrations for the textbooks show materialistic scenes from daily life — a visit to the supermarket, children stuffing themselves with ice cream, and getting new toys.

    a. _____ Encouraging the desire to consume

    b. _____ Screening students on the basis of ability

    c. _____ Building loyalty to the nation

### ANSWERS TO EXERCISE 3

1b. The activity described should lead to a better understanding of standards with which to judge reading material.

2a. Humor is often the key to encouraging children to try new materials. Discussion of humorous elements in literature is likely to stimulate interest in books.

3b. The behavior described suggests that some children are seeking prestige or a feeling of importance through the books they read.

4c. Reading beyond the lines means doing something about what one reads — a neglected aspect of reading in many classrooms.

5b. Learning letter-sound correspondence is related to acquiring the skills of reading.

6a. Content analysis of school textbooks often reveals particular cultural values, such as consumption, that are either deliberately or unintentionally being reinforced through the teaching of reading.

# Selected Readings

Bormuth, John K. "Value and Volume of Literacy," *Visible Language* 2 (Spring 1978): 119–162.

    Bormuth collects evidence that our nation's population has reached a high and increasing level of literacy, that literacy has been worth far more than it has cost to produce it, that it is one of our nation's most important economic activities, and that personal and social investment in literacy has been growing rapidly.

Some of the evidence that he marshals in support of these hypotheses includes estimates of the amount of time people spend reading, measures of the quantity of literacy materials produced and distributed, and measures of the amount of instruction people receive in literacy skills. He finds, for example, that 95 percent of the people say they can read something; that the amount of money employers pay for people to read is greater than the money spent in teaching literacy skills; and that not only individuals but society as a whole is increasing investments in literacy.

Burke, Sandra, and Duffy, Gerald G. "Do Teacher Conceptions of Reading Influence Instructional Practice?" East Lansing, Mich.: Michigan State University, Institute for Research on Teaching, College of Education, April 1979.

This paper reports upon an on-going study of teacher conceptions of reading. Data regarding teachers' conceptions were collected, followed by observations of the teachers' classroom practices. Although most teachers have multiple conceptions of reading, their views tend to fall within either a *content-centered* orientation, such as basal text and linear skills, or a *pupil-centered* orientation that encompasses natural language, interest, integrated curriculum, and self-selection of trade books.

Some teachers possess more complex conceptions than others and these conceptions appear to be related to the grade level taught and the ability level of pupils. For example, pupil-centered teachers indicate that their conceptions would change if pupils were less able.

The instructional practices of teachers reflect their stated conceptions. However, other nonreading factors also influence and frequently dominate instructional practices. To date, the data do not support the basic hypothesis that effective reading teachers are necessarily those who analyze the instructional situation in terms of a reading conception. Identical conceptions are seen to be employed in qualitatively different ways.

Guthrie, John T. "Research Views: Why People (Say They) Read," *Reading Teacher* 32, no. 6 (March 1979): 752–755.

The author reviews both a recent study about reading activities of adults in the United States and an older study of the reasons people gave for reading. The most frequent reasons given have stayed the same for more than thirty-five years: general knowledge, pleasure, and recreation.

Guthrie also points out that reading often has multiple reasons, that reasons may change as a result of reading, that personal circumstances affect reasons, and that in an interview people may not tell a stranger their real reasons for reading.

Resnick, Daniel P., and Resnick, Lauren B. "The Nature of Literacy: An Historical Exploration," *Harvard Educational Review* 47, no. 3 (August 1977): 370–385.

The Resnicks address the issue of the "back to basics" movement in education as an answer to low levels of literacy and widespread reading difficulties.

Their historical study reveals the reading goals that have dominated at different periods and suggests that older methods of teaching reading were not designed for the literacy standards sought today nor to insure successful literacy for everyone.

The authors show how reading instruction has been aimed at attaining either a low level of literacy for a large number of people or high level for an elite. The expectations of high levels of literacy for an entire population is a recent development.

# 2

# Approaches to the Teaching of Reading

When we speak of approaches to reading, we are talking about content and method as found in instructional materials. Four basic approaches to the teaching of reading are the *basal reading approach*, which is the most common practice involving the use of textbooks; the *technological approach*, which is seen in skill management reading systems and programmed instruction; the *language experience approach*, whereby pupils themselves participate in the creation or writing of their own materials; and the *individualized reading approach*, in which children select their own reading material.

You should compare and contrast these four approaches for several reasons. Ideally, you should be able to combine the best features from all, capitalizing upon the systematic quality of some approaches, the motivational aspects of others, and the richness of content in still others. Realistically, you need to see how one approach might be more useful than another in the light of a given child's preferred mode of learning. Also you should recognize the special demands each approach makes upon the teacher, thus helping you to anticipate your own role as a teacher of reading. You might find, for example, that the technological approach is the easiest for you to carry out or that the language experience approach seems more appropriate for certain pupils.

Understanding the different approaches will also be of value to you as a student of the teaching of reading. It will be much easier for you to make sense out of the tasks of lesson planning, classroom management, evaluation, sequencing of instruction, and the like once you know that each approach offers a different way of handling these tasks.

# Basal Reading Approach

Basal reading instruction involves teaching the child a number of reading skills that are common to many reading situations and to purposes such as reading for enjoyment, information, and guidance. The basal reading approach stresses continuity (reiteration and review of what has been taught previously) and sequence (increasing breadth and depth of what has been taught) in the teaching of reading skills. Vocabulary and spelling patterns are introduced in a systematic fashion. That is, words and elements of words are controlled and presented according to an assumption about the number of words that can be learned at a given time and the number of repetitions that are necessary. Comprehension, dictionary, and study skills are similarly developed sequentially throughout a K–8 basal reading series. (A list of resources, including publishers of basal readers, is given in the appendix.)

## Materials and Content

A basal reading series consists of a number of textbooks called basal readers and other materials arranged for sequential use. Although there are some differences in the scope (range) and the placement of content and in the ordering of skills, most basal reading programs include books that are ordered by levels.

**One or more readiness books**   These are books that offer opportunity for the child to acquire auditory and visual discrimination skills prerequisite to learning to read.

**Three or four preprimers, a primer, and a first reader (textbook)**   These are books for helping children learn to recognize a restricted sample of words — words composed of particular initial consonants (for example, /b/, /m/) and vowel-consonant or rhyming patterns (for example, *it sit; up cup*) and words with inflectional endings (for example, dogs, boys, going, running).[1] These books also offer practice in learning

---

[1] A pair of slant lines enclosing phonemic symbols is a graphic device to signify that the symbols are not letters but representations of sound units.

comprehension and study skills such as finding a main idea, determining cause and effect, and following directions as they apply to the restricted reading selections of the textbook.

**Two second-grade readers**[2]   These books give an opportunity for the child to maintain the skills of word recognition and comprehension introduced in previous books and to acquire additional ones. There is, for instance, more emphasis on recognizing two-syllable words, contractions, and derivatives — compound words and words with affixes. Children are given practice in the understanding of sequence and the reading of different literary forms, such as poetry. Beginning dictionary skills that involve the use of alphabetic order are featured.

**Two third-grade readers**   In these books, word recognition skills are extended to include identifying new words that have different vowel sounds for the same letter, for example, *good, food.* Opportunities are given for the child to examine root words, root changes, and endings. Comprehension skills, such as understanding sequence and finding main ideas, are more fully developed. Dictionary skills are augmented to include interpreting pronunciation symbols and other useful devices. Reading selections at this level often include a variety of fictional pieces such as narratives, poems, myths, legends, and plays as well as informational articles.

**One fourth-grade reader**   Books at this level continue to feature word recognition skills. Attention is given to the structural elements in multisyllable words and less frequent spelling patterns, such as /ui/ in *fruit* and /y/ in *rhyme.* The comprehension skills that are taught demand that pupils make inferences such as anticipating a point of view from the title of a selection. Children also learn to relate details to topic sentences. Both dictionary and study skills get further attention. Pupils are taught, for example, how to use the dictionary to determine primary and secondary stress, ways to locate information in encyclopedias, and how to interpret graphs and tables. Fictional pieces, popular science, and social studies material serve as the principal vehicles for applying the skills.

---

[2] Commercial publishers of the reading series now tend to remove the designation of a book as first grade, second grade, or other grade because much instruction is nongraded, and individual children may require a given book regardless of grade level. However, publishers still key each book to a particular level in the series. One common key for recognizing the level of a book is to note the alphabetical order of the initial letter of the title. For example, *Away* and *Begin* are the first books in one series; *Landings* and *Moments* are used much later.

**One fifth-grade reader**  Word recognition skills are maintained and expanded. New structural elements in the form of suffixes are introduced; and the teaching of spelling patterns, such as /oi/ in *choice* and /ear/ in *earn*, is common. Comprehension skills receive a greater proportion of attention than word recognition at this level. Children are expected to interpret the author's intent, mood, and descriptive language. They are asked to engage in forecasting and in reading between the lines. Study skills are extended. Children learn to use the card catalog, table of contents, index, and glossary. Selections at this level typically include biography as well as the previously introduced fictional forms, science, and social studies.

**One sixth-grade reader**  Word recognition skills are still taught. However, comprehension skills and study skills are emphasized to a greater extent than in previous books. There is more opportunity for pupils to evaluate the material read, distinguishing, for example, between fact and opinion. Study skills now include isolating key thoughts in paragraphs, skimming, surveying material, using a bibliography, and reading in different ways to fit different purposes. Dictionary skills now emphasize the selection of right meanings to match particular situations and the understanding of synonyms and antonyms. The content of selections includes more factual pieces than prior readers; yet fiction, plays, essays, and poetry still make up most of the material to be read.

Figures 2.1 and 2.2 illustrate how word recognition and comprehension are treated at different grade levels.

Most publishers of basal readers offer activity sheets, workbooks, tests, film strips, and flash cards that allow pupils to practice the skills taught in each respective reader. A teacher's manual accompanies the text at each level. This manual is rich in suggestions for presenting the selections and teaching the skills. Resources and ideas for lesson follow-up and enrichment are also found in the manual.

### Basal Method of Instruction

Typically those using a basal reader follow two related lesson formats: the skill development lesson and the directed reading lesson.

**The skill development lesson**  Most selections in the pupil's text are preceded by skill activities that prepare the child to read the selection. The skills of word recognition and comprehension are taught in a systematic way according to a sequence outlined in the teacher's guide. The skill development lesson aims at the child acquiring a particular

**FIGURE 2.1**  Basal-series content at primer level.

Source: M. S. Johnson et al., *Find* (New York: American Book Company, 1977), p. 101. *American Book Reading Program,* © 1977. Reprinted by permission.

instructional objective such as the ability to recognize given spelling patterns, base words, or dictionary skills. The skills are ordered in what the authors of a basal series believe to be a hierarchical developmental plan to teach skills to form a foundation for learning more advanced skills.

The sample illustrates a skill development lesson suggested by the authors of one basal reader.[3]

---

[3] Adapted from William K. Durr et al., Reference Handbook accompanying *Keystones*, Houghton Mifflin Reading Series. Copyright © 1976 Houghton Mifflin Company. Used by permission.

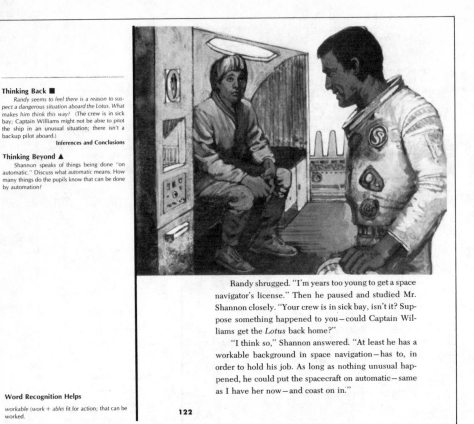

**Thinking Back ■**

*Randy seems to feel there is a reason to suspect a dangerous situation aboard the Lotus. What makes him think this way?* (The crew is in sick bay; Captain Williams might not be able to pilot the ship in an unusual situation; there isn't a backup pilot aboard.)

**Inferences and Conclusions**

**Thinking Beyond ▲**

Shannon speaks of things being done "on automatic." Discuss what *automatic* means. How many things do the pupils know that can be done by automation?

**Word Recognition Helps**

*workable* (*work* + *able*) fit for action; that can be worked.

Randy shrugged. "I'm years too young to get a space navigator's license." Then he paused and studied Mr. Shannon closely. "Your crew is in sick bay, isn't it? Suppose something happened to you—could Captain Williams get the *Lotus* back home?"

"I think so," Shannon answered. "At least he has a workable background in space navigation—has to, in order to hold his job. As long as nothing unusual happened, he could put the spacecraft on automatic—same as I have her now—and coast on in."

**122**

**FIGURE 2.2**  Basal-series content at fourth-grade level.

Source: M. S. Johnson et al., *Lanterns* (New York: American Book Company, 1977), p. 122. *American Book Reading Program,* © 1977. Reprinted by permission.

## *Example of a Suggested Skill Development Lesson*

### OBJECTIVE

Given printed words beginning or ending with the consonant *b,* the child can identify the sound value associated with this letter *b.*

1. Write the following words on the chalkboard: boy bat job cab.

2. What are these four words? (Teacher provides answers if children cannot respond.) Look at the first two words. Does each word begin with the same letter? What is the letter? Let's say these two words together and listen for the beginning sound in each. (Put a slight stress on the beginning sound as you say each word with the pupils.) Does each of these words begin with the same sound? Yes. Each begins with the same letter and the same sound.

3. Now look at the last two words. Does each word end with the same letter? What is that letter? Let's say those two words together and listen for the last sound in each. (Put a slight stress on the final sound as you say each word with the pupils.) Does each of these words end with the same sound? Yes. Each word ends with the same letter and the same sound. Is the last letter and sound in *job* and *cab* the same as the first letter and sound in *boy* and *bat*? Yes. That sound you hear at the beginning of *boy* and *bat* and at the end of *job* and *cab* is the sound that the letter *b* almost always stands for.

4. Ask pupils to circle the words in the following list that have the same sound as *b* in *boy* and *cab*:

dog      be      tot      tub      rug      pod

**The directed reading lesson**   The format for the directed reading lesson has five parts:

1. *Motivation.* The teacher tries to arouse and develop interest in the selection to be studied. This may occur by having children recall from their own experiential background incidents related to the content of the selection. Sometimes the teacher poses a problem, puzzle, some incongruity, or other need that might be resolved by reading the selection.

2. *Background preparation.* So children may be successful in reading, the teacher will define by example or have pupils derive from examples the unfamiliar words and concepts that are important in understanding the selection. The teacher may write these unfamiliar words in sentences on the chalkboard or wall chart and ask children to locate the strange words, use them in conversation, or guess their meaning from context. The skills taught in the skill development lesson are part of the background preparation.

3. *Setting of purposes.* Teacher and pupil together examine the selection and determine what purpose it might serve. Is it likely, for example, that a particular story or article is written so the pupil will enjoy the humor of a situation, learn how to make something, answer a question, or solve a mystery or problem? As children gain in reading ability, they will set purposes such as to answer their own questions about the events depicted in the illustrations or other questions generated by prior discussion.

4. *Directed silent and oral rereading.* Pupils are directed to read the selection to find answers to their questions. During this silent reading period, the teacher may go to individual pupils and ask them to read aloud, to determine what they are gaining or understanding from their reading or where they are having trouble. The teacher may help a

child having difficulty at that time or make notes of what must be taught subsequently. Various degrees of guidance are needed with children who are at different levels of competency. The teacher may direct the reading of beginners line by line, having them attempt to read silently and then orally. The teacher's manual is an excellent resource, usually providing more suggestions than any teacher could use during the directed lesson.

5. *Follow-up and extension.* The reading lesson may be followed by activities that give children an opportunity to practice the skills acquired. Teacher's manuals specify particular workbooks, self-instructional exercises, or activity sheets that allow for additional practice. Also the teacher's manual is a good source of suggestions for ways to extend the skills taught through additional projects, construction, creative writing, and the like.

### Strengths of the Basal Approach

A basal reading series allows faculty members of an individual school to work in accordance with the same instructional plan, thereby permitting a cumulative effect. A systematic and coherent reading program is associated with reading achievement. The basal approach is also valued because of its comprehensiveness, encouraging the learning of a wide range of skills and content. The teacher's manual is more than a tool; it is in a sense a complex instructional instrument filled with ideas, theories, and principles concretely expressed for teacher use.

A basal series aids in the individualization of instruction in several ways. Through the use of placement tests that accompany the texts, pupils can be placed according to a particular text appropriate to their learning levels. Usually checkup tests are also available for assessing pupil achievement with the different skills taught in the given readers. Pupil performance on these tests helps the teacher decide whether to reteach the skills to certain individuals or whether to advance the pupils in the program. Special needs of pupils are often met through suggestions in the teacher's manual for extending and enriching the lessons.

### Weaknesses of the Basal Approach

Critics say that basal readers in general are planned for average conditions and do not meet the special needs of exceptional children, such as the non-English-speaking child. Certain basal readers have been singled out as having particular weaknesses. For example, authors of several reading series have been faulted for failing to provide the same systematic attention to varied sentence patterns that they have given to controlling for the introduction of vocabulary and spelling patterns. Edys Quellmalz and others analyzed the content of four commonly used reading series and found that study skills, inferential comprehension of nonfiction material, and sentence structure receive low priority.[4] John Bradley and Wilbur Ames presented evidence showing that a basal reader's grade designation reveals little about how difficult it is for the child to understand.[5] Vocabulary burden at a given reading level varies greatly from one series to another. In fact, the variation of readability even within a single textbook can be extreme.

Teachers using basal readers sometimes do not give learners sufficient practice in applying decoding skills to unfamiliar words. Instead the pupils learn to recognize words in the textbook on the basis of sight recall after having seen the words several times during the lessons. Hence, pupils may read the selections in their own textbook quite well but do not read passages as well when they are composed of unfamiliar words appearing in other books or materials.

Unlike the technology approach, in which the focus is on the child's learning one skill at a time with mastery, the basal approach allows for the simultaneous treatment of many skills. The teacher's manual is rich in ideas regarding how several different skills can be related to a single written selection. Although this feature is desirable in terms of meeting the individual needs for given skills and for encouraging the application of many skills in a lifelike reading situation, it sometimes leads to confusion. The authors of basal materials do not intend that all of the possibilities be acted upon at once; they consider the suggestions a resource for judicious selection. Teachers, however, sometimes overlook this intention and try to teach too much at once, thereby accomplishing little.

## The Basal Approach and Your Role as a Teacher

The basal system can help you determine the concepts and skills to be taught, the activities and content to offer, and the assessment devices to use for placement and for monitoring pupil progress. The system will also suggest continuities and indicate what steps to take next. In using the basal approach, you must actively interact with pupils in the

---

[4] Edys Quellmalz, Nancy Snidman, and Joan Herman, "Toward Competency-Based Reading Systems" (Paper presented at the annual meeting of the American Educational Research Association, Chicago, March 1977).

[5] John M. Bradley and Wilbur S. Ames, "Readability Parameters of Basal Readers," *Journal of Reading Behavior* 9, no. 2 (Summer 1977): 175–183.

instructional process—motivating, eliciting pupil response, clarifying, questioning, listening, directing, evaluating, confirming, and planning.

# Technological Approach

The defining element of technology in the teaching of reading is *reproducibility*. The instructional sequence can be reproduced. It is tangible, exportable — to be followed by children in many different classrooms regardless of the teacher. Also, to a great extent, the results or objectives attained are reproducible with different learners, providing they meet the general description of those for whom the program is intended. The ideal of reproducibility of sequence and outcome is fulfilled to different degrees by the various reading programs and by the teachers who use them. Labels often associated with the technological approach include: objective-based reading systems, criterion-based programs, competency-based reading, skill management systems, and diagnostic prescriptive reading. (Refer to the appendix for a list of the materials used most often with the technological approach.)

## Materials and Content

Most technological reading materials share four components:

There is a sequentially ordered set of *behavioral objectives.* These objectives are usually ordered within two or three strands or areas, such as objectives for recognizing words, objectives for comprehension, and objectives for study skills. The continuum of skills in any strand may be appropriate for three weeks, one year, six years, or some other period of instruction. One company's objective-based system consists of 367 skills and objectives intended for pupils from first through sixth grade.[6] An example of a typical word attack objective at the primary level is: Given a picture of a familiar object and three words, one of which has the same rhyming element as the name for the picture, a child can select the word that rhymes; for example,

(fan)    dog    man    cat.

There is a *criterion test* to accompany each objective. A criterion test is a test that ascertains an individual's status with respect to a well-defined behavior domain, such as a simple skill of reading or a combination of many reading skills. This test must match the objec-

---

[6] *Fountain Valley Teacher Support System* (Huntington Beach, Calif.: Richard L. Zweig Associates, 1971).

tive for both the stimuli (for example, a picture of familiar objects) and response (for example, selecting the word that rhymes). Usually a rule states how many items on the criterion test the child must get right to indicate that the skill has been mastered.

There are *instructional strategies.* Instructional strategies are those that appear in the form of materials, programmed lessons, or activities to which children must respond and that, through prompting by examples and explanation, help them learn to achieve the task specified in the objective. Some technological instructional systems offer only a resource file listing specific workbook pages, spirit masters, games, or kits that should be useful in teaching to the objective. Others are more programmed and provide detailed lessons in the form of a script by which the teacher is told what to say, how to signal the children to respond, when to praise, and how to handle incorrect responses. Some technological materials consist of lessons on tape or in pupil booklets so no live teacher interaction is necessary for the child to achieve the objective. Figure 2.3 illustrates a programmed lesson.

There is a *record-keeping system.* This system allows for recording the skills successfully mastered by the learner as determined by performance on the criterion-referenced tests and shows the objectives and instruction to be undertaken. Subsequently, children are assessed to determine their status with respect to the objectives. If they pass the pretest, they are given a more appropriate task and are not expected to participate in instruction relevant to the objective they have already attained. If they do not pass the pretest, they are given instruction on the task. Following instruction, children are again tested, and if they are successful, they may proceed to a new objective. If they are not, supplementary instruction is given.

A record of achievement is maintained, indicating results in a form such as that shown in Figure 2.4. The checklist can be modified to show data and instruction given when there is no mastery.

## Diagnosis

Placement of the pupil in the hierarchy or continuum of reading skills is the first activity of the teacher. This is done by administering a survey test that samples performance on a range of objectives or by testing the child on specific criterion tests for each objective thought to be relevant. Should children already demonstrate mastery of a particular objective or skill, they need not receive instruction in that skill. We are not belaboring the obvious here: The diagnosis or preassessment step is one advantage the technological approach has over the basal

---

NAME _____     400-02.07-(12)-02.00

WORKSHEETS: Fundamental Stage:      Directed Lesson 1
            Primary — Step 12        Blending /A/ with m,
                                     n, p, b, d, t
                                     Step 12-Page 31

| at  | an  | am  |
|-----|-----|-----|
| mat | man | ham |
| pat | ban | tam |
| bat | Dan | dam |
| nat | tan | Pam |
| cat | Nan | Mam |
| hat | pan | bam |
| dat |     | nam |

| ab  | ad  | ap  |
|-----|-----|-----|
| cab | dad | map |
| nab | bad | nap |
| tab | mad | tap |
| dab | had | pap |
| hab | pad | hap |
| bab | Tad | dap |
| mab | nad | bap |

TEACHER DIRECTIONS — **Say to learner:** On this worksheet we are going to learn how to blend the consonants we've learned with the sound of /a/ (the short sound of a) to make words. The reason we've learned these sounds is so that we can read words. By putting different sounds together in different ways, we get many different real or silly words. If we put /a/ with /t/ we get **at**. When we have a lot of words that end with **at**, we say we have a word family. In human families we usually all have the same last names but different first names. So it is with words. Look at the **at** family in the top left corner of the page. Notice that all the words in this group have **at** for their last names. What different letters do they have for first names? (Wait.) (Response) Now let's see if we can blend these different beginning sounds with **at**. The sound of /**m**/ combined with **at** is **mat**, a mat such as we (sat or sit) upon in kindergarten. (Teacher continues the lesson with the remainder of the word families.)

**FIGURE 2.3**   Illustrative programmed lesson.

Source: *Developmental Reading Program, Worksheets Step 12* (St. Paul, Minn.: Paul S. Amidon and Associates, 1975). Reprinted by permission.

approach where children are sometimes given lessons whether or not they already know what the lessons purport to teach.

### Prescription

Once the teacher knows which objective on the continuum the child has mastered, an instructional sequence designed to teach the needed skill is provided. As indicated before, the teaching strategy can be

*Objective Number and Name*

 1. Consonant variants _____

 2. Consonant blends _____

 3. Long vowel sounds _____

 4. Controlled vowels _____

 5. Diphthongs _____

 6. Long and short oo _____

 7. Middle vowel _____

 8. Two vowels separated _____

 9. Two vowels together _____

10. Final vowel _____

*Key*

Passed preassessment ✓

Instructed and mastered O    Name _____

**FIGURE 2.4**    Teacher's checklist of skills to be mastered by primary grade children.

teacher-directed, self-instructional, or tutor-guided with the tutor using a script or other programmed material. This instruction should provide the prerequisites, prompts, examples, and explanations for learning the task and give opportunities for the learner to practice the behavior called for by the objective. *Prescriptive lessons, instructional strategies, interventions,* and *learning activities* are all terms that signify means for helping a child attain objectives.

**Posttesting and Recording**

Upon completion of the instructional component, the child is given a criterion-referenced test that corresponds to the competency described in the given objective. If the results indicate mastery, the learner proceeds to the next objective on the continuum. Unsuccessful performance requires further specific diagnosis to reveal the learner's interfering perceptions or the lack of prerequisites. Subsequent instruction is planned to remedy the revealed needs before the child proceeds on the continuum of objectives. Figure 2.5 illustrates the instructional design followed in the technological approach.

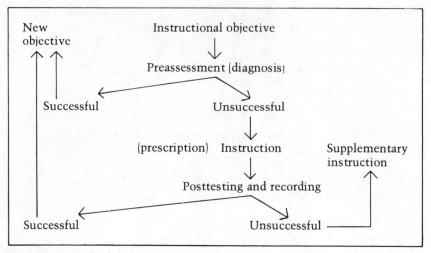

**FIGURE 2.5** Model showing procedures used with technological approach.

### Strengths of the Technological Approach

Many teachers find that the technological approach is a timesaving, focused, and effective method of teaching reading. The clarity of objectives for both teachers and pupils facilitates relevant instruction and practice. The task analysis and logical ordering of objectives and prerequisites make it possible for many pupils to succeed on a given task. The match between objectives and tests and the monitoring of instructional results enable teachers to select appropriate tasks for pupils and to know when instructional treatment has been successful. The approach allows instruction to proceed in accordance with each child's deficiencies on a continuum of reading skills and at a pace consistent with the child's ability to learn. An outstanding characteristic associated with those who develop reading materials for use with this approach is their concern for validation or reproducibility. The materials are tried out with children before being released for general use and are not judged acceptable until results from the tryouts verify the program's effectiveness.

### Weaknesses of the Technological Approach

The technological approach has been criticized for featuring questionable objectives and continua. Not all objectives included in the different programs are thought to be important in learning to read. Critics have questioned the criterion-referenced tests. The criteria for mastery (the number of test items that must be correctly answered) are often arbitrary. Children may be able to read without passing the tests or they may pass all the tests on the continuum and still be unsuccessful readers. There is little agreement among different monitoring systems about the right sequence of objectives. Some teachers do not like the structured format of programmed materials that restrict *what* will be learned and *how* it will be learned, charging that such lessons tend to restrict spontaneity among teachers and learners. Some pupils have found the narrowly focused tasks and exercises boring. Also, the teaching of reading skills apart from the reading of complete stories, articles, and other materials (as sometimes happens in the technological approach) denies the nature of language and makes it difficult for the learners to relate the skills acquired for reading in the real world.

## The Technological Approach and Your Role as a Teacher

For a large proportion of your time as a teacher using the technological approach, you must be a teacher-manager. You are a manager when administering and interpreting tests, placing pupils according to self-instructional materials, supervising pupils at work, and recording individual progress. This is quite different from the role of a facilitator who engages pupils in the planning of activities, encourages classroom projects, and clarifies purposes.

Little knowledge about linguistics and other content of the reading field is required to learn how to carry out the operation of commercially prepared programmed approaches to the teaching of reading. However, you must understand the program's purposes and components and demonstrate the ability to perform the tasks stipulated in the design. You will be provided with concepts, materials that teach, schedules, tests, and continuities. Some teachers, when given prescribed teaching sequences, attempt to change the format, materials, and instructions of the program to fit their own needs and style. Developers of the materials are opposed to these adaptations, believing the changes weaken the carefully designed instructional program and make it difficult to guarantee results. On the other hand, teachers who use canned self-instructional materials rather than generate and conduct their own didactic lessons are relieved of a difficult and time-consuming task. Hence they have more opportunity for personal interaction and discussion with pupils about problems and questions arising in the course of learning the skills from the programmed sequences and exercises.

Monitoring systems, such as the *Wisconsin Design for Reading Skill Development*,[7] enable teachers to monitor pupil progress in essential skills and also to employ basal readers and other materials to broaden the reading program. Each objective or skill has been keyed to commercially available materials for teaching this skill. In addition, there are separate loose-leaf sheets with teacher ideas that are useful in teaching a given skill.

## Language Experience Approach

The language experience approach is characterized by learning activities involving close relations between thinking, talking, writing, and reading. The teacher first stimulates children by the presence of an attention-getting item or event (animals, puzzles, problems, issues, personal concerns). Next, children are encouraged to express orally their thinking about the situation. These expressions may range from descriptions of the situation, analysis of the problem or situation, and proposed solutions to judgments about what has been seen and proposed. Those things that are said are then put in written form by the children or the teacher. What children have thought, spoken, and written they now read with meaning.

### Materials and Content

Unlike the basal and technological approaches, the language experience approach has no textbooks prescribing the vocabulary, sentence patterns, and reading skills to be taught. The approach is primarily a method. The vocabulary and sentence patterns that children read are their own. The content consists of expressions that reflect the child's own experiences and the activity that probes the expression. Resource books and kits are available for teachers suggesting activities and materials that are likely to provoke pupil expressions considered useful in learning to read (see appendix). *Language Experience in Reading*, for example, offers sets of activities by categories so there is a greater likelihood of a balanced development of reading skills.[8] One set is aimed at vocabulary development and features the sharing of personal experiences. Activities include discussing and reading individual

---

[7] *Wisconsin Design for Reading Skill Development* (Minneapolis, Minn.: National Computer Systems, 1974).

[8] Roach V. Allen and Claryce Allen, *Language Experience in Reading, Teacher's Resource Book*, Level I, II, III. (Chicago: Encyclopaedia Britannica Education Corporation, 1966).

books. Another set of activities focuses upon language patterns and gives opportunities for children to abstract relationships from speaking, reading, and writing and to generalize about sentence patterns and frequently occurring words. A third set aims at helping children relate ideas of authors to their personal experiences. These activities call for reading a variety of printed sources, reading for specific purposes, summarizing, and determining the worth of what is read.

Reproducibility is not a value in language experience. The language experience approach is not tied to a set of published books or other materials but to the individual learner's time and place. Nevertheless, teachers using the approach do teach word identification and comprehension as well as writing, listening, and speaking. The teacher helps children formulate generalizations necessary for word recognition and comprehension by having them attend to relevant instances of given generalizations as they appear in the children's stories. For example, when a teacher asks children to identify a number of words in their story that look the same at the beginning and also sound the same, they might note *black*, *blew*, and *blizzard* and learn to generalize about an important blending pattern.

Most individual and group-experienced stories can be used to teach comprehension skills. Children may be asked to draw pictures that correspond to the image presented by the written passage, answer both factual and inferential questions based upon the passage, and paraphrase the main idea of the passage.

The language experience approach is ungraded in that much of the teaching is done with material produced by the children. As soon as pupils are reading, however, they move from reading chiefly their own writing to reading that of others. By the end of the first year, pupils are reading more material written by those outside the classroom.

The approach can be used at all grade levels. Indeed, Paulo Freire used the approach in teaching reading to adults as part of his process for social change. The following are examples of Freire's assumptions that support a language experience approach for adults:

> Poor people should create texts that express their own thought language and their perceptions of the world.
>
> Words should be chosen for (a) their pragmatic value in communicating with one's group (for example, the word *soul* has special meaning for blacks); (b) phonetic reasons; and (c) generative features, such as syllabic elements by which learners can compare and read new words of importance to themselves.[9]

---

[9] Paulo Freire, "The Adult Literacy Process as Cultural Action for Freedom," *Harvard Educational Review* 40, no. 3 (1970): 205–225.

## Language Experience Method of Instruction

The method used in the language experience approach follows these five steps:

1.   Creating a need for thought and oral expression
2.   Writing the thought expressed
3.   Reading what is written
4.   Generalizing about the spelling patterns and sentences written
5.   Noting how choice and arrangement affect meaning

Procedures for carrying out these five steps vary. Individuals or groups may dictate stories or describe events to the teacher who then records them on the chalkboard or paper for subsequent reading. The stories can also be bound with tape, cardboard, and staples to give them more permanence. Large charts can be used in recording both group-composed and individually composed stories. The separate stories are often exchanged. Here is an example of such a story.

*A Language Experience Story*
*Produced by a Second-Grade Pupil*
*after Hearing a Poem about*
*Being So Quiet You Can Hear . . .*

It is so quiet that I
can hear the wind dancing
with the leaves.
I can even hear the pet
goldfish splashing their
slippery tails.

by Maybelle Gordon

New words are put on a single card for review and referral when writing later. Once a child has had occasion to use and recognize a new word, that word is printed by the teacher on a rectangular sheet of paper. The child files these word cards alphabetically in a box or word bank. In addition to using the words in producing stories of their own choice, pupils use the words for word recognition activities under teacher direction or with another pupil.

Training in word recognition can be handled in several ways. Children may be taught to recognize a word on the basis of configuration as a *sight word* (a word that is recognized by sight without using any decoding skill), or the teacher may ask pupils to look at a number of words on the experience chart whose initial letters are the same and then ask them to supply orally a new word "that begins with the same sound these letters make."

Comprehension is taught in a number of ways. For example, children may be asked to read their experience charts with different intonation patterns, noting how intonation and punctuation change meaning. They may "discover" how to find the antecedents of pronouns. They may be taught to note words in their own passages and in the passages of others that signal cause and effect, sequence, main ideas, contrasting thoughts, and the like.

Writing, of course, begins when the pupils copy the words dictated in the experience stories. As their written vocabularies expand, pupils begin writing sentences and stories of their own. The teacher initially gives help with spelling, punctuation, and capitalization. Stories to be read by others must be correctly spelled. Pupils accept this standard and see that it is necessary so others can understand what has been expressed. Usually pupils do not release their stories until they are polished. Throughout, they participate in creating group compositions, plays, scripts for puppet shows, poems, songs, reports, and directions for helping others complete interesting tasks.

## Strengths of the Language Experience Approach

The major strength of the language experience approach (LEA) is the close match between learning to read and the child's own interests, concerns, and language. The value of the approach in working with the bilingual child is a case in point. Spanish-speaking children, for example, often find it helpful to dictate something and learn to read it in Spanish; later they learn to read what they dictated in English. The fact that motivation for learning to read is intrinsic rather than dependent upon extrinsic rewards is another plus. Children believe they are controlling the situation and their own destiny; thus they are "origins, not pawns." Richard De Charms says that when people think their behavior is externally determined — pushed — they are *pawns*. Those who believe they are internally motivated by their own choices are *origins*. [10] Another strong feature of the language experience approach is that it produces an integration of all the language skills: thinking, speaking, listening, writing, and reading.

---

[10] Richard De Charms, "Pawns or Origins: Enhancing Motivation in Disaffected Youth," *Educational Leadership* 34, no. 6 (March 1977): 444–447.

## Weaknesses of the Language Experience Approach

The most serious limitation to the language experience approach is that it requires the presence of an exceptionally able teacher to assess the learner's experiences and to direct these experiences so they lead to the continuous development of language power.

There is some speculation that LEA may mask complex developmental processes. Terry Johnson, for example, suggests that the child's most preferred language ability — conversation — may actually interfere with the process of learning to read.[11] Natural conversation tends to depend on context and nonverbal body language to be comprehensible, but with written material there must be a flow of information without the aid of questions, confirmation, or encouraging words from readers. Thus, pronouncements about a child's ability to apply oral long-range skills directly to written language may be oversimplified. It may be necessary first to help pupils produce oral monologues that are more similar to writing and that, in turn, may provide them with skills more related to reading.

## The Language Experience Approach and Your Role as a Teacher

As a language experience teacher, you would try to increase the sensitivity of children to the world about them. This might mean reading literature to them; letting them express themselves through art, plays, and creative story telling; discussing topics of interest and concern to them; or helping them write what they hear, feel, imagine, and discover. It would be up to you to assume the major responsibility for making essential decisions about concepts, experiences, facts, timing, evaluations, and what to teach next.

You would also have to have a plan for developing the language competencies of the child. Classroom experiences should not be random like a diary but should flow like a novel toward some important climax. Continuity in the child's language would be enhanced if, for example, you had a plan extending the child's present vocabulary, style of expression, and use of frequently occurring words and sentence patterns.

By way of contrast, it is possible with the basal or technological approach to consider the interests, questions, and problems of children only incidentally as they can be brought into discussion of the lessons in the materials provided. Indeed some teachers give too much emphasis to the speed with which children pass through the material and

---

[11] Terry D. Johnson, "Language Experience: We Can't All Write What We Say," *Reading Teacher* 31, no. 3 (December 1977): 297–299.

the degree to which they acquire the stated objectives. Formal evaluations are usually of skills outlined by the materials rather than how these skills are used by children in facing the problems of daily living. In many ways, your role as a language experience teacher is more demanding than the roles associated with the basal or technological approaches. You must know the skills necessary for learning to read and have your own rationale about how and when to teach these skills. You must ask yourself what questions or problems your children have and how such problems can be used in developing reading skills. What kinds of learning experiences, materials, and processes are important in dealing with these skills? Are children gaining more than isolated skills? Are they gaining in competency to think, apply, generalize, and see relationships?

# Individualized Reading Approach

There are different degrees of individualization in reading. A restricted practice is to have the same objective for all pupils but to individualize the material and instructional time in light of learner characteristics. A more open practice allows individuals to select from an array of objectives and purposes and to use optional materials in attaining them. An even more open practice provides for independent reading by which the child decides *what* is to be learned and *how* it is to be learned. The latter practice seldom occurs in schools. What we refer to in this section as the individualized reading approach is an open practice but not independent reading. Accordingly children select their own reading material to match their needs, interests, and abilities. The teacher does, however, help them learn how to select books by showing how to skim and sample pages and determine reading difficulty. For example, the five-finger procedure is taught: "Pick a page in the middle of the book. Start to read it. If you come to a word you cannot read, put one of your fingers down. If you come to another, put another finger down, and so on. If you use up your whole hand, the book is too hard."

### Materials and Content

An individualized reading program, more clearly than any other, gives children an opportunity to read extensively and independently from a wide array of books and magazines. The purposes associated with this approach are (1) to effect a greater range in the child's reading interest and commitment to reading as a lifetime value; (2) to develop competency in a range of skills from simple word recognition to application of the skills with complex material; and (3) to increase the child's ability to comprehend and evaluate reading material — for example, to extend the child's ability to recall what is read to the point where he or she can grasp the thought of a work as a whole at any desired level of generality.

With respect to material used in individualized reading, trade books for children predominate. A trade book is one that is sold in bookstores and found in most libraries; trade books are not textbooks. (See the appendix for further information on materials used in individualized reading.) Magazines, newspapers, and programmed materials are also available. Paperbacks have a special appeal for children.

### Individualized Method of Instruction

Individualized reading is a method of reading instruction that relies on each child selecting a book according to interest and ability. Some children need little assistance; others initially need the teacher's help in choosing books that are in keeping with their ability to read. By design, children read independently from the materials they have chosen, setting their own purposes and reading at their own rate.

In addition to the child's self-selection of what to read, a second key feature of this approach is the teacher-child conference. Each child gets at least five minutes every three days for a personal teaching period or conference. In this conference, the teacher extends the child's involvement with words and ideas. Teacher and pupil discuss ideas obtained from a book and the implications of these ideas for the child's own life. Often the child reads to the teacher passages of special interest and importance. The pupil may show the teacher new words learned from reading. During the conference, the teacher observes many characteristics of the child's reading, such as whether the child gives broad ideas and supporting evidence or relates minute details.

Jeannette Veatch, a leading proponent of the individualized approach, holds that open-ended, thought-provoking questions are most desirable.[12] She suggests that teachers might ask questions in areas such as:

Main idea: for example, What kind of story is this? Describe the book with one word.

---

[12] Jeannette Veatch, "The Conference in IRP: The Teacher-Pupil Dialogue," *The Individualized Reading Program: A Guide for Classroom Teaching*, Proceedings of the 11th Annual Convention, International Reading Association, vol. 11 (Newark, Del.: International Reading Association, 1967). Reprinted with permission of Jeannette Veatch and the International Reading Association.

Value structure: Could you get into an argument about the book? On which side of the argument are you? Why?

Critical thinking: When you read this book, did you get any ideas that were not actually put into words? What was the story *really* about?

Sequence: If the story were a play, what main event would make up each act?

Author: If you wrote the author a letter, what would you say about the book? Did the author write the book only for children's enjoyment or to give information?

Reasons for choice: Why did you choose this book? What did you learn from this book?

Peer awareness: Who might like this book?

Word definition: Can you tell me what this word means? Use this word in a sentence.

Study skills: Tell me the theme of the story after looking at the table of contents.

Decoding: Show me a word you did not know. How did you figure out what the word was?

Details: What does it say you have to do first? What do you have to be careful about in performing the experiment?

Oral reading: What happened next? Can you read it (make it) exciting, spooky, silly?

You can augment this list by posing questions that will teach a child to set purposes for reading; to organize information; to identify literary qualities such as honesty, imagery, and characterization; and to judge the material read on the basis of completeness, accuracy, and the like.

As a result of questioning and listening to a child read, the teacher notes what is required for future action — *specific* comprehension or word attack skills that should be taught or given instruction on the spot. When two or more children have a common difficulty, interest, or purpose, the teacher may group them for instruction (more economical use of teacher time), dissolving the group when there is no longer a common problem. Frequently teacher and child prepare for sharing a book with the class. The teacher often suggests some follow-up activities and helps the child select the next book.

Most of the teacher's time is given to individual conferences; less time is spent with small groups. There is some activity involving the whole class, when children share aspects of stories, explore the meaning of a poem, or generalize how words change in structure; for example, ride/riding, hop/hopping, candy/candies.

An individualized reading program requires daily records. Teachers keep track of skills developed, words that a child learned to recognize and use, titles of books read, and anecdotes regarding the pupil's interests in books. Pupils, too, maintain records of their progress, listing the instructional objectives they have accepted for themselves. They also may keep scrapbooks of illustrations, prepare summaries of stories read, and maintain charts on which stories are evaluated according to criteria set by the class.

### Strengths of the Individualized Approach

The individualized approach is valuable in that it respects the unique needs of the learner and capitalizes on the motivational force of interest. Its advocates assume that books and materials chosen by pupils will have a more positive effect upon the child's desire to read than those chosen by teachers and that the method contributes to the child's having a personal commitment to reading as a purposeful and pleasurable activity. Individualized reading is consistent with the belief that pupils should be self-assertive rather than passive. Gains in initiative, self-management, and independence are associated with it.

In addition to allowing the individual the opportunity to learn without competition from peers, the approach lends itself to the grouping of pupils on the basis of skills needed and common interests.

### Weaknesses of the Individualized Approach

The central problem of individualized reading is that children's interests may be limited to the present. Some children may be very narrow in their choice of literature. The approach requires pupil self-direction and management. The scheduling of enough conferences with each pupil is difficult. Thirty pupils in a class and five hours weekly for teaching reading (the typical time provided for directed teaching of reading) may mean there will be no more than ten minutes of personal instruction per week, which is inadequate for teaching all a pupil needs to learn about reading. As with the language experience approach, success with this approach rests upon the teacher's ability to observe, question, and interpret. It differs, however, in that it requires that the teacher have knowledge of children's literature. Further, the teacher must be able to keep the whole class busy enough to make individual conferences possible. Hence, learning centers and projects are frequent adjuncts to individualized reading.

### The Individualized Approach and Your Role as a Teacher

Your role when using the individualized reading approach is to guide children in making selections appropriate to readability and interest. You must help them establish a purpose for reading particular books. To stimulate interest in books, you probably will try many tacks: talking about books, reading to the children, displaying new acquisitions, talking about the authors, highlighting short excerpts, and encouraging children to read aloud to the class.

Unlike the role that is taken with the basal and technological approaches, your role in the individualized approach is guided by pupils' needs, not by a standard imposed from without. Hence, you must be conscious of the skills necessary for helping each child become a better reader. Your program will fail unless you can diagnose pupils' problems and motivate them in those areas.

You will spend time under this approach in working with individuals and small, variable groups. Partly as a result of the one-to-one conference, it is likely that relations between you and the pupil will become more intimate, and you may thus become a friend and advisor. As a listener, rather than a director, you will have a good opportunity to know, understand, and encourage children as individuals.

One indispensable quality for a teacher using this approach is familiarity with books and other written materials. For example, you have to know popular books treating mature content written at a lower grade level as well as sources of paperbacks treating both fiction and nonfiction in a wide variety of subjects.

## Summary

There are four major ways of approaching the task of teaching reading.

The basal reading series is a textbook approach characterized by comprehensiveness of skills taught, directed reading lessons, systematic organization, and a variety of reading selections and activities. This approach is the most commonly used.

Technological management systems represent a more recent way of teaching reading. The practice of teaching one skill at a time to mastery has gained in popularity along with the relatively new notion that almost anyone can learn to read regardless of ability if the task is broken down into its component parts and instruction in each part is properly sequenced and paced.

The language experience approach allows for reading words of personal importance in meaningful contexts. Further, the fact that LEA encourages writing, speaking, and listening as well as reading is a compelling advantage.

Individualized reading, in which there is pupil-teacher contact for both skill development and sharing of perceptions about reading, has real merit. Allowing pupils to select their own reading materials, to read them at their own pace, and to discuss their reading with the teacher during individual conferences is desirable from the standpoint of both motivation and independence in reading.

Most teachers would like to be eclectic, to take advantage of the strengths of the various approaches. It should be recognized, however, that the underlying assumptions of the different reading programs are not the same. For example, technological systems are predicated on the belief that learning proceeds from the part to the whole; programs in language experience rest on the belief that reading must proceed from perception of the meaningful whole before it can be analyzed into parts. Nevertheless, teachers can combine the approaches subject to constraints of time, numbers of pupils, and the teacher's own abilities in employing each approach. Also there are situations when one approach may be more appropriate than the others. The usefulness of LEA for the child who is not fluent in English and programmed instruction for the transient child are cases in point.

# Self-instructional Exercises

### Exercise 1. Selecting an Approach to the Teaching of Reading Consistent with Your Own Philosophy

There are many reasons why you might choose one rather than another of the four approaches to the teaching of reading. Perhaps you believe one is easier or more challenging. Perhaps, too, you believe that one approach better meets a dynamic need that underlies your decision to become a teacher. For example, you might have a need for much personal involvement with pupils. If so, you probably would not find the technological approach as satisfying to you as the other approaches. To help you choose an approach consistent with your beliefs and needs, first define some of your beliefs by circling an answer to each of the questions below. Then select the reading approach that seems closest to your own philosophy.

| | | |
|---|---|---|
| Who should control the process of instruction? | 1. Teacher | 2. Teacher with active sharing by learner | 3. Primarily the children themselves; teacher is a facilitator |
| How should reading purposes and skills be decided for a particular grade level? | 1. Analysis of competencies needed for successful reading | 2. Children's developmental growth | 3. Individual children set own purposes and choose skills they want to learn |
| How should the child be motivated to read? | 1. Through a variety of attention-getting and maintaining methods; for example, frequent overt responses and knowledge of results | 2. Introducing a problem that requires some aspect of reading in its resolution | 3. Giving the pupils freedom to learn by removing emotional blocks and recognizing that natural motivation is always present |
| How should reading skills be sequenced? | 1. Analyze the reading task components; arrange tasks into a hierarchy and teach the basic ones first | 2. Arrange for problem-solving activities appropriate for child's stage of development | 3. Let children explore books of all kinds and then decide where they will begin |
| How important is practice? | 1. Provide much practice; practice on each skill selected | 2. Do not proceed on a skill until the child sees how this skill relates to the bigger picture of reading | 3. A single good reading experience is worth more than practice. If children need practice, they will seek it |
| How should a teacher give feedback or knowledge of results to children? | 1. Let children know if they are correct or not | 2. Do not tell children if they are right or wrong, but let them see the re- | 3. Let children judge their own responses by whether the |

| How should the teacher take into account individual differences? | 1. Let learners have their own objectives and match learning sequences based on their status with respect to hierarchy of objectives as evidenced by testing | lation between their responses and the purposes for which they are reading 2. Have a variety of approaches to allow for different learning styles and abilities | responses help them reach their purposes 3. Let learners express their own desires of what to read, how, and when |

### ANSWERS TO EXERCISE 1

If your answers tend to be in the first column on the left, you have selected the technological approach. If your answers are all in the middle column, you have selected the basal approach. Answers that fluctuate between the middle and last columns are closest to the basal and language experience approaches. If you consistently answered by selecting from the last column, you have selected the individualized approach.

### Exercise 2. Diagnosing within Four Approaches to the Teaching of Reading

This activity is presented to clarify further the distinctions of the different approaches and to introduce the crucial task of diagnosis. Diagnosis is treated in chapter eight in greater detail. In the present exercise, identify the gap between what children *can* do with respect to reading and what they *should* be able to do in reading. That is, look at each of the following accounts and, when you recognize a child's deficiency, select the reading skill that promises to correct it.

1. During a basal lesson, Tim was asked to read aloud a page from the textbook. A record of his performance is superimposed in parentheses.

"Do we have all the things we need?" asked Walter. (Tim was unable to read the word *asked.*) (Tim's voice rose with the question.)

"You know we do," said Leo. "They are all in the tent!" (Tim's voice showed emphasis.)

Walter wished his dad could see him now. (Tim was unable to read the word *wished.*)

An appropriate skill to teach is:

a. _____ To interpret punctuation marks

b. _____ To recognize the base words *wish* and *ask* and the inflectional ending *ed*

c. _____ To recognize the antecedent of the pronoun *him*

2. Before assignment of technological material, Mary was asked to take a multiple choice pretest. Her responses are circled. The first word has a line under some of its letters. Circle the word next to it that has the same sound as the underlined letter(s).

| road  | cart   | lost   | (hope) | had   |
|-------|--------|--------|--------|-------|
| knew  | change | (king) | car    | not   |
| we    | egg    | (need) | wet    | there |
| use   | bus    | up     | (few)  | lunch |

An appropriate skill to teach is:

a. _____ To recognize that certain consonants are not pronounced

b. _____ To recognize that in certain vowel combinations the second letter may be silent

c. _____ To recognize that the final *e* is often not pronounced

3. The following sentences were presented by the teacher in a language experience lesson.

"He has long legs, and he runs fast. He really does!" A black dialect speaker read the sentences as: "He have long legs, and he run fast. He really do!"

The teacher should:

a. _____ Teach the child to recognize the sound value for the consonants

b. _____ Recognize that the child is making appropriate substitutions in his own dialect

c. _____ Forbid the child to dictate stories in his own dialect

4. The following is from a teacher's record of an individualized reading conference:

Name: Gregg Lane        Date: March 6, 9:15–9:30
Material evaluated: "Get Smart"
Results: Recalled story accurately. Knew that the author was writing fantasy and could tell what indicated fantasy as opposed to reality. Used the position of a word in the sentence to interpret meaning — "You want to *slim* down." Couldn't tell whether *quiet, weak, strong,* were opposites or just different.

An appropriate skill to teach:

a. \_\_\_\_ To recognize the words *quiet, weak, strong*

b. \_\_\_\_ To recognize antonyms

c. \_\_\_\_ To recognize how context may give clues to word meaning

### ANSWERS TO EXERCISE 2

1b. Tim should learn that if he can read *ask* and *wish,* he can also read *asked* and *wished.*

2a. Mary doesn't seem to recognize that *k* before *n* is silent.

3b. The speaker is using a special dialect that differs from standard English third-person singular verbs. He has versus he have; he does versus he do.

4b. An *antonym* opposes the meaning in another word, negating the implications.

## Exercise 3. Teaching within the Four Approaches

To experience firsthand what it is like to teach within the four approaches, try to develop lessons in accordance with each of the following four assignments.

1. Obtain a basal reader and accompanying teacher's manual. After studying the suggestions given in the manual for teaching one of the selections in the reader, prepare a lesson plan. Your plan should include the following parts: background preparation, setting of purposes, directed reading, and follow-up.

2. Teach the lesson presented below that is constructed along technological principles. Note that it contains an objective, a pretest, and an opportunity for learner(s) to attain the objective.[13]

---

[13] The lesson is adapted from "Phonetic Discrimination: The Letter *c,*" *Teaching Improvement Kit* (Los Angeles, Calif.: Instructional Appraisal Services, 1972).

*Lesson*

OBJECTIVE:
Given a list of unfamiliar words containing the letter *c,* the child will be able to indicate whether the *c* takes the /k/ or /s/ sound by circling a picture of a kite or sun.

PRETEST
Look at the word and then put a circle around the picture of the kite if the letter *c* in the word should have the sound of /k/ in *kite.* If *c* should have the sound of *s* as in *sun,* put a circle around the sun.

| | | |
|---|---|---|
| cyme | (kite) | (sun) |
| lucid | (kite) | (sun) |
| pectin | (kite) | (sun) |
| rubric | (kite) | (sun) |

INSTRUCTIONAL PROCEDURES
Attainment of the objective occurs through the following:

a. Recognizing the letters *c, i, e,* and *y* in any position in the word.

b. Understanding the concepts *followed by* and *immediately;* for example, *c* is pronounced as an *s* when it is immediately followed by *i, e,* or *y.*

c. Applying the rule given in item b above; associating the pictures of the kite and the sun with the two sounds of c.

The sequence to follow is:

a. Print words containing a *c,* which sometimes is (1) followed by an *i, e,* or *y;* (2) followed by one of the other letters of the alphabet; and (3) at the end of a word.

b. Give the phonic rule and have children indicate whether *c* should have the sound as in *kite* or *sun.* Make the point that they can use the rule even in words they have never seen before. A word like *gynecomorphous* might get a chuckle.

c. Give the children practice with words like *placer, condor,* and *tunic.*

POSTTEST
Administer a test composed of new words like *cylinder, rectify,* and *tacit.* If a child gets them all correct, you can assume mastery and go on to next objective on the hierarchy.

3. Develop and teach a language experience lesson to your colleagues. Involve them in creative writing, such as writing the script for a pup-

pet show to be presented to young learners. Include in your lesson provisions for:

a. *Encouraging thought.* You may wish to stimulate them by reading poetry or other material, showing appealing pictures, asking questions, or making suggestions for imaginative topics.

b. *Discussing ideas before writing.* This is necessary so colleagues realize the range of acceptable ideas, for example, mood and messages.

c. *Writing the script.* Be prepared to answer questions regarding choice of words, appropriateness, format, and mechanics. Allow for personal choices.

d. *Sharing the creative writing.* Give an opportunity for listening, speaking, and oral reading. Focus on acceptance and language awareness stemming from the language of peers and their sensitivity to the needs of pupils for whom the material is designed.

e. *Following up.* Indicate how the script can be used in different situations.

4. Prepare an individualized reading lesson that will take the form of an individual conference. First, select a pupil or peer who has recently completed a book. You should become familiar with the book and then prepare for the conference by drafting questions that might be helpful to the reader. You might ask, for example, how the book contributed to self-evaluation: What did you like about the book? What did you not like? What do these likes and dislikes tell you about yourself?

Include in your questions some that will get at individual skill needs. If your learner is a young child, look for gaps in word analysis. If the learner is an adult, identify deficiencies in reading critically, such as whether the reader notes how well the author substantiates conclusions in the form of observation, experiments, or other data.

**ANSWERS TO EXERCISE 3**

1. Your lesson plan must make clear what pupils should learn from the lesson. Your motivation strategy may have been built upon presenting a paradox or a problem. Why do you think your strategy appealed to the learners? How did your plan prepare the learners so they would have success in their reading? Were your instructions clear? What questions did you provide for use in the discussion? Were these questions relevant to your stated objective? Were they diagnostic — a means of getting information about what

should be taught next or were they primarily intended to extend further thought and action? What follow-up activities did you plan? What materials are needed for this follow-up?

2. Confirmation of your ability to teach with the technological approach is whether or not the child acquired mastery of the task selected. One of your roles is to make sure the objective is appropriate for the learner (that is, that the learner had not already mastered the objective). Another role is to insure that the learner completed the learning sequence provided.

3. Your lesson was successful if it resulted in a high degree of involvement and progress in areas such as the ability to use reading as a medium of communication, an increase in reading vocabularies, and favorable attitudes toward reading.

4. If your lesson has helped the learner in any of the following ways, it was worth the time and effort:

    a. Identification of new skills to be learned

    b. Instruction in a needed skill

    c. Development of a new interest or extension of an old one

    d. A desire to reread a book

    e. Clarification of what was read

    f. Development of readiness not now present

    g. Recognition on the part of the reader and yourself of prejudices, fears, loves, strengths, and other attributes

# Selected Readings

Applebee, Arthur. "Environments for Learning: ERIC Resources on the Language Experience Approach," *Language Arts 55*, no. 6 (September 1978): 756–760.

Studies showing the effectiveness of the language experience approach are cited. In addition, the review calls attention to many studies giving the theoretical rationale for the approach, describing specific classroom practices, and illustrating lesson sequences.

Cheek, Earl H., Jr., and Cheek, Martha C. "A Realistic Evaluation of Current Basal Readers," *Phi Delta Kappan 60*, no. 9 (May 1979): 682.

The authors report their analysis of three basal reading series published since 1976. Contrary to the popular criticism that basal readers do not portray life as it is, the Cheeks conclude that basal reading materials have come a long way in depicting life as a series of realistic conflicts and challenges. The question is asked, however, whether teachers and parents have increased their emphasis in helping children deal with life's problems.

Cohen, Sandra B., and Plaskon, Stephen P. "Selecting a Reading Approach for the Main-streamed Child," *Language Arts* 55, no. 8 (November/December 1978): 966–970.

Learning characteristics of the educable mentally retarded child are stated, and the advantages and disadvantages of the various reading approaches for the EMR child are outlined in some detail. The authors emphasize the importance of selecting an approach that will maximize the child's desire to look for information and pleasure, basic sight vocabulary, and word analysis skills for independent reading.

Cornelius, Paula Lee. "Reading Management Systems: Solution or Problem?" *Resources in Education* 14 (January 1979): 38. ERIC Ed. 158 221.[14]

Both advantages and disadvantages of a reading management system are reviewed in this article. Advantages include the usefulness of an RMS in assessing pupil needs, for organizing the teaching of reading skills, reporting to parents, and helping teachers make decisions. Disadvantages of RMS include shortcomings of the tests, lack of flexibility for pupils and teachers, and failure to incorporate the skills taught into everyday life.

The author's recommendations center on careful choosing among management systems and incorporating the system into the existing program rather than substituting it as the entire reading program.

Pearson, David P. "Some Practical Applications of a Psycholinguistic Model of Reading." In *What Research Has to Say About Reading Instruction*, edited by S. Jay Samuels. Newark, Del.: International Reading Association, 1978, pp. 84–98.

The author presents a model of how children read and learn to read and indicates how this model can be useful to the teacher. The value of semantics, syntax, and phonics in learning to read is shown. Then six uses of the model in making practical instructional decisions are depicted. One of these uses is to pinpoint similarities and differences among approaches to reading. For example, the technological approach differs from a language experience approach, which capitalizes upon syntactic and semantic information. In contrast, the technological approach addresses directly the child's weaknesses in phonics, encouraging the child to develop phonic skills while giving little attention to semantics or syntax. Once phonic skills are acquired, however, they can be integrated with the pre-existing competence in semantics and syntax.

"Reading and Language," *Theory Into Practice* 16, no. 5 (December 1977).

This special issue of *TIP* is composed of articles by prominent reading specialists — most of whom conceive learning to read as a language experience. They believe children should be taught to read from the wholeness of the task rather than isolated decoding skills, leaving comprehension until later.

Among the authors are Kenneth Goodman, who argues for deskilling reading instruction and placing more emphasis at the beginning on building the

---

[14] ERIC materials are reproduced in microfiche and may be viewed in libraries or ordered from ERIC Documentation Reproduction Service, P.O. Box 190, Arlington, Virginia 22210.

personal-social functions of reading; Moira McKenzie, who emphasizes the importance of letting children know books in enjoyable ways; John Downing, who cites studies supporting teaching approaches that help children understand the concepts used in teaching about literacy skills and how they are related to language; Marie Clay, who indicates how writing contributes to reading; and Arthur Applebee, who shows the importance of a young child having a sense of story — or expectations — when learning to read.

# 3

# Organizing and Managing for the Teaching of Reading

Organizing the class means grouping pupils and orchestrating an array of materials and activities to facilitate learning. Organization makes it possible for you to meet many different objectives within the constraints imposed by the clock, the building, other persons, and the range in pupil characteristics. The need to manage an entire class while attending to individuals within the class can be your greatest dilemma in teaching reading.

In this chapter, we present organizational patterns and management ideas for dealing with the problem of individual attention versus the demands of the whole class. Our suggestions are calculated to make group instruction efficient and enjoyable.

## Organizational Patterns

### Basal Reading Approach to Classroom Organization

Classroom organization with the basal reading approach follows a specific pattern. Consider the case of Ms. N, a first-year teacher assigned to the third grade in a school that uses the basal reader approach for reading instruction. As she looks over the class records of her pupils, Ms. N notices a large span between reading levels. The breakdown of reading levels looks like this:

|  | Primer | Grade 1 (beginning) | Grade 1 (end) | Grade 2 | Grade 3 | Grade 4 |
|---|---|---|---|---|---|---|
| Number of students | 3 | 7 | 8 | 8 | 4 | 2 |

How will Ms. N be able to teach six groups with such varied reading accomplishments?

Traditionally, basal readers have suggested dividing a class into three groups, for this is considered the most reasonable number a teacher can instruct in one hour. While one group works with the teacher, another group follows up instruction with seatwork (workbook exercises, assignments, and other follow-up activities); a third group works independently on supplemental reading assignments.

A typical classroom setup with three groups might look like this:

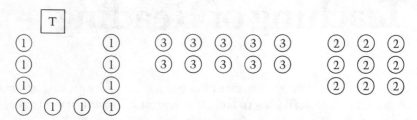

In this arrangement, the teacher is stationary and the pupils move to a new location for each reading activity.

Or the classroom furniture might be arranged in this way:

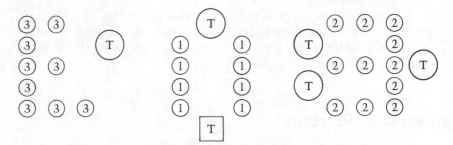

In this second arrangement, pupils retain their "home seat" for the duration of the reading period, and the teacher moves from group to group. (In this situation, experienced teachers know the value of having a chalkboard readily available for working with each group.)

Instead of using three groups, Ms. N could keep her pupils in the six groups where they seemed to fall naturally and meet with only two groups each day:

| Monday | Tuesday | Wednesday | Thursday | Friday |
|--------|---------|-----------|----------|--------|
| Primer | Primer | Grade 2 | Grade 4 | Grade 1 (beginning) |
| Grade 1 (beginning) | Grade 1 (end) | Grade 3 | Primer | Primer |

Scheduling two groups a day gives a teacher thirty minutes to work directly with the pupils when the reading period is one hour. An alternative would be to keep the twenty-minute reading time of traditional grouping and teach the whole class together during the remaining time.

Within the groups, the lower level readers will require more interaction with their teacher until their independent reading skills have advanced. Also more self-directing assignments will be necessary for the groups that meet less frequently, and arranging a variety of activities will help the teacher manage the independent workers. For example, the grade 3-level readers of Ms. N's class can read a story silently and answer written questions on Monday, work with phonics games on Tuesday, receive instruction on Wednesday, receive follow-up instruction on Thursday, and have interest reading on Friday.

An option available in some schools is a pattern that combines the pupils of two or more classes for small group instruction. For instance, the teacher next door to Ms. N may be willing to work with the grades 3- and 4-level readers in exchange for a like number of grades 1- and 2-level readers.

Other temporary methods of grouping are by interest and invitation. With interest grouping, some youngsters from all six of Ms. N's reading levels might like to read about horses. Each of these pupils would be assigned reading materials on the topic but at a different reading level. Members of an invitational group come together for experiences such as sharing their independent reading, dramatizing the stories read, working on reading projects, and engaging in choral reading.

## Technological Approach to Classroom Organization

Management systems within the technological approach are not all alike, although they share some common features. The idea of a management system is that the teacher knows the reading skill needs of each child in the classroom and that children are given differentiated reading instruction to meet those needs. Using the *Wisconsin Design for Reading Skill Development* as an example, you can see how the technological approach provides for differences in children's rates of learning and in the mode or style of learning.

The steps of this system are as follows:

1. Identify individual needs through initial assessment.   Teachers select a skill for word attack, comprehension, study skills, or self-directed, interpretive, and creative reading. The teachers then determine which tests of the skill each pupil should be given. For example, if a child can read second-grade material, you should begin to test skills beyond this level rather than go back to those skills associated with lower levels. It is important to determine the skills each student has already mastered within the level as well as the skills each one lacks. After the assessment data is gathered and scored, the results are recorded.

2. Record test results on profile cards and notch cards.   Profile cards listing specific objectives are usually used as the basis for establishing a continuous record of the child's skill development. A hole appears at the edge of the card for each skill. The card is notched open when a skill is mastered. To identify pupils with common skill development needs, the teacher selects a given skill, passes a skewer through the chosen hole in the grouped profile cards, and shakes off the loose cards. The cards that remain identify the students needing instruction. The profile card allows whoever is working with the child to determine where to begin instruction. (A computer-assisted accounting scheme for pupils is now implemented in schools that have access to computer and teletype terminals.)

3. Form instructional skill groups.   On the basis of analysis of skills that must be taught, teachers may form instructional groups. Each group consists of pupils needing instruction on the same skill. Those individuals who do not fall into any group are assigned to an instructional materials center for independent study. When a team of teachers is working together, each teacher assumes responsibility to work with one of the skill groups, and together they decide how best to provide for supervision of the instructional materials center and for those who are dismissed from skill groups because of early mastery.

4. Select appropriate instructional materials.   The instructional objectives dictate the materials to be used. The prime consideration for selection is whether the materials feature activities that will give the learner sufficient practice in doing what the objective calls for or activities that provide a prerequisite to the objective. In some schools, it has been necessary to examine existing materials and to pair them to the objectives. This has not always worked well because the match between material and objective is too loose. The same rubric or title

may be given to both the objective and the activity, but different operations may be involved. For example, *rhyming element* may be the label used in an objective calling for the child to *generate* a new word consistent with a given rhyming pattern, but an activity with the same name in the text material may require only that the child *select* a word that has a particular rhyming pattern.

Resource materials to use in teaching to a specific objective include: basal readers; textbooks in math, social studies, and science; trade books; and other printed materials. Often skill kits and games are keyed to objectives. Teachers, too, design their own activities and materials. Commercially available materials are made in accordance with technological principles, such as *patterning* (learner is given many examples with which to form a generalization), *prompting* (learner is prompted to make correct responses), and *confirmation* (learner is given feedback regarding the correctness of answers). For example, the Learning Development Center of the University of Pittsburgh has published *Individually Prescribed Instruction* (IPI). This program is aimed at specific objectives and includes diagnostic tests, teaching materials, and a prescribed methodology. Such commercial systems differ from the concept of the *Wisconsin Design for Reading Skill Development* in that they require less teacher involvement. The teacher does not have to develop materials nor personally instruct. Instead with commercially prepared programmed learning, the teacher merely assigns appropriate exercises to the child. The teacher's role, then, essentially involves the placement of the pupil and the monitoring of the pupil's progress.

The *Teacher's Resource Files*[1] is another example of material that helps teachers teach to a specific objective. This material consists of individual folders, each containing the name of a skill and instructional objective. Into each of these folders go lists of published materials related to the particular objective. Worksheets and directions for teacher-developed activities are created and placed in the folders so teachers who want ideas and activities for a given skill can merely pull the folder from the files. Of course, there must be provision for maintaining the file.

5. Teach skill groups for appropriate periods and give consideration to individual differences.  Typically, two hours a week is devoted to specific skill instruction: word attack, comprehension, and study skills. If only one teacher is doing the teaching, that teacher should expect to give six hours a week to skill development. Individuals are

---

[1] *Teacher's Resource Files for the Wisconsin Design for Reading Skill Development* (Minneapolis, Minn.: National Computer Systems, 1975).

moved out of a skills group when their performance is adequate. Working five minutes a day or 120 minutes a week for two to three weeks usually is sufficient time for acquisition of a skill, although pupils differ greatly according to the time and instruction they require.

The number of teachers available and the number of pupils needing instruction in various skills determine the scheduling of group instruction. Each teacher may present two or three skills to the same or different groups. The time for each session can vary with the task. Pupils and materials are matched so children learn in the way most appropriate for them. Some children respond best when instruction is in the form of a game; others prefer audiovisual presentation of skills. Most need interaction with other pupils, although a few work best when they are relatively isolated from the rest of the group. Self-instructional materials are preferred by some children; others would rather learn from cross-age peers who have a better grasp of the skill.

6. Assess pupils to determine mastery.   A teacher's judgment about whether a child has mastered a skill is not enough. In addition, a test is given, and children are informed of their present status. If they show mastery on the test, they are told of their progress and are given the next goal; if they fail, their difficulties with the skill must be pointed out. Often those who fail begin to work with a different skill group before returning to instruction on the unmastered skill. Usually it is better to change the teacher and the materials when teaching the skill a second time. Some children will have success the second time because the teacher capitalizes on the strengths that individual students bring to the instructional group, allowing pupils to help each other, or because the teacher varies the teaching method, perhaps giving more examples or encouraging different response modes — motor, verbal, constructed.

7. Notch profile cards when skills are mastered.

8. Return to step 3.

Objective-based systems are often associated with independent skill stations. A skill station may consist of five or six work areas in a classroom that are stocked with self-instructional materials (materials that feature a format by which pupils make many individual responses and check their own answers during half-hour periods), audiovisual materials, games, and other activities for learning specific skills. Usually each station is devoted to a single skill, and no more than eight children are assigned to a skill station at one time. The teacher circulates among the stations offering direct instruction to one group while the others work independently.

### Language Experience Approach to Classroom Organization

The language experience approach to reading takes its direction from the experiences of individual pupils. This means there will be a great deal of sharing, discussing, listening, telling, dictating, and "reading back" of written material.

For example, Ms. S has used a language experience approach with first-grade pupils for several years. How does she organize such a program with children whose English-language ability ranges from limited to fluent use of English? A look at Ms. S's classroom shows that she relies heavily upon flexible grouping patterns and aids for pupil self-direction.

Flexible grouping is essential for a reading program that centers on pupil interest and participation. Whole class instruction may indicate a multileveled assignment. Small groups may be gathered for instruction according to interest, sex, age, reading needs, or social preference.

Ms. S organizes both skill refinement groups (organized to give help with specific skills) and reading activity groups (organized not by age or ability but on the basis of being able to profit from the experience). Children are regrouped frequently during the year.

To meet the needs of a variety of groups, Ms. S sets up her classroom to allow for meeting places, teamwork positions, and private reading spots.

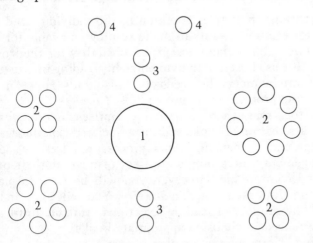

*Area 1.* Large area provides space for whole class activities or for smaller groups to spread out materials.

*Area 2.* Chairs or tables or both are arranged to allow face-to-face interaction among members of various instructive, discussion, or activity groups.

*Area 3.* Team learning or tutoring assignments may take place in semiprivate corners of the room.

*Area 4.* Every classroom needs areas where a child may work in near isolation.

Remember that the furniture arrangement of a classroom is flexible and may be changed with instructional goals. Each of Ms. S's "areas" might accommodate a learning center or a reference material center, or it might change size and location.

Teaching pupils to be self-directed assists teachers like Ms. S in the management of the classroom. The youngsters know where to find picture dictionaries to help them spell a word and whom to ask for help when they cannot read a word. A tape recorder is available for dictation. Sometimes parent volunteers or older pupils help during the reading time. As a teacher, you will think of other devices for self-direction that can be employed in a language-experience reading program.

## Individualized Reading Approach to Classroom Organization

A fourth organizational pattern is common in the individualized approach. Mr. Z, for example, wants to make reading enjoyable for his sixth graders while helping them accept responsibility for their own reading growth. He has chosen to individualize his reading instruction but wants to be sure he meets the needs of all his pupils. How can he manage this reading program so as not to "lose" readers?

One of the four major activities that comprises individualized reading is the self-selection of books and the associated experiences of sharing, visiting, and exchanging. This process requires an open classroom arrangement where pupils are free to move at their own pace, relaxed and comfortable. However, you will be wise to place some limit on the time spent for this activity. You will also find it helpful to limit the number of reading selections available until the readers are experienced in choosing appropriate books.

Silent reading is another activity that is crucial to individualized reading. To keep track of which students have read which books, involve them in record keeping. Giving book reports, making contracts, keeping personal charts, and reading for information are means for joint teacher-pupil evaluation of reading progress.

The third major activity is skill development. Whole class or small group instruction can be used in an individualized reading program if the purpose of the lesson is temporary and specific. More often skills are developed by pupils themselves using charts, workbooks, games, a buddy system, or even basal readers. Any teaching tool may be used in this program as long as direction for reading instruction comes from the individual student.

The teacher-pupil conference is the fourth major activity. During this time, you will listen to the pupil read, diagnose special needs, guide reading choices, evaluate progress, and motivate reading interests. Often the conference activity takes place while the rest of the class engages in silent reading or selecting reading matter or individual study.

You will need to plan a place for conferring that offers some privacy. To avoid interruptions, provide a signal to other students that the conversation is confidential. You will not meet with each reader every day. The cruciality of the conference makes it important that you and the pupil are able to concentrate, knowing that the other pupils can manage independently.

## Ways to Provide for Large Group, Small Group, and Individual Activities

You now know much about grouping patterns for teaching reading. You know that there are times when it is efficient to give reading instruction to the entire class. You also know that small groups of pupils joined for a common reading need or interest accomplish a great deal, and there are times when each youngster works best individually with the teacher.

What kinds of activities can you provide to stimulate interest and progress in reading while allowing for flexible grouping patterns? Seatwork, learning centers, contracts, lap packs, task cards, and games are among the answers.

**Seatwork**   Seatwork should not be busywork. Silent reading periods, written questions, phonics worksheets, dictionary assignments, and reading workbooks are all teaching tools to be employed as follow-up or reinforcing activities to enhance reading skill development. You should design "sitting down" activities to meet specific objectives and let the pupils know what those objectives are. Youngsters will respond with energy and interest to a seatwork assignment when they know it has meaning for their own reading progress.

Vary the form of this type of activity and limit the time each child spends sitting in one place. You might direct pupils to read silently for ten minutes and then move to another spot to work on phonics papers or comprehension questions.

Pupils will work more continuously on any assignment when they are expected to share the results. Dramatizing a story that was read silently, explaining a worksheet to another pupil, or giving a class report on answers to comprehension questions are all motivating ways of conducting seatwork.

Share your evaluation of seatwork with the pupils. Two-way comments from teacher and pupil will enhance a basal workbook tremendously. All written work needs some response, however brief, if it is to remain a meaningful form of learning activity.

**Learning centers**    A learning center is a place in the classroom where children engage in a variety of reading activities, such as locating information, applying reading skills in projects and games, practicing skills, and making generalizations or pronunciation rules after examining written language patterns. Classroom learning centers give the teacher versatility for instructing individuals and groups. They may be used for an entire class in conjunction with basal texts or for individual pupils and at all age levels and for all reading skills.

Open-ended activities are most useful for learning center tasks. You might provide one set of materials with a choice of directions to meet various levels of difficulty. For example, a center might include two packets of cards, each with the same vocabulary words printed on them. While one pupil would be directed to match words, another would be asked to pair synonyms, beginning sounds, or suffixes; a third pupil could use the same cards for creative writing or a dictionary activity. Another means of adjusting the level of difficulty is to use one set of directions for a variety of materials. "Read the story and choose the best title" is an assignment that can be used for stories of various lengths and reading levels.

Youngsters enjoy a change of format in reading centers. Games, worksheets, crossword puzzles, riddles, manipulative devices, pictures, flashcards, tape recorders, phonograph records, and film strips are only a few of the interesting items that can be used productively in an instructional center for reading. (Refer to the appendix for a list of books that offers ideas for learning centers.)

Each center has a performance objective if it is part of the reading instruction. To avoid creating an entertainment center that has no teaching motive, keep objectives specific and share them with the pupils. "After completing this center's activities, you should be able to distinguish contractions from other words" is an objective that will direct pupils.

For easy management of learning centers, introduce the activities that will enable pupils to complete the tasks independently and provide time for evaluation of finished assignments and recording of individual progress. Youngsters enjoy filing or displaying their work and will take more interest in a center that illustrates their reading progress.

**Contracts, lap packs, task cards, games**   Self-directing materials will free you to work with a variety of group sizes. Contracts (child agrees to complete independent study or self-instructional material designed to teach a single concept or skill), lap packs (child has a portable packet of learning tasks complete in themselves), and task cards (child functions independently following the directions given on a card; for example, to make a puppet, to find out why it takes eighteen hours to go ten miles in some locations, or to undertake other activities involving reading research or reading skill) may be easily adapted to suit individual teaching styles and pupil needs. Whichever form these materials take, each should have an instructional objective, a means of evaluation, and provisions for pupils who require special help or who complete the assignments early.

*Sample Contract*

OBJECTIVE
After completing this contract, you should be able to distinguish a compound word from other words.

|  | Completed Work | |
|---|---|---|
|  | Pupil | Teacher |

1. Use the word cards. Put two cards together to form ten new words that make sense. Write the new (compound) words on your paper; for example:

   cow   boy     cowboy

2. Look in your reading book and find ten words that are made by putting two words together. Write these compound words on your paper.

3. Play "Compound Word Bingo" with two friends.

4. Finished? Good for you! You may use the
picture cards to make *nonsense* compound words. Draw a picture to go with
each word. Need help? See David or Janet.

*Sample Task Card*

OBJECTIVE:
After completing the task card, you should be able to group words
according to feelings.

DIRECTIONS:

1. The following words may be happy or sad: good, sick, fun, bad,
   like, smile, hurt, cry, laugh, scared, school, lost. Fix your paper
   like this:

   *happy      sad*

   Now list the words that make you happy under *happy* and the
   words that make you sad under *sad.*

2. Answer these questions on the back of your paper.
   a. Do you have more happy words than sad words?
   b. What is the most unhappy word for you?
   c. Can some words be both happy and sad?
   d. Which words make you happiest?

3. Finished? Good for you! You may choose another feeling (anger,
   excitement, worry, silliness?). Make up words to go with your
   feeling. Draw a picture to go with your feeling.

Youngsters who are used to working with self-directing materials
are good resources for creating new learning activities. Show them the
format of a game board and let them design how it can be used to meet
a reading objective.

The game board may be used for almost all reading skills. Cards
are made to allow players to progress as they practice reading vocabulary, phonics, or comprehension skills at various levels of difficulty.
The child moves one space after successfully completing the task
printed on the card; that is, reading the word, making the sound, or
defining the term. Spell out the objective so the players understand
why they are playing and provide a means of evaluation. Requests such
as "Keep a list of the words that are difficult" or "Write your answers

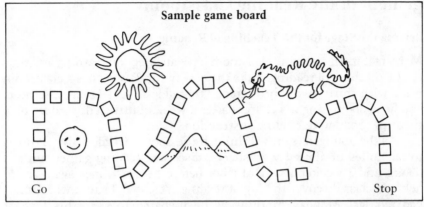

**Sample game board**

Go

Stop

**Sample cards**

| Vocabulary | Phonics | Comprehension |
|---|---|---|
| cat | ing | Tell how Johnny |
| Read the word. | Say a word that | Tremain burned |
| Move one space. | has this suffix. | his hand. |
| | Move two spaces. | Move three spaces. |

down" will give the teacher feedback on the activity as well as let the pupils know they are playing for a purpose.

### How Tutors, Paraprofessionals, and Volunteers Aid in Grouping

The reading classroom that provides more than one instructor is often the most productive. Chapter 9 explains in detail how you can extend yourself through arrangements involving other adults and pupil helpers. Adult volunteers, paraprofessional aides, and tutors may be trained to teach a particular reading skill. As resources for the teacher of reading, these people provide another means for handling activities for large groups, small groups, and individuals.

To train a volunteer, aide, or tutor, you need specific instructional objectives, clear procedures for reading activities, and a system for evaluating both pupil and aide. Have the tutors perform the learning task themselves before presenting it to the pupils. Also provide the tutor with an answer sheet or guideline for instruction. You want assurance that each skill will be taught correctly.

Classroom aides and volunteers can provide assistance to readers when you are busy with a small group or individual. However, limit the time any youngster spends with an aide or in directed reading sessions with you.

# Management of the Reading Classroom

### Setting the Stage for the Teaching of Reading

Many factors in a reading classroom have an effect on learning and thus on the teaching of reading. Take the case of Mr. P, who has a classroom filled with thirty-two fourth-grade "tornadoes." It is Friday afternoon and he is dismissing his charges after a week of futile effort to involve them in productive reading instruction.

As the youngsters crowd through the door to freedom, Mr. P turns to face piles of abused worksheets, discarded reading games, unread books, and a weekend of hard labor before he must once again try to help his class discover the joy of reading. Yes, joy! That is what Mr. P had felt last Monday morning as he prepared to share his love of reading with his pupils. He did not feel joyful today, knowing that he had shared only tension and frustration. What had gone wrong?

The school bus was late on Monday, and by the time the class was assembled, the reading period was half over. The pupils who had finished their assignment were rowdy, the newcomers were confused, and Mr. P was barely able to give hasty directions for homework. Tuesday, six pupils left their workbooks at home, and there was a fight at the listening center. Wednesday, the band rehearsed outside and glue spilled on the phonics workbooks. Thursday, the slide projector broke, and Friday, the reading groups would not follow along when one person was reading.

Mr. P needs help. What can teachers do to improve such defeating situations?

**Environment**  Noise, light, air, odors, colors, activity, space, and placement of materials are all elements that can be juggled to create a productive learning environment. You have to experiment by arranging these factors to see how they best fit your group's personality.

A well-lighted, ventilated, clean room with a minimum of outside noise or activity is a good beginning. Although even this basic requirement may not be present in some schools, it is important enough to pursue. Sometimes you will have to try to deal with outside-of-the-classroom matters as they bear upon the learning environment. Playground activities, bells, lawn mowing, and other interferences may have to be altered to lessen conflict with your reading instruction.

Certainly you should change detrimental factors within your classroom. A lethargic group of students may need only an opened window or an activity involving movement. Pupils may be asked to act out a story they are reading after a lengthy session of sitting.

The placement of materials and classroom furniture can also make a difference in the child's ability to concentrate. As a general rule, materials are well placed if everyone in the room is able to obtain work essentials, such as paper, pencils, books, and workbooks, without assistance. It does not matter whether you choose to have a central location for pencils and to store books and workbooks in the pupils' desks or vice versa.

Avoid clutter. Oral directions may be kept simple if pupils can see clearly the materials they are expected to use. The purpose of work items dictates their placement. You would not store painting equipment on the reading table or reading material on the art table.

It is important to have consistency in the location of items and to insure that the youngsters are familiar with the classroom arrangement. To determine appropriate placement of reading materials for various age levels, study the classroom from a child's viewpoint. Younger pupils may respond well to labels on cupboard doors, but older ones will require fewer visual cues to locate work items. Everyone will benefit from the establishment of a convenient system for obtaining materials that provides independence while giving direction to learning objectives.

**Patterns of movement within the reading class**   The physical location of persons in the classroom and their patterns of movement can help create a productive learning situation. A teacher who greets pupils at the door will capture more attention than one who keeps them waiting. Pupils who know where to go and what to do once they are in the room are more likely to meet classroom behavior expectations than those who must search aimlessly for direction.

You may establish patterns of movement with deliberate attention to the needs of the children. Restless little children might be assigned to work on a rug where they would have room to move around; rowdy youngsters should be separated from each other; and individual interest groups could have a corner of the room for themselves.

Used consistently, patterns of movement and positioning can help create a "mind set" for work. If the pupils are regularly taught reading instruction while seated on a chair in a circle formation, they will learn to respond to that setting with an expected standard of attention. A worksheet placed on top of a desk may be an automatic signal to begin work, and the direction "Please go to the rug" may mean "Time for phonics." Of course, children should be provided opportunities to read at other times. Reading should be an integral part of all school life. Children have the right to read for enjoyment, reaction, and entertainment as well as to learn the mechanics of reading.

**The effect of voice and body language on learning**    Your voice, hand movements, facial expressions, and physical closeness influence pupil responses. A raised voice may be very effective for hurrying a class outside for a fire drill, but it may also create tension during a reading lesson. Hand and arm movements may illustrate a story but distract an oral reader.

To hold the attention of a class, it is sometimes helpful to maintain frequent eye contact, to exaggerate facial expression, to move around the room, and to engage in touching behavior. Although it is impossible to state rules to be slavishly followed about which characteristic will result in a desired response for a particular group and situation (some Eskimos, for example, interpret direct eye contact as intimidating conduct), it is useful to be aware of how your physical presence is influencing your pupils.

One of the best ways to whet the child's appetite for reading is for the teacher who enjoys reading to read aloud stories, poems, and informative writings in a voice that conveys meaning and mood. Teachers who are good readers of stories will find that their pupils move physically closer in reading circles during the reading of scary tales.

**Children's responsibility for the learning environment**    Youngsters should learn to be sensitive to conditions that interfere with the quality of their learning and to make known their concerns so improvements can be made. Broken pencils, toilet needs, inadequate space, or a poor line of vision are distractions that pupils can change themselves without detracting from the lesson. Children should be encouraged to let you know when they do not understand directions or do not know what is expected of them. To develop a workable learning environment, you should decide with your class which kinds of problems can be solved independently and which need to be shared. This means letting pupils know the tasks to be undertaken in learning to read, planning how to get these tasks done, and feeling free to use the resources for doing the job. You must help learners know their strengths and weaknesses in reading and where to find the practice materials or other sources that zero in on a demonstrated need. Children should not have to waste time at tasks they can already do.

**Preparation of materials**    Preparation for instruction includes securing enough books, duplicating clear worksheets, sharpening spare pencils, arranging furniture, and mastering audiovisual equipment before pupils arrive to avoid classroom confusion and gain instructional time. Efficient teaching depends on the availability of extra worksheets for new students, provisions for the pupils who have been absent, and spare books for those who have left theirs at home.

To provide for interruptions, schedule and enrollment changes, equipment breakdown, and other interferences, some teachers prepare a reading emergency kit. Such a kit contains short lessons, such as those dealing in a phonics skill, independent activities, and oral language games. Directions are kept simple and easy to follow. The teacher who prepares for a routine day but also provides alternative activities for unexpected disturbances will have fewer classroom management problems and a more effective reading program.

Timing in the use of materials is equally important. Generally, materials should not be distributed before children are ready to use them. When they are distributed too soon, children give their attention to the materials rather than to the teacher's directions for using them.

## Using Time Efficiently in the Teaching of Reading

Be frugal with instructional time. Sometimes valuable learning hours are lost to administrative and controlling functions. Waiting for the completion of roll taking and announcements, for groups to gather, and for the many five-minute blocks of time when materials are being collected add up to months of wasted teaching time. Instead spare minutes may be used for activities that reinforce previous learning. As a group is gathering, pupils can practice flashcards, look up certain words in a dictionary, or play a word game. Mental exercises are useful during transition times: "Be ready to tell me two compound words when I collect your paper."

The fact that each child works at a different pace must be considered. The period between the times when the first and last students finish a task may be used by asking the first child to engage in reading of his or her own choice. Learning additional parts of a complex skill, improving accuracy, and reducing time for performance are other examples of supplemental pacing activities for dealing with learner variations.

A great deal of time is wasted when the teacher asks a pupil a question or requests a performance from a single child and the rest of the class sits passively or tunes out while the selected pupil responds. It is more economical to involve all pupils. In an oral reading situation, for example, it is sometimes better to give all listeners a task before asking someone to read. You might say to those awaiting their turn at oral reading, "While listening to Billy read, try to find out what caused the fight." Or "Think of your own question about the story and listen for answers as each pupil reads aloud in turn." In asking questions, it is often a good idea to frame them so all will have to think about the response required, not knowing who will be called upon. An example of economy in teaching is found in instructions such as: "Raise your hand if you can find the main idea in this paragraph." (All participate and the teacher is aided in recognizing those who may need help.) Occasionally questioning a child about a previous response from another child will keep the class alert and accountable between turns. At times, however, it is better for children to know when they will be called upon; for example, when it is necessary to lower the children's anxiety about being called on unexpectedly or to minimize the tendency for overeager pupils to call out answers or volunteer too frequently.

As a result of studies such as the *Beginning Teacher Evaluation*,[2] a study indicating the importance of direct instruction, concern about the use of classroom time has been expressed. Data from this study suggest that second-grade reading instruction, for example, is more effective when there is an opportunity for each pupil to have access to the teacher for instruction and correction of work and when the teacher works with an individual child or with a small group. Unmonitored seatwork or arrangements that keep pupils waiting for instruction are ineffective. At fifth-grade reading levels, too, those teaching practices that provide for the teacher's sustained interaction with pupils are more effective.

In their study of effective teachers of reading, investigators at the University of Texas also found that high-achieving first-grade teachers give pupils more opportunity to learn than low-achieving teachers.[3] High-achieving teachers maximize instructional time by:

1. Meeting with their reading groups for thirty minutes a day rather than twenty minutes a day as the less effective teachers do.

2. Starting the lesson immediately without needing to organize the class or discipline pupils.

3. Spending less time in making transitions among activities. Hence they accomplish other things, such as arranging extended reading groups, providing more content, and encouraging greater pupil participation.

---

[2] Educational Testing Service, *Beginning Teacher Evaluation*, BTES Report no. 3 (Princeton: Educational Testing Service, 1977).

[3] Linda M. Anderson, Carolyn M. Evertson, and Jere E. Brophy, *An Experimental Study of Effective Teaching in First Grade Reading Groups* (Austin: University of Texas, The Research and Development Center for Teacher Education, August 1978).

4.   Giving each child an opportunity individually to practice a new skill that was taught instead of using excessive choral responses.

**Objectives and economy of time**   Instructional objectives can make teaching more efficient. The resourceful teacher is careful to determine which objectives are appropriate for individuals and what the correct level of difficulty is for each youngster. The teacher then monitors progress toward these objectives and adjusts them continuously as needs change. It is uneconomical to spend time working on activities pointed toward objectives that have already been attained or are too difficult in light of the learners' present status. This does not mean you should not plan review lessons or provide challenging materials. It does mean you should find out what your pupils already know and plan for what they need to learn.

**Independence in use of time**   Pupils themselves may share in the responsibility for determining what takes place in the reading classroom. To include children in decision making, teach them to seek out tasks that are motivating, sufficiently difficult, and focused by instructional objectives. For example, you might introduce new vocabulary and together with your pupils establish an expected standard of performance. The pupils could then choose between a variety of teacher-planned tasks or design their own activities to learn the vocabulary. Such activities teach youngsters to use their time wisely and to select activities appropriate to their personal learning needs. Teaching for independence will in the long run free you for instructional time. Pupil teams or peer pairs are another solution to the problem of dependency on teacher presence. Learning takes place when two or more children pool their knowledge or when a child explains something to a peer in words that may communicate better than the formal language of an adult. Also, children are more apt to work independently when they select their own seating and have a variety of relevant activities available.

The practice of having pupils serve as consultants or chairmen often builds pupil esteem while lessening teacher dependency. A "word captain" may help peers with vocabulary, and a "dictionary wizard" may help the class gain a new respect for the alphabet, guide words, diacritical markings, and other reference features.

Mutual aid among classmates requires careful direction. Asking a group to "discuss this story" is a vague direction that will result in little productive work. But asking a group to "list the five characters you like most in this story and be ready to tell why" will produce thought, effort, and, possibly, a lively discussion. Clear and simple directions that include a means of feedback to you will help the pupils cooperate for a mutual purpose.

## Improving Reading Motivation

Productive activities vary with the level of reading skill, but highly motivating activities may be adapted to any skill. To initiate interest in reading or reading skills, plan lessons that include something novel, pleasant, or intriguing. Youngsters love drama. An unusual object, short role play, interesting visual aid, field trip, speaker, or improvised melodrama will capture the pupil's curiosity and can be used to connect reading with something meaningful. A treasure map could be used to introduce readers to *Treasure Island* and a braille book might help beginning readers understand that symbols can represent sounds.

Always relate your reading goals to something significant to the individual pupil. Some youngsters will work hard to experience a personal sense of success or to satisfy a natural inquisitiveness. Other pupils may need extrinsic rewards as motivators. Although stars, happy faces, grades, or other prizes may be helpful to direct attention to the pursuit of reading goals, they should be used only temporarily. Reinforcers that youngsters already enjoy — praise, rewards, even novelty as in playing music during reading or reading outside — should be used only occasionally. The main goal is to teach the pupils commitment to reading as an end, valuable for itself. One study of young children found there are fewer independent children in a kindergarten classroom where adults heap praise on children, although a positive correlation exists between praise and high scores on beginning reading tests.[4] Our general conclusion is that your use of praise should not be overdone, and it should be used discriminately. Take care to be specific about the behavior being praised.

To help youngsters develop more interest in reading and less dependency on extrinsic rewards, teach them to use their reading skills for everyday purposes. Newspapers, comic books, television guides, games, recipes, menus, telephone books, and personal correspondence are only a few of the items that can be employed to show that reading has value as part of the out-of-school world.

**Teaching pupils to direct their own reading progress**    Youngsters will be motivated toward reading activities if they are able to influence

---

[4] Jane Stalling, *Study of Children in Kindergarten Participating in Follow-Through Programs* (Palo Alto, Calif.: Stanford Research Institute, 1978).

those activities. Most pupils enjoy choosing one of two books to read and will work harder on their own selection than on one that has been assigned. Deciding whether to work with a team or independently, electing to read now and practice phonics later, and choosing between studying words on flashcards or in a book are all decision opportunities that will enhance a young reader's motivation.

Help pupils learn to evaluate and reward their own reading achievements. Opportunities to compete with oneself, to decide how much one has to do or learn to show satisfactory improvement and to set personal goals, are motivating. Peers, too, can help one learn to set realistic goals. An example has been adapted from the work of Richard De Charms.[5] After a pretest of vocabulary, the students are told they will have a vocabulary "bee" the next day, and they may study the words overnight. When it is time to play, the class is divided into two teams. As each pupil's turn comes, the child is asked, "Would you like to try an easy word for one point, a moderately hard word for two points, or a very hard word for three points? Any error in definition will be zero points." An easy word is one the child knew on the pretest, a moderately hard word is a new word the pupil had time to study, and a very hard word is one taken from a future vocabulary list. Each reader is faced with making a choice, often with pressure from teammates to increase (but not by too much) the risks he or she takes. Thus pupils learn to make wise choices while acquiring vocabulary, selecting the moderately hard words that offer a realistic chance of success.

Other ways to motivate the reading of children in elementary school are to give the children an opportunity:

1. To share a favorite passage of a book or describe an interesting character.

2. To take turns at being "story teller," reading a short, easy story or book.

3. To help an unsure reader by having him or her read to a younger child.

4. To hear a book talk by the librarian followed by browsing.

5. To hear you read from books such as *Journey to the Center of the Earth.*

6. To read a ghost story by candlelight.

---

[5] Richard De Charms, *Enhancing Motivation: A Change in the Classroom* (New York: Irvington Publishers, 1976).

7. To read condensed versions of original stories (for example, *The Invisible Man*) but make the original available, too.

8. To hear you reading a book to the class, but stopping at the climax. Have students find out for themselves what happens.

9. To learn why you think a particular book is great (invite pupils to borrow it).

10. To make "movies" of a story by mounting rolls in cardboard boxes and turning them while narrating the story.

11. To make a *collage* (a collection of fragments pasted together in an artistic composition) using pictures from magazines to illustrate feelings or ideas in a book.

12. To make a *diorama* (a small scene) illustrating incidents and characters from books.

13. To act out plays.

14. To present a story with puppets.

15. To write a letter to the subject of a biography or autobiography.

16. To write their own stories or books and place them in the class library for others to read.

17. To reveal their interest by responding to an interest inventory.

## Summary

The challenge of teaching individuals in a classroom with many children has prompted a variety of organizational and grouping practices: ungraded systems, interclass grouping, team teaching, and individualized programs. Your own commitment to a method or to a set of materials also influences the plan of organization. Organization within the major approaches to the teaching of reading tends to follow patterns. The range in goals found in a comprehensive basal reader requires a variation in grouping, and the focus on specific skills as found in a competency or technological approach calls for frequent reassignment of individual pupils. Different reading goals require different types of classroom organization. Current organizational plans emphasize ways to match instruction with the reading skills individuals need as shown by a diagnostic measure. When goals change (as has happened so often in the past), organizational patterns also change. The teaching of reading for the purposes of personal enjoyment or for resolving a problem, for instance, encourages more organization for free selection of reading material and pupil-teacher conferencing.

One key to classroom achievement in learning to read is the management competence of the teacher. Giving attention to the physical environment, using an efficient placement of materials, establishing patterns of movement and pupil responsibility, are some of the factors contributing to such competency. Others are the ability to plan ahead for routine and emergency situations, to use instructional time efficiently, and to arrange activities of high motivational value.

# Self-instructional Exercises

### Exercise 1. Matching Solutions with Classroom Problems

Check the statements that best answer each question.

1. What can teachers do to improve the environment of their reading class?

   a. \_\_\_\_\_ Punish the pupils who are tardy.

   b. \_\_\_\_\_ Prepare more difficult work for those who fight.

   c. \_\_\_\_\_ Instruct the class in purposeful placement of work items.

   d. \_\_\_\_\_ Try to have disturbances removed; for example, have band rehearsal relocated or rescheduled.

2. What can teachers do to improve the patterns of movement and physical location?

   a. \_\_\_\_\_ Instruct the pupils in movement activities and means of removing themselves from uncomfortable situations.

   b. \_\_\_\_\_ Prepare self-directing assignments for pupils who complete work early or arrive in the middle of a lesson.

   c. \_\_\_\_\_ Maintain an awareness of the teacher's influence through personal presence.

   d. \_\_\_\_\_ Use diagnostic instruments to pigeonhole the learner in relation to other children.

3. How can teachers improve their use of instructional time?

   a. \_\_\_\_\_ Plan learning activities that can take place during transition.

   b. \_\_\_\_\_ Use questioning techniques that require the total class to be involved.

   c. _____ Give silent members a listening task to be performed while a peer reads orally.

   d. _____ Provide a variety of reading materials.

4. What can teachers do to initiate an individualized-reading program?

   a. _____ Set up the classroom for freedom of movement, availability of books, and some privacy.

   b. _____ Design a joint record-keeping system.

   c. _____ Plan to have a conference with each child every day.

   d. _____ Collect a variety of skill development materials.

5. What can teachers do to provide activities for productive reading instruction within a variety of grouping patterns?

   a. _____ Determine specific reading objectives for pupils and let them know what those objectives are.

   b. _____ Instruct pupils in the use of self-directing materials and provide for a means of evaluation.

   c. _____ Design a variety of task cards, games, worksheets, learning centers, contracts, and reading assignments to meet reading objectives.

   d. _____ Let pupils know long-term reading goals and give them a chance to share their progress.

   e. _____ Ask for volunteers to come in and teach reading.

**ANSWERS TO EXERCISE 1**

1. Answers c and d will improve the environment. Children who find themselves in a lush reading environment are more likely to become immersed in reading. It helps to have many reading materials close at hand: films, encyclopedias, dictionaries, self-testing practice materials. The environment should be an invitation to read with space for solitary silent reading and space for shared reading, reading to each other and discussing what has been read.

2. Answers a, b, and c may help improve patterns of movement. Although item d may affect pupil assignment, it does not bear directly on classroom movement.

3. Answers a, b, and c relate to the economical use of the learner's time. Item d may or may not be associated with the amount of pupil time spent on a task.

4. Answers a, b, and d are useful procedures in individualized reading. Although it would be desirable, it is not practical in a large class to have a

daily conference with each pupil. The best way to schedule pupils is in alphabetical order rather than in the order they finish their books. Some pupils read short, easy books merely to have frequent conferences; others take difficult books to avoid them.

5. Answers b and c seem appropriate and consistent with the technological principle that activities must match objectives. Item a is only partially appropriate — letting pupils in on the objectives is helpful but not sufficient. Some provision must be made for how the pupils will attain the skills desired. Item d lacks provision for how goals will be achieved. In item e, volunteers need guidance in what and how to teach before instruction can be productive.

## Exercise 2. Classroom Management Patterns and Probable Consequences

Check the consequence(s) that is likely to follow each grouping practice.

1. Children are assigned to small reading groups for the year on the basis of their ability to read. Bright, high achievers are placed in one group, middle achievers in another, and slow pupils in another.

   a. _____ Difficulties of many bright students may be overlooked.

   b. _____ Strengths of many slow learners may be ignored.

   c. _____ The self-concepts of some pupils may be damaged.

   d. _____ Pupils in each group will be found to go at the same pace.

2. Children are assigned to provisional groups — groups flexible enough to allow for the shifting of individual pupils between groups depending on their progress and need for review.

   a. _____ Materials are not likely to be available for dealing with the range of individual differences.

   b. _____ The demand on teacher time is great because the teacher must plan for several groups.

   c. _____ Parents may be unhappy because their child is removed from a fast group.

   d. _____ Children cannot work by themselves on self-instructional material.

3. Children from a number of grades, all of whom need a particular skill, go to a designated learning station for instruction in that skill.

   a. _____ Reading tends to be isolated from math, science, and the other content fields.

   b. _____ The clock determines the length of the lesson, not the pupils' continued involvement and interest.

c. _____ The teacher chosen to teach the skill lesson is likely to be exceptionally prepared and competent in teaching that skill.

d. _____ Children are likely to read stories of common interest regardless of the grade level.

**ANSWERS TO EXERCISE 2**

1. Answers a, b, c, and d are all likely consequences from the grouping plan described. A two- to three-year range in reading ability is likely even with the fast group, and there is a similar range within the slow group. Even the child reading at the top of the fast group may have need for skills that will be taught in the low group. Grouping is never exact because we do not usually test for all skills and testing is not perfect for individual cases. Also, children change in their ability to read during the year because of motivational, maturational, and other factors. Some children assigned to a slow group might label themselves failures in reading and together with a teacher engage in a self-fulfilling prophesy.

2. A likely consequence is stated in answer b — the need for planning. It is true that parents often value the status that comes from their child's placement in a fast group. However, flexible grouping allows *more* children to acquire the advantages that come with membership in a fast group. The other consequences come from poor planning rather than from flexible grouping.

3. Answer a is a likely consequence. A skill taught in isolation from what the child is experiencing in math, science, and other subject groupings tends to remain an isolated skill, seldom applied in appropriate areas. Item b is probable inasmuch as scheduling often requires a return to the classes from which the pupils come at a given time. Item c is probable. Indeed teachers often volunteer to teach the skill in which they have greatest teaching ability and interest. Item d is not a likely consequence. The consequence of item d would occur if there was interest grouping rather than skill grouping.

## Exercise 3. Room Arrangement and Teaching Purpose

Check the activity most likely to be served by the room arrangement described.

1. A large, round table with seating for five to ten children and an adult

a. _____ The teacher working with a reading group poses questions to be answered from a reading selection or has a discussion about what has been read.

b. _____ The teacher administers individualized testing; each child completes a mastery test when ready.

c. _____ The teacher allows recreational reading; each child reads a book of his own choice.

2. A cubicle where a child works alone with text, workbook, programmed booklets, film strip, or tape recorder

    a. _____ The child composes stories for others to read.

    b. _____ The child receives punishment by being isolated from others.

    c. _____ The child learns a skill of personal importance.

3. Student desks in a row facing the front of the room with the teacher's desk at the front

    a. _____ Different groups of pupils analyze different parts of the same story.

    b. _____ Pupils share a directed lesson or share something of importance to all.

    c. _____ Pupils apply their study skills in individually selected learning tasks.

4. An activity center consisting of art, science materials, construction devices, boxes of odds and ends, together with cards for guiding the pupils in the use of the center

    a. _____ Children apply skills learned and follow directions.

    b. _____ Children type a story for classmates, incidentally learning an awareness of words.

    c. _____ Children develop their own interests without regard to reading skills.

5. A library center consisting of a variety of reading materials, comfortable chairs, a rug, or even pillows

    a. _____ Listening to rhymes, stories, and other oral language activity

    b. _____ Playing learning games that teach and reinforce reading skills

    c. _____ Reading books of personal interest

**ANSWERS TO EXERCISE 3**

1a. This is the purpose best served by the arrangement defined. The key to the correct answer is that a round table invites interaction between persons, not testing or other private activity.

2c. A learning cubicle best serves individual acquisition of a skill. Although it may be useful in cutting out distractions for children easily influenced by peers, it should never be punishing.

3b. The traditional classroom format is best for lecture and total class viewing.

4a. An activity center is usually associated with the purpose of application, for example, using reading skills in constructing a model or making something according to directions. The typing of a story may be part of an activity center, although some teachers organize a composing center for such activity and encourage individuals to use it as an incentive to writing and reading.

5c. Reading: free reading and reading to investigate a problem are both enhanced by a classroom library.

## Selected Readings

Atkinson, Richard C. "Adaptive Instructional Systems: Some Attempts to Optimize the Learning Process." In *Cognition and Instruction,* edited by David Klahr. Hillsdale, N.J.: Lawrence Erlbaum Associates, 1976, pp. 81–109.

This chapter is an account of how research in computer-aided reading instruction can contribute to the development of principles for teaching reading. Atkinson has devised decisive rules for optimizing learning. He has shown how decisions regarding classroom management strategies differ in accordance with external pressures placed on the teacher; for instance, if the teacher is expected to maximize average group performance when instructional time is limited. The effective teacher works first with pupils who learn most rapidly and teaches them to mastery. Then the teacher continues with small groups in order from the fastest to the slowest learners, saving little time for the slowest learners because they do little to raise the average for the given investment in time. (Obviously, this strategy is undemocratic.) On the other hand, if the teacher is supposed to get all children up to some minimum competency, the high-achieving teacher will not give special attention to those who read the minimum level until every pupil has achieved comparable gain. (This strategy is antagonistic to maximizing potential.)

Dunlin, Ken L. "Reading and the Affective Domains." In *Aspects of Reading Education,* edited by Susanna Pflaum-Connor. Berkeley, Calif.: McCutchan, 1978, pp. 106–125.

Dunlin presents "four faces" of affect: attitude toward reading, motivation to read, preference for certain materials, and critical and creative responses to specific characteristics of materials. He then describes ways each can be developed through teaching. He gives, for example, specific ways positive attitudes toward reading can occur through (1) identification with a teacher and that teacher's own responses to reading, (2) rewards, (3) successful reading experiences, (4) adaptation in response to individual needs, and (5) practices that foster the habit of reading.

Dunlin summarizes the reasons why people read at certain times, why they want to read particular materials, and how to capitalize upon the reader's patterns of preference. He concludes by presenting what is known about the skills required for creative and critical reading.

Felsenthal, Helen, and Kirsch, Irwin. "Variations in Teachers' Management of and Time Spent on Reading Instruction: Effects on Student Learning," *Resources in Education* 14, no. 2 (February 1979): 48. ERIC Ed. 159 614.

This study shows extreme variations in teacher management styles and in the amount of engaged and scheduled time in reading in fourth-, fifth- and sixth-grade classrooms. Although the investigators were unable to find significant differences in post-test performance of pupils, they concluded that differences in management style and time result in outcome differences of cognitive measures.

Fox, Anne C., and Franke, Mary. "Learning Centers: The Newest Thing in Busy Work?" *Reading World* 18, no. 3 (March 1979): 221–226.

A report on the instructional quality and effectiveness of learning packets used in selected elementary school classrooms. The criteria used by the investigators are explicit; each packet must have a goal to teach in a specific skill, and the activity must be directed toward achieving the stated goal.

Results of the evaluation indicate that nearly half of learning center packets have problems in meeting the criteria. It is recommended that teachers develop a critical attitude toward materials used to facilitate learning. Suggestions are given for modifying those packets with fewer faults.

Keisling, Herbert. "Productivity of Instructional Time by Mode of Instruction for Students at Varying Levels of Reading Skill," *Reading Research Quarterly* 13, no. 4 (1977–78): 554–582.

A report of an empirical study to determine the number of minutes of instruction each child received under large group, small group, and individualized instruction and to relate this time to reading performance. The findings indicated that reading gains were related to the number of minutes of instruction offered, especially for children at or slightly below grade level. Also, it was found that teachers gave relatively more resources (instructional time) to the lower performing children.

# 4

# Word Attack Skills

In Chapter 1 we differentiated between reading acquisition skills (skills for learning to read) of the young learner and the skills of reading from texts (reading skills that help one learn from print) as applied by the mature reader. In this chapter, we introduce word attack skills as the principal category of reading acquisition skills commonly taught in the elementary school. Three categories of skills — comprehension, study, and critical reading — are defined and illustrated in Chapters 5 and 6. Since you will be expected to teach most or all of these skills to your pupils, you should know what they are and, of course, you should have mastered them yourself.

Word attack means "figuring out" printed words. Ideally it means looking at an unfamiliar printed word that may correspond to a word in one's oral repertoire and recognizing what the printed word stands for. At times, as an enabling but not sufficient step (that is, a step that helps but cannot succeed by itself), word attack is taken to mean learning how to pronounce without necessarily comprehending such unfamiliar printed words. The latter is something like a speaker of English learning to pronounce Spanish words orally by following the rules assigning particular sound values to the letters *i, e, a, o,* and *u* without knowing what is being read.

This chapter is a partial answer to the question of *what* should be taught in reading. The skills presented have been drawn from numerous sources reflecting school practice in teaching word attack skills. We state each skill as an objective and include a sample test item and often a learning activity to clarify what is being demanded of the learner. Detailed descriptions of ways to teach the skills are presented in Chapter 7. You may want to use the present chapter as a reference rather than to try to recall all the information presented, particularly if you are not already familiar with the specialized terms associated with reading skills — *rhyming elements, consonant digraphs, consonant blends,* and the like. To help you organize your study of word attack skills, the following outline is arranged to indicate skills taught at readiness, primary, middle, and upper elementary grade levels and to show the relationships of certain subskills.

*Outline of word attack skills*

I. Prereading or readiness skills
   A. Auditory discrimination
   B. Visual discrimination
   C. Sound blending
   D. Language of instruction
   E. Supplementary skills

II. Primary level skills
   A. Basic sight vocabulary
   B. Phonic analysis skills
      1. Consonant sounds
      2. Consonant digraphs
      3. Beginning consonant blends
      4. Rhyming elements, phonograms, and "families"
      5. Short and long vowel sounds
   C. Structural analysis skills
      1. Compound words
      2. Base words and endings
      3. Contractions
   D. Contextual analysis skills

III. Middle level skills
   A. Expanded sight vocabulary
   B. Phonics analysis skills
      1. Consonant variants
      2. Consonant blends
      3. r-controlled vowels (vowels followed by *r*)
      4. *a* plus *w* or *l*
      5. Diphthongs

The central word attack or decoding task is to figure out the identity of written words on the basis of (1) associating the sounds with letters (phonics), (2) examining meaningful parts of words (structural analysis), and (3) using the meaning and grammar of sentences as clues to word recognition (contextual analysis). Good readers use all of these strategies to decode words. Although one strategy may be more useful in a given situation (for instance, contextual analysis is most appropriate when the unknown word is not spelled the way it sounds), each strategy contributes to the deciphering of a word. Contextual analysis, for example, aids in confirming a word decoded through a phonics or structural analysis strategy. We want to make it clear that the word attack skills taught as part of the three strategies differ from what is taught under a "look and say" or whole word method of word recognition. The latter is a technique for helping children recall or recognize words previously seen, not for learning to decode unfamiliar words. The whole word technique involves showing pupils printed words and having these words pronounced for them. After some repetitions, the response of the sound of the word is associated with the sight of it.

# Phonic Analysis Skills

Phonic analysis is based on the *alphabet principle* of our language. The essence of this principle is that there is a correspondence between the spelling of words and their pronunciation. In phonics one deals with the relationships between letters and sounds or what some call *phonemes* (meaningful sounds in their smallest unit), which are the individual sounds that combine to make a word, and *graphemes* (letters representing particular phonemes).

The twenty-six letters of the alphabet or their combinations are the graphemes of our language. These letters alone or in different combinations must be associated with nearly forty-five phonemes. One grapheme does not necessarily represent one phoneme, although it may. For example, in the word *hat,* the grapheme *h* does represent one phoneme; the *a,* another; and the *t,* still another. However, in the word *house,* the grapheme *h* represents one phoneme; the grapheme *ou* represents one phoneme or sound; the *s* represents one phoneme; and the *e* represents no phoneme but serves as a marker to indicate that *s* does not denote a plural or third-person singular verb. The idea of phonics instruction is to teach the child what sound values to apply to particular graphemes.

Matching of sounds to letters in English may appear difficult when you think of graphemes that are associated with a variety of sound values (*o* in *oat, though, come, hot, off*) and the phonemes that are represented by different graphemes (the phoneme /f/ as in *laugh, face, photo, muffler*).[1] Years ago George Bernard Shaw asserted that in English the word *fish* might just as well be spelled *ghoti,* because if /gh/ is sounded as in *enough, o* as in *women,* and *ti* as in *nation,* one hears *fish.* However, the linguist Carl Lefevre has pointed out that George Bernard Shaw was spoofing with *ghoti* because in practice *gh* is rarely used at the beginning of words; *ti* representing /s/ occurs as the initial part of a suffix such as *tion,* not at the end; and *o* as /i/ occurs only once in English in the word *women.*[2]

Fortunately the decoding of English is not as difficult as Shaw suggested. You probably can decode *Jabberwocky* (" 'Twas brillig, and the slithy toves did gyre and gimble in the wabe . . .") because you know that the double consonants in *brillig* signal that the sound in the previous vowel is /i/ as in *dinner;* that the *y* in the final position of *slithy* usually stands for the sound of /e/ as in *carry;* and the *g* in *gyre* stands for /j/ as in *gym* rather than /g/ as in *go* because it is followed by *y.*

## Prereading or Readiness Skills

*Readiness* means that one is prepared or has what is needed for some act. Psychologist David Ausubel defined it as "the adequacy of existing

---

[1] A pair of slant lines enclosing phonemic symbols is a graphic device to signify that the symbols are not letters but representations of sound units.

[2] Carl Lefevre, "Spelling, Word Analysis and Phonics," *Linguistics in Elementary School Classrooms,* ed. Paul S. Anderson (New York: Macmillan, 1971), p. 228.

capacity in relation to the demands of a given learning task."[3] Robert Calfee and Richard Venezky have appraised the component skills necessary in beginning reading, giving special attention to the uncovering of visual and auditory processes related to decoding.[4] These component skills are high-priority readiness skills because they are necessary if learners are to succeed in learning to decode printed words, and children are not likely to acquire them without deliberate instruction.

Most children are taught these readiness skills in preschool, kindergarten, or first grade. There are cases, however, when it is necessary to teach them to older learners. The reading specialist Donald Durrell tells of a fifteen-year-old boy who was unable to progress in reading until he learned to supply spoken words that began with the same initial sound as whatever word the teacher gave.

The following are prereading skills of high priority.

### Auditory Discrimination: Sound Matching

Auditory discrimination is more than the ability to say whether words like *Billy* and *Letty* are the same. It is also the ability to designate separate sounds in spoken words that make them different. To engage in phonic analysis, a child must understand that the sound patterns of a word are divisible into smaller units and that these units are common to the sound patterns of other words.

OBJECTIVES FOR AUDITORY DISCRIMINATION  The following objectives are useful in helping children acquire the essential skills of auditory discrimination:

Given familiar words pronounced by the teacher, the child indicates which of three words rhymes with the given word; for example,

"Raise your hand when I say the word that rhymes with *cat.*"

king     hat     top

Given a pronounced word featuring a particular phoneme in the initial position — at the beginning of the word — and pictures as choices, the child can select the picture whose name begins with the same phoneme; for example,

---

[3] David P. Ausubel, "Viewpoints from Related Disciplines: Human Growth and Development," *Teachers College Record* 60 (February 1959): 245–254.
[4] Robert C. Calfee and Richard L. Venezky, *Component Skills in Beginning Reading* (Madison, Wisc.: University of Wisconsin, Wisconsin Research and Development Center for Cognitive Learning, July 1968).

"Point to the picture whose name *begins* with the same sound as the word I say — *cup.*"

(hen)     (dog)     (cat)

Given words pronounced by the teacher, the child indicates which picture's name *ends* with the same phoneme; for example,

"Point to the picture whose name *ends* with the same sound as the word I say — *he.*"

(tree)     (hen)     (book)

Given a phoneme and three pictures, the name of one containing the sound in initial, medial, or final position, the child can select the picture whose name contains the phoneme; for example,

"One of these pictures has the sh-h sound. Point to the one that has the sh-h sound."

(ring)     (fish)     (flag)

## Visual Discrimination

Three visual discrimination skills that relate to analyzing and synthesizing printed words are letter orientation, letter order, and word detail. Can the child identify letters that are the same? Can the child identify pairs of letters that are in the same order? Can the child distinguish among sets of letters that differ only by a single letter? Operational definitions (objectives) and illustrative test items for each of these skills appear below.

### OBJECTIVE FOR LETTER ORIENTATION

Given a sample letter(s) and two other sets of letters (one set identical to the sample and the other set having at least one letter different), the child can select the set that matches the sample; for example,

"Mark the one that looks just like this one" (teacher points to the item in the first column).

| | | |
|---|---|---|
| di | bi | di |
| gi | gi | pi |
| d | b | d |
| op | op | og |
| bc | bc | dc |

### OBJECTIVE FOR LETTER ORDER

Given a sample of letters and two other sets of letters (one set identical to the sample and the other differing only in the ordering of the letters), the child can select the set that matches the sample; for example,

"Point to the one that looks just like this one."

| | | |
|---|---|---|
| gm | mg | gm |
| rf | fr | rf |
| nt | th | nt |
| bc | cb | bc |
| kw | wk | kw |

### OBJECTIVE FOR WORD DETAIL

Given a set of three letters and two other sets of letters (one set identical and the other a distracting set differing in a single but similar letter), the child can select the set that matches the sample; for example,

"Circle the one that looks just like this one."

| | | |
|---|---|---|
| oty | ofy | oty |
| uhg | ubg | uhg |
| ODA | QDA | ODA |
| hzp | hzp | bzp |
| uxs | uks | uxs |

## Knowledge of Letter Names

The ability of kindergarten or beginning first-grade children to identify uppercase and lowercase letter names is one of the best predictors of first-grade reading achievement. It could be, of course, that those children who enter school with some familiarity with letters come from homes where reading is highly valued. Hence parental influence, rather than knowledge of letters alone, would account for the greater success of these children. Nevertheless, the learning of letter names contributes to learning to read in several ways. First, there is a relation between the names and phonemes. The names of the vowels are the "long sounds" $/\bar{a}/$, $/\bar{e}/$, $/\bar{i}/$, $/\bar{o}/$, $/\bar{u}/$. Also Donald Durrell and Helen Murphy have noted: "The names of most consonant letters are syllables made up of the basic phonemes plus a vowel. The "ee" vowel follows the phonemes in these consonants: /b/ee, /d/ee, /p/ee, /v/ee, and /z/ee; while c and g are their less frequent phonemes: /s/ee and /j/ee — twenty-two letter names contain their phonemes." In saying the letter name, the child says the phoneme.[5]

OBJECTIVES FOR KNOWLEDGE OF LETTER NAMES

Given any letter name, the child can print, write, or otherwise identify the letter from several that correspond to the name; for example,

"Point to *E*."

H    E    L

Given any uppercase or lowercase letter, the child can name the letter; for example,

"What is the name of the letter?"    f

## Sound Blending

Sound blending as a readiness skill parallels a task that is to come later; namely, combining separate phonemes to form words. As a readiness skill, however, the child combines phonemes spoken by the teacher rather than looks at letters and then tries to pronounce and combine the phonemes suggested by these letters. As a readiness activity, a child listens to the teacher pronounce *segmented words* (words pronounced with pauses between phonemes) and then tells the teacher what word the sounds made. Thus the teacher might say "sa" "nd," and the child would be expected to say "sand"; or if the teacher says "s-and," the child would blend /s/ /and/ into *sand*. These differences in how the word is segmented by the teacher reflect differences in opinion regarding the proper unit for breaking down a word. Chapter 7 treats this issue fully.

It is sufficient for now to know that the task of trying to assign a sound value to each letter in a word and then to blend these separate sounds into a pronounceable word is too great for most children. There is always a distorted pronunciation of the consonant sounds /b/, /p/, and /d/ when these sounds are in isolation from words in which they appear. Hence a child who has been taught to decode by using a single letter as the unit for analysis has the additional task of learning how to combine the pronunciation of isolated sounds into a pronounceable word. A child who, for example, analyzes the word *hat* as "huh" "ah" "tuh" may have difficulty in associating these sounds with *hat*.

---

[5] Donald D. Durrell and Helen A. Murphy, "A Prereading Phonics Inventory," *Reading Teacher* 31, no. 4 (January 1978): 385–390.

Some phonic systems avoid the problem by not having the pupil pronounce a consonant without a vowel. For example, children may be taught to use a phonogram as a unit of analysis and synthesis. A phonogram is a pronounceable unit consisting of clusters of letters, the first of which is a vowel like *in*, *ip*, *at*, and *ight*. Accordingly, teachers use a consonant substitution method by which the child learns to recognize the pattern *at* in *hat*, *cat*, and *fat*, as well as other patterns, and then learns merely to blend the initial consonant with the pattern. "The word begins like *happy*, *house*, and *hair* and it rhymes with *fat* and *cat*. What is the word?"

OBJECTIVE FOR SOUND BLENDING

Given isolated sounds (a two-second pause between sounds), the child can put them together to pronounce or make a word; for example,

"Try to guess — say — the word I'm making:

mou-se, boa-t, a-pe, s-at, m-et."

## Language of Instruction

Children may not succeed in phonics instruction because they do not know what the teacher is asking them to do. Therefore a second category of prereading skills includes those tasks related to the language of instruction — special terms used in the teaching of readiness activities.

OBJECTIVE FOR MATCHING TO SAMPLE

Given a sample (sound, letter, or picture), the child can select from among several choices the one that "is the same" — identical. Matching can be on the basis of attributes such as directionality, shape, size, order, or function.

OBJECTIVES FOR POSITION

Given illustrations (pictures, letters, words arranged in left-to-right order), the child can label the illustrations as first, middle, or last.

Given expressions like *beginning*, *ending*, *sound*, the child can identify the referent (the sound to which *beginning* refers) to be used when teaching phonics.

OBJECTIVE FOR SPECIAL VOCABULARY

Given terms such as *top* or *bottom of page, line, row, checkmark,* and *word,* the child can identify the referent.

## Supplementary Skills of Low Priority

A number of other lower priority skills are sometimes found in reading readiness programs. Seven categories of low priority skills are:

Attending skills: persisting, cooperating, following directions

Motor skills: balancing, left-to-right movements, path following, drawing

Sensory skills: visual discrimination of color and geometric figures; auditory discrimination of pitch, sound intensity, sources and direction of sounds, rhythmic patterns; tactile discrimination of textures and shapes

Pattern recognition: counting, completing sequence, conserving number

Problem solving: stating rules to self, searching systematically, reducing possibilities, formulating questions, predicting outcomes, ranking alternative solutions

Memory skills: recalling an array of objects, repeating a sequence of events, using mnemonic devices

Geometric skills: identifying bare shapes, lines, determining congruence of forms

Many of these skills are useful supplementary aids in developing high priority skills. Pretraining in geometric skills, for example, identifying characteristics such as angularity, horizontality, intersection, number of strokes, curvature, straightness, or obliqueness, sometimes contributes to the child's more accurate recognition of letters.[6] However, we relegate these skills to lower priority for one or more of the following reasons: (1) they are not directly related to reading; (2) they can be acquired incidentally; (3) they are influenced more by maturation than by teaching; and (4) they can be taught more effectively in another area of the academic program — special education, aesthetics.

---

[6] Eleanor J. Gibson, "Experimental Psychology of Learning to Read," *The Disabled Reader,* ed. John Money (Baltimore: Johns Hopkins Press, 1966), pp. 41–59. John McNeil et al., "The Value of Feature Analysis in Learning to Recognize Letters," *Reading Improvement* 11, no. 2 (1974): 32–35.

# Phonics Skills at the Primary Level

## Sight Word Vocabulary

Children at the primary level may recognize words because they have seen them many times, have associated the words with something, or have noticed a familiar configuration, shape, or other distinguishing feature. Words that are recognized on sight without having to be decoded on the basis of phonics are called *sight words*. We discuss sight words under the topic of phonic skills because a sight word vocabulary is very useful in helping the child generalize about phoneme-grapheme relationships. That is, after children have learned to recognize *he, hen, hop,* and *hot*, they can generalize that the *h* in *his* is likely to have the same initial sound. After recognizing words such as *hit, hot,* and *hat*, they may generalize that the *t* in *but* will have the same sound. Sight words used in teaching phonic generalizations are, of course, phonetic or "regular" and conform to particular letter-sound patterns about which the children are to generalize. But not all sight words are phonetic. There are sight words called *structure* or *function words,* many of which do not follow a regular spelling pattern but make up a high percentage of all reading material. These words signal the relationship of words in sentences; *of, a, the, with, because, on,* and *after* are examples. Function words differ from subject or content words like *house, blue,* and *book* in that they do not have a referent or name something. Lists of basic sight words include both function and phonetic words of high frequency in the materials read by children.

Useful lists of basic sight words are Edward Dolch's "A Basic Sight Vocabulary,"[7] Edward Fry's "The Instant Words,"[8] and Wayne Otto and Robert Chester's "Sight Words for Beginning Readers."[9] Typical basic words for a beginning reading program include:

| | | | | | | |
|---|---|---|---|---|---|---|
| a | can | get | in | no | see | was |
| am | come | girl | is | on | she | we |
| and | did | go | it | or | that | went |
| are | do | good | jet | old | the | were |
| at | dog | have | just | other | them | what |
| away | down | he | little | one | there | where |
| ball | father | her | like | play | they | who |
| big | for | here | long | ran | this | will |
| boy | found | his | many | run | to | with |
| but | gave | house | make | said | too | yes |
| be | had | I | not | same | up | you |

---

[7] E. W. Dolch, "A Basic Sight Vocabulary," *Elementary School Journal* 36 (1936): 456–60; 37 (1936): 268–272.

[8] Edward B. Fry, "The Instant Words," *Elementary Reading Instruction* (New York: McGraw-Hill, 1977), p. 73.

[9] Wayne Otto and Robert Chester, "Sight Words for Beginning Readers," *Journal of Educational Research* 65 (1972): 436–443.

OBJECTIVE FOR SIGHT WORDS

Given written words selected from a list of words that appear frequently in the printed materials used by the child, the child can recognize the word; for example,

"Name these words."

with     them     bet     this     have     they     from


## Initial Consonant Sounds

Most words encountered in beginning reading begin with consonants rather than vowels. This fact plus the observation that consonant letters are more significant in the perception of a word and determine to a great degree the sound of the word make the correspondence of consonant-phoneme and grapheme an early skill to be taught. The teaching of initial consonants involves review of auditory and visual discrimination skills and association of consonant speech sounds with pictures and letters.

In teaching initial consonants, you may print and pronounce some words that begin with the /b/ sound such as *boy, bet,* and *be.* (They begin with the same sound.) Pupils then may be asked what they see that is the same. (They all begin with the same letter.) Finally, pupils may be asked how another word that begins with the letter *b* will probably sound. (It will begin with the same sound as *boy, bet,* and *be.*)

Once pupils know several initial consonants, they may engage in *phonic substitution.* You might write *ball* and *tall* on the board and discuss the similarity and difference between them. Then children might be asked to identify a third word *fall* or to indicate which word best completes the sentence: The boy is (ball) (tall).

Beginning consonant sounds are also taught through activities whereby pupils draw a line from the letter *b* to the picture whose name begins with the same sound.

OBJECTIVES FOR INITIAL (BEGINNING) CONSONANT SOUNDS

Given letters and words pronounced by the teacher, the child can identify the letter that has the same sound as the initial sound in each pronounced word; for example,

"Point to the letter that has the same beginning sound you hear when I say *Bill.*"

D     B     G

Given pictures and letters, the child can select the picture whose name begins with the same sound as each given letter; for example,

"Look at the letter and then select the picture whose name begins with the same sound."      B

(man)     (girl)     (boy)


## Ending Consonant Sounds

Techniques for teaching beginning consonant sounds apply in teaching the ending consonants, too. The teacher pronounces some words that end with /t/ like *cat, pet,* and *sit.* Children tell whether the ending sound in each of these words is the same or different and then supply other words that end with /t/. The printed words *cat, pet,* and *sat* are shown and pupils are asked to pronounce them. Finally, the teacher shows how substituting one final consonant changes the word. The word *cat,* for example, may become *car* or *can.*

### OBJECTIVES FOR FINAL CONSONANT SOUNDS

Given pictures with one accompanying letter, the child can tell whether the sound for the letter occurs first or last in the name for the picture; for example,

"Say the name of the picture and then tell whether the sound for this letter comes at the beginning or end of the picture's name."

t      (mat)

Given pictures and accompanying words missing their final consonants, the child can select the consonant that best completes the word; for example,

(car)   ca $^{p}_{r}$


## Consonant Digraphs

Reading programs at the primary level also focus on the use of consonant digraphs. As implied by its name, a *digraph* is two consonant letters. Consonant digraphs are pairs of consonants that are treated together rather than separately because they appear together so frequently. Convention reserves the use of the term to two consonant letters with a single sound value that differs from either letter comprising the pair. That is, the two letters used in combination represent a single phoneme. In a word like *shop*, for example, the *sh* digraph is not pronounced as a blend, nor are there separate sound values for the *s* and the *h*. Instead the *sh* records a single sound or phoneme /sh/. Frequently occurring consonant digraphs are ch /ch/ as in *church*, sh /sh/ as in *shoe*, th /th/ as in *thin*. Consonant digraphs often appear both at the beginning and at the end of words; for example, *ng* as in *sing*.

OBJECTIVE FOR CONSONANT DIGRAPHS

Given consonant digraphs, the child can select the picture whose name begins or ends with the sound recorded by the digraphs; for example,

"Put a circle around the picture whose name begins with the sound for these letters."

ch    (ship)    (chicken)

"Put a circle around the picture whose name ends with the sound for these letters."

sh    (chain)    (fish)

## Beginning Consonant Blends

Some words begin with consonant clusters that are pronounced as a blend. Beginning blends refer to such letter clusters that occur so frequently they are taught as a unit. These clusters are called blends because in pronouncing them, you blend or slur the two phonemes represented by the letters. A consonant blend differs from a consonant digraph in that the cluster of letters in a digraph does not signal two phonemes, as the blend does, but one. Notice, for example, that the phonemes /s/ and /n/ are both heard when you pronounce *snail*. Only a few consonant clusters are blended together at the beginning of a word. As a memory device, you may want to think of blends and their clusters as falling within three families:

An *s* plus a consonant: *spot*    *sc, sk, sl, sn, sm, sp, st, sw*

A consonant plus *r: brown*    *br, cr, dr, fr, gr, pr, tr*

A consonant plus *l: blue*    *bl, cl, fl, gl, pl*

Given words beginning with consonant clusters that are to be pronounced as a blend, the child can pronounce the words; for example,

"Say these words."

play     tree     slow     bring     cry     clown     fly

## Rhyming Elements, Phonograms, and "Families"

Many reading programs teach "families" of words. For example, the words *pan, man,* and *fan* are from the same word family "an." Families consist of a phonogram that is a vowel plus a consonant. An initial consonant or consonant cluster prefaces the phonogram. For instance, the family phonogram "et" includes *pet, net, set,* and *wet.*

Family phonograms constitute rhyming elements. Examples of rhyming elements commonly taught in beginning reading are: *ad, ag, am, ap, at, ed, eg, ell, em, en, et, id, ig, ill, im, in, it, og, op, ot, ub, ug, uh, up.*

Teachers use rhyming elements in consonant substitution exercises to help children generalize the sound values associated with given spelling patterns. Once children recognize, for example, the sound value for *et* in *net, get,* and *wet,* they can read new words composed of this phonogram and familiar initial consonants: *pet, jet, met, set, bet.*

Given spoken words that end in word patterns such as *ap, at, ed, en, ig, op,* and *ut,* the child will choose the printed word that rhymes with the spoken word; for example,

"Put a mark under the word that rhymes with *can.*"

cap     top     tan

Given a new one-syllable word consisting of letters representing familiar initial consonants and a familiar family of phonograms, the child can pronounce the new word; for example,

"Say this word."     ban

## Short and Long Vowel Sounds

Children at the primary level must learn short and long vowel sounds. Unlike consonants, each vowel letter represents two or more sounds. In phonics the sounds associated with *a, e, i, o,* and *u* as they occur with words like *am, end, it, odd,* and *up* are called *short* or *unglided* vowel sounds. In speech short vowels are characterized by lax articulation. The sound of *a* in *ate, e* in *eat, i* in *bite, o* in *coat,* and *u* in *use* are called *long* or *glided* vowel sounds. Long vowels are characterized by articulatory tension — a gliding action of the tongue and a rounding of the lips.

There are a number of ways to teach children how to tell whether a vowel letter takes a short sound or a long sound. One way is for you to pronounce words that contain a particular short sound such as *bat, cap,* and *pan* and ask pupils what they notice about the middle sounds in these words. Were the middle sounds the same or different? The children may then practice differentiating words that do and do not have the short *a* sound. They may be taught that the sound they have been hearing in certain words given by you is the short *a* sound. A second method is to give pictures, the names of some having the short *a* sound in the middle (*pan*), and ask them to identify the picture whose name has the short *a* sound.

You might also teach the different sounds by explaining that consonants and their positions often indicate whether certain vowels are long or short. For example, after seeing many instances of words that follow a *cv* (consonant-vowel) pattern — *me, he, she; go, no, so* — the child may arrive at the generalization that the vowel is long when in the cv pattern. Similarly after seeing many instances of the *cvc* (consonant-vowel-consonant) pattern — *cat, hen, hot, sit* (one-syllable words) — the child may generalize that the vowel is short in a cvc pattern. Children can also be helped through frequent experiences with words that exemplify the generalization that words in a *cvc(e)* (consonant-vowel-consonant-final e) pattern usually take the long vowel sound.

OBJECTIVE FOR LONG AND SHORT VOWELS

Given one-syllable words with cv, cvc, and cvc(e) patterns, the child can match those that have the same vowel sound; for example,

"Put a mark under the word that has the same vowel sound as the first word in each row."

| rate | rat | kite | cape |
|------|-----|------|------|
| wet  | hat | hen  | we   |
| go   | so  | got  | log  |

Thus far we have stressed skills and objectives for beginners that relate to the phonics strategy for decoding words. We now turn to those skills most useful to beginners in their development of strategies based on structural and contextual analyses.

# Structural Analysis Skills at the Primary Level

Structural analysis differs from phonic analysis in that words are not decoded on the basis of their letter-sound relationships but by recognizing some meaningful unit or units in the word. At the primary level, these units are found in compound words, contractions, affixes, and inflected endings.

## Compound Words

Teachers at the primary level instruct pupils in recognizing and forming compound words. These compound words are composed of two root words that combine to form a new word, usually having a meaning that connects the two root words: *bedbug, cannot, sunup, bookmark, upon.* You may want to use an exercise such as the following for teaching compound words:

Present children with two columns of one-syllable words and ask them to join words in column 1 to words in column 2 to form a compound word.

| *1* | *2* |
|------|------|
| pig  | fire |
| camp | pen  |
| cow  | time |
| bed  | boy  |

OBJECTIVE FOR COMPOUND WORDS

Given sentences that contain compound words, the child can pronounce the compound word and identify the two words that make it; for example, *airplane, tomcat, pancake.*

## Contractions

The use of the apostrophe with contractions is another beginning structural analysis skill. *Isn't, don't, let's, hasn't, didn't, can't, I'm, I'll, I've, haven't, isn't, wasn't, he's, he'll, she's, you'll, we're, we'll,* and *they're* are among the contractions frequently taught. Exercises similar to the following may be used to teach the simple beginning contractions:

"Draw a line from each of the two words to the contraction that means the same."

| | |
|---|---|
| does not | they'll |
| they will | doesn't |
| they are | You're |
| I am | they're |
| You are | I'm |
| I have | we'll |
| we will | I've |

OBJECTIVE FOR CONTRACTIONS

Given words with contractions, the child can pronounce them; for example, *can't, let's, what's, they're.*

## Affixes

Children begin to deal with affixes at the primary level. The combinations of affixes — prefixes and suffixes such as *un* (not), *ly* (like), and *less* (without) — and root or base words are called *derivatives.* An illustrative teaching exercise is one that requires children to identify the root word for derivatives such as *helpful, unhappy, careless,* and *quickly.*

## Inflections

Primary-level reading programs also introduce inflections. These are changes in word forms to show number, tense, possession, comparison, and gender. Inflected endings commonly introduced to beginning readers include: *s* (cars, runs), *'s* (Jim's), *ing* (jumping), *er* (faster), and *est* (fastest). An inflected ending signals its own meaning. The *'s* in boy's, for example, has relevance outside the word itself, signifying possession.

Steps in the teaching of inflected endings are as follows:

1. Read sample words in context; for example, Jim lost his *dogs.* Mary found a *dog.* The men are *working.* They *worked* yesterday.

2. Have child identify (1) the words in each pair of sentences that are almost the same and (2) the root words (*dog*) (*work*).

3. Have children identify the inflected endings and generalize what they think the endings stand for.

4. Give additional practice exercises in which they underline root words and circle inflected endings; for example, He walked a long way. That is Tom's house. She is taller than he.

Another example of an exercise to use in helping pupils recognize inflections and affixes is the following:

"Choose the word that best completes each sentence."

She has ten _____. (pens, pen)

They are _____. (sing, singing)

He is a good _____. (help, helper)

She was sad. She was _____. (happy, unhappy)

### OBJECTIVE FOR BASE WORDS AND ENDINGS

Given a list of words composed of familiar roots with inflected endings and suffixes, the child can pronounce the words; for example,

jumping      toys      called      worker

Thus far we have stressed structural analysis as a strategy for decoding words. Children who are familiar with base words and with several inflected endings and affixes have a much larger sight vocabulary than those who fail to recognize a familiar word in a changed form. We show in Chapters 5 and 7 the advantages of structural analysis for comprehending the meaning of words read.

# Contextual Analysis in Word Attack at the Primary Level

Studies have shown that children who use contextual clues to recognize words are better readers.[10] Essentially, analysis by context consists of looking at an entire phrase or sentence and then guessing the unknown word. For example, if children know all the words in the following sentence except the underlined word, they are likely to be able to determine the unknown word: Dogs bark and cats <u>meow</u>. Clues for guessing the unknown word come from semantics and syntax. *Semantics* refers to clues given by the meaning of the sentence. *Syntax* is word usage. The fact that only certain kinds of words can be used in a given position within a sentence gives a clue to the unknown word. For example, in the sentence given above, the missing word had to be a verb for the sentence to "sound right."

Contextual analysis is especially useful as a decoding strategy when new words do not follow phonic patterns for letter-sound correspondence. Nevertheless the strategy does have limitations. The child must already know most of the words in the sentence and seldom is there only one precise word that will complete a sentence. That is why most teachers encourage pupils to combine contextual analysis with phonics and structural analysis. Once the unknown word has been narrowed to a population of possible words, clues such as the sound value of the initial letter and recognition of a meaningful part further reduce uncertainty.

Lessons in contextual analysis encourage children to guess new words from what other words in the sentence suggest. The lessons may commence with oral practice in guessing missing words in sentences where the missing word is prompted by context. Subsequently, pupils may practice contextual analysis with written items.

OBJECTIVE IN CONTEXTUAL ANALYSIS

Given a sentence with one unfamiliar printed word that is in the child's oral repertoire, the child can pronounce the word; for example,

"Read the sentence and then say the new word that is underlined."

Some cars make a lot of <u>noise</u>.
She put <u>syrup</u> on her pancakes.

---

[10] H. A. Klein et al., "Utilization of Context for Word Identifications Decisions by Children," *Journal of Exceptional Children* 17 (1974): 79–86.

# Phonics Skills at the Middle Level

We can speak of phonics skills that are commonly taught at the middle grade level. Middle grade teachers give more attention than other grade teachers to the variant sounds of consonants, vowels followed by *r*, diphthongs, consecutive vowels, and silent letters. Nevertheless effective teaching of any skill depends on the child's present status with respect to that skill and readiness to learn it. In the following paragraphs, each of these terms is defined by example.

### Consonant Variants

Middle-level teachers show pupils how to recognize the consonant variants *c* and *g*. Both *c* and *g* commonly record two different sounds, known as "hard" and "soft" sounds. The hard sound for *c* is the one heard at the beginning of *cake.* The soft sound of *c* is heard at the beginning of *cent.* The soft sound of *g* is heard at the beginning of *gyp* and the hard sound of this letter is heard at the beginning of *gush*. Common one-syllable words associated with the soft *c* and *g* sounds respectively are: *bounce, cell, face, ice, nice, place, race, space, age, edge, lodge, page, gem, large, stage*. Both *c* and *g* generally record a soft sound before *e, i,* or *y,* although there are exceptions; for example, *get, girl,* and *give*.

Although the consonant sounds for *q* /kw/ as in *queen* and /k/ as in *boutique,* as well as the sounds for *x,* are also consonant variants, they are not usually treated at this level.

OBJECTIVE FOR CONSONANT VARIANTS

Given words recording variant sounds of *c* and *g,* the child can pronounce the words; for example,

"Say these words."

city     go     giant     pace     candy

### Consonant Blends

As a middle-level teacher, you may have to instruct pupils in how to recognize both beginning and ending blends. As we indicated previously, blends are two- or three-letter clusters that are taught as a unit. The letters of a blend signal phonemes that are blended or slurred in pronunciation. A good way to help children generalize the sound value for a given consonant blend is to present several examples and then ask pupils to predict the pronunciation of a new word containing the same consonant cluster; for example, "Let's say these words together: *street, strong, strap.*" "Underline the part of each word that looks and sounds the same." "Say this word: *string.*"

OBJECTIVE FOR CONSONANT BLENDS

Given words with the clusters such as *sm, st, sk, sw, sn, sc, dw, dr, fr, fl, gr, gl, tr, tw, spl, str, thr, scr, sp, mp, nd, nt, nk, ct, pt, lt, ld,* the child can pronounce them; for example,

"Say these words."

small     scream     dwarf     land     bent     act     jump
wasp

## Vowels Followed by r or r-controlled Vowels

Middle-level teachers show their pupils that when the letter *r* follows a vowel, it usually changes the recorded vowel sound so it is neither long nor short. When *r* follows a single vowel in a syllable, the vowel plus *r* usually records the same sound as the vowel sound in *her, curl,* and *sir.* However, when *a* is followed by *r,* it records either the sound heard in *art* or the sound heard in *Mary.* When *o* is followed by *r,* the vowel usually records the vowel sound heard in *lord.*

OBJECTIVE FOR VOWELS FOLLOWED BY R

Given words with *r*-controlled vowels, the child can pronounce them; for example,

"Say these words."

part     jerk     skirt     blur

## a plus w or l

Another phonic skill at the middle level concerns the use of *a* plus *w* or *l.* In the *al* combination as in *also* and *talk,* the *a* usually records the vowel sound represented by /a/ or /al/. The *aw* combination records the vowel sound for words like *draw, paw,* and *saw.*

OBJECTIVE FOR A PLUS W OR L

Given words with *aw* and *al* combinations, the child can pronounce them; for example,

"Say these words."

call      claw      awful      malt

## Diphthongs

Middle-level children are taught to pronounce words with diphthongs represented by vowel digraphs. Diphthongs are speech sounds that change continuously from one vowel to another in the same syllable. English has only two diphthong sounds: /ou/ as in *ouch* and /oi/ as in *oil*. These sounds are signaled by the vowel digraphs *oi, oy, ou,* and *ow*. The diphthong in *oil* and *toy* is the same. (*y* always functions as a vowel except at the beginning of words when it is a consonant.) The diphthong in *ouch* and *growl* is the same. Although diphthongs are represented by vowel digraphs, you should not think that all vowel digraphs signal diphthongs. There are other vowel digraphs — letters that appear together in syllables — that are not diphthongs but are to be treated as a unit: *au* as in *cause, aw* as in *paw, oo* as in *cool,* and *oo* as in *look.*

OBJECTIVE FOR DIPHTHONGS

Given words with the digraphs representing diphthongs, the child can pronounce them; for example,

"Say these words."

noise      soil      coin      blouse      owl      towel

## Consecutive Vowels

Children at the middle level should learn to recognize the major sound values for consecutive vowels. The term *consecutive vowel* includes both diphthongs and single-vowel sounds signaled by vowel digraphs (a pair of vowels that represent a single sound). The latter are illustrated by digraphs that record the long vowel sound as *ea* in *eat, ee* in *see, ai* in *fail, oa* in *oat,* and *ow* as in *own.* Consecutive vowels also include the double *o* with its two sounds as in *moon* (most frequent) and *book.* Examples of some of the major sound values for consecutive vowels that should be taught are: *ay — play; ai — rain; oa — toad; ee — seen; ea — teach, bread, great; au — laugh, caught; ou — pound, soup, would; oo — food, look.*

A practice activity for teaching vowel pairs is *paper and pencil dominoes.* One child writes a word containing consecutive vowels.

Another child uses the initial or final letter to attain another word with the same vowel pair. The last person to contribute a word is the winner; for example, *read* (ea), *bead, lead.*

OBJECTIVE FOR CONSECUTIVE VOWELS

Given words with consecutive vowels, the child can pronounce them; for example,

"Say these words."

beach    mail    road

## Silent Letters

Linguists dislike the term *silent letters* because they know no letter has a sound. Nevertheless, teachers find it useful to speak of silent letters as a way to communicate to children that some letters are not to be pronounced. Some generalizations about silent letters may be taught; for example, when a consonant is doubled, the first one is often silent, as in *sitting; b* may be silent after *m* and before all consonants, as in *bomb, debt; k* is silent before *n,* as in *knot;* and *w* is silent before *r,* as in *wrote.*

OBJECTIVE FOR SILENT LETTERS

Given words containing silent letters, the child can pronounce the words; for example,

"Say these words."

gnat    knife    bomb    knight

## Schwa Sound

One of the most common sounds in English is the schwa sound, symbolized by the phonetic notation ə. It is the initial sound heard when pronouncing words like *ago* and *alone.* It may appear with any vowel letter in words with unstressed syllables like *cola, cement, money,* and *upon.* It also occurs with words ending with a consonant plus *le* like *bubble* and *hustle.*

OBJECTIVE FOR SCHWA

Given familiar words that have a schwa sound, the child will pronounce them with the schwa sound, rather than attempt an artificial pronunciation; for example,

"Say these words."

lemon     soda     animal     butter     asleep

### Long and Short Vowel Generalizations

Our treatment of phonics skills at the middle level concludes with a summary of the more useful long and short vowel generalizations. You have noted that variability in spelling vowel sounds is much greater than in spelling consonants. Hence there are many generalizations that will not always work. However, the following generalizations have value:

1. When there is one vowel in a syllable and it is not the final letter (cvc pattern), it usually records the short sound, as in *leg* and *rat*

2. When there is one vowel in a syllable and it is the final letter (cv pattern), it usually records the long sound, as in *he* and *go*.

3. When there are two vowels in a syllable, one of which is a final *e* (vc(e) pattern), the first vowel usually records its long sound and the final *e* is silent, as in *pine* and *same*.

4. When there are two adjacent vowels in a syllable, the first often records its long sound while the second is silent, as in *seat* and *pain*.

5. When a single vowel is followed in a syllable by two consonants plus a final *e*, the short vowel sound often is recorded, as in *grudge* and *prance*.

> Objective for long and short vowel generalizations
>
> Given words that are consistent with phonic long and short vowel generalizations, the child can pronounce them; for example,
>
> "Say these words."
>
> spine     spin     ledge     leap     gum     Luke

## Structural Analysis Skills at the Middle Level

In the middle grades, structural analysis skills would be extended by introducing additional possessives, contractions, and compounds. Recognition of suffixes — additions to the end of a root word — should be taught. These suffixes may be inflected endings that distinguish gender (actor, actress); time (deal, dealt); person (I run, he runs); or common suffixes signifying special meanings; for example, *er* (doer of action); *able* (capable of being); *full* (characterized by); *ic* and *cal* (connected with); and *ness, hood, ship, ence,* and *ment* (state of).

One technique to teaching structural analysis is *word building* by which children are given a root word and are asked to extend it through the addition of inflected endings (*rub, rubbing, rubbed*); suffixes (*beauty, beautify, beautiful, beautifully*); or prefixes (*mount, remount, dismount*).

Word structure is sometimes taught as a prerequisite to syllabication or the breaking of a word into syllables to pronounce it. For instance, if children know that prefixes, suffixes, and inflections usually form separate syllables (units of pronunciation), they may have a clue to the pronunciation of an unknown word; for example, *un met; com fort able; strong er.*

To help children recognize derivatives and variants to words they know, you should teach them how many words change their spelling when affixes are added:

1. *When a root ends in a consonant followed by y,* the *y* is changed to *i* before adding *es, er, est, ly, ful, less,* or *ous;* for example, *lady, ladies; marry, married; cry, cried; busy, busiest; happy, happily; melody, melodious.*

2. The plural of root endings — *s, ch, ss,* and *sh* — is formed by adding *es;* for example, *bus, buses; launch, launches; fish, fishes.*

3. The plural of root endings is formed by changing the *f* to *v* and adding *es;* for example, *leaf, leaves.*

4. With roots that end in a single vowel followed by a consonant, the consonant often is doubled before adding *ing* or *ed;* for example, *run, running; pat, patted.*

5. With roots that end with a silent *e,* the *e* usually is dropped when a suffix or inflectional ending begins with a vowel; for example, *bake, baking; large, largest; create, creation.*

STRUCTURAL ANALYSIS OBJECTIVES

Given any familiar root word with the suffixes *ly, ful, or,* and *able,* the child can pronounce the word; for example,

"Say these words."

smoothly    colorful    actor    sinkable

Given words where spelling changes have occurred when affixes were added, the child can pronounce them correctly; for example,

"Say these words."

hidden     ladies     given     beautiful

# Contextual Analysis Skills at the Middle Level

Upon completion of the middle level, children ought to have a large sight vocabulary and be able to decode one-syllable words efficiently. In addition, they should be using context clues to figure out the meaning of new words and to identify unfamiliar words in their oral repertoire.

Context analysis is also a useful way to help children overcome problems associated with (1) *homonyms* (words that are sounded alike but have different spellings and meaning such as *blue* and *blew;* some writers call these words *homophones*) and (2) *homographs* (words written in exactly the same way but having entirely different meanings: "He was *mean.*" "What did you mean?"). Also context analysis is a good way to determine how to pronounce or stress syllables in words that are used as both nouns and verbs: "He has a *record.*" "She will *record* it."

Among the techniques for teaching context analysis are exercises that have been grouped into a hierarchy from the most difficult to the easiest:[11]

1. No clue given other than context

   The _____ of a turkey are not tasty.

2. Beginning letter given

   The f _____ of a turkey are not tasty.

3. Length of word given

   The _____ of a turkey are not tasty.

4. Beginning and ending letters given

   The f _____ s of a turkey are not tasty.

5. Choice of four words given

   The _____ of a turkey are not tasty.

   gizzard     legs     wings     feathers

---

[11] Robert Emans and Gladys M. Fisher, "Teaching the Use of Context Clues," *Elementary English* 42 (March 1967): 243–246. Copyright © 1967 by the National Council of Teachers of English. Reprinted with permission.

6.  Consonants given

The f    th  rs of a turkey are not tasty.

Given a sentence context, the child can choose between homonyms; for example,

"Read the sentence and then put a line under the word that belongs."

She    ate  eight    it.
Can we    by  buy    it?
We will    write right    the letter.
Let's    meat meet    tomorrow.

Given a sentence context, the child can place proper *accent* (stress) upon words that vary with their use in sentences; for example,

"Read these sentences and give the underlined words the proper stress."

There was no conflict between them.

These two conflict.

Do you have your permit?

I will permit you to do it.

# Phonic Skills at the Upper Level

All skills previously taught and maintained are extended to more complex word and sentence patterns in the upper grades. Further, the decoding of words with several syllables is given special attention. Every syllable is comprised of a vowel phoneme to which consonant sounds are frequently added. For example, *wonder* has two syllables; *wonderfully* has four. Only certain combinations of consonants and vowel phonemes occur in the English syllable, and the amount of stress (accent) given a syllable depends on its position in the sequence of syllables in a given word. Advanced phonics teachers have long emphasized teaching children how to divide words into syllables as an aid to word recognition and pronunciation. One problem is to determine when a consonant goes with one vowel rather than another in two-syllable words. Why, for example, does *b* go with the syllable *ot* in *robot* but with *ro* in *robin?*

Indeed, some authors have questioned the value of syllabication as a means for discovering the sounds in words,[12] arguing that syllabication is best done *after* one has already pronounced the word. This criticism may reflect the fact that children have been asked to spend more time counting the number of syllables in words and drawing lines between parts of words than in pronouncing parts in order to identify words. Also teachers should not encourage children to rely on dictionary divisions of syllables as keys to pronunciation. Such divisions are for the purposes of writing and printing (to show where a word may be divided at the end of a line), not reading. The word *vision*, for example, is divided vi-sion according to printers' usage, although it is pronounced vizh un.

Even if, in some instances, it is impossible to divide the spelling of words to agree with their pronunciation, the following generalizations often reveal cues for syllabication and for helping children realize that they can decode one part of a word at a time:

1.  Do not divide a one-syllable word.

2.  Divide a prefix from its root or base word (pre-view).

3.  When two consonants are between two vowels, divide the word between the two consonants (ad-ven-ture) (hop-ping).

4.  When one consonant comes between two vowels, the consonant is part of the first syllable if the first vowel is short (pal-ace); but if the first vowel is long, the consonant is part of the second syllable (ho-tel).

5.  When a multisyllabic word ends in *le* preceded by a consonant, divide it before the consonant (bu-gle).

There are two common ways to teach syllabic generalizations:

1.  The example generalization method: Give children a large number of words in each of the categories (for example, words having one consonant between two vowels) and then ask them to formulate the rule for dividing and pronouncing words in each category.

2.  The generalization example method: Give children the generalization and then ask them to give corresponding examples.

You may want to try one of the above methods using these words:

---

[12] Gerald G. Glass, "The Strange World of Syllabication," *Elementary School Journal* (1967): 403–405. G. D. Spache and M. E. Baggett, "What the Teachers Know about Phonics and Syllabication," *Reading Teacher* 19 (1965): 96–99.

*hero, famous, radar, money, natural, cover, peril, period, polar.* However, it does not matter where pupils divide words as long as they come up with the correct recognition of the word.

Many children are helped in pronouncing unfamiliar multisyllabic words by noting the frequently occurring *phonograms* (commonly occurring syllables). For example, in decoding the word *terminal*, children may attend to the phonograms ter-min-al. Vowel sounds are stable in most phonograms, even in multisyllabic words. When they are not, learners must use the appropriate sound derived as a prompt to word recognition.

In determining which syllables to stress, children may find the following generalizations helpful:

1. Stress the first of two syllables in a two-syllable root word:
   'pen cil      'stan za

2. Stress syllables containing long vowel sounds:
   'tri al     im 'pede

3. Do not stress a final syllable comprised of a consonant plus *le*:
   'ca ble      'lit tle

If children already are familiar with words in their oral forms and can attack them through letter-sound relation, syllabication, structural analysis, or context sufficiently well to identify the words, they will be able to pronounce them naturally without resorting to generalizations about stress.

### OBJECTIVES FOR SYLLABICATION

Given words in the vowel-consonant-vowel (vcv) pattern, the child will divide them before the consonant; for example,

a'way.

Given vowel-consonant-consonant-vowel (vccv) words, the child will divide them between the consonants; for example,

can'dy.

Given words ending in a consonant plus *le*, the child will divide them before the consonant and *le*; for example,

un'cle.

In addition, teachers in upper elementary grades should extend their phonics instruction by emphasizing dictionary skills related to pronunciation and stress.

### PRONUNCIATION OBJECTIVES FOR DICTIONARY SKILLS

Given unfamiliar words with accompanying phonetic spelling and *diacritical markings* (special marks to indicate sound values of letters in words; some dictionaries have their own special marks), the child will pronounce them; for example:

"Say these words."

impiety (im-'pī-ət-ē)    oracle ('or-ək-l)    portal ('pōrt-l)
supine (sü-'pīn)    gendarme ('zhän-,därm)

Given words with different stress marks, the child can pronounce the words with proper stress, for example:

"Say these words."

,ärt-ə-'fish-l    ik-'strak-shn    'pal-pə-bl

## Structural Analysis Skills at the Upper Level

Prefixes, suffixes, and root words are reviewed and extended at the upper level. Pupils learn to build many words from one base word. They also practice reading new words derived from familiar base words. A popular activity is to ask pupils to collect groups of words having common origins (*communicate, community, communicative*). The search for derivatives contributes to the development of both comprehension and word attack skills.

### OBJECTIVES FOR STRUCTURAL ANALYSIS

Given any familiar root or base word with frequently occurring affixes, such as *ance, ence, ight, hood, pro, col, ier, by, ward, acy, ency,* the child can pronounce it and give the new meaning; for example,

"Say these words and tell what they mean."

piracy    carrier    homeward

Given any new word derived from a familiar root word, the child will pronounce it; for example,

"Say these words."

driven (drive)    national (nation)    southern (south)
heroic (hero)

## Contextual Analysis Skills at the Upper Level

Although contextual analysis takes on increased importance as an aid to comprehension at upper levels, it continues to be taught as a tool for word recognition. Some hold that it is the sense of the text that enables readers to use spelling-to-sound correspondence effectively. Frank Smith, for example, says that encouraging a child to use context will promote the ability to make predictions about language, to comprehend, and to learn. Hence, he recommends teaching materials that have a meaningful context for learners, not single words devoid of context, not sentences that are devoid of purpose, and not paragraphs and stories that are of no concern to readers.[13]

Children should see print as purposeful and predict what words are likely to be on the basis of their setting and individual experience. In contextual analysis, meaning precedes word identification. It is easier to recognize a word when semantic and syntactic constraints are placed on it from context. That is one reason meaningful material can be read twice as fast as unrelated words.

Successful use of context analysis depends upon familiarity with sentence and other syntactic patterns. Most children in upper levels have competency in four sentence patterns: noun-verb (I see); noun-verb-adverb (He reads well); noun-verb-noun-noun (He spoke to his friend Mary); and noun-linking verb-adverb (It is under the roof). Most of them are also familiar with patterns for requests and questions. However, many children need help in understanding these constructions: passive (The teaching is done by Mrs. Jones); appositive with commas (Betty, my sister, came); infinitive as subject (to work is good); conjunctive adverbs as signals to conclusions (*therefore, hence, thus, being as*); clauses as subjects (What you think is your business); and absolute constructions (This being so, let's go).

Carl Lefevre has made the provocative suggestion that if children were taught to use five sets of structure words in relation to the words and functions they signal, great improvement in reading would follow. These five sets of markers that signal particular types of structural sentence elements are:

---

[13] Frank Smith, "Making Sense of Reading — and of Reading Instruction," *Harvard Educational Review* 47, no. 3 (August 1977): 386–395.

Signals for nouns — the, a, some, any, this, one, that, our, their, most, another

Signals for verbs — can, could, may, might, must, shall, should, will, would, am, are, is, have

Signals for phrases — down, in, above, below, beside, around, along, across, through, toward, inside

Signals for clauses — if, when, until, so, where, whose, which, before, though, like

Signals for questions — when, where, why, how, who, whose, which, what[14]

In learning to recognize the sets of markers, children are taught to note how they function in the language, not as words in isolation. Markers are always to be learned in relation to the large pattern of a sentence.

### OBJECTIVE FOR CONTEXT ANALYSIS

Given incomplete sentences written with various sentence and syntactic patterns, the child can choose the missing word; for example,

"Read each sentence and then choose the missing word."

The ball was _____ by Mike.     (hit, fast)

When the rain _____, the group went home.     (climb, came)

When there is fire, _____ is heat.     (there, this)

If he works, _____ he will be paid.     (but, then)

The above objective can be modified by using a variation of the cloze (closure) procedure by which a one-hundred-word passage featuring various syntactical structures is selected; then every fifth word is deleted and the child is asked to read the passage and write the missing words on the blank lines. Perhaps you see how the ability to comprehend a sentence or entire passage aids the decoding process. Contextual analysis helps the reader anticipate particular words and confirms the correctness of words decoded by any strategy. Through contextual analysis, the reader knows whether the decoded word "makes sense" on the basis of the grammar of the sentence, the meaning of the sentence, and the phonic or structural clues present in the

---

[14] Carl A. Lefevre, *Linguistics and the Teaching of Reading* (New York: McGraw-Hill, 1964), p. 119.

word. The key to teaching contextual analysis, however, is in providing reading material that makes sense to the child.

# Summary

The skills specified and illustrated in this chapter are not narrowly tied to a particular approach — basal reading, technological, language experience, or individualized reading; neither are they restricted to a given methodology for teaching reading — look-say technique; whole-word or sight method; phonics; structural analysis; and cognitive or meaning methods associated with contextual analysis. All are useful in helping pupils recognize words. Some letter-sound correspondences have been ignored intentionally. For instance, it is not necessary to teach the different phonemes for *s* because the English-speaking child will naturally pronounce the final *s* differently in *cats* and *dogs*.

Reasons are given for including certain skills, and a sequence is suggested. The sequence, of course, depends on what children already know and other individual differences. It may be, too, that not every child needs to learn every skill.

It should be clear that the skills discussed in this chapter relate to beginning readers rather than to accomplished readers who are more concerned with learning from print than with decoding. The intent of this chapter is to provide you with the knowledge necessary for helping children develop competency in decoding. This knowledge includes ideas about language regularity (there are more consistent spellings than inconsistent ones); generalizations about consonants in various positions in words; the phoneme-grapheme relationships for vowels as signaled by word patterns (cvc, cvc(e) patterns, for example); the value of phonograms in helping a child deal with the variability in the sound of vowels; and the structure of words, including units of meaning such as roots (in compound words), roots and affixes (derivatives), and roots and inflectional endings (variants). As an experienced reader, you already had a functional knowledge of the skills discussed; now you have more systematic and generalized knowledge of what can be taught to help children be more effective in their word recognition.

The content of this chapter is fairly difficult because of the concept density and it is unlikely to be fully understood at a single reading. In many respects, this is quite acceptable because the chapter is intended as a resource to help you in your teaching of reading and to be used as a reference for different instructional problems.

# Self-instructional Exercises

### Exercise 1. Demonstrating Knowledge of Frequently Confused Terms in the Teaching of Phonics

Mark each example that illustrates the term.

1. Vowel digraph      *oo*      *sh*      *ing*
2. Diphthong      /i/      /ng/      /oi/
3. Consonant digraph      *bl*      *ph*      *s*
4. Consonant blend      /sm/      *sh*      *oa*

**ANSWERS TO EXERCISE 1**

1. The example *oo* is a vowel digraph or vowel cluster. There are two letters or graphemes that represent a vowel sound. In this case the vowel sound can be the vowel sound heard in *cool* or that heard in *cook.*

2. The example /oi/ is a diphthong — a blend of two vowel sounds represented by the letters *oi* or *oy.*

3. The example *ph* is a consonant digraph. The sound of the single phoneme recorded by these two letters is different from those associated with either letter comprising the pair.

4. The example /sm/ is a consonant blend. This sound is recorded by the clusters of letters *sm.* It is a blend of two sounds. In a word like *small,* the *s* stands for one sound and the *m* for another.

### Exercise 2. Demonstrating Knowledge of Terms Used in Teaching Word Attack

Put a mark by each example that illustrates the term.

1. Short vowel pattern      cvc      cvc(e)      cv
2. Long vowel pattern      cvc(e)      cve      cvcc
3. Phonogram      *bl*      *et*      *pre*
4. Soft sound of *c*      lance      camel      slick

**ANSWERS TO EXERCISE 2**

1. A cvc (consonant-vowel-consonant) is a short vowel pattern. It is representative of words like *met, bat,* and *lit.* The vowel sound in a short vowel pattern is usually short.

2. A cvc(e) (consonant-vowel-consonant-final *e*) is a long vowel pattern. A vowel followed by a final consonant plus *e* is usually long, as in *fine, slope,* and *mule.*

3. The example *et* is a phonogram — pronounceable units or clusters of letters, the first of which is a vowel, for example, *ing, ang,* and *op.*

4. The example *lance* records the soft sound of *c.* A *c* generally has a soft sound before *e, i,* or *y.*

## Exercise 3. Demonstrating Knowledge of Terms Used in Structural Analysis

Put a mark by each example that illustrates the term.

1. Root or base word    speaker    speak    speaks

2. Compound word    book    booking    bookmark

3. Derivative    rewrite    write    writing

4. Inflected word    book    books    bookish

**ANSWERS TO EXERCISE 3**

1. *Speak* is an uncompounded word, without prefix, suffix, or inflectional ending. Hence it is a root or base word.

2. *Bookmark* is a compound word because two roots are combined to form a new word in which the pronunciation of both is maintained and there is connected meaning.

3. *Rewrite* is a derivative because it is composed of a root word and a prefix. (If it had a suffix, it also would have been a derivative.) *Writing* is an inflected word because the letters *ing* have been added to indicate tense.

4. *Books* is an inflected word. The added *s* to book indicates number. Other inflections indicate gender, tense, voice, and comparison.

## Exercise 4. Recognizing the Sounds Associated with Particular Letters on the Basis of Letter Position, Surrounding Letters, and Spelling Patterns

Look at each synthetic (artificial) word and the letter underlined. Then circle the word that has a letter with the same sound as the underlined letter on the left.

1. c̲igal    sure    sale    king

2. g̲ac    gym    gem    dig

3. la̱t late awl ran

4. bry̱ baby shy yet

**ANSWERS TO EXERCISE 4**

1. The *c* in *cigal* has the same sound value as *s* in *sale.* When *c* is followed by *e, i,* or *y,* it usually has a soft sound.

2. The *g* in *gac* has the same sound value as *g* in *dig.* When *g* is followed by *e* or *y,* it usually has a soft sound.

3. The *a* in *lat* has the same short vowel sound as *a* in *ran* because most vowels in a cvc (consonant-vowel-consonant) pattern mark the short vowel sound.

4. The letter *y* in the final position of a word functions as a vowel. In one-syllable words, if the letter preceding *y* is a consonant, the *y* records the sound heard in *cry, by,* and *shy* (long *i* sound). As the final letter in words of two syllables, it records the sound heard in *baby, lady,* and *happy* (long *e* sound).

## Exercise 5. Recognizing Structural Elements

Affixes and inflected endings are meaningful as are sound units. Put a circle around the meaningful part of each synthetic word.

1. unwrab

2. cepn't

3. glinks

4. toving

5. ruborful

**ANSWERS TO EXERCISE 5**

1. *un* — the prefix signifying *not*

2. n't — contraction for *not*

3. *s* — added to nouns to indicate number; to verbs to indicate person

4. *ing* — added to verbs to indicate tense

5. *ful* — a suffix meaning full of

## Exercise 6. Anticipating Words from Context

Guess the missing word.

1. Synonyms are two or more _____ having nearly the same meaning.

2. Blends are to consonant digraphs as _____ are to vowel digraphs.

3. The root word is *short*, *er* is its inflected ending, so the word is _____.

4. Contextual _____ is figuring out a word by the way it is used in a sentence.

**ANSWERS TO EXERCISE 6**

1. *words* — prompted by the term synonym and by context

2. *diphthongs* — prompted by analogy

3. *shorter* — prompted by logic

4. *analysis* — prompted by definition

# Selected Readings

Calfee, Robert C., and Drum, Priscilla A. "Learning to Read: Theory, Research and Practice," *Curriculum Inquiry* 8, no. 3 (Fall 1978): 183–249.

This extensive article is divided into five sections: the historical antecedents of ideas about how best to teach reading, theories for integrating what is known about reading and the implications of these theories, research on reading acquisition within particular theoretical models, the relationship between individual differences in reading achievement and variations in teaching practices, and future research and practice.

With respect to approaches to the teaching of reading, the authors treat the age-old question of whether initial emphasis should be placed on the child learning to grasp the "meaning of the message" or on learning to pronounce the message with accuracy and fluency: "direct perception versus hypothesis testing; bottom-up versus top-down processing; decoding versus whole word and look say; joyful and meaningful experience versus drill and skill." The authors throw historical light on these issues and illustrate how formal models of reading and learning may lead to better critical tests of the various views.

Research studies are reviewed as they bear upon such questions as prerequisites to decoding, the value of the alphabetic principle in learning to read, and whether a pupil must master decoding in order to comprehend. The authors believe that the skill of bringing meaning to the text is what must be taught in reading comprehension — the capability of putting oneself in the position of the writer. Hence, they question the language experience approach because instead of helping pupils think about how the text relates to their own experiences and knowledge, LEA turns the problem around and creates materials that spring directly from the individual child's experience.

Cunningham, Patricia M. "A Compare/Contrast Theory of Mediated Word Identification," *Reading Teacher* 32, no. 7 (April 1979): 774–778.

This study supports a compare/contrast theory of word identification. Briefly, the theory is that instead of going through the process of dividing unknown words into syllables and applying phonic generalizations to the letter combinations, readers are more likely to compare an unknown word with the store of words and word parts in the reader's memory. An unfamiliar word that cannot be recognized as a whole is segmented into the largest manageable units and compared to known words or fragments. The study indicates that using a compare/contrast strategy can result in an increase in the ability to decode unfamiliar words.

Gibson, Eleanor J., and Levin, Harry. "Beginning to Read." In *The Psychology of Reading.* Cambridge, Mass.: MIT Press, 1975, pp. 264–332.

In this chapter the authors review research related to beginning reading and draw conclusions such as:

Learning to read is learning rules and strategies for extracting information from text.

The child's own curiosity is the best source of motivation to learn.

The issue of finding a single unit to use in decoding is a false one — instruction should allow the child to use sentences, syllables, letter clusters, and the like. The teaching of spelling patterns and the rulelike structure of words is helpful. It is also important that children learn to notice structure within words.

Simply telling children rules does not work. Younger children profit from instructions to search for invariant patterns, but the learner must discover the patterns himself, with time, exposure, and active search.

Ives, Josephine P., Bursuk, Laura Z., and Ives, Sumner A. *Word Identification Techniques.* Chicago: Rand McNally, 1979.

The authors describe seven techniques for identifying written words: visual configuration clues, picture clues, semantic clues, syntactic clues, morphemic clues, phonic clues, and pronunciation spelling using the dictionary or glossary. The advantages and disadvantages of each technique are given, and the value of using a technique in combination with others is stressed. Situations that favor the use of one technique over another are described. For example, phonic analysis is not likely to be effective in interpreting structure words. This book offers activities for teaching the techniques and practice exercises illustrating how each technique may be used in identifying words.

Rinsky, Lee Ann, and Griffith, Barbara. *Teaching Word Attack Skills.* Dubuque, Iowa: Gorsuch Scarisbrick Publishers, 1978.

This manual focuses on five kinds of word attack skills: phonic analysis, basic sight words, structural analysis, contextual analysis, and dictionary skills. Definitions are given for the elements to be taught in each skill along with suggested procedures for teaching these skills. The manual is noteworthy for additional features such as overviews of major topics, short reviews, and self-checks. In addition, a separate section deals with areas of differences of the dialect-speaking and English-as-a-second-language child.

# 5

# Skills for Comprehension in Reading

Historians tell us that at one time, teachers of reading made no attempt to emphasize comprehension but only accurate and fluent pronunciation.[1] The prevailing notion was that reading consisted of nothing more than the power to utter certain sounds when perceiving certain letters. The idea of gaining understanding, meaning, or knowledge from reading was not emphasized. Today a dominant goal of reading is comprehension — the ability to find meaning in what is read.

Perhaps you think that if children can comprehend oral language, they are then able to comprehend written words, sentences, and paragraphs, too, provided they can decode them. This may be so in part, for some of the abilities required to process speech are necessary to process written language. Yet important differences occur between the processing of oral and written information. Children understand much of what they hear because of the voiced intonation — the pitch, stress, raising of voice, and separations of some words and syllables. To read, however, they must learn how these same intonation patterns are signaled by printed symbols. Also the language of spontaneous speech has a less varied vocabulary, less subordination, and less redundancy, thus making it easier to comprehend. Other cues in oral communication, such as facial expressions and gestures, also make the decoding of speech less difficult for the beginner.

---

[1] Daniel Resnick and Lauren Resnick, "The Nature of Literacy: An Historical Exploration," *Harvard Educational Review* 47, no. 3 (August 1977): 370–385.

It is true, however, that once children acquire competency in both decoding and reading comprehension skills, many of them are better at comprehending tasks, such as understanding mathematics and science, from print than from speech. This may be due to the fact that when reading, as opposed to listening, one can control the rate at which the information is given and review all or part of it as often as necessary.

In this chapter, we focus on those specific comprehension skills and techniques that will help children understand what they are reading. These skills help them deal with explicitly stated information — *literal comprehension* — and draw deeper meanings about what is read — *inferential comprehension*. The contrast between literal and inferential comprehension can be seen in the following illustration:

Sentence from text: Jim was the only one there without a friend.

Who was without a friend?
(Answer is explicitly given, hence it requires literal comprehension.)

How did Jim feel? (Answer must be inferred on the basis of reader's own experiential background.)

To comprehend at a literal level, one must know the meaning of the words read (vocabulary knowledge); know how to follow the structure of a passage — to identify modifiers, antecedents of pronouns, and so on; and know how to locate answers to specific questions. To make inferences about what is read, one needs to have a general ability to reason with the information presented, to be sensitive to subtle linguistic clues, and to draw from personal experiences in deriving the full significance of what the author has written.

# Specific Comprehension Skills

### Understanding Sequence

The ability to understand the sequence of events is necessary if one is to comprehend a variety of reading material. Items as different as solving arithmetic problems, understanding the causes and effects of historical events, following written directions, and interpreting a story, play, novel, or poem depend on the ability to note sequential order. The following are illustrations of sequence objectives as they might appear at different levels of a reading program:

OBJECTIVES FOR UNDERSTANDING SEQUENCE

Given pictures showing a sequence of events, the child can determine which events came first and last; for example,

"Look at the three pictures and then put a mark by the one that happened first and last."

"Look at the three pictures and then put a mark by the one that happened first."

(house painted)     (house half painted)     (house unpainted)

Given either a story or a set of directions, the child can repeat or recall the events as they appeared in the material; for example,

"These three pictures show what happened in the story you just read. Which one shows what happened first, next, last?"

Given a list of words, the child can identify those that signal chronological order; for example,

"Put a circle around the words that tell *when* something happened."

first     then     later     next     finally

Given scrambled sentences, the child can order the sentences on the basis of tense and words that signal sequence; for example,

"Put a mark by the sentence that tells what happened last."

a. _____ Tesla thought of a way to make lights brighter.

b. _____ Later there were dim electric lights.

c. _____ Once there were only candles.

Given a narrative, the child can order events in the sequence in which they occurred; for example,

"Read the story about the twelve deeds of the king and list them to show the order in which they were done."

Given selections containing instances of the techniques of *foreshadowing* and *flashback*, the child can identify the techniques and explain these techniques in relation to the interpretation of the selections. The ability to order events chronologically even when they are not presented in the order of their narration is useful in interpreting many literary forms.

The manner in which sequence skills are taught depends on the reading approach taken. For example, if you use a basal reader, you will probably teach sequence through exercises consistent with events in a story; if you use a language experience approach, you will teach sequence by having children repeat for dictation the proper sequence of an activity in which they have participated; when using the technological approach, you are more likely to make sure that pupils demonstrate mastery of a sequence skill before proceeding.

The following illustrates a typical teacher-directed lesson:

*Skill — Noting Correct Sequence — Clue Words*

In most stories, authors don't tell you that one thing happened first, that another happened next, and so on. They do give clues, however.

Look at these sentences:    The girl left before the bell rang.
                            The girl left while the bell rang.
                            The girl left after the bell rang.

Do you notice that all three of these sentences are the same except for one word? What are the two things that happened in each sentence? (the girl left; the bell rang) In the first sentence, what happened first? . . . How do you know? . . . Yes, the clue word *before* lets you know that the girl left first. Which action happened first in the second sentence? . . . Yes, they both happened at the same time. How do you know? . . . In the third sentence, which action happened first? . . . How do you know?

## Interpreting Sentence Structure: Semantics and Syntax

The semantics (meaning) of sentence structure depends on the word order in a sentence. Syntax refers to the way the words are put together.

OBJECTIVE FOR WORD ORDER

Given two sentences that are the same except for word order, the child can state the difference in meaning of the two sentences.

The writing mode of language can serve to teach the semantics of sentence structure. After sentences are built, ask children to change the word order to give another meaning; for example, The girl who is in my room gave the toy to the boy *versus* The boy who is in my room gave the toy to the girl.

Written language tends to be more formal and constrained than oral language. Some of the language structure in school textbooks is likely to be unfamiliar to pupils. Hence objectives that aim at helping the child comprehend the less familiar sentence patterns and structure words — the passive voice sentences, sentences with clauses, and antecedents of pronouns — are necessary.

**Active and passive voice**  The active sentence pattern (noun-verb-noun) is a basic structure: Mary saw the car. By inverting the word order and adding a form of the verb *be* and the preposition *by*, the sentence is changed to a passive sentence: The car was seen by Mary.

OBJECTIVES FOR ACTIVE AND PASSIVE VOICE

Given a passage written in the active voice, the child can select an answer to a question using the literal information found within the passage. Passages can be written at the grade level desired.

Given a statement written in the passive voice, the child can identify another sentence that expresses the same idea in an active pattern; for example,

"Put a mark by the answer that means the same as the first sentence."

Tom wasn't found in the tree by Bill.

a. _____ Bill didn't find Tom in the tree.
b. _____ Tom found Bill in the tree.
c. _____ Bill found Tom in the tree.

The exercises for teaching comprehension of the passive voice as well as the teaching of other comprehension skills are closely aligned with testing. The chief difference between teaching and testing in comprehension is that in the former, the teacher gives more immediate confirmation to the child. A typical exercise:

"Read the story and put a mark by the answer that best answers the question."

Tom has a dollar. Now all he needs is one more dime and he can buy that new toy he saw in the window.
Tom has _____ .

a. _____ a dollar     b. _____ a dime     c. _____ a toy

**Sentences with clauses**  Some sentences contain groups of words (clauses) that are in a noun-verb pattern; for example,

The play *we saw yesterday* was interesting.

They were hungry *so they went home.*

*If you go*, you will be sorry.

The boys were wrong, *since the dog came anyway.*

Many clauses are signaled by words such as: *because, unless, until, who, what, which, before, though.*

OBJECTIVE FOR INTERPRETING SENTENCES WITH CLAUSES

Given a sentence containing one or more clauses, the child can answer questions using information given in the sentence.

"Read the sentence and then answer the question below it." We lost the game because Susan dropped the ball thrown by the new pitcher.

Why did they lose the game?

a. _____ Susan dropped the ball.
b. _____ There was a new pitcher.

**Antecedents of pronouns**  Children sometimes have difficulty in comprehending because they do not identify the referents (antecedents) for pronouns. Thus pupils should acquire the generalization that some pronouns refer to persons or things and that others refer to ideas. You might give exercises like these:

1. Tough little germs can cause anything from boils to blood poisoning. *They* are dangerous. (What is dangerous?)

2. The little boy found *it* helpful to count on his fingers. (What is helpful?)

3. It is possible to change a vapor to a liquid. *This* is done by condensation. (What is done by condensation?)

Beginning readers learn to read pronoun referents on the basis of number and gender; for example,

My friend went. He had a good time. (What does *he* stand for?)

My friends went. They had a good time. (What does *they* stand for?)

One readiness exercise is to write common pronouns on the board — *they, some, his, her, we, our, that, it, both, many* — and then ask the pupils to supply the pronoun referents; for example, *they* — Mary and Carla.

OBJECTIVES FOR DETERMINING ANTECEDENTS OF PRONOUNS

Given sentences containing a subject pronoun, the child can select the referent on the basis of agreement in number and gender; for example,

"Put a mark by the picture that goes with the underlined word."

<u>We</u> eat ice cream.    (boy)    (girl)    (children)

Given selections containing subject or object pronouns, the child can identify referents; for example,

"I'll be here for a month," Mr. King said, "to see how Mr. Queen and the pets get along. *He* will be staying in the old south house."

*He* refers to:    a. _____ Mr. King    b. _____ Mr. Queen

Given selections containing demonstrative or possessive pronouns (*this, these, those*) and pronouns that indicate ownership (ours, its), the child can identify the referents; for example,

*This* is not allowed. Mary, stop those children from running. What is not allowed?

## Interpreting Meaning through Punctuation

Punctuation, which signals the emphasis and meaning of words, is a key to the interpretation of meaning. Italics and boldface type, for instance, indicate stress or emphasis. Type size, commas, semicolons, periods, and question marks also indicate pauses (juncture) and pitch (high and low emphasis).

OBJECTIVES FOR PUNCTUATION AS A COMPREHENSION SKILL

Given words in context and punctuated by different typographical devices, the child can pronounce the word as indicated by the typographical markings; for example,

"Read these two sentences aloud."

That is MY dog.
That is my dog?

Given sentences that are identical except for punctuation, the child will read the words with proper intonation; for example,

"Read these sentences aloud."

Run, fast man.
Run fast, man.
Run fast? Man!

Given sentences that differ only in the use of ellipses, dashes, and signals for titles (italics, quotation marks, underlining), the child can interpret the different meanings conveyed by the typographical devices; for example,

"Tell what is on the TV as indicated by each of these sentences."

The "Lost Girl" is on the TV.
The *lost* girl is on the TV.
The lost girl is *on* the TV.

To sensitize pupils to the meaning of typographical devices, you might ask questions such as whether a particular use of a *dash* shows a break in thought, a comparison, an emphasized conclusion, or something else; whether *ellipses* — dots — are being used to indicate a pause, an interruption, or reluctance; and whether the italics in a sentence signal a title, a foreign word, or the use of a word as an example.

### Deriving Meaning of Words through Affixes

A few affixes and roots can be helpful in determining the meaning of many thousands of words. *Affixes* include both *prefixes* (which are put before the main part of a word) and *suffixes* (which come at the end of the main part). The root or base word is the main part. Frequently used prefixes are *trans*, across; *re*, back; *non*, not; *inter*, between; *de*, from; *com*, with; *dis*, apart; *mis*, wrong; *sub*, under; *un*, not. Important suffixes are *able*, capable of; *ance, age,* state or quality of; *ar, er, or,* agent; *fy*, to make; *ism*, being; *less*, without; *et*, small; *tion*, action or state; *ward*, toward.

OBJECTIVE FOR DERIVING MEANING THROUGH AFFIXES

Given words with prefixes or suffixes, the child can recognize the definition of the affix; for example,

"Put a mark by the best definition for the italicized affix."

*tele*meter  a. _____ superior
            b. _____ in the center
            c. _____ at a distance

trait*able*  a. _____ having characteristics
            b. _____ fit for
            c. _____ belonging to

## Recognizing Main Ideas in Paragraphs

Once pupils can identify the topic of a paragraph and then determine the most important statement about the topic, they are able to find the main idea. The ability to differentiate a general statement from statements that give supporting details is part of this process. Often the main idea is found in a topical sentence at the beginning of a paragraph or in a conclusion at the end.

### OBJECTIVES FOR RECOGNIZING MAIN IDEAS

Given statements, the child can identify the most general or encompassing statement among them; for example,

"Put a mark by the sentence that is most general."

1. _____ They play with a cat.
   _____ They play with a dog.
   _____ They play with pets.

2. _____ Dogs pull sleds.
   _____ Dogs work.
   _____ Dogs watch sheep.

Given paragraphs, the child can select the answer that best expresses the main idea or general synopsis of the paragraph's information; for example,

When a bee wants to lead other bees to flowers, it does a dance. A *wagging* dance means that the flowers are far away. A *round* dance means that the flowers are a hundred yards from the hive. A *fast* dance means that the supply of nectar is very big.

a. _____ Bees enjoy dancing.
b. _____ Flowers have nectar.
c. _____ Bees "talk" by dancing.

When additional instruction is given in teaching main ideas, it usually consists of a suggested strategy. "Answering two questions can often give you clues to help you recognize the main idea of a paragraph: (1) What is the topic of the paragraph? and (2) What is the most important thing said about the topic?"

One reason reading for main ideas is such a difficult comprehension task is that it requires placing details in proper relationship to each other. A technique for helping pupils to see such relationships is *paraphrasing main ideas.* Pupils are given material that contains a central thought or main idea and then are asked to state in their own words what they thought the author was trying to say.

Also you may want to provide pupils with factual pieces or short, informational paragraphs and ask them to generate headings or titles that would be appropriate for these passages. A more challenging activity is to give a story, fairy tale, or fable and ask them to go beyond the specifics in the selection to draw a universal generalization or moral from what is read; for example, that money does not always bring happiness, that one must risk something to gain something, or that surface appearances do not reveal the inner worth of a person.

## Drawing Logical Conclusions

The skill category identified as drawing logical conclusions includes inferring outcomes and noting cause-and-effect relations. One way to help pupils draw conclusions from their reading is to sensitize them to words that serve as supports or signals to the ideas that are to be presented. For example, cause and effect is often signaled by words like *if-then; because, so, therefore,* and *hence.* The drawing of conclusions also requires that children have sufficient experiential background and maturity to synthesize information and logic.

OBJECTIVES FOR DRAWING LOGICAL CONCLUSIONS

Given several pictures, the child can select the picture that shows the most probable outcome from a described event; for example,

"A child is playing with a ball near a window. Which picture shows what might happen next?"

(broken window)    (broken chair)

Given a fact, the child can logically infer another fact; for example,

"Complete the sentence."

Juan and his cat are having a race. Juan's cat _____ .

a. _____ is black.
b. _____ is fat.
c. _____ runs.

Given descriptions of a natural event, the child can select the answer that best describes the cause; for example,

"Complete the sentences."

The clothes are drying fast because _____ .

a. _____ the wind is strong.
b. _____ Mother is in a hurry.
c. _____ there are few clothes.

The tree blew down because _____ .

a. _____ the clouds were blue.
b. _____ the wind was strong.
c. _____ the tree had no leaves.

Given paragraphs containing facts, the child can select the conclusion that best takes into account all relevant information; for example,

There is much water in the world. Salt water seas make up 97.27 percent of the water in the world. We can't drink salt water. We have shortages of drinking water because:

a. _____ Most water is too salty for drinking.
b. _____ People drink too much water.
c. _____ There is not enough water in the world.

## Obtaining Meaning of Words through Context

Children should infer the meaning of an unfamiliar word by using context clues. These clues include (1) those where the new word is defined by the sentence itself: "She was *puissant*, a powerful and mighty person"; and (2) the use of a comparison and contrast to signal opposite meanings. Children may comprehend an unknown word because it is likened to a familiar term. Also they may understand an unfamiliar word because they know the opposite: It wasn't temporary but *permanent*. Comparison and contrast are often signaled by words such as *like, as, but*, and *on the other hand*.

OBJECTIVES FOR OBTAINING WORD MEANING THROUGH CONTEXT CLUES

Given sentences that include an unfamiliar word, the child determines the meaning of the unknown word on the basis of known information in other sentences; for example,

"Choose the answer that best completes the sentence."

1. It was a two-legged animal. It was a *biped*. A _____ is a biped.
   a. _____ dog
   b. _____ man

2. *Auks* are diving birds that breed in the colder part of the North. Auks _____ .
   a. _____ fly
   b. _____ rob

3. It is *irrespirable* here; life cannot go on. We can't _____ .
   a. _____ laugh
   b. _____ breathe

Given sentences that include an unfamiliar word, the child determines the meaning of the unknown word on the basis of contrast as a context clue; for example,

"Tell what the underlined word means."

1. Some cheeses are good to eat after a long time; but butter becomes <u>rancid</u> in a few days.

2. In contrast to the staying power of Mike, Harry was known for his <u>evanescency</u>.

3. This one was not far away; it was <u>proximal</u>.

Basic to interpreting the language used by authors are opportunities for children to become familiar with language expressions such as:

*Idioms or dialects*: "start from scratch," "means business."

*Figurative language*: one thing is expressed in terms that are analogous but normally used in another context. "They moved, *uprooting* the children from their neighborhood."

*Metaphors and similes*: suggest a likeness or analogy. "The ship *plowed* the sea." "The boat skimmed like a water bug."

# Newer Ideas in Reading Comprehension

Current research focuses on the ways good and poor comprehenders differ in their approach to the reading tasks and on the possibility of encouraging children to control their own cognitive processes and to learn strategies for reading different kinds of materials. Tentative findings from such research indicate the importance of teaching language constraints, self-mediated learning strategies, elaboration, and the use of *schema* for relating reading to one's life experiences.

## Language Constraints

Good comprehenders are sensitive to language constraints in sentences but poor comprehenders seem to ignore semantic and syntactic cues and treat words as individual entities.[2] This finding points up the need for teaching children to (1) integrate semantic, syntactic, and phonic cues, (2) associate meaning with printed passages, and (3) test the resulting meaning to see if it corresponds to what they expected to learn from the passage. Exercises with connectives help sensitize children to semantic cues. Try giving exercises to children in which they are asked to explain the differences between several paragraphs, all of which are the same except for the substitution of connectives — *but, and, yet, so, nor*: I wanted to go on (but, so, and, yet) she didn't.

The use of *cloze exercises* is another way to help children anticipate meaning from context. The essential feature of the cloze technique is the deletion of words in a passage that the child is to fill in on the basis of context clues. Although the procedure is used often in the measurement of comprehension, it is also a device for teaching pupils to anticipate meaning from context.

The following is an illustration of a cloze exercise:

"Read the selection all the way through and then fill in the missing word in each blank."

Frank met Sue and Stan on his __1__ home from school.
"Guess __2__!" he said. "I have a straw man __3__ my yard."
"A straw man?" asked Sue. "__4__ mean a strong man, __5__ you?"
"No," Frank said, smiling. "Not a strong man, a straw __6__."

---

[2] Richard Isakson and John W. Miller, "Sensitivity to Syntactic and Semantic Cues in Good and Poor Comprehenders," *Journal of Educational Psychology* 68 (1976): 787–792.

"What is he doing in your __7__?" asked Stan.

"What is he like?" asked Sue.

"What does he __8__?" asked Stan.

"He doesn't eat! He doesn't even __9__. He just stands there."

"Oh, he must be very __10__," said Sue.

"Not at all," Frank said. "You should see the way he scares away the __11__."

Key:
1. way; 2. what; 3. in; 4. you; 5. don't; 6. man; 7. yard; 8. eat; 9. move, play or any other answer consistent with context; 10. boring; 11. birds, children, or any other defensible answer.

You may find the exercise above too difficult for your pupils. The optimum ratio of deleted words to running text depends upon the children's maturity and familiarity with the material. In using cloze exercises for teaching context clues, be sure the deleted words can be correctly identified without too much difficulty, even if it means deleting only one word out of twenty or more.

## Self-mediated Learning Strategies

There is a need to differentiate the instruction for children who comprehend poorly and have poor word recognition skills and those who comprehend poorly but have adequate word recognition skills. The latter may be given training in translating strategies into self-statements or sentences to say to oneself when reading:

> I've learned three things; first, to ask myself what the main idea of the story is — What is the story about? A second is to learn important details of the story as I go along. The order of the main events and their sequence are especially important details. A third is to ask how the characters feel and why?

Two sequences for helping children learn what to say to themelves before performing a reading task are:

*Sequence One*

1. Stop and think before I begin.

2. What plan can I try?

3. How would it work if I did that?

4. What shall I try next?

5. Is it right so far?

*Sequence Two*

1. What is it I have to do? (problem identification)

2. Repeat the instruction. (focusing attention)

3. Good, I'm doing fine. (self-reinforcement)

4. That's OK. It's all right to make a mistake. (coping skill)

## Elaboration

Asking pupils to elaborate on what they read aids comprehension. Reading comprehension occurs when readers actively construct meaning from the text. Marleen Doctorow and others have found that the reading comprehension of children is enhanced by having them first attend to one- or two-word paragraph headings and then asking them to construct original sentences summarizing events described in each of the paragraphs of a text. Examples of questions eliciting elaboration are:

> Tell why you think this is true or not.
>
> What would be the next thing to happen?
>
> This is the theme — extend it.
>
> Tell how this relates to your past experiences."[3]

Children also are more successful in recalling what they read when they are given the opportunity to reflect upon what they read, using the factual information read to defend positions of importance to them.[4] Thus you might provide pupils with factual pieces on topics such as pets and sports and then have them say how they would use the information in treating controversial issues like vivisection and non-competitive athletics.

Since comprehension is facilitated when learners are stimulated to construct elaborations of what is read,[5] there is value in helping them

[3] Marleen Doctorow, M. C. Wittrock, and Carolyn Marks, "Generative Processes in Reading Comprehension," *Journal of Educational Psychology* 70, no. 2 (1978): 109–118.

[4] Donald S. Biskin et al., "Prediction, Reflection, and Comprehension," *Elementary School Journal* 77 (1976): 131–139.

[5] M. C. Wittrock et al., "Reading as a Generative Process," *Journal of Educational Psychology* 67 (1975): 484–489.

form mental pictures. Asking children to provide more detail about a character or situation than is given in the text is one way to help them form such mental pictures. Drawing pictures to illustrate an important aspect of their reading is another way. Elementary school children are rich in the means for making concrete descriptions of events, actions, states, and objects. In addition to encouraging visual imagery of what is read, you also should ask them to associate personal experiences to what they read.

## Schema Theory

Skillful readers read to verify what they already know. Current theory suggests that to comprehend well one must have schematic or cognitive patterns that can be filled in with specific content and embedded upon each other. There are different schemata for different types of prose. In approaching a narrative, for example, you might use the story schema of a setting and episode. Children can be taught to use the same schema employed by the author or to use a different schema to organize the information for processing and storage in memory. Having children learn to write stories may help them learn the schema used by authors, thereby improving the children's ability to comprehend when reading. The schema theory of reading comprehension suggests that good readers have a set of scenarios in their heads (for example, the four basic plots used in television soap operas) and all that one does when reading is to fill in the blanks. Having a schema or pattern helps one *chunk* information — relate a lot of information to a single concept, idea, or symbol. The relating of information to the schema is thought to be the basis for understanding — for making sense of what is being read.

It is likely that many teaching techniques will follow the development of schema theory. Already the following procedures are suggested:

1. Teach children to chunk by going from one word to a phrase, to a sentence, and to a paragraph at a single glance.

2. Ask children to predict what will be found on a page.

3. If children do not have their own schema or cognitive organizer for reading a selection, you might provide a preview of the content using concepts and generalizations. The preview will serve as an ideational framework for subsuming the detailed information.

4. Teach children that testlike questions presented *before* passages will enhance their learning and retention of answers to these ques-

tions, but that questions placed *after* passages will help them retain both the question's specific information and additional information.

5. Teach children to formulate their own questions and read to answer these questions. For instance, after children have responded to your formulated questions at various levels of thought, they should be encouraged to use your questioning model in formulating questions appropriate to a given kind of book or selection.

6. Children should know whether they are expected to read for main ideas or specific facts and detail because the purpose determines how they are to read. They should also be told if they are to recall the information without referring to the text and whether the question will require an inference or not. As indicated previously, it is a good idea to let children themselves prepare their own questions in a variety of forms and then read to see how fully the questions are answered. One word of caution: There should be a manageable number of pre-reading questions for any one selection, usually not more than three.

7. Introduce reading materials that have simplified syntax but take care to instruct children in how to comprehend both complex sentence structures and cues within sentences, such as terms that signal cause and effect, contrast, descriptions, and appositions.

8. Provide children with the relevant background for understanding the content of what they are to read. Children appear to be dependent on the interplay between their preexisting knowledge and the text content.[6] Before giving a passage to be read, you might excite the right background expectations by providing pictures, precis, examples, or brief descriptions so the child can make inferences while reading. Training children to generate appropriate contexts for material they must comprehend is likely to be a fruitful way for improving understanding of what is read.

9. We have mentioned how written and spoken language differ. Listening to written language is an excellent way for children to learn how to comprehend its characteristics. Children will acquire understanding of written language when listening to you read aloud. Listening to others read may be one reason why children who become proficient readers often come from homes where parents have read to them. A wide range of material can serve in reading aloud. Both traditional material — fairy tales, adventure stories, myths — and the contemporary writing found in newspapers and magazines provide the language complexities necessary for comprehending written language.

---

[6] Ann L. Brown and Sandra S. Smiley, *The Development of Strategies for Studying Prose Passages* (Champaign, Ill.: University of Illinois, Center for the Study of Reading, October 1977).

Comprehension skills can be acquired through indirect procedures that encourage pupils to process print into meaning. Helping children select books they can read is an indirect approach to comprehension. If children do not have to attend to the decoding process because of familiarity with the material, they can attend better to the comprehension task — the implication of what is being read. Other indirect approaches are dictating and reading children's stories and having pupils frame their own purposes for reading. It is not enough to ask children questions after they have read. They should be encouraged to state what they expect to gain from their reading and then focus on both the expected and the unexpected.

## Summary

Learning to read is much more than learning to read words quickly and efficiently. It is deriving meaning from what is read. Although a comprehension of spoken language is basic to the comprehension of printed material, it is not sufficient because spoken and written language are not the same. The vocabulary and grammar for the two language systems are distributed diversely and each makes different demands upon one's memory.

We began this chapter with a distinction between comprehending written language at a literal level and making inferences about what is read. Prerequisites to both of these tasks were given. Then we focused on specific comprehension skills that can be taught and that contribute to literal and inferential reading ability. Categories of comprehension skills — sequence, syntactical structures, punctuation and typographical devices, affixes, main ideas, logical conclusions, context clues — were defined and illustrated to show how these skills might be dealt with at the beginning, middle, and upper stages of learning to read. Newer ideas and research about what should be taught in reading comprehension were presented: language constraints, self-mediated learning strategies, elaboration, and schema theory.

Although techniques for helping children use comprehension skills in concert are treated in Chapter 7, the present chapter has a number of suggested practices. Our suggestions include forming mental pictures of what is read, employing a variety of questions, generating contexts for material to be read, completing cloze exercises, paraphrasing main ideas in passages, interpreting language, and hearing written language read aloud.

# Self-instructional Exercises

### Exercise 1. Distinguishing Between Questions That Call for Explicitly Stated Information and Those That Require an Inference

Label each question below either (a) *literal* if its answer is likely to be given directly in printed material or (b) *inferential* if its answer requires the making of an inference.

1. _____ From your reading of the story, do you think the Fosters were happy?

2. _____ How many children did Mr. Foster have?

3. _____ What was the name of Mrs. Smith's cat?

4. _____ What might have happened if the train had not been late?

5. _____ How are camels able to survive in the desert?

6. _____ How did Lucy probably feel after her meeting with Rose?

**ANSWERS TO EXERCISE 1**

1. Inferential: one must "put two and two together" to arrive at a conclusion.

2. Literal: one can expect to find the answer directly stated.

3. Literal: the question is a factual one.

4. Inferential: one must draw from personal experience to answer the question.

5. Literal: the question suggests that the answer will be directly stated in the text.

6. Inferential: to understand how Lucy felt, one would have to know the total situation and identify with Lucy.

### Exercise 2. Recognizing Meanings Signaled by Words

Match each set of words in column 1 with the meaning it signals in column 2.

1. then, later, during          a. Cause and effect

2. besides, under, into          b. Sequence

3. because, if-then, since       c. Compare and contrast

4. although-still, more-than, not-but       d. Conclusion to follow

5. hence, therefore, so                                  e. Position

**ANSWERS TO EXERCISE 2**

1b. These words signal sequence or chronology.

2e. These words are prepositions indicating positions.

3a. These words indicate that reasons or conclusions follow.

4c. These words introduce comparisons.

5d. These words signal conclusions and indicate a relationship between sentences.

## Exercise 3. Recognizing Words That Signal Different Kinds of Sentences or Sentence Elements

Match each set of words in column 1 with the kind of sentence or element it signals.

1. who, why, when            a. Noun to follow

2. above, below, in           b. Phrase to follow

3. our, the, few                 c. Question to follow

4. am, could, did               d. Clause to follow

5. until, if, who                 e. Verb to follow

**ANSWERS TO EXERCISE 3**

1c. The five W's — *who, what, where, when, why* — and *how* signal questions.

2b. These words introduce prepositional phrases.

3a. These words are noun determiners indicating to readers that they should grasp the word and the following noun as a whole within the pattern of the sentence.

4e. These are verb markers. Forms of *be, have,* and *do* along with helpers such as *can, may,* and *might* are typical verb markers.

5d. These words and others like *when, once,* and *now* signal that a clause is about to unfold.

## Exercise 4. Identifying Clues to Comprehension Problems

Put a mark by the answer most likely to be the key to comprehending each of the following statements.

| Problem | Key |
|---|---|

1. To know which of the two is superior: "She was a tujam, but he was only a rikum."

   a. _____ Verbal clue *only*
   b. _____ Opposite clue found in tujam/rikum
   c. _____ Contrast clue *but*

2. To know the cause: "Also, since it didn't rain, the crop failed."

   a. _____ Verbal clue *also*
   b. _____ Reasoning clue — crops need water
   c. _____ Verbal clue *since*

3. To know the order of events: "During our time there, we threaded a projector, operated the latest videotape, and, finally, lost ourselves in a display of talking books."

   a. _____ Verbal clue *during*
   b. _____ Verbal clue *latest*
   c. _____ Verbal clue *finally*

4. To recognize conclusions: "The costs of converting brine to fresh water are high; hence we don't know if the new process will be a boon or bust."

   a. _____ Verbal clue *or*
   b. _____ Verbal clue *hence*
   c. _____ Verbal clue *if*

5. To determine the meaning of an unfamiliar word: "She always wore gimcracks, showy ornaments of little worth."

   a. _____ Context clue-definition within sentence
   b. _____ Verbal clue *always*
   c. _____ Context clue — contrasting ideas

6. To determine the main idea: "Strange things happen in fairy tales. A frog turns into a prince and witches play around with magic apples."

   a. _____ Factual and emotionally loaded statements
   b. _____ Statement of fact and statement of opinion
   c. _____ General and specific statements

**ANSWERS TO EXERCISE 4**

1a. The word *only* as used signals depreciation.

2c. *Since* is a signal word for cause and effect.

3c. *Finally* signals chronology.

4b. *Hence* indicates a conclusion follows.

5a. *Gimcracks* is defined within the sentence.

6c. To differentiate between general and specific statements is one way to find main ideas.

## Exercise 5. Recognizing Instances of Terms Used in Teaching Comprehension

Match each term in column 1 with a sentence in column 2 that illustrates the term.

1. Contrasted ideas
2. Analogy
3. Classification
4. Figurative language
5. Definite and indefinite terms
6. Idioms

a. The ship's wake looked like a giant snake zigzagging across the ocean.

b. The farmers had barley, wheat, and other grains.

c. Light is free when it comes from the sun, but it is costly when converted into electricity.

d. Some came versus ten came.

e. "The last one home is a wet goose," he yelled.

f. In my lifetime, I've peeled mountains of potatoes.

**ANSWERS TO EXERCISE 5**

1c. Contrast is signaled by *but*.

2a. The ship's wake is analogous to a snake with respect to pattern of movement.

3b. Barley and wheat are instances within the category *grain*.

4f. This is flowery language and expresses something in terms normally denoting something else.

5d. Words used to define precisely are definite terms. Other examples of indefinite terms are: *many, soon, far, near, large, small, fast.* Ability to translate indefinite terms into definite terms often aids comprehension.

6e. This is language peculiar to a limited setting. In this case, the words must be understood as a challenge to race.

# Selected Readings

Gowie, Cheryl J. "Psycholinguistic Strategies for Improving Reading Comprehension," *Elementary School Journal* 79, no. 2 (1978): 67–73.

The author cites studies which show that children's comprehension of sentences and passages is greatest when the text is in harmony with what the reader expects to find in the print. Expectations are rooted in experience. Implications for teaching comprehension are that the teacher should assess prior knowledge and establish expectations appropriate to the material. If children do not have enough information, add it. Further, it is important to provide children with prior knowledge, such as what the reading material is about, and to build the experiential background with which to set appropriate expectations. (Make sure the child has enough knowledge to understand the text.)

The author argues that teachers should help children be more sensitive to what they know before and after reading a passage.

Pany, Darlene, and Jenkins, Joseph K. *Learning Word Meanings: A Comparison of Instructional Procedures and Effects of Comprehension with Learning Disabled Students.* Technical Report No. 25. Cambridge, Mass.: Bolt, Beranek, and Newman, March 1977. 34 pp. ERIC Ed. 136 237.

Five learning disabled children were given different treatments for learning word meanings. One treatment involved no direct teaching and the child was expected to learn unfamiliar word meanings from inferences from passage context (meaning from context). Another treatment called for the teacher telling the child the meaning of unfamiliar words during oral reading of stories (meaning told). A third treatment consisted of the teacher presenting unfamiliar words on cards, giving the definitions plus a sentence containing the word. The child was then asked to read each word and repeat its meaning (meaning practiced). The meaning-practiced treatment was associated with the greatest acquisition of word knowledge but did not improve story understanding. (The unfamiliar words composed only a small percentage of the words in the stories.)

The study is important in that it raises questions about common practices in reading instruction and how word meaning might contribute to comprehension.

Spiegel, Dixie Lee. "Ten Ways to Sort Out Reading Comprehension Problems," *Learning* 7, no. 7 (March 1979): 40–41.

When a child fails to respond correctly to a reading comprehension task, the teacher should not necessarily give more instruction in reading comprehension skills. Instead, the author recommends that the teacher consider other causes for the failure to respond correctly — inability to decode, to follow directions, to express what is comprehended, to understand the questions asked, to remember what has been comprehended, to be interested in what is being read, to relate to the material for lack of background information, to understand a specialized vocabulary, to interpret faulty passages. Further, the child's own response may be valid but not the one generally expected. The article includes specific suggestions for determining whether one of the foregoing is a cause for error, and for helping the child with the problem.

Weaver, Phyllis, and Shonkoff, Fredi. *Research within Reading–A Research in Guided Response to Concerns of Reading Education.* Washington, D.C.: Dept. of Health, Education, and Welfare, October, 1978.

Pages 87–105 of this document describe reading comprehension and its instruction, question-asking strategies, cloze tasks for improving reading comprehension, and ways to improve reading comprehension scores. The authors believe that reading comprehension can be improved if pupils acquire rapid word recognition skills, vocabulary knowledge, background experience, and knowledge of text organization. They recommend that teachers ask varied questions — literal, inferential interpretive, evaluative. Postquestioning is valued more than prequestioning. Practice with cloze passages is ineffective, but instruction on completing cloze passages for specific purposes may be beneficial. Scores on reading comprehension tests may be enhanced through exercises that reproduce the format, instructions, and time constraints of the tests by making pupils less anxious and test-wise.

# 6

# Critical Reading and Study Skills in the Content Fields

Reading material used in the teaching of reading — whether with a basal, technological, language experience, or individualized approach — chiefly involves stories or narratives, a connected succession of happenings. The familiar vocabulary, sentence patterns, and organizational schema (setting, development, resolution) of narrative material make it ideal for teaching word recognition and comprehension skills whenever these skills are being emphasized more than the content of what is being read. However, there is another reading goal: to learn how to gain and evaluate information from reading. Children are expected to learn from materials that are filled with the vocabulary, concepts, and generalizations from literature, science, social studies and mathematics — the content fields.

Fundamental to reading in the content fields are the previously mentioned skills of word recognition and comprehension, but in addition, there are the skills of critical reading and study. Critical reading requires that children do more than read the lines (literal comprehension) or even read between the lines (inferential comprehension). They must read beyond the lines (make judgments about what is read and react to the content and to the author's use of language). Study skills help one locate, select, and evaluate information, organize information for retention, understand graphic aids, and follow directions.

There are signs that teachers have not been as successful in teaching these higher level skills as they have been in teaching word recognition and reading comprehension. Results of the National Assessment of Educational Progress, for example, indicate that comprehension ability falls off as reading tasks become more difficult.[1] Further, elementary teachers themselves score low on tests of the study skills intended for use with children.[2]

This chapter, then, is presented in response to the need for increased effort in strengthening the critical reading and study skill area of teacher education. The focus is on *what* to teach, although techniques for teaching the skills are illustrated. This chapter, together with the methods for teaching given in Chapter 7, presents the best of what is known about critical reading and study skills, recognizing that more research is needed to understand mature reading and how to promote it.

## Critical Reading

When reading critically, a child evaluates the material, judging the quality, worth, accuracy, and truthfulness of what is read. At all grade levels, pupils can be helped to read critically. Young children will respond to questions such as these:

> This page told how to make a puppet. Did it tell you everything you need to know to make it? What else do you want to know?

> Which of these two books do you think Maria would like to read? Why?

> Did this story tell about something that could really happen? What were the things that helped you know it was make believe?

Older children reveal their attitudes and accuracy of ideas and information when you ask questions such as these:

> How do these two authors differ in what they say about _____?

> How can we find out which one is correct? What additional information do we need?

> Did the author write this to inform, entertain, persuade, or for some other purpose? How do you know?

---

[1] Thomas R. Schnell, "Identifying the Basic Elements of Critical Reading," *Reading Horizons* 19, no. 1 (1978): 34–40.

[2] Eunice N. Askov, Karlyn Kamm, and Robert Klumb, "Study Skill Mastery Among Elementary School Teachers," *Reading Teacher* 30, no. 5 (February 1977): 485–488.

What is there about the background of these authors that might make you suspect bias in their writing?

Compare the words these two authors used in writing about nature: "We hear the anguished cry of the fox caught in the jaws of the iron trap." "The wolf gave a vicious snarl when Shirley shot him." How do the attitudes of these authors toward nature seem to differ?

To determine whether material read is fact or opinion, to determine the accuracy and adequacy of material, to recognize gross overstatements with unfounded claims (propaganda), and to analyze the author's values are among the most frequently mentioned skills of critical reading.

## Recognizing Fact and Opinion

The recognition of fact and opinion is difficult because there is no clear idea of what constitutes a fact. In one sense, a factual statement is one that can be verified. But there are many ways to verify something: observing directly, checking historical records, establishing logical proof, using conventional wisdom, and reading the findings of scientists. The teaching of reading does not often aim at having children apply the canons of evidence needed to establish truth in a fundamental sense. Instead, children are taught to recognize when writers appear to be stating facts and when they intend to give their opinions. Opinion statements are often identified by their qualifying words: *believes* (He believes that — ); *think* (We think); *could* (It could happen); *perhaps* (Perhaps this is so); *probably* (That probably was the case).

Statements that appear to be facts are often recognizable because they do not require an inference and they describe what can be seen and heard. The following sentences are either factual or inferential:

The boy was not paying attention. (inference — opinion)

The boy was looking out the window. (observable behavior — fact)

They were angry. (inference — opinion)

They threw the paper on the floor. (observable behavior — fact)

Opportunities for pupils to compare editorials with news items reporting the same event help to clarify writing that is factual from that based on opinion or facts plus opinion.

OBJECTIVE FOR RECOGNIZING FACT AND OPINION

Given statements of facts and opinion, the child can differentiate among them; for example,

"Which of these is a factual statement?"

It is the most beautiful car in the world.
Today's temperature was 10°C.

## Recognizing Accuracy and Adequacy

In addition to having pupils learn to apply the criteria of *relevancy* (the title has a significant connection to the purpose), *recency* (timeliness in date of publication), and *comprehensiveness* (wide range of content on the topic) in recognizing the adequacy of material, teach them to attend to the author's purpose and point of view: Is the author a writer with original views or a typist following a party line? This last question implies that it is desirable for a writer to express opinions and have original ideas.

It is an extension of the skill of recognizing fact and opinion to make the point that opinions are important, especially when they rest on facts. You will want to teach children how to find information about the author's background: experience, qualifications, and affiliations. An unusual exercise is to present an article — for example, one that gives an account of the value of toy trains in the teaching of reading, math, and science — and then present information showing the connection between the author and the ideas offered: The author is the owner of the toy train company.

OBJECTIVE FOR RECOGNIZING ADEQUACY OF MATERIAL

Given a purpose for reading and several reading materials, the child can select the material most appropriate for the purpose; for example, "If you are looking for information about how a volcano is formed, which title is likely to be most useful?"

By-products of an Eruption
Volcanoes Around the World
Underground Gases

"If you are looking for information about the current government of Japan, which book is most likely to be useful?"

*Japanese Life Today,* by a Japanese author, published in 1965

*History of Japan,* by a European, published in 1979
*The Politics of Japan,* by an American, published in 1979

Recognizing accuracy and adequacy also depends on one's ability to determine bias. There are two dimensions to the problem of determining bias in material: the reader and the author. Readers may bring their own biases or attitudes to what they read. When the author's ideas are congruous with those of the readers, the readers are likely to be pleased with the point of view and to assume that the writer is not biased but fair-minded. On the other hand, if the author's ideas are not congruous with those of the readers, the readers may reject them as biased.

Your response to *reader bias* might be to encourage children to challenge their own positions as well as the views of others. Opportunities for pupils to read alternative points of view are essential. Asking pupils to distinguish between logical and emotional arguments and between facts and allegations may help. Time should be set aside to read and analyze opposing accounts of issues and incidents.

Your response to *author bias* might be to give pupils practice in judging whether writers present both sides of an issue. You might, for instance, let pupils determine the number of favorable, unfavorable, and neutral headlines and photographs and the space allowed by a newspaper for treatment of a controversial issue.

OBJECTIVE FOR RECOGNIZING PROPAGANDA

Given advertisements, articles, and other written material, the child can identify persuasive propagandistic devices, for example,

"What propaganda technique is illustrated by this sentence?"

All Indians walk single file — I know, I saw one.

The Institute for Propaganda Analysis has provided categories of persuasive devices:

Name calling: The propagandist seeks to influence one person against another person or group by using a derogatory label based on religion, race, political belief, or other category (for example, *egghead, leftist, Nazi*). Typically name calling is based on a single attribute and its intent is to generalize badness to all aspects of the person or group.

Plain folks: This is an appeal to readers by relating a proposal with the common people to gain their support or to associate the values of the common people with the proposal.

Testimonial: This device associates a proposal with some highly respected or disliked person as a way of getting acceptance or rejection of the proposal.

Glittering generalities: This is a device by which one associates a proposal with glowing terms that overgeneralize; for example, *democratic, educated, efficient,* or other value terms. Such generalities are intended to prevent examination of the person, idea, or product promoted.

Card stacking: The selection of facts, opinions, and examples for the purpose of making a one-sided case.

Bandwagon: This is the "everybody does it" technique by which one is encouraged to join a winning side or trend.

To teach to this objective, ask pupils to find instances of these propaganda techniques in articles and advertisements of newspapers, magazines, and other sources.


## Analyzing Values

The critical assessment of reading material requires an ability to recognize implied values conveyed by the author. Studies of children's reading material reveal values such as the importance of human personality, devotion to truth, respect for excellence, moral equality, brotherhood, civic responsibility, good manners, honesty, initiative, and loyalty.[3]

### OBJECTIVE FOR ANALYZING VALUES

Given materials in which indicators of value are present in the form of language, characterizations, ideas, actions, tone, illustrations, and other persuasive strategies, the child can identify the implicit values.

We recommend a questioning strategy to use in teaching to this objective:

---

[3] Ruth Kearney Carlson, "A Baker's Dozen of Personal Values in Children's Literature," *New Horizons in Reading,* ed. John Merritt (Newark, Del.: International Reading Association, 1976), pp. 49–59.

1. The first step is to have pupils identify the author's values through questions such as: What does the author value (for example, freedom, health, nature, friendships, money, and so on)?

2. After pupils identify the value, ask them to note how the author defines it through examples and direct statements. Typical questions to use are: What does this character in the story do that is connected with the value? How does the author tell what honesty means to him?

3. Next, ask pupils to find reasons for the value and the feelings that are connected with it: Why does the author think the family is so important? What reasons do the characters give for valuing animals? Is the author ashamed, proud, aggressive, or defensive about the values of money and work? Why do you think the author has these values?

4. Then, have pupils compare different views of the same value: How does this book differ from other books in its regard for conservation of natural resources?

5. Finally, ask pupils to draw a conclusion about the material and the value: On the basis of what the characters showed us, their reasons for doing what they did and their feelings, what do they tell us about _____ as a value? In view of what the different authors say about _____, what can we conclude? Is there some way to decide which value is most important? Is there any way we can have both *productivity* and *conservation?*

# Study Skills Common to All Content Fields

Study skills common to all content fields can be taught from two directions: (1) You can commence with the teaching of content fields — social studies, math, and science — and find ways to teach children the skills for using text and reference books, organizing and recalling information, and following directions; or (2) you can teach these same skills through focused skill lessons and then provide sufficient opportunities for children to apply them when reading content fields. In either case, the following skills dealing with the location of information, reading strategies for study, and organizational techniques should be taught.

### Location Skills

**Using book parts** A knowledge of the parts of textbooks — table of contents, index, title page, glossary — helps pupils learn how to learn from text material.

The *table of contents* is an outline of the major topics treated in the book. It gives a preview and overview as well as the general location of the various information. Children who know how to use the table of contents can decide whether a book has the information they require and where in the book it can be found. In teaching about the table of contents, we suggest that pupils be given books whose format for the table of contents differs — some with chapter heads alone, others also listing the topics covered in each chapter. Ask pupils to use the table of contents in determining the number of pages given to a topic and the relevancy of a book for a given problem.

The *index* functions as a quick way to find facts, names, dates, and specific details. Entries in the index are alphabetically ordered. To use an index, the pupil must know how to determine the key word to find the information wanted. A good way to teach pupils how to find the key word is to ask them to read a paragraph in a textbook, write down what they think are the key words, and then check the index of their book to see whether their words correspond to the entries in the index.

The *title page* gives information such as the title, the authors, and the publisher of the textbook. The copyright date may also appear on the title page. Otherwise it appears immediately after the title page on the *copyright page*. (The copyright date is often a clue to the recency of the content.) In teaching about these pages, you might ask pupils to identify which of their textbooks has the latest copyright date, the qualifications of the authors, and the location of the publisher.

*Glossaries* are really short dictionaries of special words used in the textbook. You should refer pupils to the glossary whenever an assignment introduces unfamiliar terms.

OBJECTIVES FOR BOOK PARTS

The child can identify textbooks by their title and can locate parts of the books by using the table of contents and the index; for example,

"What is the name of the author of the book you are reading?" "On what page in this book is there information about the care of trees?"

The child can use the glossary to look up meanings of unfamiliar words that appear in the textbook.

The child can use indexes of books to locate specific information about subtopics.

**Using dictionaries**    Upon completion of elementary school, children should be able to use the dictionary for finding meanings and the pronunciation of unfamiliar words. Effective use of the dictionary includes the ability to use its special sections: geographical terms, biographical dictionary, foreign words and phrases. Children should also know how to locate words alphabetically, to find words with the help of guide words, and to use the boldface entries to determine spelling, pronunciation, meaning, and form.

### OBJECTIVE FOR LOCATING WORDS ALPHABETICALLY

The child can locate words in the dictionary using alphabetic order to open the dictionary to the right place; for example, if the word begins with *m*, the child will open the dictionary near the middle and then locate the particular word by recalling the alphabetic order of the first three or four letters — *mingle* comes before *miniature* but after *mine.*

An illustrative activity for teaching alphabetic order is to ask children to look at pairs of words like *adjust* and *admiral* and tell why *adjust* appears first. Continue with other pairs of words until children can generalize that if the first two letters of two words are the same, the third letters determine the position in the dictionary.

### OBJECTIVE FOR USING GUIDE WORDS

The child can locate words in a dictionary using guide words; for example,

"Look at these two guide words — *gunny* and *gypsy.* Which one tells you the first word on the page of the dictionary?"
"Which guide word tells you which word is last?"
"Using these guide words, would the word *gutter* be on this page?"
"Would the word *gyrate* be on this page?"

Dictionary entries show spelling, pronunciation, meaning, and form. All dictionaries give the pronunciation after the spelling. These pronunciations are given by means of symbols or diacritical marks that stand for sounds. In bŭ ń dl, ˘ is a symbol. Children should not have to memorize the meanings of such symbols in a pronunciation key, but they should know how to use them. That is, you should give them the pronunciation key and then ask them to use it in pronouncing words.

### OBJECTIVE FOR USING DICTIONARY ENTRIES

The child can use the boldface entry to determine spelling, pronunciation, meaning, and form; for example,

"Look at this entry — bun dle    bŭ ń dl    a number of things together. Now tell how the word is pronounced. What is its meaning?"

Sometimes several meanings are given for a word. Pupils should know that the different meanings appear either in the order in which they came into the language or in their order of frequency of use.

Another feature that can be described in connection with entries is the *stress mark*. A dictionary may show a high mark before the part of the word said more strongly and a low mark before the part said less strongly. Other dictionaries may show stress marks after the stressed part.

OBJECTIVE FOR USING STRESS MARKS

The child can use stress marks to determine emphasis in pronunciation; for example,

"Which part do you say more strongly in these words?"

exploit ('eks-,plóit)    confess (kən-fes')

**Using encyclopedias**   Like words in dictionaries, the topics found in encyclopedias are in alphabetical order. If children cannot find the topics they are looking for, they should refer to the index of the encyclopedia. The index tells both the specific book and the page of the book where they will find the information needed.

OBJECTIVE FOR ENCYCLOPEDIAS

Given topics, the child can find information about them in encyclopedias.

One way to teach children how to use the encyclopedia is to pose riddles and questions along with the topic under which the answers can be found; for example,

A tomato is not a vegetable. What is it? (Look under *tomato*.)

How do fish sleep? (Look under *fish*.)

Another way is to ask pupils where they would find information to problems such as these:

If the flame of a candle is held too close to glass, carbon forms. What kind of chemical change has taken place? Give the answer and reference.

In what volume of the encyclopedia would you find information about jumping beans? A carnival?

**Using various guides and sources** Children should learn how guides and sources differ and how to find information in each. Sources of specialized information include *The World Almanac, Who's Who, Bartlett's Familiar Quotations,* atlases, newspapers, magazines, and the like. After explaining the differences among references, you might ask children where they would find information such as: the average rainfall in California, the baseball scores for a recent game, the population of Scotland, and the weather prediction for tomorrow. To use a particular reference, pupils must know how it is organized. In learning to use the newspaper, for example, give children practice in using the *Index of Features* as a guide to the information sought. For schedules, pupils should be able to take a simple schedule, determine its purpose, and be able to answer appropriate questions; for example,

What time does the Number 7 bus leave the beach?

Which airline has the most flights to Miami?

Which train will you take to get to a certain place at a designated time?

OBJECTIVE FOR USING GUIDES AND SOURCES

Given an almanac, atlas, directory, newspaper, periodical, and schedule, the child can state the kind of information likely to be found in each source and extract facts when needed.

**Using library reference skills** Children should develop library reference skills; for example, the ability to read shelf and floor plans; the ability to use the Dewey Decimal System, the Library of Congress system, or some other method or facility to locate material; and the ability to use indexes such as the *Readers' Guide to Periodical Literature,* a thesaurus, biographical dictionaries, and the *Subject Index to Poetry.*

OBJECTIVE FOR ILLUSTRATIVE MATERIAL

The child can find materials using the *Subject Index to Children's Magazines;* can find specific collections — for example, books dealing with holidays, astronomy, sports, biography, and Indians, using the Dewey Decimal System; and can locate a book or other material appropriate for a given purpose using information given in the card catalog.

Library skills are best taught when pupils have a real reason for using them — a question, interest, or concern to pursue. Also it is important in teaching library skills to insure that children have success in using the tools available. This means that you must explain facts such as: (1) three types of index cards are found in a card catalog — the author card, the title card, and the subject card; (2) when *a*, *an*, or *the* is the first word of a title, one should disregard these words in title cards; and (3) books of fiction are not numbered according to the Dewey Decimal System but instead are listed in the card catalog and arranged on the shelves according to the system indicated on the card.

## A Reading-Study Strategy

Upper grade teachers should prepare children for using PQRST or other reading-study techniques. The steps in PQRST are as follows:

Step one is *P* — to preview. Children should preview the reading assignment by reading the first paragraph to get a view of the author's purpose, scope, and direction. They also should learn to preview by reading the title and thinking about its significance, guessing what the text material is about, examining headings to find the major organization and thought divisions, and reading the last paragraph to see what conclusions to expect.

Step two is *Q* — to question. Titles and subheadings can be converted into *who, what, where, when, why,* and *how* — the five W's plus *how*. For example, subheadings like "The Use of Reclaimed Water" might suggest questions such as: What is reclaimed water? How much does it cost? Who is doing it? What are the advantages and disadvantages of using reclaimed water? Questions about facts: What are its characteristics? How does it compare with something else? Questions about problems: What is the problem? How can it be resolved? Questions about relationships: How does it interact or relate to other factors, events, or things? Questions about values: Is it a good thing for you? For others? Why? Why not? Questions posed should be of personal importance to the child.

Step three is *R* — to read. Reading should answer the questions posed. When the material is difficult and the goal is full comprehension, children should test themselves for comprehension, asking: What examples can I cite and what can I do with this information?

Children should read with flexibility, varying reading style according to purpose and the nature of the material. For example, if one is preparing for an essay examination, it is better to read for main ideas. If one is preparing for a multiple-choice test, it is better to read for details.

Step four is *S* — to state. Children should give in their own words the answers to the previous questions. Reciting answers clarifies ideas and fixes them in one's memory.

The final step is *T* — to test. Children should learn to test themselves to see if they understand and remember the important information read. They can test themselves by trying to make use of the information provided or by summarizing or explaining the principal ideas. They can also test themselves by trying to infer implications of what is read or to provide a judgment about the value of the material. A test of remembering demands recall of the specifics read whether they are terms, facts, trends, categories, methods, principles, or generalizations.

## Skimming

Children should be able to skim material when looking for something to read or when reviewing what is read. Skimming is a procedure for getting a general gist of reading materials. A useful objective is that the child can quickly skim materials and assess their general purpose, content, and appropriateness. The most important part of skimming is to anticipate the main ideas and general content by noting things such as the title, author, first and last paragraphs, headings, and charts and tables.

In teaching children to skim, encourage them to make quick assessments of material. Ask them questions such as:

If you wanted to learn about playing better ball, would this article help?

What would be a good title for this paragraph?

Would you want to read this article?

Is this newspaper in favor of the candidate?

Take just two minutes to read this and tell me what it is about.

## Scanning

Scanning is a procedure children can use to locate an answer to a specific question. It is an economical procedure in that one's eyes are spread out across the page focusing on phrases, lines, and entire paragraphs. Further, in scanning, the mind is focused on what is being sought; it does not abstract any information, word, or phrase that does *not* answer the specific question the reader has in mind.

To scan, children must anticipate the form or type of answer expected. For example, when children want to know when something happened, they should scan looking primarily for a date. Listings, definitions, facts, conclusions, principles, are the kinds of answers sought when scanning.

Children who can scan begin, first, by stating the question they want to answer from their reading; next, they frame the form of the answer; then, they run their eyes down the center of the page permitting their peripheral vision to pick up whatever fits the answer format — headings, numbers, words, or phrases.

## Adjusting Reading Rate to Purpose

Reading material itself should guide children in deciding how fast to read. When it is clear that an author is sharing an experience (there may be clues such as the use of personal pronouns: *I, we, our*), the children should know they can relax and read quickly to enjoy the author's experience. When an author begins a paragraph with a question or uses a question in a title or heading, the children should also read quickly. They merely have to read the question and then glance through the text until they find the answer. It is unnecessary for them to formulate their own question.

### OBJECTIVE FOR ADJUSTING READING RATE

> When seeking to verify or locate specific information, the child reads at a very rapid rate; when seeking a review about content, the child reads at a rapid (but slower) rate; and when trying to acquire new concepts and recall factual information, the child reads at a relatively slow rate.

Slow, careful, and detailed reading is necessary when the material imparts information in the form of many factual details. Few words can be ignored in such writing. Similarly material that begins with a conclusion or a statement of fact and is followed by reasons for the conclusion must be read slowly. Substantiation for the conclusion is usually in the form of observations or experiments that must be read carefully.

We recommend that you give children a variety of material and ask them to determine the style of reading required by each so they can see how flexibility is important in proficient reading.

## Organizational Skills

Developing good organizational skills will help children read effectively for specific purposes. Underlining, notetaking, outlining, and summarizing are organizational devices for helping one write reports and recall information.

**Underlining and note taking**   Underlining and note-taking skills may help pupils improve their academic performance. However, the experimental literature on the effects of these skills shows mixed results.[4] Indeed work by Ann Brown and Sandra Smiley indicates that although a certain proportion of children from fifth grade and up profit because they spontaneously underline or take notes during study, pupils who are induced to adopt one of these strategies are less likely to be sensitive to the important elements to be underlined or recorded.[5] Successful underlining and note taking seem to depend on the ability to identify the main points for special study (relevant underlining and note taking) and to know when to use such study strategies. We recommend, then, that in teaching these skills you give children an opportunity to predict ahead of time what the important elements of a text are and to say why they are important.

**Outlining and summarizing**   Outlining and summarizing are based on the comprehension skill of recognizing main ideas. Outlining is a way to show the relationship between main ideas and supporting details. The first step in forming an outline is to identify the main ideas and to list these ideas beside roman numerals in the order of occurrence. Supporting details for each major idea are indented and listed beside capital letters below the idea supported. Details, subordinate to the main details, are further indented and preceded by arabic numerals.

In teaching outlining, begin by giving pupils partially completed outlines of chapters in textbooks and ask them to fill in the missing parts. Subsequently leave more and more details out of the outline until the pupils complete the outline by themselves.

---

[4] Thomas H. Anderson, "Study Strategies and Adjunct Aids," *Theoretical Issues in Reading Comprehension*, ed. Rand J. Spiro, Bruce Bertram, and W. F. Brewer (Hillsdale, N.J.: Lawrence Erlbaum Associates, 1978). W. J. Browning, "A Critical Review of Research and Expert Opinion on the Underlining Study Aid," *Reflections and Investigations on Reading*, ed. Wallace D. Miller and George H. McNich (Clemson, S. C.: National Reading Conference, 1976).

[5] Ann L. Brown and Sandra S. Smiley, *The Development of Strategies for Studying Prose Passages* (Champaign, Ill.: Center for the Study of Reading, University of Illinois, October 1977).

A summary consists of the main idea of a selection. Illustrations and elaborations of the main idea are not included. In teaching children to prepare summaries, begin by having them look at three summaries for a text passage and tell which one is the best and why. Next, you might give them news stories without headlines and have them create headlines that summarize the main ideas of the stories. Finally, present passages and have them provide summaries of the main idea(s).

# Skills Required for Reading Content Fields

What are the important differences in the specific content fields that require adjustments in the application of reading skills? First, each subject field has a specialized vocabulary — familiar words used in a new way (*operation* in math) and unfamiliar words that represent key concepts in the material to be read (*molecules* in science). Second, the style of writing differs among the fields. For example, mathematics is written more tersely and precisely than most literature. Third, the content fields differ in the kinds of graphics used. Social studies textbooks have a variety of maps; those of mathematics and science have more diagrams and charts. Thus three categories of skills useful in making adjustments for reading in the content fields are: developing a specialized vocabulary, recognizing writing patterns, and reading maps, globes, graphs, and tables.

## Developing Specialized Vocabulary

A specialized vocabulary may consist of terms with technical or scientific meanings or general words that take on a specific meaning or connotation in context. Examples of the former are *boycott* (social studies), *colloquialism* (language), *binary* (mathematics), and *bacteria* (science). Examples of the latter are *minority* (social studies), *tone* (language), *product* (mathematics), and *charge* (science).

Several techniques are available for teaching technical and special vocabularies. One involves relating conceptual terms to actual experience in the form of field trips, demonstrations, and experiments that illustrate the processes and concepts denoted by the terms. A second technique is to provide examples of the terms and ask pupils to define them in their own words. A third technique is to teach the prefixes, roots, and suffixes common to a particular subject. There are, for example, useful root stems in social studies — *port*, carry; *reg*, rule; *equ*, just, equal; *voc*, call; *cap*, head; *cred*, believe; language — *graph*, write; *logi*, speak; *nomin*, name; *vis*, see; mathematics — *dia*, through; *pos*, place; *sign*, indicate; *struct*, build; *cir*, ring; and science — *syn*, together; *mon*, one; *photo*, light; *micro*, small; *part*, share.

Upper grade children should know prefixes involving numbers from one to ten as found in familiar words such as *unicycle, tricycle, quadrangle,* and *pentagon*. They also should learn to recognize how words have been made negative by prefixes such as *a* or *an, anti, dis, il, in, im, ir, non,* and *un.*

Gaining meaning from context is an effective technique for both general and technical vocabulary development. You can create context exercises to help pupils extrapolate word meanings by selecting brief passages and then developing multiple-choice or completion questions. The following is an illustration:

> Since there are wide variations in reading abilities, a *model* or construct can be used to make the textbook more meaningful and a purpose in reading can be established. Pupils should first be asked to function only at the literal level — to say what the author actually said. Later, they should be asked to interpret what the author meant and to recognize generalizations in broader contexts.

In this paragraph, *model* means:

a. A set of plans for a building
b. A person who poses
c. A pattern to follow

Vocabulary development in content fields has two dimensions. On the one hand, children learn new words; they first learn the frequently used meanings of new words and then, for some of these words, they learn additional meanings as found in different settings. On the other hand, children learn how to learn words — processes that facilitate the learning of vocabulary. Glennon Rowell has suggested instructional strategies for dealing with the different dimensions.[6] Examples of these strategies as applied to the teaching of social studies and their relation to the different dimensions are as follows:

*Classification strategy for developing processes that help children learn new words.*

This strategy deals with the relationships among groups of words;

---

[6] Glennon Rowell, "Vocabulary Development in the Social Studies," *Social Education* 42, no. 1 (January 1978): 10–14. Reprinted with permission of the National Council for the Social Studies and Dr. Rowell.

for example, "Examine each of the words below and then regroup them under the headings *rainfall, coastline, voted, armistice.*"

| | | | |
|---|---|---|---|
| governed | mountainous | ruled | lowlands |
| negotiate | elected | settle | Senate |
| represented | terrain | disputed | peninsula |
| highlands | humidity | Congress | island |
| moor | treaty | arbitration | precipitation |

After grouping the words, children tell why they placed words under a given heading.

*Wide-reading strategy for developing processes that help extend meaning of known words.*

The wide-reading strategy features activities such as charting words from library books and using resource books. In charting words, you provide pupils with several books on an area of study, such as the Revolutionary War. From these books, you might compose six to eight headings, such as kinds of government, taxation, and leisure activities. Then tell pupils:

"As you read the library books provided, add words that you find under the headings given."

In using resource books, you might place several different resource books on a table, above which there is a sentence such as:

"Did you know that another name for _____ is _____?"

Blank cards should be available for pupils to write answers to complete the sentence form; for example, "Did you know that another name for *tariff* is *duties?*"

*Use of games for learning the most frequently used meanings of words.*

An example of a gamelike activity for vocabulary building is to place on the outside of an envelope a word to be learned. Other words on small cards are placed inside the envelope. The pupils are expected to arrange the cards so they define the word on the envelope.

Thus if *island* is the word, the cards should be arranged as:

island is a body of land surrounded by water

*Use of games for learning the meanings of known words in different contexts.*

Ask pupils to find a headline in a newspaper about people helping other people or topics related to what is being studied. The words should be ones that are used differently from common usage. Place pupils in small groups where they take turns showing the headlines and reading no more than three or four beginning lines from the news stories to give clues to the unknown word. The definition, if guessed by a participant, is verified by the presenter; for example,

"We're *soft* on truth."

The teaching of vocabulary in mathematics presents a special problem. Apart from the definition of the term, there is little helpful context. Word problems, for example, are usually very succinct and lacking in contextual clues. Hence, you must either start with the definition, then illustrate, and explain, or start with examples, appeal to past experience, and then arrive at a suitable definition.

These are examples of exercises for developing vocabulary in mathematics:

"Draw a circle around the symbol that stands for the expression on the left."

1. Is equal to $\quad \cap \quad > \quad < \quad \cup \quad =$
2. Is less than $\quad \cap \quad > \quad < \quad \cup \quad =$
3. Is greater than $\quad \cap \quad > \quad < \quad \cup \quad =$
4. Is not less than $\quad > \quad \not< \quad \neq \quad \leq \quad <$
5. Is not equal to $\quad = \quad \in \quad \neq \quad \cup \quad \cap$
6. Is congruent to $\quad < \quad \cong \quad = \quad \not< \quad \cup$

"Match each expression on the left with the correct symbol on the right."

1. Intersection $\quad \cup$
2. Union $\quad \emptyset$
3. Is a subset of $\quad \in$
4. Is an element of $\quad \subset$
5. Empty set $\quad \cap$

"Write the symbol for the operation suggested by the expression."

1. The sum of _____

2. Take away _____

3. Altogether _____

4. Quotient _____

5. The difference _____

"Draw a circle around each group of terms that includes all of the others."

| 1. sum | | product | quotient | answer |
|---|---|---|---|---|
| 2. addend | | sum | addition | plus |
| 3. whole numbers | zero | | one | counting numbers |

Certainly if your children are expected to read terms like *acre*, *quart*, and *rod* and terms for the concepts of the metric system like *meter*, *kilo*, and *kilometer*, you should provide opportunities for them to measure these units.

Language studies require more interpretation of figurative language than other school subjects. Poetry, drama, the short story, and the novel present the most difficult vocabulary in literature. Often it is helpful to read selections from these literary forms aloud to the class, clarifying the vocabulary. Teach children that the context of an entire passage will probably be of more help than the individual sentence in determining the meaning of a difficult word. If after instruction in context, a pupil still has trouble with certain words, these words should be listed and dealt with by definition, example, dictionary, explanation, and discussion. Writing and dramatics also can aid. A weekly round-table discussion about words is often helpful. Ask pupils to keep notebooks of unfamiliar words met in reading and each week have everyone choose one word to share in discussion, explain why the word was chosen, use it in context, and define it. When doing creative work, children are likely to use new words more frequently. As an interim step to creative work, give pupils practice in expanding word meanings through connotation. For example, have each pupil select a word and use it in two or more sentences, giving a different meaning in each. Words such as these might be used: *back, book, level, fit, track, sun, latch, nose*. Have each child describe how the meaning of a word changes in different contexts; for example, "Describe the ball in each sentence. The baby kicked the ball. The punter kicked the ball. The golfer kicked the ball."

### Recognizing Writing Patterns in the Content Fields

After analyzing two hundred textbooks to find out what children had to do in reading literature, science, social studies, and mathematics, Nila Banton Smith discovered that these subjects made use of different patterns that called for different reading skills.[7]

**Writing patterns in literature**   The short story or novel, essay, drama, poetry, and biography are examples of established writing patterns. A story is read to enjoy plot, character, and setting; an essay, to gain a perspective on an aspect of life; and drama, to interpret character through dialogue and to visualize action.

Children understand stories better if you ask them questions about the setting, characterization, sequence, plot, and theme. Children should recognize that an essay can be humorous, persuasive, and informative. They also should be asked to speculate about the characteristics of the writer. Children understand plays better if you develop background for the play first and give them practice in visualizing the action as it is read. Best of all, let the children act out the play in the classroom.

Poetry uses rhythm, rhyme, and repetition to create its impressions. Encourage children to read poems orally at the elementary level. Poetry is intended for the ear. Children need not analyze poetry although you may want to note whether they can identify the words that create particular images and feelings or can find a message in the poem.

Biographies afford opportunities for teaching critical reading. Invite children to find out about the biographer and to look for evidence of bias.

**Writing patterns in science**   The *classification pattern* is seen when living things, materials, liquids, forces, and so on are classified into headings and subdivisions. Children should read materials written in this pattern by grasping the common element of the classification and the chief characteristics of the subdivisions.

The *explanation of a technical process* is a difficult pattern to read. Usually a diagram accompanies the text and requires special reading skills. The child has to learn how to read the text and the diagram alternately as one contributes to the other.

---

[7] Nila Banton Smith, "The Classroom Teacher's Responsibility to the Able Reader," *New Horizons in Reading,* ed. John E. Merritt (Newark, Del.: International Reading Association, 1976), pp. 229–241.

The *didactic explanation* is a common pattern in science textbooks and consists of definition, example, additional factors, explanation, and generalization. In reading this pattern, children should be looking to see how each of the parts in the pattern contributes to the whole.

The *detailed statement of facts* is another pattern. In science materials, the density of facts per page is often high. These facts may illustrate a principle or definition. In reading the pattern, the child should look for the most important thought and then find details that reinforce it, noting definitions and principles.

**Writing patterns in social studies**    The *chronological pattern* divides topics into periods arranged in chronological order. This pattern presents events in a time sequence accompanied with dates. As an aid to helping children understand the pattern, try asking them to make time lines or an outline of dates and events in their appropriate locations.

The *comparison pattern* is used to compare policies, views on issues, functions of agencies, and the like. If pupils know they are about to read a comparison chapter or paragraph, they can approach it with the purpose of noting likenesses and differences.

The *cause and effect pattern* is frequently used in accounts of historical and current events. Major events are explained in terms of some cause or set of causes. Recognition of this pattern enables one to read specifically to ascertain causes and effects.

**Writing patterns in mathematics**    The *problem pattern* is found in paragraphs setting forth a situation or condition followed by a series of numbers or values; the reader is told what to find. *Peanuts'* Peppermint Patty provides a good example.

The reading of such problems involves five processes: (1) reading the entire problem as a whole; (2) attending to the question at the end that tells what to find; (3) deciding which operations to use to find the answer; (4) determining whether all necessary information is given; and (5) reading the numbers and symbols needed to solve the problem.

The *explanatory pattern* is usually recognizable by its format: a reference to past experience, a discussion of the problem, a discussion of its solution, a practice problem or an example "worked out" that illustrates the "key ideas," and suggested exercises. In reading this kind of pattern, pupils should follow the given example step by step, referring to the explanation to find out why the step was necessary.

## Reading Maps and Globes

Three basic levels of skills in reading maps and globes are the ability to perceive and recognize information on the map or globe, the ability to understand relationships among data, and the ability to make inferences from the data.

Before pupils leave elementary school, they should be proficient in (1) noting direction, (2) recognizing the scale of maps and computing distance, (3) locating places on maps and globes by means of grid systems, (4) recognizing and expressing relative locations, (5) reading map symbols, and (6) making inferences from patterns that appear on maps.

The following are typical elementary school instructional objectives for reading maps.

OBJECTIVES FOR READING MAPS

Given simple maps in which pictures, semipictorial symbols, or color keys indicate various objects on the map, the child can locate points on the map and tell what specific symbols mean; for example,

"What is near the house?"
"Look at the key (legend) and then tell me which symbol represents a boat. Which symbol represents a lake?"

Given maps containing nonpictorial symbols, such as dots representing cities and lines representing roads, the child can use the map and key to answer questions; for example,

"How many cities are there in Smith County?"
"Point out the most direct route from A to B."

Given maps, the child can answer questions that require the use of cardinal directions and units of distance; for example,

"Toward which city would you be going if you leave City A and go south?"

"How far is it between City A and City C?"

Given maps or globes, the child can use lines of latitude and longitude to locate points; for example,

"What city is located at 40° north latitude and 74° west longitude?"

Given a variety of maps (topographic, climatic, political), the child can make inferences based on the information presented; for example,

"Point to the area that has the greatest rainfall."

Given maps drawn to different scales, the child can answer questions that require comprehension of sizes; for example,

"Although the maps of Venezuela, Mexico, and France are the same size, which country is much larger?"

As indicated in Table 6.1, types of maps have specific uses.

Application of the map skills is more important than acquisition of the isolated skill. To this end, map reading and map thinking are inseparable. Map reading involves the following steps:

1. Looking at the map's title to find out what area is depicted and to note features of the map.

2. Looking at the legend and trying to visualize the things for which

**TABLE 6.1**  Maps and their uses

| Type of map | Principal use |
| --- | --- |
| Street maps | Show streets in a city, study of local problems |
| Road maps | Show routes of travel by land, settlement of areas, present and past travel routes |
| Relief maps | Indicate elevations of land by use of changes in color as height increases; show why travel routes were chosen, why population centers developed |
| Physical maps | Use symbols to indicate mountains, plateaus, political boundaries and physical characteristics, type of land area and population development |
| Vegetation maps | By color, lines, and symbols, indicate forests, deserts, jungles, grasslands; compare ways of life around earth, similarities in climate, housing, and dress |
| Land use maps | How land is used in specific areas; compare use in 1900 with use of land in 1961; what are reasons for change? |
| Political maps | Through color and division lines, show political divisions of cities, counties, states, and countries; indicate shifts in political control, reorganization characteristics of government |
| Product maps | Specific crops or goods of an area; compare principal products of countries and how terrain influences economy |
| Pictorial maps | Pictures or cartoons that illustrate the particular point the map is trying to make; pictures of poets of world in their respective countries, native dress, animals and birds, famous battles |
| Population maps | Distribution of earth's people, rate of population increase, shift of population by country |
| Historical maps | Show explorers' concepts of the world or indicate historical events such as acquisition of territory, explorations, changes in national boundaries |
| War maps | Areas where battles have been fought; how strategy, terrain, equipment influence wars |
| Weather maps | Indicate air pressure, winds, types of precipitation, temperature, and the movement of weather; study of weather and significance of high and low pressure areas, warm and cold fronts |
| Blank outline maps | No words, few symbols, outlines of territory, useful in evaluating pupil understandings |

Source: Edward G. Summers, "Utilizing Visual Aids in Reading Materials for Effective Learning," *Perspectives in Reading No. 4., Developing Study Skills,* ed. Harold Herber (Newark, Del.: International Reading Association, 1965), pp. 97–155. Reprinted with permission of Edward G. Summers and the International Reading Association.

the map symbols stand — when looking at thick lines on a road map, one should see the major highways.

3.  Finding north. North is usually, but not always, at the top of a map. Many Mercator maps, as well as locally drawn maps, do not put north at the top. In addition to north as a cardinal direction, there is magnetic north.

4.  Finding out how big or far something is from the scale of the

map — a small scale map depicts a large area made smaller and a large-scale map depicts a small area made larger.

5. Looking at the grids that section maps into smaller segments by the use of horizontal or vertical lines. City maps and atlases, for example, section by using marginal letters and numbers. Parallels and meridians help one locate places by latitude and longitude.

Map interpretation means deriving a reasonable conclusion from an analysis of the relationships shown on a map or between different maps. For instance, after looking at both population and economic maps, the child should be able to say where most of the people live and to make inferences about the geographic features that account for the distribution of population.

Examples follow of activities for teaching map skills at different grade levels.

### Orienting in relation to the environment

Locating oneself in relation to door, windows, or furniture
Locating office, lunchroom, hall, in relation to classroom
Locating home in relation to school, hospital, and other community landmarks
Locating one's town, county, and state on a map of the United States
Locating the United States on a world map

### Orienting in terms of direction

Locating direction in relation to the sun
Locating north by compass
Locating direction on a community map
Locating positions on a route, noting changes in direction in terms of parallels, meridians, latitude, and longitude

### Recognizing scale and distance

Observing relative distances and time for travel
Recognizing linear units and their relative length — foot, block, mile, knot, meter
Exploring ways to express scale
Drawing maps of the community and sketching routes

### Reading map symbols

Devising a key for one's own map
Introducing symbols for lakes, oceans, bays, and so on

Comparing pictures of landscapes with aerial photographs and later with symbols on large-scale maps

Constructing transportation maps to show routes of ships, railroads, airplanes, highways, and so on

Reading weather maps for atmosphere and climatic information

## Reading Graphs

Graph reading includes many kinds of nonword reading, such as schematic drawings, tables, charts, and diagrams found in newspapers, news magazines, and in history, geography, social science, and science books. Graphs show at a glance how certain numbers are related, facilitating the comparison of areas, distances, numerical values, and other quantitative information. Although all graphs have certain things in common, each has characteristics that make it best for a given purpose. The *bar graph* is good for comparing quantitative data; the *circle graph* shows parts of the whole; the *line graph* is useful for indicating the relation between any two quantities.

The first step in interpreting graphs is to survey the graph for a general impression and then to read for specifics. Three skills are of most importance: reading the information from the graph, analyzing the information, and interpreting it.

### OBJECTIVES FOR READING GRAPHS AND TABLES

Given a simple vertical picture graph in which each symbol represents a single object and there are no more than five columns of pictures, the child can determine the purpose of the graph; for example,

"From the graph showing school absences, can you tell me the days when there were the fewest and the most absences?"

Given a vertical bar graph that has one group of bars and a small interval on the coordinate, the child can determine the purpose, compare relative amounts, and extract information directly from the graph; for example,

"Look at the title and contents of this graph. Which bar shows the most? the least? How much is shown?"

Given a circle graph with four divisions, the child can determine the purpose and compare relative amounts; for example,

"Which division shows the greatest amount? the least?"

Given a single-line, noncumulative line graph, the child can determine the purpose, compare amounts, extract both directly and by interpolating, and determine differences between numbers extracted; for example,

"How many more cars were sold in January 1979 than in January 1978?"

The process of teaching graphs calls for helping children attend to five elements:

1. What type of graph is used and what data are presented? What is the graph attempting to accomplish? What are the names of the variables graphed?

2. What is the unit of measurement? Does the scale indicate degrees, numbers, fractions, percentages, hours, or other units? What are the largest and smallest amounts involved?

3. What symbols are used? A key or legend should state what each symbol represents. Often no symbols are used when the axes are labeled.

4. What do the column headings represent? In most instances, the vertical scale indicates the items to be compared and the horizontal axis shows the relationship that exists.

5. What does the information on the graph mean? To answer this question, refer to the text description that accompanies the graph.

Look at the graph in Figure 6.1 and use the preceding questions to guide your own interpretation of the graph.

Your answers should be similar to these:

1. The graph is a bar graph presenting past, present, and predicted population of the world's largest centers. The graph is attempting to show the rate at which the world's urban areas are growing.

2. The unit of measurement is millions of persons (population) as indicated on a scale from 0 to 35. The largest amount showing future population is 33 million; the smallest future population is less than 10 million.

3. The only symbols used are color and shading to indicate population at three points in time.

4. Three horizontal columns appear for each major city. The columns show the relative gain in population.

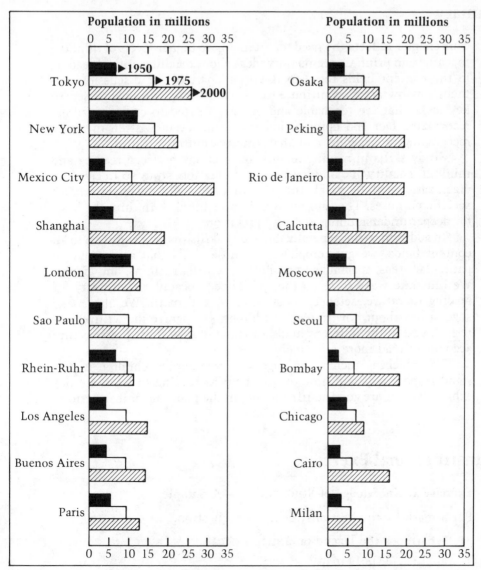

**FIGURE 6.1** Growth of world urban centers. Twenty largest centers by 1975 population with 1950 and year 2000 estimates.

Source: Population Reference Bureau, Inc., 1978. 1337 Connecticut Avenue, N.W. Washington, D.C., 20036.

5.  The graph shows that the world's urban areas are growing rapidly. In 1950 there were 71 cities with populations of 1 million or more and by 1975 there were 181. Mexico City, one of the fastest growing cities, is projected to increase its population and become the largest urban area in the world.

# Summary

This chapter reflects the need for attending to higher levels of thinking to learn from print. Contemporary ideas about teaching critical reading in the content fields form an important part of the discussion. Although many factors contribute to critical reading, we have presented key tasks that are teachable and directly related to critical reading: recognizing fact and opinion, judging adequacy of written material, recognizing propaganda, and analyzing the author's values.

Study skills in reading require an interplay between reading and thinking. Facility in using sources of information, study strategies, and organizational skills enable the pupil to read widely and effectively for specific purposes. The information thus acquired is, in turn, the basis for deeper understanding and interpretation.

In addition to the generalizable study skills that are common to all content fields, we give emphasis to those skills that are unique to particular areas, specialized vocabulary, writing patterns, and graphs. We illustrate ways to teach the specialized vocabulary necessary for reading literature, science, social studies, and math. We also make suggestions about how to teach children to recognize the writing patterns found in the different fields and how to take these patterns into account to read more effectively.

The teaching techniques suggested for helping children understand graphic aids and how to use them in reading to learn are not exhaustive but are good starting points in the planning of instruction.

# Self-instructional Exercises

### Exercise 1. Knowledge of Study Skills — A Sample

Put a mark by the best answer to each question.

1. What does the legend on a map indicate?
    a. _____ Type of map
    b. _____ Symbols used
    c. _____ Direction

2. Which reference skill should be taught first?
    a. _____ Recognizing alphabetical order
    b. _____ Using the indexes of books and encyclopedias
    c. _____ Locating words in a dictionary

3. When using a study technique like PQRST, what should occur first?

   a. _____ Ask questions before reading.

   b. _____ Read before asking questions.

   c. _____ Skim material and then ask questions.

4. What gives the best clue to the writer's organization of a book?

   a. _____ Index

   b. _____ Table of contents

   c. _____ Glossary

5. Which graph shows parts to the whole?

   a. _____ Bar

   b. _____ Line

   c. _____ Circle

6. Which graph pictures the progress of some trend?

   a. _____ Pictorial

   b. _____ Line

   c. _____ Bar

7. What determines method and rate of reading?

   a. _____ Material to be read

   b. _____ Purpose for reading

   c. _____ Both purpose and material

8. Which illustrates alphabetization of names in a card catalog?

   a. _____ McGhee before MacNab

   b. _____ MacNab before McGhee

   c. _____ MacNab before McLean

9. What is the quickest way to find out whether a book tells about a particular subject?

   a. _____ Refer to the glossary.

   b. _____ Refer to the table of contents.

   c. _____ Refer to the index.

10. Which word would *not* appear between the guide words *smooth* and *snark*?

   a. _____ Snail

   b. _____ Snipe

   c. _____ Snap

ANSWERS TO EXERCISE 1

1b. The legend or key indicates what the symbols on the map stand for and the scale of the map.

2a. Alphabetical order is a prerequisite skill.

3c. When using PQRST, first preview and then question.

4a. The table of contents shows the organization of the book according to chapters, units, or other major divisions. The table of contents also is an outline of major topics treated in the book.

5c. The circle graph shows relationships among parts and the whole. To understand circle graphs, children must understand the use of fractional parts — that the size of the part devoted to a particular item indicates the relationships to the whole represented by the circle.

6b. The line graph pictures progress of a trend. In interpreting this graph, children have to attend to both the vertical and horizontal scales as well as to steepness of the line slope and the internal size of the scale.

7c. Both one's purpose for reading and the nature of the material to be read require an adjustment in rate.

8a. Names beginning with Mc are filed as though spelled Mac.

9c. The index is a shortcut to details, facts, names, dates, and specific pieces of information.

10b. Guide words are the first and last words on a page and are useful in locating a word quickly.

## Exercise 2. Matching Purpose with Teaching Activity

Put a mark by the purpose most likely to be fulfilled by the teaching activity.

1. Children are asked to write the antonym to words like *gentle* and *courteous.*

    a. _____ To recall word definitions

    b. _____ To extend vocabulary

    c. _____ To recognize multiple meanings of words

2. Children are asked to read familiar words in a new context and tell what the word implies in the context. *yellow* — He turned *yellow* and ran.

    a. _____ To develop multiple meanings of words

    b. _____ To learn the origin of words

    c. _____ To derive lexical (dictionary) meanings of words

3. Children are asked to tell whether the author is trying to inform rather than to entertain or move them emotionally.

a. _____ To read critically

b. _____ To read quickly

c. _____ To read for information

4. Children are asked to characterize persons described in such sentences as: "Harris's eyes shot dots of fire whenever anyone disagreed with him."

a. _____ To read critically

b. _____ To read inferentially

c. _____ To read literally

5. Children are asked to tell whether differences in two poems are due to differences in the poets themselves — their attitudes and beliefs — or to differences in the periods in which they were written.

a. _____ To read critically

b. _____ To read inferentially

c. _____ To read creatively

**ANSWERS TO EXERCISE 2**

1b. Activities calling for synonyms, antonyms, and analogies for given words are used to expand vocabulary and to show the functional relationships of familiar words.

2a. This activity is an illustration of word study through *connotation* (words in context giving implied emotional meanings) as opposed to relying only on *denotational* activities such as matching words with definitions and deriving meaning from affixes.

3a. To assess the author's purpose is a critical reading skill.

4b. This activity requires an inference based on personal experience.

5a. Although this activity does call for making inferences, it also demands judgment about the harmony or lack of harmony in two poems. To do such thinking while reading constitutes critical reading.

## Exercise 3. Interpreting Graphs and Tables

Read each graph or table and then answer the questions.

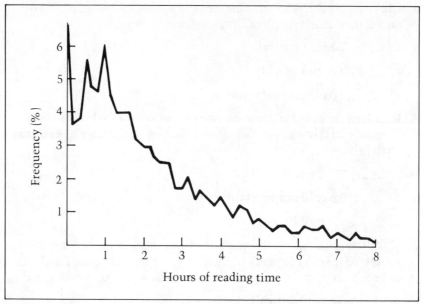

Source: Amiel T. Sharon, "What Do Adults Read," *Reading Research Quarterly 9*, no. 2 (1973–1974):157. Reprinted with permission of Amiel T. Sharon and the International Reading Association.

1. Frequency distribution plot of reading time for total population of readers

    a. _____ About how much time does the average reader in this sample spend reading on a typical day?

    b. _____ About what percentage of readers read eight hours or more daily?

    c. _____ About what percentage of readers read less than five minutes daily?

    d. _____ Do many read for long periods?

2. Effect of publishers' guidelines on sex and ethnicity of major characters in children's textbook stories

    Which of the following conclusions are warranted?

    a. _____ There has been a substantive attempt to eliminate inequities.

    b. _____ There have been only minimal changes in male-female bias.

    c. _____ There has been much more elimination of minority male inequity than minority female inequity.

    d. _____ "Other" must refer to situations where major characters

| Before guidelines (1958–1970) | After guidelines (1974–1976) |
|---|---|
| 14% Female | 16% Female |
| 2% Minority female | 4% Minority female |
| 15% Other | 7% Other |
| 60% Male | 61% Male |
| 9% Minority male | 12% Minority male |

Source: Gwyneth E. Britton and Margaret C. Lumpkin, "For Sale: Subliminal Bias in Textbooks," *Reading Teacher* 31, no. 1 (October 1977): 40–45. Reprinted with permission of Gwyneth E. Britton and Margaret C. Lumpkin and the International Reading Association.

were not identified by sex or ethnic background; for example, animals, inanimate objects.

3. Means for ratings[a] that two groups of children assigned to stories

| | Type of Character/Setting | | | | | |
|---|---|---|---|---|---|---|
| | Realistic | | Animal | | Fantasy | |
| | Mean rating | Number of children wanting to hear more stories of this type | Mean rating | Number of children wanting to hear more stories of this type | Mean rating | Number of children wanting to hear more stories of this type |
| **Group** | | | | | | |
| **Grade 1** | | | | | | |
| Story 1 (Slapstick) | 4.9 | 6 | 4.6 | 7 | 3.3 | 7 |
| Story 2 (Comic plot) | 4.0 | 8 | 4.3 | 7 | 4.4 | 9 |
| Story 3 (Peer relationship) | 3.7 | 5 | 4.7 | 8 | 3.7 | 7 |
| **Grade 3** | | | | | | |
| Story 1 (Slapstick) | 3.3 | 6 | 2.3 | 2 | 3.8 | 8 |
| Story 2 (Comic Plot) | 3.0 | 4 | 2.7 | 1 | 3.3 | 7 |
| Story 3 (Peer relationship) | 3.8 | 6 | 3.7 | 5 | 3.7 | 6 |

[a] 5 = "Super," 1 = "No Good"
Source: Lin Oliver, "The Reading Interests of Children in the Primary Grades," *Elementary School Journal* 77, no. 5 (May 1977): 401–406. By permission of the University of Chicago Press. Copyright © 1977 by the University of Chicago.

Which of the following conclusions are warranted?

a. _____ The preference ratings of first graders are higher than those of third graders.

b. _____ Interest in peer group stories decreases from first to third grade.

c. _____ Interest in slapstick and humorous plots decreases from first to third grade.

d. _____ Stories for first graders should feature many kinds of settings and characters.

**ANSWERS TO EXERCISE 3**

1.a. 1 hour and 46 minutes.
 b. Less than 1 percent.
 c. 6 percent.
 d. Relatively few read for very long periods. Only 45 percent read for 2 hours or more daily.

2.a. Not warranted.
 b. Warranted. There have been only minimal changes in male-female bias.
 c. Not warranted.
 d. Warranted. "Other" does not relate to sex or ethnic background of major characters in stories.

3.a. Warranted. The preference ratings of first graders are higher. Third graders are less enthusiastic about having a story read to them.
 b. Not warranted. Peer relationships keep high rating between first and third grade.
 c. Warranted. Interest in slapstick and humorous plots decreases from first to third grade.
 d. Warranted. First grade children like stories that feature a variety of settings and characters.

# Selected Readings

Capiobianco, Sharon, et al. *Study Skills: The Key to Reading in the Content Area.* Providence: Rhode Island State Dept. of Education, Division of Development and Operations, April 1977. ERIC Ed. 159 586.

This manual focuses on the step-by-step development of study skills related to the mastery of content area reading materials. The major portion of the manual identifies objectives and activities related to skills such as locating, selecting, and organizing information; using graphic aids; following directions; and developing flexibility in reading. Among other features, the manual offers advice for organizing teaching stations, pretesting skills, evaluating study skill competencies, and for conducting a study skills workshop.

Gagné, Ellen, D. "Long Term Retention of Information Following Learning from Prose," *Review of Educational Research* 48, no. 4 (Fall 1978): 629–665.

This review focuses on factors that bear on reading retention. Studies are cited which show that prior knowledge relevant to a passage to be read generally has beneficial effects on long-term retention. Among the conclusions drawn, several have practical significance: (1) Reminding learners of relevant knowledge prior to reading may have dramatic effects. (2) Good comprehenders use the author's passage structure to organize the information read. (3) The purpose for reading affects the information retained. (4) Any strategy that encourages elaboration of information should improve retention. Hence, the teacher should have pupils (a) ask themselves how what they are reading relates to their past experience and how each sentence relates to the main idea, (b) image the passages read, and (c) make repeated use of the information acquired.

Koenke, Karl. "Teaching Reading in the Content Areas," *Journal of Reading* 25, no. 5 (February 1978): 460–462.

A review of articles that have been indexed in ERIC on the topic of reading in the content areas. The articles include one that offers a checklist of twenty teaching practices regarded by reading specialists as important, such as knowing the reading levels of both pupils and texts, illustrating the style of writing used in the subject, demonstrating study skills, encouraging reading in related materials, and grouping pupils for differentiated instruction. Other articles include a report on a project to improve a variety of language skills, a description of a handbook which focuses on reading skill development, and accounts of teachers who teach pupils to read through the teaching of art, business education, physical education, science, math, and other subjects.

McConkie, George W. "Learning from Text." In *Review of Research in Education*, edited by Lee S. Schulman. Ithaca, Ill.: F. E. Peacock, 1977, pp. 3–48.

This extensive review reports on sophisticated research on learning from texts It includes studies indicating ways to describe text materials, ways to question to find out what has been learned from passages, what is remembered from one's reading under various conditions, how to use textual patterns to increase comprehension, and the effects of questions, underlining, notetaking and the like under different conditions. The effects of individual differences in retention are also treated. A glimpse at the future suggests that research on learning from text may help in understanding the mental activities involved in comprehension so that we will know better how to prepare written materials and how to teach pupils to gain information efficiently from text.

# 7

# Instruction at Different Grade Levels

This is a chapter on teaching methods. More than a single method is presented because different methods are needed as dictated by differences in children, in reading materials, and in reading goals. Although some general principles of instruction are discussed, the emphasis is on optional methods for teaching reading at the readiness, beginning, middle, and upper levels.

One general principle of instruction is the *principle of advance organizers*. Advance organizers are statements that link what the learner already knows with what is to be learned. Such statements serve as an outline or structure within which the new learning is embedded. The principle holds that most teaching is more effective when the teacher uses advance organizers. We will practice what we preach by using an advance organizer as the introduction to this chapter.

*You already know*

That teachers employ different methods in teaching the same reading skill and in trying to reach similar goals.

*You will learn*

That a teacher's methods and style of teaching depend on his or her orientation to instruction — behavioral, cognitive, humanistic.

That there are many principles of instruction and guidelines for developing lessons.

That most lesson plans should provide ways to gain the learner's attention, to help the learner know what to do — to note the key features, to practice what is taught, to confirm the correctness of responses, and to gain satisfaction in the task.

That there have been great debates about how best to teach beginning reading — through phonics, "look-say" methods, and modified alphabets.

That the conflict over methods for teaching decoding is now being resolved by teaching children different strategies for recognizing words — a phonic strategy for words that follow a consistent spelling pattern, a structural analysis strategy for words composed of familiar parts, and a contextual strategy in which the child tries to figure out a new word by drawing upon the meaning of what is being read (semantics and syntax).

That those teaching in the middle grades are especially interested in developing the reading comprehension of children.

That different views of comprehension require different methods — literal comprehension depends on a knowledge of vocabulary and syntax; the inferring of deeper meanings requires the ability to reason with the information presented.

That teachers in the upper grades are increasingly interested in comprehension and study skills as they apply to reading in the content fields.

That adapting speed of reading to purpose is one reading-study skill. Others are: how and why to skim and scan, how to turn titles into questions, and how to recognize the patterns of writing in different subject fields.

# Orientation to Instruction: Effects on Teaching Style

Your knowledge and beliefs concerning the process of learning will be reflected in the lessons you teach. Many teachers prefer to be eclectic in their orientation toward reading, believing it is possible to assume different roles depending on what is to be taught and to whom. As we discuss instruction at different levels, it is helpful to understand the major positions on learning and instruction.

Each of the three positions — cognitive, behavioral, humanistic — tends to be associated with the different approaches to teaching reading. The cognitive orientation may be successfully employed by those using the basal or language experience approach; the behavioral orientation is usually associated with the technological approach to the teaching of reading; and the humanistic orientation is best represented through individualized reading.

## Cognitive Orientation

Teachers with a cognitive orientation emphasize the learner's growing cognitive capacity. Reading is seen as a process of acquiring information, organizing and storing knowledge, discovering new perspectives or questions, and learning how to learn. As a cognitivist, the reading teacher is a guide who clarifies questions, suggests activities, helps children evaluate their progress, and teaches general patterns of learning. The cognitive-oriented teacher wants pupils to learn to be self-directed in processing information. To cognitivists, motivation is an important element for learning. They hope children will find reading exciting and important. However, they offer no extrinsic reinforcers (rewards) to conflict with the reward of learning for learning's sake.

## Behavioral Orientation

Behaviorists hold that teaching is changing behavior. Teaching is not successful unless children acquire new skills. Reading objectives are broken down into subskills or behaviors that must be mastered sequentially. As children perform each subskill satisfactorily, they proceed along a continuum toward more encompassing goals. Techniques for keeping tasks meaningful, providing varied and extensive practice, reinforcing or rewarding appropriate behavior, and providing sufficient guidance are in accordance with the behaviorist's orientation.

The behaviorist pays attention to the motivation of pupils and continually attends to the responses of children, both to maintain the children's interest and to insure that they are eliciting correct responses needed for mastery of a skill.

### Humanistic Orientation

Humanists believe the learning experience must be significant and personal. Reading is viewed as an experience of the realities of life. There is no separation between cognitive and affective processes; reading involves both simultaneously. Humanistic teachers of reading share their own feelings of joy, frustration, success, and disappointment as they introduce children to the experiences of reading. The humanist believes that motivation is the natural result of facing the concerns of life. Happiness and sorrow, social expectations and rewards, nature and the senses, anger and curiosity, are all part of the child's world. If reading is taught as an expression of interaction with that world, it will necessarily be motivating and meaningful.

## Principles of Instruction to Use in Designing Reading Lessons

Most teachers design their own lessons, although some prefer to use lessons designed by product developers or authors of basal textbooks. In any case, well-designed lessons provide for:

1.  Getting *attention* to channel children's interests and motivating forces

2.  Guiding a *presentation* by which children can be helped through examples, cues, patterns, prompts, rules, and the like to notice the key features or attributes of what is being taught

3.  Giving children an *opportunity to respond and to practice*

4.  Giving children an *opportunity to apply* what they have learned to new situations

5.  Allowing children to find out whether their *responses are adequate* and to *gain satisfaction in achieving*

### Attention

Children's attention is required if you are to be successful. Although some children are basically interested in learning to read and will pay attention to your directions, others require more effort to attract them to the task at hand.

There are many different ways to help the learner attend to a task. Some teachers arrange sensory stimulations; for example, presenting something novel or surprising, showing incongruous items, using humor, or introducing a quandary. Others make challenging comments such as: "See if you can do this!" or "I'll bet you can't do this!" Still others use reassurance: "This is very difficult, but I'm sure we can do it together," or "You are such good pupils, let's do some harder work today." It often helps to clarify the difficulty of the task. Individual learners may perceive differently on the basis of experience and background; hence you might ask, "How difficult is this task for you?" and "How difficult is this task for the other children?"

Theatrical devices can be useful in arousing attention: "Goodness! There are only ten minutes until recess, and you haven't been told about the suffix *ing* yet," or "Even some college students don't know this skill." At the primary level, puppets or dolls may "speak" for the teacher: "I'm Evil *E* and I'm going to make some sounds for you." Older pupils may be attracted to lessons conveyed through posters, songs, and puzzles.

Part of the process of gaining attention involves directing the children's physical movement. It helps to ask them to point out or underline something: "Look at this word. Put your finger on it. This word is *man*."

Asking pupils to describe what they see in a picture and what they want to know about the picture is another way to get attention and set purposes.

## Presentation

In presenting lessons, you must try to lead the pupils to make appropriate responses. For example, in teaching young children to recognize a word by sight alone, you might say: "This word is *toy*. When I look at this word, I say *toy*. Now you look at the word. What is this word?" In this instance, you want the children to respond verbally to the configuration and shape of a printed word. Your questions will elicit a particular response because a prompt has been given. As the desired responses become more sophisticated, so does the presentation. In teaching how to isolate the main ideas of paragraphs, for instance, the presentation might show how this is done: "As you look at these possible answers, you see that only one of them is consistent with all facts contained in the paragraph — that it is a general synthesis of the paragraph's information." Now, of course, you need not always give the rule but may instead give several examples and then let the pupils generalize their own rule: "Each of these answers corresponds to a main idea in a paragraph. Each of these does not. What is different about the answers that give the main idea?"

The success of any presentation is indicated by the pupils' response. If there is not an appropriate response, the fault probably lies with the presentation, and a different and more simplified form for leading the youngsters to the response or generalization must be given. This new presentation may simply consist of providing information or understandings prerequisite to the task that was incorrectly assumed to be in the learners' repertoire. For instance, after trying unsuccessfully to teach children to read paragraphs orally with proper intonation, a teacher discovered that the children were unable to interpret typographical clues to interruptions, pauses, and emphasis (ellipses, dashes, and italics). Once the prerequisites were taught, the children achieved the objective.

A presentation may be very straightforward and didactic: "Look at this compound word. See the small word *cow*; see the small word *boy*. *Cowboy* is a compound word because it is made up of two familiar words that make a new word. Tell me why *cowboy* is a compound word."

Or a presentation may allow the learners to generalize for themselves: "Look at the words *cowboy, fireman, sidewalk*, and *something*. These are compound words. What makes these words compound words?"

Another way to elicit desired responses is through modeling. *Modeling* means demonstrating the task for the learners to imitate. "In each of these sentences, there are some unfamiliar words. Watch how I figure out what the first word is by using both phonics and context." (Teacher demonstrates.) "Now you show me how you would figure out the next unknown word."

Since the success in mastering a skill depends upon how clearly the skill is presented, the crux of instruction is the presentation. Ability to answer fresh questions about a factual paragraph, to interpret new metaphors, or to identify the author's tone is evidence that the children have learned (assuming the pupils could not do any of these things before instruction). The presentation need not be a one-way lecture. Instead pupils can be encouraged to respond overtly to maintain their attention and to show that they are comprehending. During the presentation, you might invite a variety of responses: raising hands or fingers, winking, standing up, speaking fast, reading in a whisper, writing with colored pens, recording on tape, role playing, and mimicking.

## Opportunity to Practice

Pupils need an opportunity to practice performing newly learned responses. This is done by providing fresh examples in a variety of contexts. Teaching for independence, too, requires that children respond without teacher assistance. Games, worksheets, written exercises, and homework activities provide an opportunity to practice. You must be careful, however, not to confuse practice activities with teaching activities designed to guide children in making generalizations. Children should not be assigned practice without the benefit of prior teaching.

## Application

Application is an advanced form of practice. Once a lesson has been conducted and the children have practiced the skill in isolated exercises, there remains the need to apply the skill in more complex situations. To help pupils carry over their newly acquired skills to reading, plan reading activities that require application of the skill taught in isolation. When presenting a lesson, direct the learners' attention to ways in which the skill will be useful. Give assignments in which children relate the reading instruction to textual material in school and to other reading material in the home and community. Let children apply the skill in reading trade books, other textbooks, and in the reading matter found in daily living outside the school. Children who have learned to identify and read isolated compound words but who stumble over such words in a library book have not successfully learned to apply that skill.

## Reinforcement

Reinforcement is another principle for designing lessons. Essentially, reinforcement means that the learner obtains satisfaction from the learning task. There are a number of ways to increase the chance that an activity or lesson will be satisfying. On the one hand, knowing that one has mastered a reading task can be rewarding. Hence the teacher should let the child know what the criteria are (what determines whether an answer is right or wrong) when decoding words, finding main ideas, adjusting reading rate to purpose, or using other skills. On the other hand, satisfaction is likely to result if the lesson is appropriate to the child's present attainment, interests, and own purposes.

There is controversy about whether the teacher should give external reinforcement to the child for engaging in reading tasks or whether these tasks themselves should be inherently rewarding. External reinforcers are often tangible: something to eat, a toy, a handshake, being able to sit at a teacher's desk or go outside for a drink of water. Other external reinforcers are smiles, high grades, written comments, praise, teacher's congratulatory phone calls to parents, and special reading materials.

Some teachers object to giving external rewards in return for compliance in reading tasks, saying that external rewards smack of manipulation, that the child should enjoy reading for its own sake, and that it is wrong to give a child the idea that reading is so distasteful that external rewards are necessary. Also external rewards may be dysfunctional. One expert maintains that those who need to try the hardest (low-ability pupils) are given less incentive for doing so because the top third of the class stands a better chance of getting better grades and other reinforcers.[1] This objection, of course, might be overcome by procedures to increase the success of poor performers and to note all significant gains, rather than pitting poor performers against good performers for scarce rewards.

It is important to recognize the part that internalization plays in all human affairs. The more effective rewards are intangible relationships with others. What our parents, brothers and sisters, teachers, and peers wish for us, we eventually come to wish for ourselves. Although the goal is to help learners set their own reading tasks and standards, tangible reinforcers for desired reading activity are at times effective.

An illustration of how the five features just described are combined in a lesson can be seen in this sample lesson plan.

*Sample Lesson Plan Illustrating Principles of Attention, Presentation, Opportunity to Practice, Application, and Reinforcement*

OBJECTIVE

Given words likely to be unfamiliar to the pupil and containing the affixes *re*, *ex*, and *less*, the child can choose the best definitions for the words and select examples most consistent with the definitions; for example,

SAMPLE TEST ITEM

*loveless*:

| a. One who loves | b. One who has no love | c. One who is loved |
|---|---|---|
| a. Friend | b. Lover | c. Devil |

---

[1] J. W. Michaels, "Classroom Reward: Structures and Academic Performance," *Review of Educational Research* 47, no. 1 (Winter 1977): 87–98.

INSTRUCTIONAL PROCEDURES

*Attention.* Write words like *reverberate, exhume,* and *ruthless* on the board. Say: "Look at these unfamiliar words. How do you suppose you can guess the meaning of these words? Can you find the clue?"

*Presentation.* Show children several familiar words containing the affixes *re, ex, less — return, renew, exit, expel, homeless, toothless —* and ask what these words mean. What parts look alike? What are the meanings of these parts? Ask the children to point to the words that mean (1) without something, (2) out of something, and (3) back from something. Explain that there are two answers required to make each item right and that the correct example may not be directly under the correct definition; for example,

*exile*:

|   |   |   |
|---|---|---|
| a. To invite to your home | b. To stay still | c. To send away |
| a. One who must leave his country | b. One who never moves away | c. One who visits other countries |

*Opportunity to practice.* Provide examples of words that include base words that are common (*careless, reread*) and uncommon (*witless, reprise*). Help children recognize that when they are not sure about the meaning of the base word, they should study the choices and select the one most consistent with the affix.

*aimless*:

|   |   |   |
|---|---|---|
| a. With careful plans | b. Outline or work | c. Missing an aim |
| a. A plane going to New York | b. A doctor going to a hospital | c. A leaf blowing in the wind |

*reforge*:

|   |   |   |
|---|---|---|
| a. To never do | b. To do once | c. To do many times |
| a. Read a Chinese newspaper | b. Write your name | c. Finish these sentences |

*expurgate*:

|   |   |   |
|---|---|---|
| a. To keep something good | b. To get rid of something bad | c. To wish for something wonderful |

a. Cleaning a    b. Not spend-    c. Pretending to
dirty cut       ing your        be able to fly
                money

*Application.* Find examples in newspapers and magazines of words using the affixes and write or orally give definitions for the words found. Or create fresh definitions and examples for words with the affixes (pupils may use the dictionary).

*Reinforcement.* Children in the class might enjoy conducting the application as part of a group activity. Teams may be set up and team members encouraged to help each other. Group activity often helps individuals to evaluate their own and others' work and to review feedback in an objective, productive fashion.

## Teaching Reading Readiness

Theories about when it is best to start teaching reading relate to the concept of reading readiness, the practice of preparatory skills before formal reading instruction. The present consensus is that the teacher or parent, not nature, is responsible for equipping the child with the skills necessary for learning to read and that readiness is not something to wait for but to produce. Educators and psychologists like Benjamin Bloom and Jerome Bruner emphasize the importance of the learning environment to the very young child's intellectual development. They hypothesize that children at any age can learn something from deliberate instruction that will move them toward ultimate objectives more rapidly than if they are left to unguided activity.

A minority view maintains that delaying the onset of reading by one or several years will not retard the rate at which the component skills of reading are acquired.[2] Indeed one psychologist opposes an early start in reading because, he says, it may be detrimental to cognitive growth.[3] Usually the holders of this view conceive of readiness as a maturational state rather than as a deficiency amenable to instruction. Maturationists are pessimistic about instruction aimed at preparing children for reading. They believe the intellectual development for reading depends on the individual's internal biological mechanism, and that the necessary growth will proceed in an orderly way — spontaneously with time rather than through external manipulation.

The final verdict about the value of specific training in prereading

---

[2] W. D. J. Rohwer, "Prime Time for Education: Early Childhood or Adolescence?" *Harvard Educational Review* 41, no. 3 (1971): 316–341.

[3] Hans G. Furth and Harry Wachs, *Thinking Goes to School: Piaget: Theory of Practice* (New York: Oxford University Press, 1974).

skills is not yet in. Lawrence Kohlberg, for example, finds value in the early teaching of reading, but not because it is likely to lead to greater cognitive development. Rather he believes the child might enjoy learning reading skills early, especially since many of the early reading tasks are more interesting to younger children than to older ones. Also the child who begins school with many prerequisite word attack skills may be freed for more cognitively valuable activities. In fact, studies have shown a positive effect from early training.[4]

Although we believe all children at every age are ready to learn something of importance to reading, our purpose in this section is not to argue when to begin formal reading instruction. Rather we want to illustrate the kinds of activities that are useful in helping children acquire both the general language and experiential background for learning to read and the specific, high priority prereading skills described in Chapter 4.

## Developing Language and Experiential Background

High achievers in reading tend to have an enriched verbal environment with more books available and more opportunity to have adults read to them than low achievers. A. H. Koppenhauer found that the home environments of high-achieving readers differed from those of low achievers in these ways: (1) parents gave the children more opportunity for verbal development — instead of saying, "Bring me a glass," they might say, "Please get the blue glass in the upper right-hand corner of the cabinet"; (2) parents encouraged pupils to share in adult activity — fathers of high-achieving pupils, for instance, deferred repairing of household items until the child could be present to observe and help; (3) parents stimulated educational growth — whenever the family had occasion to take a trip or even a short ride, they first considered the potential educational value that could be acquired en route, for example, during a visit to a historical site.[5]

An opportunity to talk with adults is important to children's language development. This fact emphasizes the value of your encouraging conversation, story telling, discussion, and listening to

[4] Joseph Brezeinski, *Summary Report of the Effectiveness of Teaching Reading in Kindergarten in the Denver Public Schools* (Denver, Colo.: 1967). Dolores Durkin, "What Does Research Say about the Time to Begin Reading Instruction," *Journal of Educational Research* 64, no. 2 (October 1970): 52–56. Marjorie Sutton, "Children Who Learned to Read in Kindergarten: A Longitudinal Study," *Reading Teacher* 22 (April 1965): 595–602.

[5] A. H. Koppenhauer, *Reading and the Home Environment*, Claremont Reading Conference, 38th Yearbook (Claremont, Calif.: Claremont Graduate School, 1974), pp. 122–130.

someone read as a basis for reading. One prominent reading specialist claims that the essential antecedents of reading consist of two cognitive insights: written language is meaningful and written language is different from spoken language.

The first insight can be acquired by drawing upon the interests of children in written language: "The wealth of print found in every product in the bathroom, on every jar and package in the kitchen, in the television guide and television commercials, in comics, advertising fliers, street signs, storefronts, billboards, supermarkets, and department stores."[6] Children should have the chance to hear comments such as: "That sign says *stop*," and "There's the *bus* for downtown," just as they should have the chance to test hypotheses about the meaning of printed words on their own: *Toys* — Is this word the clue to the location of the toy department? Does the word *Men* on a door mean that I should or should not enter?

To acquire the second insight — recognition that print is different from speech — the child must hear written language read aloud. Such an insight may explain why children tend to become proficient readers if they come from homes where a good deal of reading occurs — "the school of the mother's knee" (or "the school of the father's knee," as in the case of Mexican-American homes, where the most successful male readers are taught by their fathers). Traditional stories — fairy tales, adventure stories, history, myths — and contemporary material found in newspapers and magazines may be used in reading aloud to children. Whatever is read should be something the parent or teacher, too, will enjoy, something that will make the children laugh, cry, or give them "gooseflesh and glimpses of glory." It does not matter that large parts of the language read are incomprehensible, as long as the general theme carries the listener along. Through such exposure, the child learns to interpret written structures that are not common in everyday speech: the passive voice, clauses, appositives, and paired conjunctives.

To encourage language development, you must provide children with something to talk about. As one child said, "Boy, when I have something to tell, I can sure tell a good story." Both walks in the natural world and bringing nature into the classroom can assist children in sequencing, distinguishing similarities and differences, separating inferred causes from convincing evidence, and abstracting common elements — all of which are necessary for future reading comprehension. Art, music, and poetry are good sources for children's oral language experience. Similarly, cooking with a group of children, par-

---

[6] Frank Smith, "Making Sense of Reading — and of Reading Instruction," *Harvard Educational Review* 47, no. 3 (August 1977): 386–395.

ticipating in dramatic plays, and having telephone conversations can improve oral language at all age levels.

Children's favorite language-development activities are providing endings to stories and retelling them, describing objects and letting others guess what is described, reciting rhymes, putting on puppet shows, pantomiming descriptive words and stories, interviewing, and following directions — "Simon says."

Materials for helping children acquire specific objectives related to language improvement include oral drills, games, and programmed materials.

**Oral drills**   Pattern drill exercises are helpful in reinforcing children's predetermined linguistic structures. These drills may be humorous and should proceed at a fast pace. The teacher gives a stimulus phrase and the children make a response that is appropriate to a particular language pattern.

| | | |
|---|---|---|
| Pattern inversion: | The ball throws Bill. | (teacher) |
| | Bill throws the ball. | (pupil) |
| Pattern transformation: | Is it raining? | (teacher) |
| | It is raining. | (pupil) |
| Pattern elaboration: | She had a party. | (teacher) |
| | She had a party Friday. | (pupil) |
| Pattern negation: | Are you a girl? | (teacher) |
| | No, I am not; I'm a boy. | (pupil) |

**Gamelike activities**   Gamelike activities can be helpful for teaching various word forms. Comparative and superlative forms of adjectives, the past tense in verbs, and the transformation of an active sentence into a passive construction can be taught through simple games in which children are given examples of the pattern and then are asked to "play the game" by contributing examples that match the pattern.

Teacher: "The cat is big, but the dog is bigger." Or "The car is fast, but the plane is faster."
Pupil:    "The bread is hot, but the soup is hotter."

Creating chain stories is an enjoyable activity whereby the teacher starts an eventful story and children continue it. As the children progress through the chain of events, the story can be taped for replaying.

**Programmed materials**   Programmed booklets for use with children by teachers, parents, or peer tutors offer reproducible sequences of instruction leading to attainment of specific reading readiness skills. One such set of materials offers instructional sequences for fifty-two prereading skills.[7] The program provides practice in responding to a variety of verbal directions involving negation, labeling, categorizing, rhyming, numerals, language of instruction, and concepts required for following teacher directions (top, bottom, first, middle, last, and so on). As indicated in Figure 7.1, each frame has printed on it the instructions to be read to the child. Tutor and child sit together and work through the items one at a time.

### Teaching High Priority Reading Readiness Skills

**Auditory discrimination**    Auditory discrimination in reading readiness is the ability to recognize spoken words beginning or ending with the same sound. Initially children might be taught the concepts *same* and *different*. Children quickly learn these concepts when shown items that are identical and items that are not: "These two are the same; this one is different. Now you point to another one that is the same."

Although some teachers teach the concepts *same* and *sound* by having pupils identify similar gross environmental sounds — keys jingling, windows opening, coins dropping on the floor — most find it less time-consuming to move directly to having children identify words that begin and end with the same speech sounds.

At times teachers prefer to introduce the concept of rhyme before introducing *beginning sounds*. The term *rhyming part* is used to let children know they must attend to final sounds of spoken words instead of initial sounds. The concept of rhyme is easily taught by first repeating words such as *stop, cop,* and *drop,* explaining that they rhyme, and then presenting other rhyming words such as *note, vote,* and *tote* and *cry, sky,* and *my.* Finally, children should be asked to identify which word pairs rhyme: *toy, boy* or *toy, head; free, fun* or *free, key.* Pictures may be substituted for the teacher's oral pronunciation. Accordingly children are asked to: "Circle the pictures whose names rhyme" (car), (moon), (star). In such an activity, it is important that the child know the intended labels for the pictures.

---

[7] J. D. McNeil, *The ABC Learning Activities* (New York: American Book Company, 1966).

---

**FIGURE 7.1**    Example of programmed material offering instructional sequences for ▶ prereading skills.

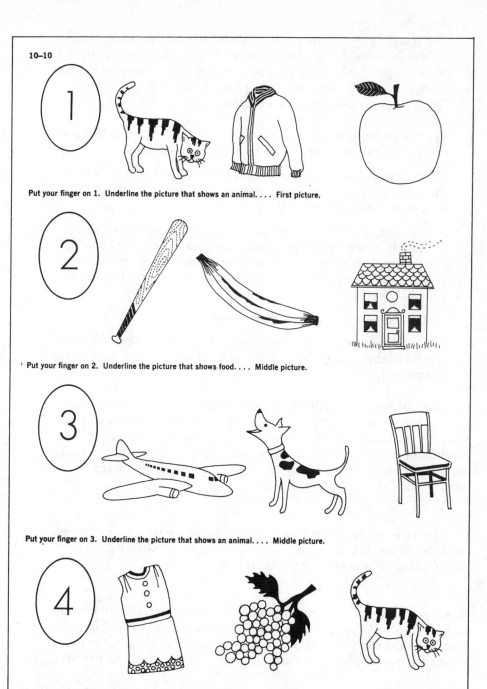

10–10

1. Put your finger on 1. Underline the picture that shows an animal. . . . First picture.

2. Put your finger on 2. Underline the picture that shows food. . . . Middle picture.

3. Put your finger on 3. Underline the picture that shows an animal. . . . Middle picture.

4. Put your finger on 4. Underline the picture that shows clothing. . . . First picture.

The teaching of auditory discrimination of beginning sounds in spoken words is similar to the teaching of rhyming parts. Figure 7.2 gives an example of a lesson aimed at helping children identify spoken words with the initial sounds of /c/, /p/, /j/, /l/, /d/, and /r/.

Other ways of teaching aspects of auditory discrimination include:

1.  Verifying a child's name: "Are you Betty or Netty?" (a technique for introducing the concept of beginning sounds).

2.  Asking pupils to clap each time they hear a word that begins with the same sound as the first word in the sentence: "Betty saw a baby bird that was not very big."

3.  Exaggerating an initial sound and then asking children to identify the one of two words that begins with the exaggerated sound: "The Campbell soup song: mmmmm, mmm good, mmmmm, mmm good, that's what Campbell soups are, mmmmm, mmm good."

    mmmmm — man      mmmmm — ran

4.  Distributing pictures or small objects and asking pupils to name them and then group them on the basis of the initial sound in the names assigned.

**Visual discrimination**   Although there may be children who profit by being asked to match gross shapes — stars, circles, arrows, and cars going in particular directions — as a prerequisite activity to discriminating among letters, children gain more by proceeding directly to matching letters with samples: "Which letter on the right is the same as the first letter on the left?"

Y:  R  H  Y  E

The task of matching letters can be made easier by first having children choose the match from distracting letters that are different with respect to angularity or other features:

O:  X  O  Y  E  H

However, the work of Joanna Williams has shown that children who are taught to make simple comparisons do not achieve as well in letter discrimination as those who are taught to make difficult comparisons.[8] Nevertheless, it is sometimes useful to have children learn to attend to

---

[8] Joanna P. Williams, "Training Kindergarten Children to Discriminate Letter-Like Forms," *American Educational Research Journal* 6, no. 4 (November 1969): 501–514.

features such as curvature, straightness, and obliqueness before asking them to discriminate among letters.[9]

Although the naming of letters is more than a simple visual discrimination task, most exercises for teaching letter discrimination involve labeling. Assigning names to letters facilitates letter recognition. The following lesson is a case in point:

OBJECTIVE

The child will match capital letters Y, N, and B with initial capital letters in words; for example, the teacher prints on the chalkboard:

| Y | To | Not | Yes |
|---|-----|-----|-----|
| N | You | Be | No |
| B | But | Nut | Yes |

The teacher asks pupils to name the first letter in the first row (capital Y). "Now look at the first letter in each of the three words in this row." (Indicate the first letter in each word.) "Which word begins with a capital Y?" Encourage pupils to come to the board and draw a line under the word. Have a pupil name the first letter in the word (capital Y). Continue in the same manner for capital letters N and B.

Examples of other letter discrimination activities are as follows:

1. "Circle the pairs of words that are the same."
   can   ran      pat  pat      hot  hot      hop  hog

2. "Circle the pairs of letters that are the same."
   db      dd      db      pp

3. "Circle the word that begins the same as the first word."
   far      fog      jar      tar

4. "Find the word that is different from the others."
   and      can      and

5. "Take these two mixed sets of alphabet cards and find the letters that match, placing one on top of the other."

6. "Underline the word in the big box that begins with the letter in the little box."

   | b | | dog   go   bit   hot |

---

[9] E. J. Gibson, and Harry Levin, "A Theory of Perceptual Learning and the Relevance for Understanding Reading," *The Psychology of Reading* (Cambridge, Mass.: M.I.T. Press, 1975), pp. 13–45.

Lesson for Page 79                     Beginning Sounds                              Section 6

**OBJECTIVES**
The learner will identify words that contain the initial sounds \c\, \p\, \j\, \l\, \d\, and \r\.

**MATERIALS**
Picture cards: initial consonants \c\, \p\, \j\, \l\, \d\, \r\.

On Your Own

## TEACHING THE LESSON

### Step One

Initial \c\
   Auditory Perception: Have ready the picture cards for initial \c\. If you do not have a set of picture cards, you may substitute any pictures of objects whose names begin with \c\. Display, in left-to-right order, two of the picture cards: *calf* and *can*. *Look at these two pictures. Listen carefully as I say their names: calf, can. Now I'll say the words again: calf, can. Both of these words begin with the same sound: calf, can. Let's say the words together. Listen for the sound the words begin with:* calf, can.

   Add the picture of the *cactus* to the right of the other pictures for initial \c\. *Listen as I say the names of all three pictures:* calf, can, cactus. *Cactus begins with the same sound as calf and can. Let's say all three words together. Listen for the sound the words begin with:* calf, can, cactus.

   Auditory Discrimination: Next, add the picture of the *cot* to the right of the other three. *Listen as I say the names of all four pictures:* calf, can, cactus, cot. *Does* cot *begin with the same sound as calf, can, cactus?* (yes) *What can you tell me about all these words?* (They all begin with the same sound.) *Let's say all four words together. Listen for the sound the words begin with:* calf, can, cactus, cot.

   Remove the picture of the *cot* and in its place, put the picture of the *ring*. *Now listen as I say the names of these four pictures:* calf, can, cactus, ring. *Does* ring *begin with the same sound as calf, can, cactus?* (no)

   Continue in this manner, using the following pictures in the fourth position:
      *duck* (no)
      *coat* (yes)

   Finally, display at random all the pictures used thus far—except the *calf*. Place the *calf* on a separate section of the chalkboard, felt board, pocket chart, or table. Direct the pupils to find and identify the pictures whose names begin with the same sound as *calf*. Once identified, the pictures whose names begin with \c\ can be grouped under the picture of the *calf*.

### Step Two

Initial \p\
   Follow the procedure suggested for initial \c\, using the following picture cards:
      Auditory Perception: *pie, pig, pan*
      Auditory Discrimination: *pail, dish, peach*

### Step Three

Initial \j\
   Follow the procedure suggested for initial \c\, using the following picture cards:
      Auditory Perception: *jeep, jet, jar*
      Auditory Discrimination: *rake, calf, jacks*

### Step Four

Initial \l\
   Follow the procedure suggested for initial \c\, using the following picture cards:
      Auditory Perception: *lamp, lion, lock*
      Auditory Discrimination: *dish, leg, rug, leaf*

### Step Five

*Begin,* page 79
   Distribute copies of *Begin*. Help the pupils to locate page 79. Allow them a few moments to explore the page. Then direct their attention to Box 1.

   *Put your pencil under the numeral 1. Look at the two pictures in the box. Listen as I say their names:* cake, candy. *Now say these words with me. Listen for the beginning sound in each word:* candy, cake. *Do the words* candy *and* cake *begin with the same sound?* (yes) *Take your pencil and ring the word Yes in Box 1.*

   *Now find Box 2. Put your pencil under the numeral 2. Look at the pictures in this box. Listen as I say their names:* ladder, cup. *Now say these words with me. Listen for the beginning sound in each word:* ladder, cup. *Think: Do the words* ladder *and* cup *begin with the same sound? If you think they do, ring the word Yes. If you think they do not, ring the word No. The correct answer is No. Ladder and cup do not begin with the same sound. Proceed in this manner with the rest of the page.*

   Picture names and correct responses are as follows:
      Box 3: *pie, lamp*          (No)
      Box 4: *cap, leaf*          (No)
      Box 5: *jeep, jack-in-the-box* (Yes)
      Box 6: *pencil, penny*      (Yes)

**FIGURE 7.2**   Example of a lesson designed to help children identify spoken words.

Source: M. S. Johnson et al., *Begin*, Teacher's Edition (New York: American Book Company, 1977), pp. 78a–79. American Book Reading Program, © 1977. Reprinted by permission of American Book Company, New York.

1   Yes   No

2   Yes   No

3   Yes   No

4   Yes   No

5   Yes   No

6   Yes   No

7. "Find another word in the chart (or book) that begins with the same letter as the one I've printed on this card."

8. "Trace this word."

It does not matter whether you introduce the discrimination of capital or lowercase letters first. In fact, some teachers prefer to teach both forms of each letter together; for example,

"Draw a line from the capital G to the small g."

G
    f
    h
    e
    g

"What is the name of the letter in the box? (Capital A) Now find a small a in the same row. It is the first letter in a word. Draw a line under the word that begins with small a."

| A |     go     with     and

# Reading Lessons in the Primary Grades

Word attack skills constitute a major target for beginning readers. Chapter 4 details *which* decoding and word recognition skills are essential for reading. However, the teacher of beginning reading also needs to know *how* word attack skills are taught efficiently. Rather than delineate a single prescription for teaching the beginning skills, we introduce a variety of methods, new and old, for teaching word attack skills so that you will be knowledgeable about reading and have an increased repertoire of methods to use in varied stiuations. Our focus here is on specific *methods* for teaching decoding, not general approaches to the teaching of reading.

### Synthetic and Analytic Methods

Conventional methods of teaching word recognition in beginning reading are classified as *synthetic* and *analytic*. Synthetic methods are inductive in that they begin with the smallest possible unit, such as a letter and its corresponding sound, and build up to a larger unit, such as syllables and words. Children might, for instance, be taught (after they had learned the letter-sound relationship for *h, a,* and *t*) to attack an unfamiliar word, *hat*, by synthesizing the sounds associated with the separate letters, huh-a-tuh = *hat*.

Analytic methods start with units that can be broken down or analyzed into smaller parts, such as a phrase being analyzed into words, the words analyzed into syllables, and the syllables analyzed into letters. For example, children may learn the words *hot, he, hand*, and *happy* and then be helped to generalize that all of these words begin with the same sound and letter and that this written letter represents the same sound at the beginning of each of these words.

Let us now consider various reading procedures that epitomize the synthetic and analytic methods.

**Alphabet method**   From about 1600 to 1840, Americans learned to read by this synthetic method. According to the alphabet method, the child first learned the names of the letters and their order in the alphabet. Then combinations like *ab, eb,* and *ib* were spelled out and pronounced. Later, three-letter combinations such as *glo, flo,* and *pag* were spelled; and finally, monosyllables and longer words were used. Spelling the word preceded its pronunciation. "M-a-n spells *man"* is one example of reading by the alphabet method. Spelling out has the disadvantage of teaching children to identify letters instead of reading words. How many words can a person remember this way? Although allowing for accurate word recognition and nearly perfect spelling, this method is limited in regard to teaching children the generalizations needed for decoding unfamiliar words.

**Phonetic method**   This is another synthetic method. The phonetic method differs from the alphabet method in that words are spelled out by sound rather than letter name. Accordingly the child is expected to associate individual sounds with given letters and then to blend them together to read words: "muh-a-nuh = *man*." The drawbacks to this method are that (1) it is difficult to give the appropriate sound value for letters in isolation; (2) saying sounds in isolation makes blending difficult (children who have been taught to respond "huh-a-tuh" when seeing the word *hat* often cannot associate these sounds with the orally familiar word); and (3) generalizations about letters and sounds do not apply in decoding common beginning words that have irregular spelling patterns; for example, *some, have, of*.

A number of attempts have been made to change the traditional spelling of the English language to help beginning readers acquire mastery of sound-symbol correspondence. The *Initial Teaching Alphabet*, or ITA, for example, is a procedure that for a short time was popular in a few American cities. This procedure augments the alphabet by adding a number of characters.[10] Long vowels in this system have their own symbol. In addition to the added characters, spelling has been reformed; for instance, *said* becomes *sed*. Hence, children learn to read a phonetically regular symbol system and are weaned to traditional print when able to cope with its spelling irregularities. The main argument in favor of the Initial Teaching Alphabet was that it allows the youngsters who are capable of memorizing some forty symbols to read words and sentences written in these symbols without stumbling over strange new combinations of letters. Opponents of ITA held that it sidetracks young readers from their true goal and leads to future problems in spelling.

On balance, there seems to have been little difference in results from using ITA as opposed to other methods. The children taught by this method usually made the transition to the regular alphabet without significant difficulty about the end of the second or the beginning of the third grade. However, if it had been as effective as its champions claimed, it would not have withered so soon.

Other attempts to make the language more phonetic include "Words in Color," a set of twenty-one charts in which letters of different colors indicate different sounds. The child drills on the charts, reading words and parts of words, and then reads books in a single color, black. For example, letters with the sound /f/ — *f, ff, ph, fe, if, gh, ffe, ft* — are coded in mauve, thereby indicating that the sound /f/ can be spelled in different ways. A particular sound is always represented by the same color regardless of its spelling. Again there is no evidence to show the superiority of this method although some argue that it helps avoid reversals (*was* for *saw*), since sounds are connected with written speech from the beginning.[11] Arguments against the use of "Words in Color" are that some children may have trouble discriminating among the similar hues and that it is restricted to phonic color code charts, making application to out-of-class reading slower.

The phonetic method is adapted at times to feature the teaching of "rules" such as: "When two vowels go walking, the first one does the talking." This rule is thought to help in sounding out words like *seat*. The difficulty with this approach is that there are many exceptions to the rules and some rules have limited utility. Rules for word attack work best for the most consistent and frequently used phonic patterns. When they are applied to complicated spellings, they are too unwieldy to be useful; for example, "*y* has its own consonant sound at the begin-

---

[10] Maurice Harrison, *Instant Reading: The Story of the Initial Teaching Alphabet* (London: Pitman, 1964).

[11] Harriett Bentley, "Words in Color," *Elementary English* 43 (1966): 515–517.

ning of a word, the long vowel sound of *e* or *i* at the end of a word, and the long or short vowel sound of *i* in the middle of a word."

In brief, the alphabet and phonetic methods are synthetic approaches to teaching beginning reading. Their advantages are several: the teaching of smaller units first may provide a simpler task for some children; recognizing letter-sound correspondence may help children become independent readers in attacking words that have regular spelling patterns; and when combined with other decoding methods (structural and contextual analysis, for example), synthetic methods may help children retrieve or recognize words about which they are uncertain. Disadvantages to teaching word attack synthetically are: the units are not familiar and meaningful to young children; for example, the letter and corresponding sound for *t* does not communicate to the child the way the word *toy* does; the method distorts sound values — "duh" is not the sound one hears when pronouncing *dog;* and the rules governing letter-sound correspondence are difficult to learn and apply.

## Whole Word Method

A reaction to the inadequacies of the alphabet and phonetic methods is the whole word method. The whole word method is a "look and say" technique for showing the child a word and modeling its sound; for example, *"stop —* This word is *stop.* Say *stop."* This method is based on the assumption that the sound of the word is already familiar to the child and that we do not read by spelling or sounding out syllables and letters but that we read entire words or phrases. Accordingly, a new word is presented over and over until the child learns it. The child is supposed to concentrate on the visual aspects of the word and simultaneously listen as the teacher pronounces it. Following the "look and listen" phase, the child concentrates on the visual aspects of the word while pronouncing it aloud. The look and say method is accompanied by flashcards and configuration cues; for example, *go to,* "You can tell by seeing how the *g* goes down (descender letter) and the *t* goes up (ascender letter)." Youngsters, nevertheless, often confuse words that are similar in form: *came = come, Mike = Mark.*

Many children learn to "read" words by associating them with their real-life context. *Stop* and *hot dog* are examples of this. The labeling of items, such as chairs and tables, can also help children associate words with concrete objects. However, there have been cases when children learned to say *house* when that word is shown only because they identified it with a spot or smudge on the flashcard. When the word appeared in another context, they could not read it. The word method is used most often as a means to help children recognize by sight, without using any word attack skills, common words that appear frequently in their reading materials. This method is particularly appropriate for use with the language experience approach. When the whole word method is used in that way, children learn to recognize their own words written on experience charts.

### Phrase, Sentence, Paragraph, and Story Methods

Another set of methods focuses on the use of phrases, sentences, paragraphs, and stories as the basis for teaching words. The basic idea of these methods is that the child learns to recognize words more quickly if they appear in meaningful or natural speech rather than as isolated words. As implied by the name, the unit first presented is a phrase, sentence, paragraph, or complete story. These methods can be analytic when large units, such as sentences and phrases, are analyzed into words and words into either syllables, phonograms, or spelling patterns. Nevertheless unless there is a systematic effort by the teacher to provide sufficient instances of particular patterns in the larger units, the use of these methods tends to result in memory reading with the child either unable to read the words out of their original context or unable to read words never seen before. Such methods do have the advantage of being meaningful for the child and, therefore, usually promote fluency in reading. Sentences such as "I like to go on picnics" or other natural expressions are easy for the child to say. The teacher typically points to each word when the sentence is read initially and then the child repeats this procedure, thus learning that reading is language and avoiding word-for-word reading. The phrase, sentence, paragraph, and story methods are analytical whenever these large units are analyzed to reveal smaller units, such as phonograms, syllables, spelling patterns, or other letter-sound relationships. Ideally, the process becomes circular. After recognizing phonic elements through analysis of the large unit, the child is given an opportunity to practice decoding new words composed of the now familiar elements; that is, a synthetic activity.

### The Patterning Method

The patterning method for teaching word recognition is a good example of a method that combines both analysis and synthesis. The procedure consists of the introduction of groups of words that follow a consistent pattern of sound and spelling. Examples of patterns are *w — we, will, with* (initial consonant); *et — pet, get, set* (rhyming elements or phonograms). Pupils abstract the common phonic and structural elements in each group (*w* and *et*). They learn the pattern in known words and apply it first in decoding known words. Once the application process is understood, pupils practice decoding new words composed of known patterns.

Pattern words are introduced in an oral language activity (to provide meaning) and then are presented in written context. Subsequently, these pattern words are isolated and children are helped to generalize observations from questions such as: "What do you notice about these words when you say them?" (They all sound alike at the beginning (end).) "What do you notice about these words when you look at them?" (They all have the same letters at the beginning (end).)

After patterns are analyzed, pupils synthesize them in reading a new word. For instance, after the *w* pattern is abstracted from *we*, *will*, and *with*, and the *et* pattern is abstracted from *pet*, *get*, and *set*, the child is asked to decode the new word *wet*.

If a pupil has difficulty decoding a new word, the teacher helps the child abstract the key pattern for decoding it. Thus, if a child cannot recognize *led*, the teacher might say: "What word begins like *let*, *look*, and *lot* and rhymes with *bed*, *fed*, and *shed*?" Beginners learn to use rhyming patterns — *e*, *et*, *en*, *ot*, *op*, *y*, *ish*, *ay*, *al*, *it*, *un*, *ug*, *alk*, *oll*, *ell*, and so on — and initial consonant spelling patterns — h, g, t, n, r, m, d, s, l, c, p, b, f, v, w — to read many new words like *he*, *get*, *pen*, *got*, *top*, *my*, *wish*, *may*, *sat*, *bit*, *fun*, *dug*, *talk*, *sold*, and *tell*. The pattern method can also be used with more advanced readers to teach vowel patterns like *et*, *en*, and *ed* (*get*, *hen*, *bed*) and syllable patterns like *de* (*declare*, *deliver*, *department*) and *tion* (*action*, *motion*, *direction*).

### Activities for Teaching Sight Recognition

There are unlimited activities for reinforcing general word perception. Consider these opportunities for children to "see" a word and "say" it:

*Card drawing.* The teacher prints words needing practice on cards. Children in a group take turns drawing cards and reading the words. If a mistake is made, a card is returned face down to the bottom of the pack. The winner is the person with the largest number of cards.

*Word bingo.* Each player has a card marked off into twenty-five square blocks. In each block, a word is printed. There is also a small pack of word cards, each the size of a block. The teacher shows a card and the child who has the displayed word pronounces the word, points to it, and is given the small card to place over the appropriate block. The child with five words covered in any direction is the winner.

*Wheel of chance.* A child flicks a cardboard hand on a wheel to get a number that corresponds to a number on a card with a word or phrase to be read.

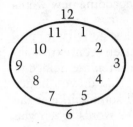

1. come; 2. the; 3. with;
4. is; 5. have; 6. has;
7. little; 8. said; 9. can;
10. run; 11. that; 12. was

*Building sentences.* Each child is given a card bearing a word in a sentence. The child who has the first word in a sentence stands and shows a word for others to see. The child who thinks he has the second word stands next to the first child and shows his word, and so on until the sentence is made.

*Answering with phrase cards.* Short phrases that relate to a story are placed along a chalkboard ledge. The child is asked to identify the phrase that best answers a question; for example, "Where was the little dog running?" The child would be expected to pick out a phrase like "down the street."

### Activities for Teaching Phonics Analysis

You may want to use the following activities to develop recognition of letter-sound combinations and for teaching pupils to blend separate sounds (decoding):

*Relating letters to beginning sounds.* Present letters — initial consonants and common blends — and ask the children to identify the picture whose name begins with the sound represented by the letters; for example,

m    (monkey)    (dog)    (cat)

*Making predictions.* After noting that *at*, *cat*, and *hat* end the same (*rhyme*) and have the same ending letters, ask the children to predict what other words will end with the same sound and have the same letters: *fat*, *sat*, *bat*, *mat*, and so on.

*Finding final digraph patterns.* Write words such as *bang*, *song*, and *ring* on the board. Ask the pupils to say the words and to generalize that they all end with the same sound even though they do not rhyme. Next, lead the children to see that each of the words end with the same letters, *ng*. Give the children a new word, *long*, and ask them to say how its ending will probably sound (with the same ending sound as *bang*, *song*, and *ring*). Finally, ask the pupils to label the pattern (*n-g* because *ng* spells the sound heard at the end of words like *song*).

*Recognizing vowel patterns.* After noting that the words *mat*, *can*, and *bag* have the same vowel sound and that a consonant follows the letter *a* in each case, ask the children to supply other words that have the same vowel pattern: *sat*, *pan*, *rat*, and *tag*.

*Synthesizing patterns.* Present new words composed of familiar patterns. Review the familiar patterns and then ask the children to figure out the new word; for example,

Print on a card or on the chalkboard the word *big*. "Here is a new word."
"You already know all the patterns in this word."
b: *boy*, *ball*, *bet*.    i: *sit*, *fish*, *win*.    g: *leg*, *dog*, *tag*.
"Which word begins like *boy*, has the vowel sound of *sit*, and ends like *leg*?"

*Word building.* Place a number of phonograms and three or four sets of consonants in envelopes and give them to the children. The first child who correctly assembles all the words wins.

*Generalizing about the final e.* List familiar words like *can*, *rat*, *Tim*, and *cod*; and then list words like *cane*, *rate*, *time*, and *code*. Ask the pupils to tell how the two parallel sets of words differ in spelling and in meaning and then ask them to generalize the effect of the final *e*. List *Sid*, *side*, *far*, and *fare* for decoding.

Perhaps you have already drawn the conclusion that all letter-sound patterns can be taught by using the following model:

1. Present several instances of the letter-sound patterns; for example, *she*, *show*, *shoot*, and have pupils pronounce the words. (Pupils can do so if the words have been presented as sight words previously.)

2. Determine auditory similarities of the words; for example, ask pupils what they *hear* that is the same in the words *she*, *show*, and *shoot*. (Each word begins with the same sound.)

3. Determine visual similarities; for example, ask pupils to identify the part of each of these words that is the same: *she*, *show*, *shoot*. (Each word begins with *sh*.)

4.  Make predictions; for example, ask pupils to tell which of the following words begins with the same sound as *she: ship, school, show, shoot, Sunday.*

5.  Label the pattern; for example, ask pupils to label the pattern in the words *she, show,* and *shoot* and tell why they chose that label. (The letters *s-h* stand for the same sound heard at the beginning of each of the words.)

### Activities for Teaching Structural Analysis

You can do a great deal to reduce children's uncertainty about unknown words by helping them identify the parts of the words: root words, affixes, and inflectional endings.[12] Practice in building new words from known words is one technique for teaching this skill; for example,

"You know the first word in each list. See if you can read the other words in each list."

| *long* | *like* | *kick* | *go* | *play* |
|---|---|---|---|---|
| longest | liked | kicks | going | plays |
| longer | liking | kicked | gone | playing |
| | likes | kicking | goes | played |

Some lessons in structural analysis emphasize changes in word forms, such as doubling a consonant, adding *ed* or dropping a final *y* and adding *ly,* and combining two root words to make a new word. These lessons give children an opportunity to identify the base words from which the changed words are derived and to use the base words in composing new ones:

"From what root words were these words made — *tapped, begged, clotted?*"

"Say these words — *mapped, logged.*"

Another teaching technique:

---

[12] Structural analysis depends on a knowledge of either inflection or derivatives. The inflectional system consists of *s* in the third-person singular (she eat*s*), *s* in the plural (key*s*), *s* marking possession (the lad*'s* hat), *ed* in the past tense of verbs (he want*ed*), and *ing* as the progressive form of verbs (he runn*ing*). The derivation system consists of spellings that derive one part of speech from another (happy-happen, small-smaller, haste-hasten, and so on).

"Sometimes you can pronounce a new word because it is made from a word you know. Look at the word you know and then read the new word."

drive — driven      drop — dropped
move — movement   kit — kitten

Note that structural analysis means finding meaningful parts in unfamiliar words: plurals (dog-dogs); tense (burn-burned); comparisons (old-older); compounds (overshoe). This is not the same as "looking for little words in big words," which is a questionable practice because it is likely to mislead the child with respect to the meaning and the pronunciation of the unfamiliar word: *hot*el, *fat*her.

### Activities for Teaching Contextual Analysis

Children should learn to anticipate and surmise new words on the basis of context clues — semantics and syntax. The strategy of guessing an unfamiliar word from the surrounding context is a useful one. When this strategy is combined with phonic and structural strategies, one can greatly reduce the uncertainty about an unfamiliar word.

A good way to teach the contextual strategy is to begin with oral exercises in which the child guesses a missing word: "My new _____ has tall handlebars. What word did I leave out?" (semantic clue) "She always went _____ him to the store. What word did I leave out?" (syntax clue)

Oral exercises should be followed, first, by simple printed sentences in which the unfamiliar word is heavily prompted. Later, less prompting is necessary.

"Sometimes you can guess new words from what the other words say. Read the sentences and guess the new underlined words."

The dog can bark.
The bird can sing.
The cat can meow.

He cut himself with a knife.
The belt had no buckle.

Although word attack skills are very important for beginning readers to acquire, a complete reading program will also include instruction in comprehension and study skills. Defining words, interpreting syntactical structures and punctuation marks, determining sequence, drawing conclusions, making inferences, and following directions are activities that will prepare the beginning reader for the development of advanced reading skills in the middle grades.

# Reading Lessons in the Middle Grades

As you read the following sections, note that methods for teaching word recognition are featured in the primary level, methods for teaching comprehension in the middle grades, and methods for teaching study and critical reading in the upper grades. Although this assignment of methods according to grade level reflects the current emphasis in teaching reading, we do not want you to think that these methods apply only at those given levels. On the contrary, the learner is the point of reference. Comprehension, study skills, and critical reading are taught at all levels with modification in the way they are presented and with consideration for the different abilities of individual pupils. The comprehension skills that receive the greatest attention during the middle and upper grades, for example, are introduced and taught in simpler contexts during the child's first year of reading instruction.

You must be careful not to let the comprehension of specific words or sentences take priority over the larger task of learning how to comprehend words and sentences in general. One way to help the learner acquire transferable skills, such as finding a main idea or determining the sequence of events, is to present enough instances where these skills apply so that the child can see the common attributes. Another way is to encourage the habit of asking questions when reading. Children who have been trained only to answer teacher-posed questions about what they have read may not know how to formulate their own questions about other materials.

Harry Singer holds that teacher-posed questions are inadequate for the development of comprehension.[13] To complete the instructional procedure, Singer recommends stimulating pupils to formulate their own questions before, during, and after reading. When pupils start to ask their own questions, they are developing what Singer calls *active comprehension.* Children learn to ask questions by (1) modeling the teacher-posed questions, (2) being asked questions that require a question, not an answer in return — "What would you like to know about this magazine?" — or (3) pretending to be the teacher and asking their peers questions.

---

[13] Harry Singer, "Active Comprehension: From Answering to Asking Questions," *Reading Teacher* 31, no. 8 (May 1978): 901–909.

Reading comprehension has many dimensions, ranging from simple recall of what is stated in a passage to the making of inferences. Practice should be given in each dimension. If a passage says that Tom went to the top of the mountain, a literal comprehension question might be: "Who went to the top of the mountain?" To reason beyond what is explicitly stated at a higher form of comprehension, an appropriate question might be: "Why did Tom go to the top of the mountain?" In this case, the learner might seek clues such as the characterization of Tom that would indicate whether he went to satisfy his curiosity or to meet a challenge. Answers derived from the making of inferences are judgments requiring personal experience, logic, and interpretation of subtle linguistic clues.

Recent studies of reading achievement suggest that intermediate and older students seem to be performing adequately on literal comprehension tasks but not so well on tasks involving implied meanings.[14] Opportunities for pupils to practice drawing implications and evaluating critically are needed.

Reading specialists do not agree about whether reading comprehension is best achieved through development of a single ability composed mainly of verbal reasoning or whether it can best be enhanced by acquiring separate skills such as understanding word meanings, getting the main idea, and detecting the author's mood. We believe that activities consistent with both positions are desirable — developing reasoning ability by reading and teaching specific comprehension skills. Teaching techniques toward these ends have been presented in Chapter 5 and are elaborated in the following paragraphs.

## Strategies for Teaching Reading Comprehension Skills

Teach children to draw on their own experience for understanding. To acquire inferential skills, children might identify with the characters they are reading about and their feelings. For example, when reading the sentence, "Her anger made Sue's face *hideous*," you might ask: "Have you ever been really angry? Tell us about it. How do you think your face looks? How do you think Sue's face looks?"

When learning from the text, children must extract the information needed and then assimilate it into their previous knowledge. Instructions asking that children generate original sentences using paragraph headings greatly facilitate (nearly double) comprehension;

---

[14] I. E. Aaron, "Today's Reading Achievement with Suggestions for Improving Tomorrow's Performance," *Reading: Directions for Change, Journal of Research and Development in Education* 11, no. 3 (Spring 1978): 3–11.

for example, "Make up and write your own sentences about what happened in each of the paragraphs, using the headings given."

Teach pupils to classify. Readers who develop their own classification system for ideas, objects, events, terms, or language structures are on their way to understanding word meanings, main ideas, and conclusions. Help the children learn to classify by pointing out details, labeling similarities and differences, looking for a common denominator by which concepts may be grouped, and creating relationships between ideas, objects, or events. The ability to classify is essential if one is to identify main ideas.

Exercises for teaching classification can range from the simple to the complex:

> "Listen while I say some words. Tell me which one does not belong — *violet, pansy, geranium, collie, rose.*"

> "Read this paragraph and then list the sentences that go with the idea of *variation,* with the idea of *courage,* and the idea of *loneliness.*"

Teach children techniques to use when reading for different purposes. Learning to read for a central thought may occur through activities in which the child reads a paragraph and gives the main idea, chooses an appropriate title for a selection, or gives an original title for a selection. On the other hand, learning to read for details is enhanced when children answer specific questions or give the facts found in a selection. In contrast, learning to follow directions in reading is unlike other reading tasks in that the child is not to try to recall what is read but to comply with each direction as given, whether the directions are for making something or doing an experiment. When learning to read to discover cause and effect, the child should be asked to answer specific questions about a selection and analyze reasons for or causes of major events. In Chapter 6 we indicated how children can learn to recognize common writing patterns and to match their style of reading to each. When reading materials written in the *shared experience pattern,* for example, pupils should relax and read quickly, enjoying the author's experience. On the other hand, when reading materials written in the *imparting information pattern,* few words can be ignored. Children should attend to many factual details and attempt to associate them with each other, usually by relating the details to the main idea of the passage. They should also read slowly when reading materials characterized by conclusions or statements of fact followed by substantiation in the form of observation, experiment, or other data (*sub-*

*stantiated facts pattern*). A suggested teaching procedure for the latter is to have children, first, understand the author's conclusions; second, challenge the author to prove it; and third, read to see if the proof is sufficient.

Teach children to attend to linguistic clues. Sentences with the following word structures require special attention:

Sentences using *unless, then,* and *if* clauses: *I will go unless it rains.* "Will he go?"

Sentences using passive voice: *The book was given to him by Dora.* "What did Dora give him?"

Sentences with negation: *I didn't want to go and neither did Bill.* "Did Bill want to go?"

Sentences where one word changes the meaning: *She was a wahoo but he was "only" a walap* versus *She was a wahoo but he was a walap.* "Which writer thinks a wahoo is higher on the social scale than a walap? How do you know?"

Teach children to develop word meaning through context clues, word structure, and extended meanings. One way to teach the use of context clues is to give children practice in guessing the meaning of unfamiliar words from surrounding familiar words; for example, "*Auks*, like the razor bill and the dovekin, are diving birds that breed in the colder part of the north." ("What is an auk?")

Contrasts or opposites are useful context clues. Children should learn that if they know one of the pair of opposites, they can infer the second; for example,

He wasn't a miser but a *prodigal.*

She wanted to be at a distance, not *proximal.*

Instead of hardening the skin, it was an *emollient.*

For children to learn that words may change their meaning as the context changes, we recommend using exercises whereby you ask pupils to select from among different dictionary meanings of a word the one that best fits the context; for example,

The *stroke* of the oar from the front boat began to pick up.

*Stroke* means:  a. movement  b. shock  c. rub

Teach prefixes and suffixes to develop word meaning. A typical instructional procedure:

"If *prearrange* means to arrange beforehand, and *preassemble* means to assemble in advance, what does *preview* mean?"

"If *prewar* means before the war, and *preadult* means before adulthood, what does *preelection* mean?"

The above procedure can be used with many affixes such as: *anti, ex, circum, pro, ill, per, com, dis, hyper, inter.*

Parallel to the use of affixes, it is helpful to teach root words as clues to meaning. "*Med* means to heal, so what do these words have in common — *medication, medical, medic*?" Among the useful root words to feature are these: *fac, cop, duct, mor, spe, ver, graph, reg, ject, mis.*

The elementary pupil needs to master the skill of interpreting extended meanings, such as figures of speech in which a word literally denotes an object or idea and is used in place of another, thereby suggesting an analogy; for example, "The moon is our stepping-stone into space." The child reading that "Joe stood ten feet tall that day" must understand that Joe did not suddenly shoot up physically, but that he performed in an outstanding fashion.

Children enjoy deriving meaning from exercises that include items like these:

She had the look of white china. (Describe her.)

Some people are hands or feet; but she is a shoulder to weep upon. (What is she like?)

The city rose to its feet as one person. (Was the city united?)

This great business is the lengthy shadow of one person. (What made the business great?)

Vary the level of difficulty of activities. To make certain that pupils learn to use their comprehension skills independently, plan lessons that use the same skills in many different ways. Activities should reflect a spectrum of levels of difficulty. "Count the number of root words on this page" is certainly less difficult than "Invent ten new words that have roots and write down their definitions." Although the difficulty level of activities will be determined somewhat by the reading or maturity level of the youngsters, plan for variety within levels. The same skill might be practiced through writing, speaking, listening, acting out, reading, or game playing.

Materials may be varied also. Choose reading selections to teach the same skill at different levels. Children who do not understand a concept at the independent reading level may find that they do understand it at an instructional level. Another way to vary materials is to change the familiarity of the subject matter. Pupils who have learned to apply their comprehension skills with familiar subjects will be challenged when asked to use the same skill in a new subject area; for example, "How does the root word you have just learned help you to understand this math term — *polygon?*" The following lesson illustrates the use of varied activities in the teaching of a comprehension skill.

*Sample Lesson for a Comprehension Skill*

OBJECTIVE
Given scrambled sentences, the child can determine an appropriate sequence of events.

PRESENTATION
"Look at these two lists of words and tell me which list is in the best order. Why?"

| | |
|---|---|
| first | afterwards |
| then | next |
| last | later |

"Now look at the following three sentences. There is a missing word before each sentence. You must put the right sequence word before each sentence."

_____ the fireman finds six empty banana peels and sees something strange on the firehouse pole.

_____ the zookeeper sees the gorilla leave the zoo.

_____ the gorilla takes something from the grocery store.

"If you put the sentences in the right order, you will have an idea where the gorilla is. After you have written the right sequence word before each sentence, tell me where the gorilla is." (On the firehouse pole.)

PRACTICE

1. Using a story from a basal text, write down the five most important events in the order they occurred.
2. Cut up a cartoon strip and see if a friend can put the frames back in order.
3. Ask another pupil to tell you a story using first, next, and last sentences.

4. Listen to scrambled-up sequences on the tape recorder. Try to figure out the correct order of events.

5. Make a time line showing major events of your life.

APPLICATION

1. Watch TV news broadcasts. Are the events reported in the order they occur?

2. Write a story to present to the class on a scroll.

3. Read a mystery. List the clues in sequential order and see if a friend can solve the puzzle.

4. Listen to another pupil, sibling, parent, or friend read a story. Then ask him or her to tell you what happened first, next, last.

5. Find out which classmate's birthday will be celebrated first, next, and so on.

6. Scramble the events of a newspaper story and see if a friend can tell the correct story.

7. Draw three pictures that show a sequence of events and let a pupil put them in order.

In the sample lesson, the level of difficulty of the task varies in that the several basal texts, newspapers, pictures, and oral reading selections are of different complexity. The youngster who sequences cartoon frames easily may have difficulty listening to scrambled sentences on a tape recorder. By changing the context in which the comprehension skill is to be used, pupils may be helped to apply their new skill in independent learning. Making a time line of major events in a person's life is a long way from tracking down a gorilla. As our goal for teaching comprehension skills is to give youngsters techniques for understanding all reading, this lesson illustrates the use of sequencing for comprehending newspapers, dates, stories from basal readers, stories shared by friends, current events, and creative writing. Dictionaries, encyclopedias, magazines, textbooks from content field areas, comic books, poems, and songs are only a few of the many other items that could be used in teaching this transferable comprehension skill.

A recent emphasis in the teaching of reading comprehension warrants attention — the use of imagery. By age nine or ten, children can benefit from instruction involving the construction of mental images corresponding to the text they have read: "Make up pictures in your head about the story." Some types of learners benefit more than others from such directions. In particular, children who do not spontaneously integrate text material learn more when given an imagery instruction. Those who comprehend poorly because they lack decoding skills or vocabulary knowledge are not helped by being told to form pictures of what they read.[15] Imposed images (pictures) can increase children's learning if the pictures accurately depict the information in the text. However, pictures can have an adverse effect on children's learning if they depict inaccurate or irrelevant information.

Perhaps the most important development in teaching comprehension is the attention being given to the child's own meaning of what is read. Current research suggests that many children cannot relate what they are reading to the knowledge they already have.[16] The implications for teaching are that before giving material to these children to comprehend, you should (1) provide pupils with the background knowledge necessary to comprehend the passages, (2) help them relate the personal knowledge they already have to the passages, and (3) find out how what a child reads is interpreted in light of the child's own point of view and do not call the child's interpretation an error just because it does not match your or the textbook writer's schema.

# Reading Lessons in the Upper Grades

Upper grade reading instruction tends to shift from learning to read to reading to learn. That is, the focus is not so much on the skill for recognizing words and processing sentences and paragraphs but rather on gaining information from the text. The oral repertoire of beginning readers is much greater than their reading vocabulary. However, in the upper grades, children's comprehension of written words begins to be greater than their oral vocabulary. Critical reading, by which the pupils begin to weigh the validity of what they read, also takes on more importance.

## Application of Thinking to the Teaching of Study Skills

The mastery of study skills allows pupils to obtain information and solve problems through their own reading efforts. As an extension of the reading skills of word attack and comprehension, study skills

---

[15] Michael Pressley, "Imagery and Children's Learning: Putting the Picture in Developmental Perspective," *Review of Educational Research* 47, no. 4 (Fall 1977): 585–622.

[16] Richard Anderson et al., "Frameworks for Comprehending Discourse," *American Educational Research Journal* 14, no. 4 (Fall 1977): 367–381.

include reacting to what has been read. The emphasis is on active rather than passive reading. Youngsters who read actively read for a purpose, think about what they read, and apply their reading skills to their purpose.

**Vocabulary building as a study skill**   Study skills apply to reading in the areas of mathematics, social studies, the sciences, and other subject areas. Such skills depend on acquisition of a special vocabulary and syntax. In fact, there are four kinds of vocabulary that must be taught: (1) words unique to the subject area; for example, *molecule* in science, *latitude* in geography; (2) common words with a special meaning in the subject area; *current* in science, *clash* in social studies; (3) a group of words with a single concept; "Along the perpendicular to the diameter of the circle is the axis" is one concept; and (4) symbols in mathematics; for example, an equal sign (=).

As indicated earlier in this chapter, we recommend the development of vocabulary through many different kinds of activities. Some pupils derive the meaning of content words from the study of root words and affixes. Others rely on deriving the meaning of new words from context. *Explication de texte* is an old and effective method by which pupils and teacher analyze a literary work to see how the language works. Explication of text is a form of literary criticism involving a detailed examination of each part of a book and an exposition of the relationship of the parts to each other and to the whole book. Accordingly, pupils might be helped to perceive subtle distinctions in terms that appear to be *synonyms: naive* versus *ingenuous*, *murder* versus *execute.*

Dictionary study whereby one looks at the etymology (origin), the denotation (explicit meaning), and the connotation (implicit meaning) of words is worthwhile for the development of vocabulary in the subject fields. Directly teaching terms is helpful, too. This usually takes the form of defining the term or concept so that the essential attributes of the concept are recognized. For some terms, you must show many instances of the concept, labeling each instance as an example, but for other concepts, you can provide a straightforward definition: "*Otitis media* is an infection in the ear that can cause fluid to build up, causing deafness."

Vocabulary that can be figured out from the context should not be explained beforehand since pupils should apply their skill in extracting meaning from contextual clues. However, ambiguous terms should be introduced before asking pupils to read the material. Activities calling for the use of a glossary and the grouping of synonyms and antonyms also may build understanding of vocabulary.

A most important suggestion is that you arrange sensory experiences by which the child can learn firsthand what the specialized vocabulary of a given subject matter means: *"Role* may be defined by pupils after activities in which they note the rights and duties assigned to medicine men, doctors, patients, nurses, and others in the health field."

To facilitate the teaching of study skills, plan reading lessons that include a variety of thinking skills. To reach the goal of integrating higher level thinking skills into the teaching of reading, you need a frame of reference for identifying different categories of thinking. The authors of the *Taxonomy of Educational Objectives*[17] delineate six areas of thought processes:

(lowest level)    1. Recall: Pupil recognizes or recalls information.

2. Comprehension: Pupil knows what is being communicated.

3. Application: Pupil solves a problem that requires use of knowledge gained.

4. Analysis: Pupil studies problem with knowledge of its parts and relationships.

5. Synthesis: Pupil solves a problem by using original thinking.

(highest level)    6. Evaluation: Pupil makes a judgment according to standards.

How can these six areas be used in teaching reading study skills?[18]

---

[17] B. S. Bloom, ed., *Taxonomy of Educational Objectives, Handbook I: Cognitive Domain* (New York: David McKay, 1956).

[18] Thomas C. Barrett has adapted taxonomies of objectives to provide specific types of questions for eliciting different levels of comprehension in reading (taxonomy of cognitive and affective dimensions of reading comprehension). T. Clymer, "What Is Reading? Some Current Concepts," in *Innovation and Change in Reading Instruction*, ed. H. M. Robinson National Society for the Study of Education, 67th Yearbook, pt. 2 (Chicago: University of Chicago Press, 1968), pp. 19–23.

Robert B. Ruddel has found that approximately 70 percent of teacher questions are at the factual- or literal-comprehension levels. Disturbed by the heavy reliance on factual questions, he offers a question-asking framework in which teachers ask pupils questions demanding recall of facts, interpretations, drawing of inferences, and application (transform or use the information obtained in a new situation). Ruddel's unique contribution is that his framework calls for asking high-level questions when teaching a range of reading skills such as sequence, cause and effect, main idea, valuing, and problem solving. In addition, he reports that four questioning strategies are most significant for developing the

**Recall and comprehension**   The recall and comprehension levels of thinking, which include remembering, translating, and interpreting, bear upon each of the other levels of thinking. Some assignments in thinking at these initial levels are:

1.   Locate Charles Dickens's *A Tale of Two Cities* in the card catalog; then find it on the library shelf.

2.   Read this story and then tell it in your own words.

3.   Read these directions for building a model ship.

4.   What kind of horse is this? How do you know?

**Application**   At the recall level of thinking, children are expected to know abstract information well enough to describe its use when prompted. At the application level, children are expected to use abstract knowledge without direct assistance. Application includes the skills of experimenting and constructing with knowledge, recording or reporting information, and the testing of skills. Some sample activities at this level might be:

1.   Make a diorama that illustrates the location of the pirates on *Treasure Island.*

2.   Plan a lesson to teach the Dewey Decimal System to another group of pupils.

3.   Tape-record the reading of a poem the way you think the poet meant it to be read.

**Analysis**   Although application activities make use of known facts in lifelike situations, the analysis level of thinking requires the taking apart of known facts and the understanding of the relationships of the parts that make up knowledge. The pupil using this level of thinking must be able to categorize, compare, and break down information into its basic elements. Some sample activities requiring analysis skills would be:

---

child's comprehension abilities. (1) *focusing* — posing a question that sets a purpose for reading, establishing a mental set; (2) *extending* — eliciting additional information on the same subject at the same comprehension level; (3) *clarifying* — returning to a previous response for further clarification, explanation, or redefinition; and (4) *raising* — asking the child for additional information but at a higher comprehension level. R. B. Ruddel, "Developing Comprehension Abilities: Implications from Research for an Instructional Framework." In *What Research Has to Say about Reading Instruction,* ed. S. J. Samuels (Newark, Del.: International Reading Association, 1978).

1. Study a graph of United States imports and determine which countries do the most trade with this country.

2. Analyze survey data from the school library to find out trends in reading of Newbery Medal-winning books.

3. Read the classified section of the newspaper and determine how many classifications it has. Are these categories sufficient, appropriate, and so on?

4. Read Robert Frost's poem, "Stopping by Woods on a Snowy Evening," and tell what fact of life the "woods" might be describing.

**Synthesis**  At the synthesis level of thinking, pupils are expected to put elements from many sources together into a new pattern or structure. This requires original thinking and creativity as well as the abilities of retaining information, using information, and taking information apart. Some possible synthesis assignments might be:

1. Choose a favorite poem and add another verse to it.

2. Write a recipe using favorite ingredients of five classmates.

3. Design a game to teach dictionary skills to other pupils.

4. Make a thesaurus of words defined by younger pupils.

**Evaluation**  The evaluation level of thinking, which requires the use of evidence-determining judgments, also includes the other four levels of thinking. The pupil may combine affective values, such as liking and enjoying, with cognitive behaviors, such as applying or creating with knowledge. You might assign activities similar to these:

1. Determine ten new books for the school library to purchase and be ready to support your recommendations.

2. Role play the court scene of *Johnny Tremain*.

3. Discuss *The Red Badge of Courage* from the point of view of a modern soldier.

4. Decide which reference tools will help you the most in studying famous artists, the history of coins, Africa, Chinese cooking, Edgar Allan Poe, and ecology.

### Teaching Study Strategies in Reading

**Preview**  Good readers do not try to absorb difficult new material with a single reading. Instead they preview the material to get a general overview of what they are about to study. A preview gives them purpose and direction, prepares them for the important ideas, and indicates how they should organize these ideas. Previewing involves forming questions and anticipating conclusions.

**Form questions**   When teaching previewing, ask pupils to look at the title and headings in the reading material (headings are the author's way to signal organization, content, and major thought divisions) and to predict or anticipate the content that will follow the headings: "Take the headings in this article and invert them into questions. You may use the five W's plus *how* to frame questions — who, what, where, when, why, and how? — or you may want to make up factual questions (What are the characteristics of _____?); questions about relationships (How does it relate to _____?); questions about values (Are the ideas good or bad?); or questions about problems and solutions (What is the problem? How does the author solve the problem?)."

**Anticipate conclusions**   Other ways to preview are to ask pupils to read the first and last paragraphs first so that they can see what conclusions to expect, or to present some final paragraphs and ask pupils to select the answer that best represents the conclusions; for example,

> We wonder if television is not becoming blind to freedom, pushing us in unhealthy ways, or are we getting what we want from it? Sad to say, police dramas on television put the safety of people before the freedom of individuals.
> a. Television is only concerned with stopping crime.
> b. Television puts the need for catching criminals ahead of civil rights.
> c. Crime will be reduced when the police have more freedom.

**Answer questions**   Once pupils have their questions, they should read to answer them. A most appropriate activity is to give children short articles, have them pose questions, and read for the answers. Questions should be answered in the order in which they occur. The learners should be encouraged to be aggressive in reading the author's ideas, challenging the author to give adequate reasons and evidence.

Ask pupils to *scan* to answer a particular question. Verify whether they can disregard the reading of irrelevant information.

**State aloud or write the answers to questions**   Putting answers to questions in one's own words clarifies the ideas gained and fixes them in memory. Give children paragraphs with questions and ask them to state aloud in their own words the answers after reading the paragraph; for example,

What are we learning about solar energy?
Many people believe that solar energy is too expensive and that it does not work. However, a recent survey shows that many solar heating systems are low in cost, work, and that an increasing number of families are depending on the sun for their energy needs.

**Test**  Learners must test themselves on whatever they want to remember. If they want to remember details, they should recall details. This self-testing should occur at varying times — hours, days, weeks — after reading the material. Often such testing suggests a need for reviewing pertinent parts of the material.

### Techniques for Taking Tests

Children can apply several techniques to do well on comprehension sections of reading tests, and there may be times when teaching such techniques will be in the child's interest. Activities for developing "testwiseness" include: (1) practice in recognizing the four standard types of questions used on standardized tests — main idea, direct information, inference, and vocabulary; (2) practice in translating main idea questions like "What is the author's main point?" and "What is the best title for this passage?" into the more understandable question, "What does the paragraph talk about the most?" (3) practice with direct information questions by substituting words in the multiple-choice answers for words in the paragraph itself; and (4) practice with vocabulary questions by reading sentences with the new word substituted to make sure the syntax is correct ("that it sounds right").

Teachers may want to let children know the importance of (1) not doing anything until they know the instructions; (2) reading questions first and then going back to the passage to find the answers; (3) allocating time properly by answering all the questions they are sure of first and eliminating a few of the answers before guessing; and (4) making blind guesses — answering all items — since reading tests are usually scored on the basis of correct answers with no penalty for wrong ones.

### Activities for Stimulating Critical Reading

Critical reading requires that one make a judgment about the quality, value, accuracy, and truthfulness of what is read. To encourage critical reading, teachers must demonstrate that they are as much interested in *why* something is said as in *what* is said. Indeed they should be slightly suspicious of the author's biases. Pupils should be asked to check copyright data, the author's reputation, as well as to look for errors in reasoning, overgeneralization, oversimplification, and distortion. Relevant activities are:

1. Determining the accuracy of information; for example, comparing information in two science books or two history books; noting authors' disagreements about a particular topic or event — "Mars," "Westward Expansion."

2. Comparing something that really exists and something imaginary.

3. Differentiating between literal and nonliteral passages; for example, reading articles where the author "makes fun" of persons, manners, or things through satire.

4. Detecting an author's bias; for example, asking children to determine how the author feels about different characters in a story and then to explain how they could tell the author feels that way.

Group discussions are one way to examine critically underlying assumptions. To analyze critically a story, article, essay, or the like requires a perspective. For example, if you analyze particular syndicated editorial writers from a conservative political perspective, the results will differ from those obtained by using a liberal political orientation. Hence it is necessary first to clarify which perspective will be used in the analysis. Without such a clarification, misunderstanding occurs between pupils and teacher.

Specific analysis should follow identification and clarification of the perspective. Pupils should be asked to identify important items in the writing as seen from the chosen perspective and then compare the writing with other writings based on what they do and do not find.

The following is a recommended teaching sequence:

| *Teacher* | *Pupils* |
|---|---|
| 1. What perspective will you use in examining this writing: religious, economic, social, political, other? | State the point of view or orientation to be used. |
| 2. What are the advantages and disadvantages of using this perspective? | Give reasons for using the perspective. |

| | |
|---|---|
| 3. What points in this writing are most important to your selected perspective? | Identify and describe aspects of the writing that bear on the perspective. |
| 4. From your selected perspective, how does this writing compare with other writings? | Compare and contrast the writing with other familiar writings. |
| 5. What important points have not been mentioned in the article that should have been from your perspective? Why are these points important? | Identify missing points and tell why these points are important. |
| 6. On the basis of the above, what do you think about the writing? | Evaluate the writing. |

Having analyzed a selection from one perspective, ask pupils to analyze from another position. Further, pupils should be asked: (1) to consider the probable consequences of ideas expressed; (2) to compare their judgment of the particular writing with judgments made about other writings (are pupils consistent in their judgments?); and (3) to state how the authors know what they purport to know (is it from personal experience, authoritative source, or other?).

The critical reading skills of distinguishing factual statements from opinion and recognizing propaganda techniques can be developed through many types of activities as illustrated in the sample lesson.

*Sample Lesson — Fact versus Opinion*

OBJECTIVE
Given sentences, the child can distinguish between those that state opinions and those that state facts.

ATTENTION
The three sentences on the board are from advertisements. Choose one of the products you might be likely to buy and tell why.

1. X candy is best.

2. Y candy has more sugar than brand Z candy.

3. Olympic winners eat Z candy.

PRESENTATION
Think about the product you have selected. What does this advertisement statement tell you about your product? Have you learned

something new from this ad? Do you think the ads are telling the truth? Which statement(s) is using a propaganda technique? What is the technique — name calling, glittering generalities, card stacking, testimonial, plain folks, prestige identification, bandwagon? Can the advertiser prove any of these statements? Note that both statements 2 and 3 can be facts but that only statement 2 is relevant to the choice of the product. Statement 1 is an opinion. If one could indicate the criteria that makes something "best," then a statement about the criteria would be factual in that it permits one to check out the extent to which the product meets the criteria.

Facts can be verified; opinions can't. Facts help people form opinions. Some advertisements give us facts and let us determine our own opinion. Other advertisements give us someone else's opinion. Many statements of opinion are introduced with expressions like: *I think, It seems to me, We believe.*

PRACTICE

1. Compare two newspaper editorials with respect to their use of propaganda techniques. (analysis)
2. Write an advertisement for a product you have created using opinions, then write one giving only facts. (synthesis)
3. Write a letter to an editor telling him what you think of a given editorial and why. (evaluation)

## Summary

This chapter dealt with methods and activities for teaching reading at different levels. Methods are ways of proceeding — often systematic procedures according to principles. Activities are arrangements devised in harmony with fundamental principles for facilitating particular reading skills.

The initial part of the chapter described how one's style of teaching is affected by a personal orientation toward learning. Different conceptions of the teaching role were presented. The second part featured general principles of instruction and illustrated how these principles apply in lesson plans aimed at given reading skills. The third part addressed the question of what a teacher might do in teaching reading at readiness, primary, middle, and upper grade levels.

In the readiness section of this chapter, both activities and models for teaching reading prerequisites were described in detail. The suggested practices relate to the development of the experiential back-

ground for learning to read and the high priority readiness skills —
auditory and visual discrimination.

The section treating reading instruction in the primary grades
emphasized how to teach word recognition skills, explaining both
synthetic and analytic methods as well as describing a method that
combines the two — *patterning.* Methods for teaching structural and
contextual analysis were introduced along with a variety of classroom
activities.

The portion focusing on reading lessons at the middle level offered
strategies for the teaching of reading comprehension. The value of
imagery and attending to the child's schema were stressed. Sample
lessons and activities to teach reading comprehension were included.

The section on teaching reading at higher levels illustrated how to
teach study skills and the skills of critical reading. Models and sequences for developing critical reading competencies were delineated.

In brief, the content of this chapter can be regarded as a
resource — suggestions, models, strategies, lessons, instructional principles, activities — to use in designing your own reading instruction.
The breadth of treatment, including an account of the strengths associated with the varied procedures, is intended to increase your
knowledge of both the practice and the principles of teaching reading.

# Self-instructional Exercises

### Exercise 1. Identifying Methods for Teaching Word Recognition

Put a mark by the answer that best illustrates the method.

1. Synthetic method
   a. _____ Children begin by noting how sentences are made up of
      words and words of syllables.
   b. _____ Children begin by noting how phonetic elements (letter-
      sound correspondences in spelling patterns) form words.
   c. _____ Children begin by learning to recognize a number of fre-
      quently used words.

2. Initial teaching alphabet (ITA)
   a. _____ Children read a uniform phonemic representation using
      uppercase letters of the alphabet.
   b. _____ Children read colors and diacritical marks cuing sound val-
      ues of letters in the alphabet.

    c. \_\_\_\_ Children read new symbols that augment letters in the alphabet.

3. Whole word phonics

    a. \_\_\_\_ Children are asked to look at words already known (*cat, fat, fan*), to say the words, and then to tell what sounds and letters are alike in the words.

    b. \_\_\_\_ Children are asked to look at the word *fat* and to remember that it is a cvc (consonant-vowel-consonant) word.

    c. \_\_\_\_ Children are asked to look at the word *fat* and sequentially to say the word with the teacher, fuh-aah-tuh.

4. Substitution method

    a. \_\_\_\_ Children are asked to look at the word *fat* and say whether it takes a long *a* or short *a* sound.

    b. \_\_\_\_ Children are told, "This word is *cat;* so what word is this?" (*fat*)

    c. \_\_\_\_ Children are told to write down words that rhyme with *cat*.

5. Structural analysis method

    a. \_\_\_\_ Children decode a new word after being prompted by a familiar, meaningful word part.

    b. \_\_\_\_ Children decode a new word after being prompted by the syntax of the sentence.

    c. \_\_\_\_ Children decode a new word by sounding out the initial letter and blending it to the phonogram that follows.

**ANSWERS TO EXERCISE 1**

1b. Synthetic methods, such as the alphabet and phonetic method, begin with the smallest possible units — letter-sound — and build up to syllables and the word.

2c. The ITA contains forty-four symbols — one for each phoneme (twenty-four taken from the traditional alphabet with *q* and *x* omitted). Children synthesize the letter-sound combinations to form words.

3a. The whole word method calls for the learner to identify words by sight. This approach is then combined with the phonic method by which the word or words are examined for their letter-sound elements.

4b. The substitution method usually means changing a beginning consonant or blend while keeping a particular phonogram the same (*at, cat, sat, fat*). Sometimes, however, word substitution is used for teaching contextual

analysis: "Which words can we put in this sentence? The boy is _____."
*ran big happy*

5a. Meaningful word parts (morphemes) include root words, affixes, and inflectional endings. When one recognizes a meaningful part in a new word, it is a prompt in recognizing the new word; for example, *walk* (familiar root word); *walked* (a new word composed of familiar word and familiar inflectional ending).

## Exercise 2. Matching Purpose and Activities for Comprehending Printed Material

Put a mark by the option that best completes each sentence.

1. The ability to use context clues for the meaning of words comes chiefly from lessons where pupils:

   a. _____ Study word prefixes and suffixes.

   b. _____ Group lists of words under different categories or headings.

   c. _____ Recognize word definitions within sentences, regardless of form.

2. The ability to recognize conclusions may be improved by lessons where pupils identify the function of these words:

   a. _____ thus, so, therefore, consequently

   b. _____ yet, nevertheless, however, although

   c. _____ moreover, furthermore, also, likewise

3. Outlining is most often undertaken to help pupils improve their ability to:

   a. _____ Determine cause and effect.

   b. _____ Interpret an author's style.

   c. _____ Recognize main ideas.

4. The ability to determine main ideas in passages is taught by having pupils:

   a. _____ Read a passage and then pantomime what they "saw."

   b. _____ Read a passage and then create a title for it.

   c. _____ Read a passage and then ask them to predict what will happen next.

5. A teacher has children characterize paragraphs on the basis of patterns such as *shared experience* (use of personal pronouns),

*question-answer* (use of question as a title), and *opinion-reason* (use of such phrases as "as I see it"). The teacher is helping children:

a. _____ Note important details.

b. _____ Recognize author's purpose.

c. _____ Identify paragraphs that restate the essential ideas.

**ANSWERS TO EXERCISE 2**

1c. The meanings of unfamiliar words are often given within the sentence itself; for example, "A cold front or *air mass* over the entire region." "The *papaya*, a large yellow fruit, is eaten in Mexico." The study of prefixes, suffixes, and roots is an excellent way to increase word comprehension but is not a context clue.

2a. Pupils are learning that words such as those given in item (a) mark the beginning of important ideas, summaries, and conclusions. Words in item (b) signal a change in thought — a negation of what has been said before. Words in item (c) signal that more is to be added to the thought expressed.

3c. Separating main topics from supporting details is taught through outlining.

4b. A title should capture the essence, theme, or most important point in a passage.

5b. Each paragraph pattern signals a purpose — to entertain, to inform, to persuade, and so on.

## Exercise 3. Choosing the Most Effective Study Skill Activity

Put a mark by the best completion of each sentence.

1. The most effective reading study skill is:

   a. _____ Reading assignment material several times

   b. _____ Outlining all headings before reading a chapter

   c. _____ Posing questions from headings before reading

2. A teacher who illustrates the concepts of directional lines, degrees, scale, and legends is preparing a child to read:

   a. _____ Graphs

   b. _____ Maps

   c. _____ Tables

3. The most effective technique for teaching an index is to:

   a. _____ Study the Dewey Decimal System.

    b. _____ Explain the *Readers' Guide.*

    c. _____ Have pupils look up topics in indexes.

4. Which of the following questions should be asked first when teaching children to read graphs, tables, and charts?

    a. _____ Questions demanding extrapolation

    b. _____ Questions with answers

    c. _____ Questions requiring judgment

5. A teacher who has pupils recognize organization patterns — a chronological pattern (events are in a time sequence), a spatial pattern (gives rise to mental pictures), and an enumerative pattern (ideas are numbered or lettered) — is trying to help pupils:

    a. _____ Evaluate materials.

    b. _____ Understand cause and effect.

    c. _____ Follow the writer's organization.

**ANSWERS TO EXERCISE 3**

1c. Posing questions and reading to answer them is the most effective study technique.

2b. In teaching maps, the teacher would draw attention to elements such as: concept of degree (compare to a circle), scale (compare to a building plan), legend (compare to words). In teaching the reading of a graph, table, or chart, the teacher would draw attention to the title, the values that are being compared, and the meaning of symbols.

3c. Opportunity to practice using an index is directly related to learning how to use an index.

4b. The drawing of inferences and the making of judgments depend on facts given in the passage.

5c. Recognition of the organizational structure indicates the reason why the passage was designed and makes it easier to derive meaning from the material.

# Selected Readings

Berg, Paul C. "There Was A Door to Which I Found No Key," *Resources in Education* 14, no. 2 (February 1979): 49. ERIC Ed. 15 9625.

    This paper suggests that certain teaching practices may discourage pupils from reading: visual aids that are similar in format to television, prepackaged materials that are irrelevant to individual needs, programmed materials used to the exclusion of interesting reading materials, and language tapes that cause listening confusion. Accordingly, the author recommends that teachers base reading instruction on pupil needs and interests, allow for skill practice in a meaningful context, build a program based on guided free reading, and stimulate creative responses to reading.

Ewing, James M. "Attitudes of Pupils to Reading," *Resources in Education* 14, no. 2 (February 1979). ERIC Ed. 159 624.

The author regards attitudes to reading as well as components of beliefs, experiences, interests, expectations, and the like that contribute to the child's disposition to reading.

Examples of attitude components include: how much the pupil looks forward to reading, the extent to which the pupil is prepared to share his reading experiences, the child's preferences for types of reading material, the pleasure the child derives from reading, how relevant the pupil feels a reading task to be.

Other factors contribute to the pupil's attitude toward reading such as his or her relationship with the teacher, the attractiveness of the reading material, the degree of support from the teacher, and the relationship between reading instruction and other classroom activities.

Internal factors bearing on the child's disposition to read include such examples as the child's preconception of what reading is and the extent to which the child considers himself successful in reading.

The author describes techniques for assessing attitude — scales, self-reports, interviews, semantic differentials, and repertory grids. He concludes with the interesting proposition that teachers might place more emphasis on factors related to positive attitude formation, focusing more on creating situations that will appeal to the child than on the reading task alone.

Koenke, Karl. "Motivation and Reading," *Language Arts* 55, no. 8 (November/ December 1978): 998–1002.

The author reviews studies of human motives and reports of school practices aimed at increasing pupil involvement in reading. Some of the suggestions for teachers are to create reading lessons that take into account the personal needs and attitudes of the pupils, to make pupils aware of their successes, to use pupils with high achievement standards as models for others to imitate, and to use folklore and poetry for helping pupils understand themselves while developing their reading interests.

Ripley, William H., and Blair, Timothy R. "Characteristics of Effective Reading Instruction," *Educational Leadership* 36, no. 3 (December 1978): 171–174.

The authors cite studies leading to the following conclusions: Effective teaching patterns differ by topic and grade level. In second grade reading, for example, the pattern that allows teachers to be accessible to pupils for instruction, work in small groups, and use a variety of materials is effective. In fifth grade reading, teacher practices that sustain interaction about ideas are most effective. These variables related to reading achievement gain are time engaged in moderately difficult tasks, content covered, and provisions for direct instruction.

Travers, Robert M. W., et al. *Children's Interests.* Kalamazoo, Mich.: Western Michigan University, College of Education, 1978.

A review of research on children's interests with respect to the problem of identifying universal patterns that have implications for curriculum design.

Travers identifies the origin of interests in the child's search for structure in the physical and social environment. He explains both the cognitive basis of childhood interests and the development of social interests from infancy to ten years of age. Childhood interests related to later adult and occupational interests are also identified. Learned helplessness and other phenomena that bear upon the failure to develop interest are treated.

Among the educational implications that follow from the conclusions are the importance of giving the child control over aspects of the learning environment; helping children find objects and events in which they can discover structure and learn to understand; introducing the child to stories such as fairy tales that both illuminate the structure of society and help the child attain the confidence to function within the society; and letting the child pursue self-selected study so that enduring interests develop.

# 8

# Diagnostic
# Evaluation

The thought of evaluation may conjure up many mental pictures. Perhaps you recall the weekly reading tests administered to you during your childhood. After the regimen of a week of repetitious oral reading, perhaps one session was graded. Did you make errors? Did you understand the materials? Could you answer the questions put forth so routinely by the teacher? There were formalized tests as well — paper and pencil reading tests — that your teacher devised. After all, the teacher needed some measure of student progress to know what grade to place on each student's report card. Perhaps the word *evaluation* also makes you think of the published reading tests required by the state and given each year in late May or early June. Or perhaps your heart pounds at the sound of the word because *evaluation* suggests *teacher evaluation.*

Although there are many forms of evaluation, we are not concerned in this chapter with the evaluation that tests students' performance to assign letter grades, nor with the evaluation of teachers. The focus of this chapter is on testing (or acquiring diagnostic and evaluative information) for the purpose of improving reading instruction.

From our point of view, diagnostic evaluation is inextricably linked to instruction. Effective reading instruction cannot take place unless evaluation precedes it. Diagnostic evaluation should be used to provide information regarding a child's progress and should be done continually throughout the school year.

Understanding the purpose of evaluation is important, as is an appreciation of the various instruments for collecting evaluation information — tests. Tests serve different purposes. In large part, the purposes of the various tests are determined by the intent of the test makers — by their frame of reference and reasons for testing.

What kinds of instruments might be used for evaluating students? We have purposely chosen the word *instruments* instead of the more commonly used *tests* because we want to emphasize that evaluation is not restricted to the use of printed tests. Diagnostic evaluation incorporates information from a range of sources — from formal testing and informal reading exercises to accidental observations that supply information relevant to the teacher's instructional purposes. The purpose is to obtain information that can help in devising appropriate instructional sequences for each child.

In this chapter, we discuss the various categories of diagnostic evaluation, and for each of them, we describe the major instruments used for gathering data.

## Reference Bases

Evaluation requires that a comparison of some type be made. In essence, the thing being used as a basis of comparison forms a frame of reference (the *reference base*) for making judgments about achievement. What makes evaluation so confusing to many people is that beginning teachers are usually bombarded with evaluation techniques, books, and measures that make no attempt to state the kind of reference on which each test is based.

Think for a moment about the various kinds of evaluations that you encounter and are aware of every day and that might be found in the typical classroom.

> On the last vocabulary test I gave, Johnny's score was better than 60 percent of the students in the class. (The reference base is the scores of other students in the same class. The comparative standard is the "normal" or typical performance of classmates.)

> Johnny is reading at the third-grade level. (The reference base is again a comparison with other students, but in this instance, the "normal" performance is defined not as that of Johnny's classmates but as that of a larger, nationwide sample of students who took the test.)

> Johnny has not mastered the consonant digraph *th*. Given new words beginning with this cluster, he cannot pronounce them. (The reference base is a specific skill or objective. This objective might be an appropriate one to teach.)

Johnny's reading demonstrates a lack of understanding of contextual cues; for word recognition he relies on phonic strategy, even when it is not appropriate. (The reference base is not a particular set of instructional materials. Instead it is the use of instructional strategies, which may be applicable to a number of different objectives.)

Johnny seems to do better at oral reading when he is not called on first. (None of the reference bases discussed previously is the basis for comparison. Instead the statement constitutes evaluation information about Johnny himself and his personality characterisics — perhaps nervousness at being first or some other individual or situational factor.)

Johnny believes he is doing well in reading. (The reference base is pupil self-evaluation — the student's own placement of value on his performance.)

The preceding examples showed five categories of diagnostic evaluation that are valuable for teaching reading. These categories are norm-referenced, criterion-referenced or objectives-based, materials-referenced, strategy-referenced, and person-referenced evaluation. As can be seen in Table 8.1, each category of diagnostic evaluation points to a particular referent, answers different questions, and uses specific kinds of instruments.

# Norm-referenced Evaluation

The typical published standardized test that you are likely to be familiar with is called a *norm-referenced test.* The Stanford Achievement Test and Metropolitan Reading Test are examples of norm-referenced tests. These tests compare a student's performance with that of a so-called norming population — a sample of students who have taken the test at its inception. Such tests are constructed to provide scores that can be translated into percentiles or grade-level norms that compare a student's performance to what is normal; in this case, *normal* means typical. If a student obtains the same number of points as the typical (meaning statistically average) student in the third grade, his or her performance is described as being at the third-grade level. A set of standards has been established in each norm-referenced test to translate scores into grade levels.

### Survey and Diagnostic Norm-referenced Tests

One of the two types of norm-referenced tests is the *survey test*, which is designed to provide a general indication of reading ability. Typically,

**TABLE 8.1**  Categories of diagnostic evaluation with examples of questions and instruments

| Category | Reference base | Questions | Instruments |
|---|---|---|---|
| Norm-referenced evaluation | Other students (the norm group) | How well is this child doing compared with others? | Standardized tests (survey test, diagnostic reading) |
| Criterion-referenced or objective-based evaluation | Instructional objectives | What objectives has this child mastered? | Objectives banks with criterion-referenced tests |
| | | What skill should be taught next? | Customized computer criterion-referenced test |
| | | | Criterion-referenced tests that accompany basal readers and management systems |
| Materials-referenced evaluation | Instructional materials | What reading materials are appropriate for this child? | Informal reading inventory, cloze test |
| Strategy-referenced evaluation | Instructional strategies | What reading strategy does this child need to use? | Miscue analysis |
| Person-referenced evaluation | The individual student | What is the child's preferred learning style? | Mills Learning Methods Test[a] |

[a] Robert E. Mills, *The Learning Methods Test* (Ft. Lauderdale, Fla.: The Mills Educational Center, 1970).

this is the kind of test the school district might require that all students take (or all third-grade, fourth-grade, sixth-grade students, or whatever). Examples of tests of this type are the Comprehensive Test of Basic Skills (CTBS) and the Iowa Test of Basic Skills (ITBS). Survey tests are used for purposes of accountability. The school board simply wants to know, "How are our students doing compared with other students nationwide?" This is an appropriate use for norm-referenced survey tests. However, data from this kind of test is subject to some misinterpretation: the objectives implicit in the survey test may not correspond precisely with the reading objectives of the school district, and there may be problems related to the appropriateness of the norming population as a basis for comparison with the school district. Yet the comparison to a norm population is precisely the reason for these tests.

Most norm-referenced survey tests give subscores in each of several categories: vocabulary, comprehension, and so on. The technical manual for most norm-referenced tests also has a *table of speci-fications* showing the number of items represented on the test in each of the subcategories measured by the test. Typically, however, these tables of specifications do a poor job of noting precisely what it is they are measuring. Thus, the use of survey tests for diagnostic evaluation purposes is fraught with danger. The norm-referenced test score, and even the subtest scores, provide very little information that is helpful to teachers in diagnosing the specific instructional needs of children.

The other type of norm-referenced test is the *diagnostic norm-referenced test*. Examples of such tests are the Diagnostic Reading Tests and the Stanford Diagnostic Reading Test. Diagnostic norm-referenced tests typically are designed in the same way as the survey tests. Both kinds of tests use the national norming population as a reference. However, diagnostic norm-referenced tests supposedly emphasize the identification of specific skills and abilities. What is most important for you is the extent to which the scores reported within the test measure aspects of reading attainment that are relevant for your instructional purposes.

Norm-referenced diagnostic tests generally are more specific in the skills and abilities that are evaluated than are survey tests of general reading ability. For example, the Stanford Diagnostic Reading Test measures scores for comprehension, vocabulary, auditory dis-crimination, syllabication, and beginning and ending sounds. Thus the test scores are more likely to correspond with the dimensions of read-ing instruction considered relevant by the teacher. Because of the time and money spent on the tests, diagnostic tests are typically used only in situations requiring in-depth supplementary information on stu-dents having reading difficulty.

Several criticisms have been leveled against norm-referenced tests of both types. One criticism relates to the way in which items are selected or rejected for the test. For the test makers to develop the norms in a norm-referenced test, students must receive a range of different scores. It is not possible to develop grade-level expectations if all students or most students get approximately the same total score. Thus the specific test items *discriminate* (show differences) among students. If a potential test item is missed by all or most of the students, it is typically eliminated from the test since it does not properly discriminate. Moreover, if an item is answered correctly by all students, or most students, it, too, is eliminated from the test since it also does not help to show differences among students.

The process of eliminating such test items and replacing them with others that do discriminate may result in the elimination of test items that are very appropriate. The fact that all students are missing a particular item might point to a deficiency in instruction. In addition, the discriminating test items that displace them may be related to objectives that are not as relevant to reading.

Does this mean that the teacher should ignore all norm-referenced data as a source of diagnostic evaluation information? We think not. Although we would not recommend administering a survey test to obtain diagnostic data, neither would we recommend that the teacher ignore such data if it is already available. Since survey tests are routinely administered and even required in many states, the information they provide is available at the beginning of the year. (For an example of a class record sheet provided by the testing companies, see Figure 8.1.). This information, although not specific enough to be used in making individual instructional prescriptions for students, can nonetheless be used for certain decisions that are of concern to the classroom teacher.

In a general way, the norm-referenced survey data can indicate the grade-level reading ability of the students. Knowledge of the grade-placement scores can serve as an initial basis for placing students in reading groups. For this purpose, however, most teachers prefer to use the data available from survey tests only to confirm their own diagnostic assessment.[1]

## Criterion-referenced Evaluation

Criterion-referenced evaluation is the process of testing to obtain information related to a child's status on a predetermined objective or criterion of performance. The reference base in criterion-referenced evaluation (or objectives-based evaluation) is the extent to which the student has met an established objective, and judgments are made simply on this basis. How many other people have also attained the objective is irrelevant; the reference base is the objective itself and not the normative performance of others.

### Selecting or Stating Objectives

An essential element of criterion-referenced tests is the establishment of specific standards of performance, defined as the indicators of the

---

[1] Another procedure that might be used to obtain an estimate of the students' general reading level involves the use of graded word lists. Students are asked to read from cards, each with ten words at each grade level. The procedure and graded lists, called The San Diego Quick Assessment, yields an estimate of the child's grade placement in reading. See Margaret La Pray and Ramon Ross, "The Graded Word List: A Quick Gauge of Reading Ability," *Journal of Reading* 12 (1969): 305–307.

CTBS Comprehensive Tests of Basic Skills

# CLASS RECORD SHEET

| | | | | |
|---|---|---|---|---|
| TEACHER NO 1 | ◀ TEACHER | TEST DATE ▶ | 11/77 | COMPREHENSIVE TEST OF BASIC SKILLS, LEVEL 2, FORM S |
| SCHOOL NO 1 | ◀ SCHOOL | GRADE ▶ | 05.2 | BATCH 0003 |
| DISTRICT # 3 | ◀ CITY | STATE ▶ | ST | SCHOOL/GROUP NO. 001/001 PAGE 001 |

| NAME | A/B | LANGUAGE C/D | NON-LANGUAGE C/D | TOTAL C/D | READING: VOCABULARY 1 2 / 3 4 | READING: COMPREHENSION 1 2 / 3 4 | READING: TOTAL 1 2 / 3 4 | LANGUAGE: MECHANICS 1 2 / 3 4 | LANGUAGE: EXPRESSION 1 2 / 3 4 | LANGUAGE: SPELLING 1 2 / 3 4 | LANGUAGE: TOTAL 1 2 / 3 4 |
|---|---|---|---|---|---|---|---|---|---|---|---|
| STUDENT NO 1 | 8-11 | — | — | — | 32355 / 16 3 | 42425 / 37 4 | 37381 / 26 4 | 18323 / 5 2 | 43459 / 40 4 | 51453 / 50 5 | 38414 / 32 4 |
| STUDENT NO 2 | 11-09 | — | — | — | 46412 / 39 4 | 40417 / 34 4 | 43408 / 37 4 | 42445 / 39 4 | 46468 / 44 5 | 53461 / 54 5 | 50448 / 49 5 |
| STUDENT NO 3 | 11-01 | — | — | — | 32355 / 16 3 | 25329 / 8 2 | 28330 / 10 2 | 15300 / 3 1 | 35430 / 27 4 | 26368 / 13 3 | 27354 / 11 3 |
| STUDENT NO 4 3 | 11-09 | — | — | — | 58461 / 64 6 | 15256 / 1 1 | 37381 / 26 4 | | 35430 / 27 4 | 11271 / 1 1 | |
| STUDENT NO 5 | 10-10 | — | — | — | 27334 / 10 2 | 25329 / 8 2 | 24317 / 7 2 | 18323 / 5 2 | 37440 / 31 4 | 48445 / 46 5 | 35402 / 27 4 |
| STUDENT NO 6 | 11-11 | — | — | — | 32355 / 16 3 | 47441 / 44 5 | 39390 / 29 4 | 38429 / 32 4 | 35430 / 27 4 | 23350 / 9 2 | 30376 / 17 3 |
| STUDENT NO 7 | 10-02 | — | — | — | 29345 / 13 3 | 69504 / 71 6 | 49427 / 47 5 | 31397 / 21 3 | 35430 / 27 4 | 35411 / 29 4 | 34398 / 25 4 |
| STUDENT NO 8 | 10-10 | — | — | — | 40390 / 29 4 | 30366 / 17 3 | 35371 / 22 3 | 27380 / 16 3 | 28399 / 16 3 | 23350 / 9 2 | 26349 / 10 2 |
| STUDENT NO 9 | 9-11 | — | — | — | 36373 / 22 3 | 32377 / 20 3 | 34365 / 20 3 | 34412 / 26 4 | 18335 / 3 1 | 35411 / 29 4 | 28367 / 14 3 |
| STUDENT NO 10 | 10-02 | — | — | — | 34364 / 19 3 | 49448 / 47 5 | 41399 / 33 4 | 34412 / 26 4 | 65506 / 63 6 | 24359 / 11 3 | 37410 / 30 4 |
| STUDENT NO 11 | 10-08 | — | — | — | 32355 / 16 3 | 21301 / 5 2 | 24317 / 7 2 | 31397 / 21 3 | 21363 / 7 2 | 35411 / 29 4 | 29372 / 16 3 |
| STUDENT NO 12 | 11-06 | — | — | — | 49426 / 46 5 | 51454 / 50 5 | 51434 / 50 5 | 72507 / 65 6 | 40449 / 35 4 | 51453 / 50 5 | 50448 / 49 5 |
| STUDENT NO 13 | 11-10 | — | — | — | 25322 / 8 2 | 23315 / 6 2 | 22303 / 5 2 | 31397 / 21 3 | 20349 / 5 2 | 24359 / 11 3 | 25340 / 8 2 |
| STUDENT NO 14 | 10-08 | — | — | — | 38382 / 25 4 | 32377 / 20 3 | 35371 / 22 3 | 42445 / 39 4 | 43459 / 40 4 | 39428 / 37 4 | 43429 / 39 4 |
| STUDENT NO 15 | 10-01 | — | — | — | 23310 / 6 2 | 21301 / 5 2 | 20288 / 3 1 | 31397 / 21 3 | 26388 / 13 3 | 10238 / 1 1 | 16275 / 1 1 |
| STUDENT NO 16 | 12-09 | — | — | — | 14249 / 1 1 | 30366 / 17 3 | 21296 / 4 1 | 21344 / 8 2 | 24376 / 10 2 | 24359 / 11 3 | 24335 / 7 2 |
| STUDENT NO 17 | 10-03 | — | — | — | 38382 / 25 4 | 28354 / 13 3 | 33360 / 18 3 | 25363 / 12 3 | 30410 / 19 3 | 17317 / 4 1 | 23330 / 6 2 |

| NAME | MATH: COMPUTATION 1 2 / 3 4 | MATH: CONCEPTS 1 2 / 3 4 | MATH: APPLICATIONS 1 2 / 3 4 | MATH: TOTAL 1 2 / 3 4 | *TOTAL BATTERY 1 2 / 3 4 |
|---|---|---|---|---|---|
| STUDENT NO 1 | 24293 / 2 1 | 27337 / 12 3 | 29336 / 13 3 | 22290 / 3 1 | 33 333 / 16 3 |
| STUDENT NO 2 | 37365 / 20 3 | 34370 / 23 4 | 39385 / 29 4 | 37361 / 21 3 | 43 380 / 34 4 |
| STUDENT NO 3 | 36358 / 17 3 | 24320 / 8 2 | 49422 / 46 5 | 36357 / 19 3 | 30 315 / 11 3 |
| STUDENT NO 4 3 | 50410 / 48 5 | 27337 / 12 3 | 33354 / 18 3 | 41376 / 28 4 | |
| STUDENT NO 5 | 39371 / 23 4 | 27337 / 12 3 | 26317 / 9 2 | 32340 / 13 3 | 32 326 / 14 3 |
| STUDENT NO 6 | 51414 / 51 5 | 42399 / 36 4 | 26317 / 9 2 | 44387 / 35 4 | 38 359 / 25 4 |
| STUDENT NO 7 | 52419 / 54 5 | 38385 / 29 4 | 42398 / 35 4 | 49403 / 44 5 | 44 385 / 36 4 |
| STUDENT NO 8 | 34345 / 11 3 | 24320 / 8 2 | 19273 / 3 1 | 26306 / 5 2 | 28 304 / 8 2 |
| STUDENT NO 9 | 37365 / 20 3 | 14261 / 2 1 | 49422 / 46 5 | 34349 / 16 3 | 32 330 / 15 3 |
| STUDENT NO 10 | 29316 / 4 1 | 38385 / 29 4 | 42398 / 35 4 | 32340 / 13 3 | 37 356 / 23 4 |
| STUDENT NO 11 | 46389 / 34 4 | 24320 / 8 2 | 33354 / 18 3 | 36357 / 19 3 | 31 319 / 12 3 |
| STUDENT NO 12 | 39371 / 23 4 | 24320 / 8 2 | 26317 / 9 2 | 32336 / 12 3 | 43 381 / 34 4 |
| STUDENT NO 13 | 36358 / 17 3 | 24320 / 8 2 | 39385 / 29 4 | 33345 / 15 3 | 27 293 / 7 2 |
| STUDENT NO 14 | 41377 / 26 4 | 21301 / 5 2 | 23296 / 5 2 | 31331 / 10 2 | 36 351 / 22 3 |
| STUDENT NO 15 | 28309 / 3 1 | 21301 / 5 2 | 13222 / 1 1 | 18262 / 1 1 | 17 212 / 1 1 |
| STUDENT NO 16 | 39371 / 23 4 | 11239 / 1 1 | 23296 / 5 2 | 27312 / 6 2 | 24 271 / 4 1 |
| STUDENT NO 17 | 47394 / 37 4 | 34370 / 23 4 | 26317 / 9 2 | 37365 / 23 4 | 31 319 / 12 3 |

| NAME | REFR 1 2 / 3 4 | SCIE 1 2 / 3 4 | SOC ST 1 2 / 3 4 |
|---|---|---|---|
| STUDENT NO 1 | 36394 / 25 4 | 29360 / 15 3 | 26340 / 8 2 |
| STUDENT NO 2 | 33373 / 19 3 | 40409 / 32 4 | 37393 / 24 4 |
| STUDENT NO 3 | 36394 / 25 4 | 29360 / 15 3 | 29359 / 13 3 |
| STUDENT NO 4 3 | 25326 / 9 2 | 43423 / 38 4 | 40408 / 30 4 |
| STUDENT NO 5 | 25326 / 9 2 | 36394 / 26 4 | 29359 / 13 3 |
| STUDENT NO 6 | 44430 / 38 4 | 47436 / 44 5 | 37393 / 24 4 |
| STUDENT NO 7 | 40412 / 32 4 | 43423 / 38 4 | 26340 / 8 2 |
| STUDENT NO 8 | 33373 / 19 3 | 33378 / 20 3 | 22319 / 5 2 |
| STUDENT NO 9 | 29351 / 14 3 | 15280 / 2 1 | 33377 / 18 3 |
| STUDENT NO 10 | 18267 / 3 1 | 43423 / 38 4 | 33377 / 18 3 |
| STUDENT NO 11 | 25326 / 9 2 | 33378 / 20 3 | 14274 / 1 1 |
| STUDENT NO 12 | 58482 / 59 5 | 36394 / 26 4 | 33377 / 18 3 |
| STUDENT NO 13 | 22298 / 5 2 | 26342 / 10 2 | 14274 / 1 1 |
| STUDENT NO 14 | 22298 / 5 2 | 50448 / 49 5 | 26340 / 8 2 |
| STUDENT NO 15 | 22298 / 5 2 | 15280 / 2 1 | 22319 / 5 2 |
| STUDENT NO 16 | 29351 / 14 3 | 54460 / 55 5 | 40408 / 30 4 |
| STUDENT NO 17 | 25326 / 9 2 | 22322 / 7 2 | 14274 / 1 1 |

CHRON. AGE A/B C/D

GRADE EQUIVALENT 1 | 2 SCALE SCORE
NATIONAL PERCENTILE 3 | 4 NATIONAL STANINE

*TOTAL BATTERY INCLUDES READING, LANGUAGE AND MATHEMATICS/ARITHMETIC ONLY.

**FIGURE 8.1** Class record sheet.

Source: CTB/McGraw-Hill, Del Monte Research Park, Monterey, California, 93940. Reprinted by permission.

attainment of objectives. For some, these standards imply the necessity of first developing statements that depict precisely what the student would be able to do to demonstrate mastery (or achieve the standard). An example of a precisely stated objective (or "behavioral objective") is: The student will be able to pronounce correctly nine out of ten four-letter words containing a single long *a* or long *o* vowel sound and ending with a silent *e*. In theory, the notion is a good one. Attention by teachers to the consideration, determination, and precise behavioral statement of the objectives they have in mind for their pupils is certainly an excellent basis for commencing instruction. Further consideration of the ways of determining whether the objective has been mastered — the criterion-referenced test items — could only help teachers clarify their classroom purposes.

Carried by the tide of behavioral-objective enthusiasm, criterion-referenced tests have steadily engulfed the educational community. This has been a mixed blessing. Part of the problem with criterion-referenced tests is that they became popularized too quickly; with this popularization came mistaken notions of what they were and simplistic assumptions about the ease of their construction.

Criterion-referenced tests have much to commend them to teachers for diagnostic purposes. However, we would encourage the teacher of reading to use existing criterion-referenced test systems for the diagnosis of pupil needs, rather than devise their own criterion-referenced system. In our view, the results of individually devised criterion-referenced tests have not been rewarding, and the time that teachers spend on this effort could be spent far more profitably. A number of criterion-referenced testing systems in reading now marketed are worthy of consideration and use.

The first step for teachers using an existing criterion-referenced test in reading is to determine the objectives. Write the objectives for a reading course at a grade level you are familiar with or that you are about to teach. If you plan to use a basal text or reader extensively, examine the objectives stated by the text's publisher or implied in the grade-level materials. Make sure you consider the objectives that are implied but are not well stated or not stated at all. Perhaps your school or district has prepared objectives for the grade level you are teaching. They should be considered as well.

## Selecting a Criterion-referenced Test

Armed with some idea of the objectives of a reading program, reading teachers can take the next step in a variety of ways and select the criterion-referenced tests they will use. Consider some of the options available.

1. Some test-development firms list objectives for reading with matching criterion-referenced test items related to each objective; for example, Instructional Objectives Exchange (IOX), and Westinghouse PLAN (Program for Learning According to Need). Thus, a teacher might find the objectives listed that correspond with those that have been selected or devised. The items made available from this list can be supplemented by other items if desired.

2. Another available option is a computer-printed test based on the objectives selected. Some test development firms (for example, Science Research Associate's (SRA) System for Objectives Based Assessment in Reading — SOBAR) now allow teachers to select the objectives they want to have tested from a list of objectives (something like a menu) and to obtain a computer-printed test that looks like other published tests but is based on the objectives selected by the teacher. This option is undoubtedly too costly for a teacher to implement for a single classroom. Criterion-referenced tests prepared for a whole school or school district, however, are feasible.

3. Some publishers (for example, IOX and SRA) have available criterion-referenced subtests that consist of a single sheet of test items related to a single objective or to a small cluster of objectives. Thus, by using the test sheets, you can devise your own criterion-referenced test appropriate for the objectives you have selected.

4. Many publishers of basal reading series now provide criterion-referenced tests for each of the basal readers in their series. If the basal series is being used as the prime basis for instruction, associated criterion-referenced tests certainly have the advantage of using relevant instructional content. The problem is that many of these tests are poorly constructed and the extent to which they are really criterion-referenced is open to question. We urge you to examine them very carefully before using them.

5. A final example is presented to indicate a kind of criterion-referenced test that we suggest you definitely should *not* use. When a publisher has prepared a single so-called criterion-referenced test that purports to measure third-grade reading, for example, and your option is "you either buy the test or you don't," we suggest that you don't. One of the great strengths of criterion-referenced tests is that they are geared to the *specific* objectives of your program of instruction. When you find a test reputed to be "criterion-referenced" but that nonetheless claims to be an adequate indicator of all objectives for all reading programs, irrespective of approach or instructional series, suspicion is called for.

How do you know a "good" criterion-referenced test when you meet it on the street? Is it the angelic look? Is it the pretty pictures? Is it the layout? No! Maybe! And, partially! The first thing to look at is whether the objectives are well stated, clear, and unambiguous. If the objective, as stated, could be tested in any number of ways, this is usually a sign of the lack of a clear definition and of a sufficiently delimited objective. If test items are available in the sample materials, why not look at them and consider whether they correspond to the objective and whether they appear to be valid indicators of competence.

Something else you will want to look at in making a selection among various criterion-referenced tests is whether a sufficient number of items are available per objective. What is a sufficient number? This question has fostered a great amount of discussion (not to mention a great number of virtually unreadable technical papers) in the educational measurement community. Clearly, one item is not sufficient. You would not want, or be able, to make a judgment, based on one item, that a child has mastered the following objective: "Given a word that ends with a single consonant sound, the pupil will identify a word that has the same final consonant sound." Surely, if we were to suggest that you give fifty test items for each behavioral objective, you would throw up your hands in alarm and give up testing as hopeless. For the range of items per objective, taking into consideration not only technical questions but feasibility as well, we suggest the Woolworth Model (five and ten). Certainly no less than five items are needed. (Refer to the appendix for a list of publications that provide evaluations of criterion-referenced and norm-referenced tests.)

## Materials-referenced Evaluation

When the teacher wants to know what reading materials are appropriate for particular children, it is not enough to know that the child scores at the 3.2 grade level on the CTBS norm-referenced reading test, because grade placement scores may not correspond well with basal reader placement. Also knowing that Johnny has not mastered objective number 23 but has mastered objective number 19 on some criterion-referenced test still does not tell you whether he should be reading *Green Grows the Grass* or *Lovely Little Lilacs*. What is required is an evaluation that is specifically referenced to instructional materials such as a basal reader series. In this kind of evaluation, the reference, the basis for comparison, is the extent to which the child can read "successfully" and "profitably" (more on this later) from a given text.

Two instruments are commonly used in materials-referenced testing: the informal reading inventory and the cloze test.

## Informal Reading Inventories

An informal reading test or inventory is usually used for the purpose of learning about a child's reading level. Informal inventories typically consist of a reading passage the student is to read orally and some related comprehension questions to be answered. The term *informal* is derived from the fact that most of these tests, when they were first developed, were not administered or used in a standardized way. (That is, the statements made by test administrators and the way in which testing took place differed from school to school, classroom to classroom.) Today many informal reading tests have been published and are standardized in their administration, scoring, test construction, and other things. A typical example of a standardized, informal reading test is the Gilmore Oral Reading Inventory. To a great extent, tests of this type are not "informal" in the sense of lack of standardization, but they continue to be designated that way.

One of the advantages of using published reading inventories is that they are readily available and the teacher does not have to develop the instrument. A second advantage is that the procedures for test administration and scoring are usually well explained. The disadvantage, of course, is that the more standardized an instrument becomes, the more the test publishers need to be concerned that it will be useful in many situations. In turn, the more that this occurs, the less value the test may have as a source of information related to a *particular* set of instructional materials.

Most teachers will opt for developing and using a locally constructed, informal reading test that is directly relevant to *their* needs and to the specific instructional materials used. In developing such an inventory for an elementary school or for a classroom, the first thing to do is select appropriate passages for the inventory. Typically, the passages to be read are taken either from several readers representing a range of difficulty of materials used in the classroom or from materials that correspond very closely with those in the basal reader. The process of administering a series of such informal tests at different levels constitutes an inventory of a child's reading skills.

For now, let us present a simplified list of the steps you might follow for an informal reading inventory in your class.

1. Perhaps the school or school district has an informal reading inventory already constructed and geared to the reading-instructional materials available at the school sites. Why not check on this?

2. If no such inventory is available, consider developing one by yourself or with other teachers at the school.

3. Given the array of instructional materials available at the

school, select randomly one (or perhaps two) passages of about one hundred words. By random selection, we mean that the passage chosen should be picked in a way that it can be considered typical of the material in the book. It should not be chosen because it represents a unique challenge; nor should it be selected because it is especially interesting or appealing.

4. Next, you will need to frame some questions about the passage that indicate the student's comprehension. We recommend that a minimum of six questions be considered. Three of these may be factual — to be answered directly from information in the passage. Three may require that the student make an inference from what is in the passage.

5. Now are you ready to begin? What next? Before you decide, consider the following situation.

Picture yourself in the classroom. Imagine that you have taken a passage, sat individually in the corner with Susie, and had her read the passage to you. How will you know if Susie can read the material *successfully* and *profitably*? Suppose you had a passage of about one hundred words and Susie read every word correctly except one. You would certainly admit that she had read the paragraph "successfully." But would it be "profitable" for her to spend time reading more material at that same level of difficulty? Would it be instructionally beneficial? Probably not. Although Susie could read the material successfully, the experience is not likely to be profitable for her; she apparently can read the material quite well without assistance or instruction. Instruction using that particular material is not likely to benefit her greatly.

On the other hand, if we were to select a passage from more advanced material and asked Susie to read it, we might find that on this more difficult passage (also of approximately one hundred words), she failed to recognize or had difficulty with about fifteen words. In this instance, there is certainly no lack of new material to learn and benefit from. The question is whether the advanced material is likely to be so frustrating to Susie that her potential as a successful reader has been set back.

The key is to give Susie *precisely* the book she is capable of reading and learning from but that is not so difficult it will frustrate her. This problem was faced by E. A. Betts, who published what is still the standard for evaluation in informal reading tests. Betts described three reading levels:

1.  The independent level, at which children's word recognition and

comprehension are high and they are able to read the book largely by themselves

2. The instructional level, at which children are unable to read the material independently but can read with the teacher's assistance and instruction

3. The frustration level, at which the material is so difficult that if it is used for instruction, the children will be frustrated

The criteria established by Betts[2] for the determination of each of the levels is as follows:

| Level | Word recognition | Comprehension |
|---|---|---|
| Independent | 99% correct | 90% correct |
| Instructional | 95% correct | 75% correct |
| Frustration | 90% correct | 50% correct |

The informal reading test works by the process of *successive estimation*. At the start of each inventory, you select a passage that you anticipate to be somewhat easy for the child. This, of course, also has the beneficial effect of starting the test on a positive note. (Billy will feel good about himself.) An appropriate starting point can be determined either from the results of standardized norm-referenced tests given the prior school year or from other information available in the child's records. The process might be continued until a passage is reached that the teacher believes is the appropriate instructional level based on the criteria of 95 percent correct in word recognition or 75 percent correct in comprehension. The instructional level is reached when, in a typical passage of one hundred words, the child makes *approximately* five word recognition errors and answers correctly five of the six comprehension questions.

The kinds of things thought of as errors are mispronunciation of words, unknown words, substitution of inappropriate words for other words, reading extra words into a passage, repeating words, and omitting words or phrases. Alternatively, even if the child is recognizing more than 95 percent of the words in a passage, you might decide that the passage represents the child's instructional level if the comprehension is at or less than the 75 percent level (25 percent errors). Consider, for example, a case in which a student misses only two words in a hundred-word passage and yet misses three of the six comprehension

---

[2] E. A. Betts, *Foundations of Reading Instruction* (New York: American Book Company, 1946), pp. 438–485.

As Liz dashed toward the colt, she came to the barbed wire fence that had been put up to keep Nitwit away from the swamp. Duchess, Nitwit's mother, had never needed a fence. She knew the swamp and knew how to pick her way through it with special care. But Nitwit hadn't learned that lesson yet.

Liz saw that a fallen tree branch had pushed one of the fence posts to the ground. Nitwit had been able to step right over the barbed wire.

"If only Duchess had been here," Liz said to herself. "She would have watched her colt and kept him out of the swamp."

**FIGURE 8.2**   Informal reading inventory.

Source: *Keystones*, American Book Company Reading Program (New York: American Book Company, 1977), p. 160. Reprinted by permission of American Book Company, New York.

questions. Or consider the situation where a child makes seven word recognition errors but gets all of the comprehension questions correct. The nature of the teacher- or school-devised informal reading inventory demands a certain amount of judgment on the part of the teacher. If you understand the characteristics of an informal reading inventory and the Betts (rough) guidelines, we are confident that you will be able to adapt these to your needs in providing student evaluation information referenced to instructional materials.

An example of a teacher-made, informal reading test is found in Figures 8.2 and 8.3. You will note in Figure 8.2 that the student copy of the informal reading test consists of a passage to be read orally by the student. The scored examiner sample in Figure 8.3 includes a set of comprehension questions and a guide, based on Betts's criteria for determining the reading level of the passage for the student. Also included in Figure 8.3 is a key to the notation system used for recording student errors.

## The Cloze Test

Another materials-referenced evaluation procedure is called the cloze test. Like the informal reading test, the cloze test can be used for

**FIGURE 8.3**   Scored sample of an informal reading inventory.  ▶

Student's Name  *Sara Davis*

    As Liz dashed toward the colt, she came to the bărbed wire fence

that had been put up to keep Nitwit away from the swamp.  Duchess,

Nitwit's mother, had never needed a fence.  She knew the swamp and

knew how to pick her way ~~through~~ it with special care.  But Nitwit

hadn't learned that lesson yet.

    Liz saw that a fallen tree branch had pushed ~~one~~ *some* of the fence

posts to the ground.  Nitwit had been able to <u>step</u> right over the

bărbed wire.

    "If only Duchess had been here," Liz said to herself.  "She

would have watched her colt and kept him out of the swamp."


QUESTIONS

C 1. Why was a barbed wire fence put up?   (Factual)
        TO KEEP NITWIT AWAY FROM THE SWAMP.
C 2. How did Nitwit get out?   (Factual)
        SHE STEPPED OVER THE FENCE.
C 3. Why didn't Duchess need a fence?   (Factual)
        SHE KNEW HOW TO PICK HER WAY THROUGH THE SWAMP.
C 4. Why was Liz hurrying?   (Inference)
        SHE WANTED TO FIND NITWIT; SHE WAS AFRAID NITWIT WAS IN
        THE SWAMP.
C 5. What could happen to Nitwit?   (Inference)
        HE COULD GET LOST; HE COULD GET HURT IN THE SWAMP.
C 6. What might have been different if Duchess had been there?
    (Inference)
        NITWIT WOULDN'T BE IN THE SWAMP.


| READING LEVEL | SCORING KEY |
|---|---|

READING LEVEL

    Independent
    0-1 Oral Reading Errors
    0  Comprehension Errors
✓  Instructional
    2-5 Oral Reading Errors
    1  Comprehension Error
    Frustration
    6+  Oral Reading Errors
    2+  Comprehension Errors

SCORING KEY

Insertions = ∧
Hesitation over 4 seconds = **H**
Repetition = underline twice
        <u>pretty</u>
Self-correction = sc
Substitution = draw  line through
    original; write in substitution
  home       ă
  ~~house~~     pĭn


COMMENTS

*needs work on "ar" vowel sounds and fluency.*
*Good comprehension; oral errors didn't interfere*
*with meaning.*

estimating the difficulty children will have in reading material. Thus, it is a testing procedure that is primarily materials referenced; its use by elementary school reading teachers will be to determine the appropriateness of reading materials for given students.

The cloze procedure is appealingly simple and therein lies its advantage. To develop cloze tests for a book, the teacher needs only to select two or three passages, preferably from the front, middle, and near the end. Each of these passages should be about one hundred words long. For each passage selected, every fifth word should be deleted. You are left with readings in which every fifth word is represented by a blank space. Simple enough? That represents the total preparation of the test.

To administer the test, each child is asked to read a cloze test passage and to supply the missing words. You as a teacher (or a classroom aide or a parent volunteer) might present various reading passages to individual students and ask them to determine what the missing words are. A great part of the interest in cloze tests probably relates to the gamelike atmosphere it presents.

Experts disagree on the way that cloze tests should be scored. Some maintain that the exact replacement of words is not necessary and that provision of a synonym or of any other word that makes sense should be counted as a correct response. Cloze test purists, as well as the developers of the procedure, maintain that only an *exact* replacement may be counted as correct. We agree with the latter position, not because we are purists but rather because we believe that one of the main virtues of this procedure for classroom use is its ease of administration and scoring. Use of synonyms makes the scoring more difficult and takes away one of the procedure's great advantages. Only when exact replacements are used can cloze tests be easily scored either by the teacher, an aide, a school clerk, or a parent volunteer. W. L. Taylor has demonstrated that accepting synonyms as correct did not improve the performance of the measure; the easier scoring procedure provides a measure of the readability of the passages that is just as appropriate.[3]

When a student has read a passage and given responses, and the responses have been scored by the number of exact replacements that have been made, a judgment must be made from the score produced about whether the material was readable for the child. Based on statistical analysis involving correlation of scores with other known measures, the traditional standard for readability has been set at 45 percent of the missing words replaced correctly. That is, the passage is consid-

---

[3] W. L. Taylor, "Cloze Procedure: A New Tool for Measuring Readability," *Journalism Quarterly* 30 (1953): 415–533.

ered to be readable by the child if he or she is able to supply the exact replacement word approximately four or five times for every ten blank spaces. Some believe this standard may be high, and our judgment is that a 40 percent standard would be acceptable, providing that the exact replacement of words is maintained within the scoring.

One advantage of this procedure has already been noted — the ease of scoring. Another advantage, which is appropriate for elementary school teachers who may have no expertise in testing and evaluation, is the ease of constructing the test.

To give you a better opportunity to become familiar with the cloze procedure, we present a passage prepared as cloze test, in which you may attempt to supply the exact replacements for the missing words (see box). To offer a greater challenge and more of a sense of excitement to this exercise, we depart from the typical procedure of using materials from children's books (which of course you *could* read) and instead present a passage from a famous story by Edgar Allan Poe.

---

*A Teacher-developed, Cloze Reading Test.*

DIRECTIONS:   Read the following short passage and insert the missing words.

The room in which _____ found myself was very _____ and lofty. The windows _____ long, narrow, and pointed, _____ at so vast a _____ from the black oaken _____ as to be altogether _____ from within. Feeble gleams _____ encrimsoned light made their _____ through the trellised panes, _____ served to render sufficiently _____ the more prominent objects _____; the eye, however, struggled _____ vain to reach the _____ angles of the chamber, _____ the recesses of the _____ and fretted ceiling. Dark _____ hung upon the walls. _____ general furniture was profuse, _____, antique, and tattered. Many _____ and musical instruments lay _____ about, but failed to _____ any vitality to the _____ .

The exact replacement words are: I, large, were, and, distance, floor, inaccessible, of, way, and, distinct, around, in, remoter, or, vaulted (you probably didn't get that one), draperies, the, comfortless, books, scattered, give, scene. For the student who had some difficulty with this passage, we suggest that perhaps you have been reading too many standard educational tests and you ought to take time off to go back to reading some of the classics.

Source: Arthur Hobson Quinn and Edward H. O'Neill (eds.), "The Fall of the House of Usher," *The Complete Poems and Stories of Edgar Allan Poe* (New York: Knopf, 1958).

# Strategy-referenced Evaluation

Teachers want to know whether a child needs instruction in one or more strategies for recognizing words. Is the child relying only on contextual clues, word memorization, phonics, or structural analysis? To gain such information, we recommend the use of miscue analysis.

## Miscue Analysis

The miscue analysis procedure provides a basis for viewing the *pattern* of errors made by students in reading a passage. We have already discussed informal reading tests and their use in determining a child's reading level and noted that the basic practice is to record the number of errors made during the child's oral reading of a selected passage. Errors were of a number of types, including substitutions, omissions, insertions, and so on. In scoring reading inventories, the *number* of errors made by students is tabulated to determine an error rate for the passage. This error rate, thought of as a word-recognition score, is one of the major bases for determining the appropriateness of reading material for children.

About 1968 Kenneth Goodman conducted a series of U.S. Office of Education-sponsored research studies. Out of these came the notion that in the analysis of pupils' reading of selected passages, it is not relevant simply to indicate the number of errors made by the students. Rather Goodman believes it is imperative to consider these errors in a patterned and more structured way. In part, he believes that errors do not occur at random but follow patterns for students. This view led him to replace the word *error* with *miscue* and, more important, to think not only of the number of miscues but of the *nature and type* of miscues made by children during their oral reading.[4]

## Why Miscue Analysis?

At first, you might wonder why we are placing this discussion in a separate section, rather than treating it under the topic of informal reading tests and treating the miscue analysis devised by Goodman as another kind of scoring technique that might be used in the examina-

---

[4] Kenneth S. Goodman, ed., *Miscue Analysis* (Urbana, Ill.: National Council of Teachers of English, Educational Resources Information Center/Reading and Communication Skills (ERIC/RCS), 1973). Kenneth S. Goodman and Yetta M. Goodman, "Learning about Psycholinguistic Processes by Analyzing Oral Reading," *Harvard Educational Review* 47 (1977): 317–333.

tion of these tests. There is no question that the use of the Goodman miscue analysis procedure on an informal reading test presents an alternate scoring form for materials-referenced evaluation. The reading miscue analysis procedure could be used simply to determine whether a child can read a specific passage.[5] However, miscue analysis is intended to go beyond this kind of gross information. Indeed it would be an enormous waste of energy and time to use the miscue procedure simply for determining readability of a set of materials by a child (something akin to using a sledgehammer to split a pea).

The reading miscue analysis procedure was converted into a formal inventory in the Reading Miscue Inventory (RMI).[6] In this inventory, miscues are classified into nine categories to provide further insights into the nature of misresponses made by students. The categories include things such as dialect, graphic similarity, grammatical function, and semantic acceptability. For example, the miscue might be analyzed to determine whether it is a dialect variation, the extent to which the miscue looked or sounded like the appropriate word, or whether the miscue involved a semantically acceptable substitution. For each of the nine categories, questions are framed and the possible significance of each miscue type is considered.

It is precisely the way of scoring that makes miscue analysis different from other procedures. The change of scoring, in essence, creates a different purpose for the test. Implementation of the reading miscue inventory furnishes a descriptive profile of the reader's deficiencies with respect to specific reading strategies, although the RMI and miscue analysis in general are difficult and time-consuming to employ. Nonetheless, the procedure offers the promise of going beyond the provision of materials-referenced information and supplies information about a child's strategy in developing words. Unless the procedures are revised and simplified, it is not likely they will be used by classroom teachers. But knowledge of the availability of the procedure and instrument is an important part of the repertoire of even the beginning teacher of reading; perhaps the miscue analysis will be used only by the beginning teacher in consultation with district reading specialists. We believe that may be the case, but we also believe that the potential rewards are great.

---

[5] In fact, the passages used in the reading miscue analysis differ from typical passages selected for use in an informal reading inventory. The reading miscue-analysis procedure sets certain limits on the material that may be used. The length of a reading selection would be longer than most selections employed in informal reading tests, and other provisions describe further characteristics of the passage.

[6] Yetta Goodman and Carolyn Burke, *Reading Miscue Inventory Manual and Procedure for Diagnosis and Evaluation* (New York: Macmillan, 1972).

# Person-referenced Descriptions

As the name implies, person-referenced descriptions are statements about some characteristics of the individual student. Descriptive statements do not have standards of acceptability or of excellence. Students do not "pass" or "fail," do well or do poorly. Instead students are simply described in a number of important dimensions. One basis for description is the mental and cognitive aspects of students. Physical and emotional dimensions is another descriptive basis. A final descriptive basis is the self-judgments of students themselves.

## Mental-Cognitive Descriptions

One consideration in person-referenced descriptions is the child's preferred learning style — the modality most likely to be effective for a given child. Some children are thought to learn best visually. Some may learn best by hearing what it is they are to learn. Still others may require *kinesthetic* involvement to learn; this group profits by being physically involved through writing, using fingers, and so on.

We know some teachers who start the school year by giving a *learning modality test* to each student to determine the child's primary modes of learning so this information can be used as part of the diagnosis and prescription in the months ahead. Some of these teacher-made modality tests are quite simple. One of them involves the use of colored squares that are lined up and shown to the students for a few moments; then students are asked to match the sequence that was shown to them. This is primarily a test of visual memory. In a second part of the exercise, the auditory portion, the teacher recites a number of colors in a certain order and asks the students to repeat the order that was cited. In the test of the kinesthetic learning mode, students are given a somewhat longer list of items and are asked to write them down on a piece of paper. The exercise involves the replication of the written list on another piece of paper, without seeing the original written list.

Other cues should be watched for in determining the preferred learning modality of children. Visual learners may close their eyes and attempt to picture the thing that is to be remembered. Audio learners might be observed moving their lips slightly or whispering as they try to memorize. Kinesthetic learners might use their fingers or simulate writing in the air as an aid to their memory. Teachers who do not want to devise their own learning modality test might examine the Mills Learning Methods Test obtainable from the Mills Educational Center, Ft. Lauderdale, Florida.

Another aspect of mental-cognitive descriptions is evident in brain-hemisphere studies. A good deal of current discussion can be found in the literature on the results of such brain-hemisphere research. Essentially, this research seems to show that the extent to which persons are oriented toward using one of the two hemispheres provides an indication of their learning tendencies. People whose left hemisphere is dominant tend to be more analytic and rational and people whose right hemisphere is dominant are thought to be more creative and holistic in their thinking.[7] An easy way to obtain a rough estimate of a child's left- or right-hemisphere dominance is to ask a question: the left-hemisphere-dominant children will move the pupils of their eyes to the right; the right-hemisphere-dominant children will move the pupils of their eyes to the left. Although this is not a completely accurate test of brain-hemisphere bias, it does provide the teacher with a possible indication of learning tendencies.

Many teachers may decide they do not want to collect learning modality data on all students. But it is nevertheless important to recognize these potential sources of information so the meaning of characteristics observed during normal classroom instruction will not be lost. In fact, informal data on preferred learning modalities might well be acquired by teachers in the course of their regular observation of students.

## Physical-Emotional Descriptions

Physical and emotional factors are also important considerations when evaluating a child. What is a child's general physical health? Are there indications of inadequate nourishment? Does the child get drowsy, possibly because of a lack of sleep? Is the child temperamental or do other characteristics seem to require special handling?

Two obvious physical factors that influence reading success are vision and hearing. A child must see the print clearly to read it correctly. Teachers need to be alert to signs of possible vision problems, such as holding a book very close to one's face or squinting when reading from the chalkboard. Good hearing is essential for a child to be able to discriminate sounds, an important reading skill. A child who frequently does not respond when spoken to, who often appears distracted during class discussions, or who speaks loudly even during normal conversations may be manifesting symptoms of a hearing im-

---

[7] J. S. Chall and A. F. Mirsky, eds., *Education and the Brain*, Seventy-seventh Yearbook of the National Society for the Study of Education (Chicago: University of Chicago Press, 1978). M. C. Wittrock et al., *The Human Brain* (Englewood Cliffs, N.J.: Prentice-Hall, 1977).

pairment. A teacher who suspects a child of having a vision, hearing, or other health-related problem should refer the child to the school nurse or doctor for further evaluation.

Despite visual and auditory acuity, a child may still have difficulty with some reading tasks due to perceptual problems. *Perception* refers to the way information received by the senses is organized and processed by the brain. In sighted children, vision and hearing are obviously the two senses most involved in the reading process. A child who has a visual perception problem may look at the word *saw* and, despite normal vision, perceive the letter order as w-a-s and read "was."[8] An inability to state correctly whether two distinctly different sounding words presented aurally are the same is a sign of a possible problem with auditory perception. A child with a perceptual-motor disorder may have difficulty copying words or may be extremely clumsy.

If a child displays symptoms that lead a teacher to suspect a perceptual problem, the teacher first should refer the child to a school nurse or doctor for an examination. The possibility of a physical disorder (such as impaired vision or hearing) causing the problem needs to be determined before proceeding with an assessment of perceptual abilities. If after the physical examination the perceptual evaluation is warranted, the child should be referred to support personnel trained to assess perception, such as the school psychologist or a learning disabilities specialist.

Emotional and personality factors may also influence children's learning. Children who are extremely shy may resist reading aloud in a group, and errors when doing so may result more from anxiety than from reading problems. We are not advocating that you attempt to become a junior psychiatrist or school psychologist, but instead that you observe and record simple information that might be relevant in the teaching of reading. Are certain children nervous when called on first? Do they work best in groups composed primarily of boys or girls? Do they perform better in smaller groups or larger groups? Do they have quick tempers? Are they easily frustrated and upset by challenging activities? You need to take a child's temperament into consideration when interacting both instructionally and personally with that child. Children with signs of severe emotional disorders should be referred to the school psychologist or counselor for assessment.

---

[8] Recent studies have shown that children who mistake "b" for "d" or "saw" for "was" do so not because these figures are literally misperceived but because these children have difficulty remembering their names. See Frank R. Vellutino, "Alternative Conceptualizations of Dyslexia: Evidence in Support of a Verbal-Deficit Hypothesis," *Harvard Educational Review* 47 (1974): 334–354.

Speech is another area of concern. Children may refuse to participate in oral reading due to speech problems. Do certain children stutter or stammer when speaking? Do they frequently mispronounce words? Do they have difficulty pronouncing certain letter or letter-combination sounds? These are all symptoms of possible speech disorders. Children with speech problems may need speech therapy and should be referred to your school or district speech specialist for evaluation.

## Self-judgments

Richard De Charms makes the point that students attain the greatest motivation when they function as their own evaluators.[9] Self-evaluation occurs in all situations. It is a very natural tendency. We constantly are aware of our status, our achievements, and our attainments. When some students in a classroom get an 88 percent on a teacher-made test, they may view that as either a magnificent achievement or a miserable failure depending on their conception of who they are, what they are capable of, and what their own aspirations are as well.

Self-judgment always takes place, but in some instances, it is inhibited by the extent to which external evaluators have already made a value judgment. The way in which a piece of test information (such as a test score or the percent correct on a test) is viewed by students is partially determined by the evaluative statements made by the teacher. Thus when teachers say "over 85 percent is an 'A' on this test," a child might tend to view an 88 percent score more favorably. In part, the child is removed from active participation in making a judgment about the extent to which the performance is satisfactory because the valuing has already been done. De Charms maintains that greater pupil involvement in the valuing process leads to greater commitment by the student and in turn greater motivation.

We may use diverse methods of collecting information about pupils' performance, and we may present this information in a multiplicity of ways, but inevitably the individual person must make a judgment. Two children receiving the same information may react with diametrically opposite judgments. Sometimes these are verbalized ("oh shoot!"), sometimes they are internalized (leading to inflated egos or adult ulcers). Likewise judgments made by oneself modify one's sub-

---

[9] Richard De Charms, *Enhancing Motivation: A Change in the Classroom,* in collaboration with Dennis J. Shea (New York: Irvington Publishers, distributed by Halsted Press, 1976).

sequent judgments. Feelings of defeat and insignificance may nurture reinforcement of that view. Feelings of success, importance, and self-confidence may provide the basis for future growth and reading improvement.

## Summary

In this chapter the major aspects of diagnostic evaluation have been discussed. The purpose of diagnostic evaluation is to provide information that can lead to improved reading instruction. We pointed out that evaluation is not confined to the use of printed or published tests: it includes a variety of sources of information to find out what skills each child already has and what skills he or she needs to acquire.

Since evaluation is a process of comparison, the basis of comparison forms a frame of reference. These reference bases help one to make judgments on performance, success, and the general status of the child's reading. We discussed five reference bases: the norm-referenced, criterion-referenced, materials-referenced, strategy-referenced, and person-referenced categories. These categories, with sample questions and instruments, are summarized in Table 8.1.

In norm-referenced evaluation, such as published standardized tests, the reference base is external normative standards such as the typical performance of students in the United States.

Criterion-referenced evaluation is based on measuring a child's attainment of a certain established objective (or criterion). Use of a criterion-referenced base carries with it the concern about which objectives have been achieved. The selection of a "good" criterion-referenced test requires ascertaining that objectives are stated clearly, that appropriate measures are chosen, and that there are a sufficient number of items per objective.

In materials-referenced evaluation, the object is to measure the extent to which a child can read successfully and profitably from a given text. The reference base for measuring success is the material itself. Two of the instruments generally used for materials-referenced evaluation are the informal reading inventory and the cloze test. In the informal reading inventory, the teacher listens to a child read specific preselected passages from a text, notes the number of errors, and asks questions to check comprehension. The cloze test is a relatively simple procedure in which two or three passages of about one hundred words in length are selected and every fifth word is deleted. The child is asked to supply the missing word.

In strategy-referenced evaluation, an attempt is made to discern whether a child needs instruction in one or more strategies for word recognition. The use of miscue analysis is recommended. In this method, the emphasis is on not only the number of errors or miscues but the nature or type of these errors. In the Reading Miscue Inventory, the miscues were classified into nine categories. The scoring process is involved and the test is time-consuming to administer. However, this does provide the teacher with an additional diagnostic tool in determining appropriate instructional strategies for individual students.

Person-referenced evaluation is not comparative but is a diagnostic tool in which children are described by their capabilities and needs. Teacher observations are often helpful in understanding the reading needs of children: Do they perform better in small groups? Do they often volunteer? It is also useful to note whether children function better as oral, visual, or kinesthetic learners.

Learning tendencies were discussed as they relate to whether children are right- or left-brain-hemisphere dominant. Children's learning will also be influenced by their vision, hearing, speech, and general health. In addition, children always engage in some form of self-evaluation. How children see themselves is important. It is essential to foster positive feelings in a child; these good feelings serve as a basis for future growth.

The total reading diagnosis of children encompasses all evaluation techniques from the externally devised tests such as norm-referenced tests to the individual informal observations made by the classroom teacher. It is important that you be aware of these information sources to make more comprehensive diagnoses.

# Self-instructional Exercises

### Exercise 1. Determining the Child's Reading Level Placement from Different Diagnostic Procedures

In each of the following cases, indicate the level of text that should be used for *instructional* purposes.

1. Mike was given a cloze test composed of three passages. Each passage was drawn from a different grade-level text. The results were first-grade passage, 90 percent; second-grade passage, 70 percent; third-grade passage, 50 percent. Mike should be given a:

   a. First-grade text

   b. Second-grade text

   c. Third-grade text

2. Sarah read aloud several paragraphs of varying grade difficulty while the teacher recorded Sarah's errors in pronunciation — an informal inventory. The results were third-grade paragraph, 95 percent accuracy; fourth-grade paragraph, 90 percent accuracy; fifth-grade paragraph, 75 percent accuracy. Sarah should be given a:

   a. Third-grade text

   b. Fourth-grade text

   c. Fifth-grade text

3. Chris answered a number of comprehension questions following the reading of passages on an informal inventory. The results were first-grade passage, 90 percent; second-grade passage, 80 percent; third-grade passage, 60 percent. Chris should be given a:

   a. First-grade text

   b. Second-grade text

   c. Third-grade text

4. Meg was given the San Diego Quick Assessment, which is a graded word list presented on cards, ten words to a card. Meg was asked to try every word on several cards. She began with the card for grade 1 and proceeded through card 3. These were the results: grade 1 word list, 100 percent accuracy; grade 2 word list, 90 percent accuracy; grade 3 word list, 80 percent accuracy. She should be given a:

   a. First-grade text

   b. Second-grade text

   c. Third-grade text

**ANSWERS TO EXERCISE 1**

1c. A cloze score of 35 percent is equal to 70 percent on a multiple-choice comprehension test. Scores between 45 and 55 percent of the possible total indicate the instructional level. A score of 55 percent or better (using every fifth word delete) is similar to the 90 percent level on multiple-choice comprehension tests indicating the independent level.

2a. If a child makes two to five pronunciation errors in every one hundred running words, it indicates that the material is instructional for the child. If more than five errors are made, the material is too difficult, and if there is only one error in every one hundred words, the child can handle the material independently.

3b. If a child comprehends material at 75 to 80 percent accuracy, it indicates that the material is instructional for the child. Below 75 percent comprehension, the material is probably too difficult. Ninety percent comprehension or more indicates that the material is suitable for independent reading.

4c. The grade level is ascertained by noting the grade level on which the child misses two or more words.

### Exercise 2. Interpreting the Child's Performance on Diagnostic Tests of Word Recognition

Look at the marked passages indicating how the child read them. Then put a mark by the inference that is warranted by the data.

1. Many dogs (dog) learn to work for man. A good work dog is not hard to train. But a trainer (train) must work with him from the time he is just a pup. The child needs help with:
   a. Structural analysis
   b. Phonetic analysis
   c. Basic sight words

2. What? You don't want to try it? (What you don't want to try it.) The child needs help in:
   a. Recognizing words that signal questions
   b. Interpreting the meaning of different word order
   c. Interpreting punctuation

3. The broadcast (boardcast) was heard in the little village. The child may need help with:
   a. Initial consonants
   b. Consonant blends
   c. Vowel digraphs

4. The Indian threw his bow and arrow ($\bar{a}$ / row). The child needs help with:
   a. Phonetic analysis
   b. Structural analysis
   c. Contextural analysis

#### ANSWERS TO EXERCISE 2

1a. The child needs to learn how to decode the inflected form of familiar base words.

2c. The child needs to learn how punctuation signals intonation patterns such as pitch and pauses.

3b. An inability to decode the letters *br* may indicate a problem with blends.

4c. The child should be taught to use context as a clue to pronunciation. He or she already knows the *ow* pattern option as /o/.

### Exercise 3. Judging Diagnostic Procedures

Read the following dialogue and then answer the questions appraising the teacher's practices.

*Author*: OK, class. We've had some opportunity to look at the various instruments that are used for diagnostic evaluation. I've described the frame of reference and how that can be used as a basis for depicting the various kinds of evaluative instruments in terms of the function that each one serves. And we talked about five basic frames of reference for testing instruments. You may remember that our discussion focused on norm-referenced testing, criterion-referenced testing, and materials-referenced testing, which included informal reading tests and cloze tests used for placing students on particular sets of instructional materials. We also discussed miscue analysis in assessing the relevance of employing different reading strategies. A final category of reference base we discussed during these sessions was person referenced. I pointed out that everything is to some extent person referenced, but that one could also look at information related to describing the pupil in terms of himself or herself, without reference to anyone else. This kind of person-referenced evaluation produced information that would help us make instructional decisions about better ways of teaching that particular child. I also pointed out that we ought to consider ways to help pupils make judgments about themselves to control their own behavior.

Now, let us turn to an examination of some of the things you do in your classrooms. The description of diagnostic instruments presented to you here may look good in theory but the actual teacher in the classroom probably wouldn't use all of them or might place different emphases on the various diagnostic instruments. Let's now consider some of the ways in which you do diagnostic evaluation in your classroom. Ok, who's first? Betty? Let's see now, you're a second-grade teacher, right? What kinds of things do you do in your classroom?

*Betty Benson*: I feel most fortunate to be in a good school where a major source of help for the teacher is a district-constructed, developmental reading program. As a part of this program there are placement tests to be given to students when they first arrive in September. These are called entry-level tests. All students take these tests, even if they aren't new to the school. For those students who are continuing students we are able to have a cross-check on a teacher's judgment from the previous June. And, then, we can also find out what students remember or have forgotten over the summer.

*Author*: What kinds of tests are these entry-level tests?

*Benson*: The entry-level tests are from the developmental reading program; there are test sections on decoding, vocabulary, and comprehension — with a few questions in each of these categories.

*Author*: These are given at the beginning of the school year?

*Benson*: Yes. And then from that entry level, we can zero in on a specific skill, perhaps.

*Author*: Who administers the entry-level tests?

*Benson*: The teacher. I do.

*Author*: You do. At the first week of school?

*Benson*: Yes, and I have to do most of it in small-group situations, so that means I have to organize the other children into other kinds of activity.

*Author*: How much testing time does it take?

*Benson*: Well, it probably takes about one-half hour for about one to fifteen children, and then I have to do some more the next day.

*Author*: I see. So it takes you about two to three days.

*Benson*: Yes. That's right.

*Author*: In terms of the reference bases we discussed earlier, how would you classify these entry-level tests?

*Benson*: They are criterion-referenced tests. There is a stated number of answers that must be correct to achieve competency on an objective.

*Author*: And so there are specific, stated objectives for the second grade and for overlapping grades?

*Benson*: Yes.

*Author*: And the tests are keyed to those objectives? How many items are there per objective?

*Benson*: Four to about six.

*Author*: How do you as a teacher use the diagnostic-evaluation information that you get from this test?

*Benson*: Well, I have a reading inventory sheet for every child in the room and I record what that child has done on the diagnostic test so it will, then, enable me to prescribe and to organize into groups the different pupils according to what they need. I sometimes group by a common skill that they need to work on, like the long vowel sound. If I have three or four children that need that particular skill, I'll group them together. If there happens to be a case where one child is at a different level and needs to be worked with on an individual basis, then I'll work with that child individually or have my aide or a volunteer work with that individual child until he or she can master that objective and be with the group. So, in other words, it allows for the grouping of children as a teaching strategy or working with the children individually.

*Author*: I see, so it's helpful, then, for you, for purposes of grouping. Now in terms of the materials you would use for conducting the instruction related to the objective that has not been attained, what materials do you use? Are the objectives of this district-made, criterion-referenced test compatible with your basal reader series, or do you use some other kind of supplementary materials?

*Benson*: We use all of these things. There are workbooks published with the program. Say the child is in the second grade working on step 13 with long vowel sounds. In that case, there would be a workbook that would provide appropriate practice for that particular skill. Then, in addition to that, we are fortunate because the reading resource teachers have put together all the materials that would be available to teach that long vowel sound. In other words, there are manipulative types of games for the teaching of that sound, and there are audiovisual activities — tapes and slides.

*Author*: Is there any other kind of diagnostic instrument you use during the course of the school year?

*Benson*: Yes, I use informal types of diagnosis where a child reads to me a certain paragraph and I keep track of how many words he or she misses — to determine reading ability, fluency, speed, and so on.

*Author*: Are the informal reading inventories you use teacher-made or are they published instruments?

*Benson*: Usually I select passages from the textbook and prepare my own questions. On some occasions, I have used published inventories.

*Author*: When do you conduct this kind of diagnostic evaluation?

*Benson*: I like to do it periodically — at the beginning and then as we move along with particular skills, I do it again, say after five weeks. I do diagnostic evaluation of this type whenever I think it is an appropriate time.

*Author*: The purpose of this informal reading assessment is what?

*Benson*: It not only allows a student to find out what skills he or she needs to work on but helps to strengthen the pupil's self-image, so the child will feel that someone cares about his or her reading ability, cares enough to work with the child for a while; and it helps a pupil to know what kinds of materials he or she can read easily, so the child can then select appropriate materials to read during free periods.

*Author*: Wouldn't the child already know that from the reading group he or she was in or from the basal reader the child was on, or from something of that sort?

*Benson*: I would give the pupil material other than the basal so the child would have another type of material. It might be similar to the basal in terms of syntax and vocabulary.

*Author*: I see. So you would do that for a leisure reading type of material to induce the child into recognizing that this is something he or she could read independently?

*Benson:* Right.

*Author*: In what way do you use information from diagnostic evaluation in making decisions about children?

*Benson*: With a beginner, I am mostly concerned with whether the child is having trouble with initial letters. Does a pupil have any word attack skills? Were there some skills that we had missed teaching somewhere along the line? Is the child able to retain the kinds of things we've been teaching?

*Author*: Betty, I wonder if you could tell me about some of the ways you collect information or some of the kinds of person-referenced information that you collect.

*Benson*: I suppose that much person-referenced information is collected by my observation of the child in many different situations. Records of this kind of information have to be stored in my head until the end, or at least until there is a break when I can go and pick up a card and write a couple of anecdotal incidents to which I can refer later.

*Author*: What kind of information do you record or collect in your head?

*Benson*: Well, for a second-grade pupil, I'd want to know what the child is most interested in during learning center time, for instance. What types of activities has the child primarily been concerned with and enjoyed? Was it perhaps because the child was successful or was it because that was his or her interest? I want to find out about the interest level of the child. Then I can gear some of the materials in accordance with this particular interest. And if there is group activity, I want to record socioinformation such as: Did the child pair off with someone? Did the child like to work with groups? Did the child prefer to work alone? Was the child a loner? I can then use the information in arranging learning experiences that match the child's interests and perhaps extend those interests. I would record whether the child was squinting or whether there were indications of failure to hear. I would make note of indications of physical problems so I could refer the child to the nurse if necessary. I even notice things such as whether a child is particularly pale or looks anemic — especially if the child is having learning problems. I note, too, how a pupil talks to other kids: Is the child kind? Does the child have a chip on his or her shoulder? Does the child seem to be happy? I used to feel that children always had to be speaking in group situations but I think there's much to be said for good listeners as well.

*Author*: That was certainly helpful, Betty. Now, let's turn to another topic. I know that your school is in a Title I Program. You've mentioned it several times during the course of this semester. Undoubtedly some norm-referenced testing is part of the Title I compensatory education requirement and the reporting to the state. In what ways, if any, do you use this information diagnostically as a teacher?

*Benson*: I use the state-mandated, standardized test, the Comprehensive Test of Basic Skills, CTBS, as a pretest to find out if a child might be having problems in recognizing some of the words or in comprehending. I use it sort of as a pretest in planning for the next year, since the testing is done in the spring.

*Author*: I guess I'm getting old and my brain a little addled. Could you state that a little more simply so I can understand it?

*Benson*: We want to find out how well our schools are doing.

*Author*: Do you use the data from the pretest given in the fall in the same way?

*Benson*: We usually don't get the results back until late October or November. By then our students already would have been placed in reading groups and according to instructional materials. So the data would really be almost too late for any kind of diagnostic purpose. But we use it to confirm whether we are on the right track — kind of a validation of our previous judgments.

*Author*: I see, so when you get the scores back you might look at them, and say, "Oh my! I didn't realize that Johnny had done so poorly on this; here I've got him placed in the Beaver's reading group and, you know, it may be that that's too difficult for him." But recognizing that this is a norm-referenced test with all kinds of biases that are in norm-referenced tests, you wouldn't take it too seriously, but you'd use it as another kind of indicator to make you *think* some more about Johnny's reading group placement.

*Benson*: That's exactly right; you said it better than I did.

*Author*: OK, Betty, thank you very much. That was very helpful to me and I hope to your fellow classmates as well.

Answer these questions:

1. For which evaluation reference base did Betty Benson do no testing?

2. What kind of test, appropriate for materials-referenced testing, did Betty not use?

3. Do you think norm-referenced testing was valuable to Betty Benson as a source of diagnosis? Discuss.

4. How adequate were the criterion-referenced tests used by Betty? Discuss.

5. Was Betty Benson sensitive to the importance of developing pupil self-evaluation skills? Discuss.

6. How important is it to record all person-referenced information? What do you think a teacher can and should do in recording such information?

**ANSWERS TO EXERCISE 3**

1. Betty Benson did not indicate the use of any evaluation information from a strategy-referenced evaluation base.

2. Although Betty Benson used an informal reading test for materials-referenced evaluation, she did not indicate the use of a cloze test. This is not to imply, however, that both tests were necessary.

3. Certainly norm-referenced testing was not one of the most valuable diagnostic instruments available to Betty. However, as a source of readily available data collected for another purpose, Betty attempted to use the norm-referenced test data to confirm her prior assessments of students.

4. The criterion-referenced tests that Betty used were certainly very adequate to the extent that they provided diagnostic information that was integrally related to student learning systems. In fact, the materials Betty was using were a part of a skills-monitoring system (see the discussion on technology-based instruction in Chapter 2). One deficiency of the criterion-referenced testing system that Betty used was the number of test items per objective. Within the chapter we indicated that an acceptable number of test items per objective would typically be no less than five and perhaps closer to ten.

5. Apparently Betty was very sensitive to the importance of developing pupil's self-evaluation skills. She seemed to be very cognizant of this kind of evaluation information. You will note that she used the informal reading assessment not only as a source of materials-referenced information but also to help in building student's self-awareness.

6. It is undoubtedly not possible to record all person-referenced information collected by the teacher. It is important, however, to be systematic in the collection of this information. This is especially true with respect to person-referenced evaluation where sources are so varied and much of the data can be serendipitous or a function of the observation of normal activities. Does it all get recorded? Undoubtedly not. We would hope the teacher would record as much as is useful. More important, we hope the teacher would become sensitized to thinking of day-to-day occurrences as evaluation information.

# Selected Readings

Allen, Virginia F. "Riddle: What Does a Reading Test Test?" *Learning* 7, no. 3 (November 1978): 87–89.
    Allen describes the results of an analysis of the tasks demanded on a stan-

dardized reading test showing that many of the test items are not relevant to the kind of reading needed for getting information from the printed page. For example, only 60 out of 232 items on the test are designed specifically to assess reading comprehension.

Evidence also suggests that many pupils can handle the reading comprehension items but not perform satisfactorily on subtests such as auditory discrimination tasks thought to be prerequisite to reading comprehension, thereby indicating that the subtests are dubious instruments for measuring prerequisite skills.

The results of this study suggest that teachers should be wary of relying on standardized tests for guidance in designing remedial programs for below-grade level readers. Further, the study indicates that newspaper accounts of how well pupils read as measured by standardized tests may be misleading.

*Assessing Comprehension in a School Setting,* Linguistics and Reading, Series 3, edited by Peg Griffen. Arlington, Va.: Center for Applied Linguistics, 1978.

This book is to help teachers build reading tests. The tests are uncommon ones. They are not tests of subskills. Instead they focus on how the reader understands written texts. Further, the tests aim at providing information useful in designing instructional strategy for particular pupils. A careful reader of this book will learn how to prepare modified cloze tests appropriate for a wide range of children. Teaching suggestions are included for dealing with the kinds of miscues or deficiencies revealed by the tests.

"Reading and Measurement," *Reporting on Reading* 4, no. 5 (August 1978).

The entire issue of this publication contains articles on tests and the quality of reading instruction. One article focuses on the failure to recognize that some important educational objectives have no effective measures, and that some tests do not offer reasons for the results produced. Further, some tests are used in ways they were not intended, and the test results do not indicate *why* the child was or was not correct.

Another article describes the reading tests given in the 1979–1980 *National Assessment of Educational Progress.* These tests call for reading all types of material and grasping the meaning of words, sentences, and paragraphs. In addition, the tests attempt to measure the value children place on reading and literature. For example, children reveal whether they value literature as a source of enjoyment or a means to self-understanding or understanding the diversity of cultures.

Roettger, Doris, et al. "Validation of a Reading Attitude Scale for Elementary Students and an Investigation of the Relationship Between Attitude and Achievement," *Journal of Educational Research* 72, no. 3 (January/February 1979): 138–142.

The authors describe the development and validation of an instrument for measuring attitude toward reading and attempt to throw light upon the relationship between attitude and reading achievement. The investigators found little relationship. They explain that some children may think reading is important but dislike it because it is difficult; others who read well may not consider reading as valuable as other activities. They also speculate that the failure to find a relationship between achievement and attitude may be due to the fact that all aspects of attitudes have not been consistent or that the instruments used to measure attitudes are weak.

Weaver, Constance, and Smith, Laura. "A Psycholinguistic Look at the Informal Reading Inventory: Part II. Inappropriate Inferences from an Informal Reading Inventory," *Reading Horizons* 19, no. 2 (Winter 1979).

The authors discuss the kinds of inferences that may be inappropriately drawn from an informal reading inventory. They illustrate a number of ways teachers might misinterpret children's responses, such as assuming that substitutions indicate the child does not know certain words. Phonics errors may indicate a child is getting too much phonics instruction and not enough instruction in reading for meaning. Some structural analysis errors are not teaching errors but rather indicators that the child is a good reader.

# 9

# Meeting
# Special Needs

Everyone is special. However, in teaching reading some children seem more special than others. In typical classrooms, most children have about the same ability to learn to read from conventional instruction, although a few have much greater or much less ability. A normal distribution of an average fourth-grade class of thirty-two pupils, for example, would look like this:

|  | 1 Pupil | 3 Pupils | 7 Pupils | 10 Pupils | 7 Pupils | 3 Pupils | 1 Pupil |
|---|---|---|---|---|---|---|---|
| Mental age | 7 | 8 | 9 | 10 | 11 | 12 | 13 |
| IQ | 70 | 80 | 90 | 100 | 110 | 120 | 130 |
| Reading grade expectancy | 1st grade | 2nd grade | 3rd grade | 4th grade | 5th grade | 6th grade | 7th grade |

Grouping practices may narrow the range within a class. However, policies mandating integration of children from various socioeconomic backgrounds and mainstreaming (placing in regular classrooms) children with exceptionalities, including the retarded and emotionally maladjusted, mitigate against homogeneous grouping.

The dimensions that make a child special in learning to read are many, but the factors most frequently used to distinguish the special learner are low intellectual ability, emotional immaturity (such as

**285**

difficulty in paying attention), physical limitations (poor hearing, vision, and general health; and disruptive or disabled brain and neurological processes). Special learners are classified according to five general categories.

*Disabled readers* are children who perform below their intellectual abilities. Even a six-month lag between achievement and potential may indicate disability.

*Retarded readers* are pupils who are below grade level in reading for whatever reason, including poor teaching. Incidentally, Richard Allington found that teachers are more likely to interrupt poor readers than good readers who err when reading aloud. Good readers also get to read over twice as many words per lesson as poor readers.[1]

*Slow readers* are those who are below grade level in reading but are performing according to intellectual ability.

*Reluctant readers* are pupils who show erratic performance. Sometimes they read up to grade level but often do not. As might be expected, most suggestions for motivating such readers involve strategies that will give them a feeling of accomplishment and satisfaction: placing them with books that match abilities, encouraging them to develop individual purposes for reading, introducing a variety of reading materials, and reading orally to them.[2]

*Superior readers* are fast learners who have a voracious appetite for reading. Although many of these children rely on their own resources in learning to read, they still need instruction — conferencing, diagnosing, and teaching of reading skills as well as guidance in selecting reading materials and an opportunity to share with others.

Although this chapter has many suggestions for you to use in meeting special needs, we want to emphasize that the suggestions also are applicable to those who are not recognized as special. A desirable consequence of attending to those with obvious special needs is that one becomes more sensitive to the fact that most children have similar needs, albeit not to the same degree as the special children.

We have three types of suggestions: (1) *heuristics* — guidelines by which you can discover your own answers to questions about how to teach individuals with unique needs; (2) *extensions* — ways by which you can extend your capacity to meet the special reading needs of large numbers of pupils through innovations involving parents, aides, and tutors; and (3) *tips* — techniques that have been successful with poor readers.

---

[1] Richard Allington, "Are Good and Poor Readers Taught Differently? Is That Why Poor Readers Are Poor Readers?" *Resources in Education* 13, no. 9 (September 1978): 37.

[2] Jerry L. Johns, "Motivating Reluctant Readers," *Journal of Research and Development in Education* 11, no. 3 (1978): 69–73.

# Heuristics for Discovering Answers to Problems in Meeting Special Needs

Heuristics are methods for discovering answers to problems. A useful heuristic for generating creative solutions to problems of individual needs is to reflect on four options for treating differences in learning to read and to think of practices that fall within each of the options. These options are circumventing, reducing pressure, transvaluating, and closing gaps.

## Circumventing

Sometimes it is best to go around a deficit rather than try to remove it. The practice of teaching a blind child braille rather than conventional material is an extreme case. We do not expect many teachers to teach braille, but since many pupils lack perfect sight, it is useful to take a cue from those who instruct the blind and teach these children to employ tactile cues through kinesthetic techniques (such as tracing letter shapes in words). You may use sandpaper letters or merely write words or sentences in large cursive (handwriting) or manuscript (disconnected letters) style. Children then may trace the letters with their fingers, saying each word as they feel it. The use of several senses in tracing, touching, saying, and hearing offers an option to those who might not otherwise learn.

Similarly one can circumvent by teaching non-English-speaking children to read in their own language rather than English. Again, not all teachers are expected to teach reading in languages other than English; however, you can adapt and supplement materials to accommodate many learners with limitations in English. Nonreaders should not be deprived of participating in classroom activities. Their inability to read can be circumvented through games, movies, filmstrips, picture books, discussions, and the like, which also build their readiness for reading.

A radical but timely circumvention is seen in the practice of teaching parents, not just the children, to read. The evidence is strong that development of attitudes and achievement in reading are associated with the home background. Parent-training programs can affect parental behavior and thus indirectly influence the reading behavior of the child. When parents acquire desired outlooks and ways to share them with their children, reading instruction becomes more effective.

### Reducing Pressure

Children who sleep in the classroom because their parents make them stay up to do schoolwork under parental supervision feel pressure. The sleepy ones who stay up because they are having so much fun with their folks are not under pressure. It is not always easy to get parents to reduce pressure. Sometimes it requires only a suggestion to parents that their children should decide when they have had enough of a given instructional activity. Other times, the help of a trained counselor is necessary. Clinical help may be in order, too, for example, when capable children will not learn because they are angry with their parents.

Parents are not the only source of pressure. The classroom is sometimes a cause. Classroom pressure can be reduced by substituting competitive groupings with friendship, interest, and skill groupings; designing instructional games whereby pupils compete only with those of comparable ability; being sensitive to differences in learning styles by adopting methods consistent with the learners' expectations; and allowing learners to set their own criteria for successful reading performance.

The introduction of humor reduces pressure. Children's humor tends to be unrealistic. They enjoy puns, verbal juggling, silly jokes, and visual incongruities (dogs in overshoes). Such humor serves as a social signal to children that they can relax and free themselves from the burden of anxiety, confusion, and cruelty. Figure 9.1 is an example of reading material for reducing tensions while learning to read.

### Transvaluating

Transvaluating is finding worth in what has been previously disparaged. It occurs, for example, when teachers are daring enough to question their negative judgments about some aspect of the learners or the materials. The process is as follows:

State the negative judgment. For example: "Even though they are bright, those kids insist on reading their own story into the story on the page. Their lives are so circumscribed that they cannot accept the interpretations the author might have expected but must substitute their own matter-of-fact interpretation."

Reverse the negative judgment. For example: "These bright kids

**FIGURE 9.1**  Examples of humor in teaching reading.    ▶

Source: From *Insults, 2* by Irving Wasserman et al. *Interaction: A Student-Centered Language Arts and Reading Program*, James Moffett, Senior Editor. Copyright © 1973 by Houghton Mifflin Company. Reprinted by permission of the publisher. "No matter how important you are, you may get the measles" from *The People, Yes* by Carl Sandburg, copyright 1936 by Harcourt Brace Jovanovich, Inc.; copyright 1964 by Carl Sandburg. Reprinted by permission of the publishers. "Your mother should have thrown you away and kept the stork" from *Wipeout*, copyright © 1969 by Al Boliska. Reprinted by permission of Simon and Schuster, Inc.

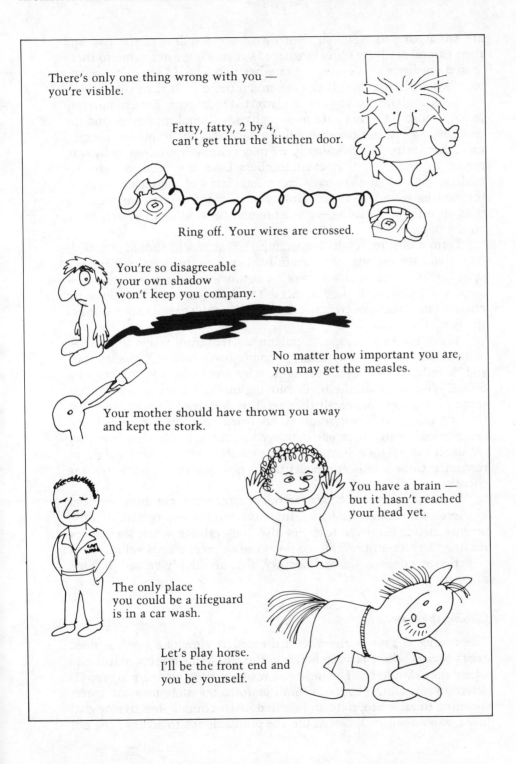

are attempting to establish their own understanding of the text and their careful scrutiny of its language is of much greater value to them than a teacher's version (mine) of what they should see in the story, even when the teacher (I) can see much more in it than they can."

Seek evidence to support the inverted judgment. For example: By looking closely at what authors actually say (literal meanings) and the way they say it, our understanding grows and our responses become more discriminating. Eventually we may perceive meanings, fully supported by the text, that even teachers have not seen. Sometimes readers spot things that have crept into texts of which the authors themselves were not aware. However, in making our own meaning from an author's meaning, we must remember to stick to what is there on the page.

Form a new principle. For example: Teachers (I) should give children credit for reading facts carefully. Teachers (I) should not impose their (my) own interpretations of an author's meaning upon the children, and teachers (I) should encourage their (my) pupils to look for unstated meanings, referencing their views to the literal expressions of the text.

There are many negative judgments requiring transvaluation — judgments about "bookworms," "comic-book readers," "escapists," and "vocalizers" are cases in point. Why not make a virtue out of a defect? Yes, even vocalizing or moving one's lips while reading has some advantages. We recall that good readers tend to vocalize when they encounter difficult reading and when they want to recall and comprehend material rather than read it quickly. Children who say words aloud as they learn to read probably will be better able to recognize these words subsequently in new sentences when reading silently.

Transvaluation can be seen in our acceptance of children who read in their own dialects and who substitute words appropriately while reading aloud. Sensitive teachers also transvaluate when they adopt reading instruction to reinforce previously unrecognized values, such as patience, cooperation, and docility, that are highly valued in some minority cultures.

## Closing the Gaps

The closing of gaps is allied with the deficit view of a need. A need exists because there is a gap between the children's present status and where they *should* be. The most promising way to close a gap is to (1) determine when the learner cannot perform on some measure corresponding to an appropriate and desired instructional objective or goal (need, assessment), (2) determine the prerequisites to achieve the objective (task analysis), and (3) give the learner guided practice in learning both the en-route and terminal tasks (appropriate practice). Most suggestions for teaching reading are focused on closing the gaps.

# Extension as a Way to Meet Individual Needs

A big worry of neophytes (and many experienced teachers) is how one person can simultaneously deal with nearly thirty individuals, each with a particular need. An important answer lies in *extension*, managing the resources and efforts of others. Successful teachers multiply their power by eliciting and directing the cooperation of parents, aides, volunteers, and tutors. The following discussion shows how this is done.

### Suggestions for Helping Parents Meet the Reading Needs of Children

**Giving parents reasons to help**  Why should parents help their children learn to read? Our country spends enormous sums of money preparing schools and teachers to teach this skill. Many people feel that parents have a big enough job keeping their children rested, fed, healthy, and happy and giving them moral training and direction for adult living. Let the teacher take care of their reading!

Of course, you as a teacher must accept responsibility for instructing children. But reading is a skill of communication. Parents who share in their children's reading development gain an understanding of their offspring; they see them as individuals with personal feelings and unique thoughts to contribute to the family and the world. To deny children the opportunity to share their reading knowledge with the family prevents them from fully understanding a major purpose for reading — communication.

**Sharing the range of ways to support reading**  Parents can help children learn to read. However, too often they feel frustrated in teaching their children and become angry and unhappy with the school or, worse, with the child. The teacher loses valuable reinforcement, and the child loses motivation. In creating a supportive relationship between home and school, it is most important that parent and child enjoy the reading activities they share. Thus, your invitation to parents must consider individual family preferences.

A parent can support reading in countless ways. Some parents enjoy listening to their child read daily; others feel more comfortable helping in the classroom; and still others help by keeping a record of the books the child has read. It is up to you to let the parent know the kinds of activities that will assist their child the most. If the parent and child do not work well together on certain types of activities, you should suggest optional activities.

**Telling parents what they may do to help**    Flyers, back-to-school nights, afternoon meetings, parent education courses, phone calls, personal notes, and parent-teacher conferences are all means of letting the parents know what the child is learning in reading and how to help. The more parents know about the reading instruction program, the more ways they will discover to help their own children. One first-grade teacher sends home an "Ideas for Helping Your Child with Reading" notice on the first day of school:

> *Ideas for Helping Your Child with Reading*
>
> Mark the ideas you want to use.
>
> _____ Read stories aloud to child.
>
> _____ Take child to public library and check out books.
>
> _____ Practice reading street and store signs.
>
> _____ Tell rhymes, riddles, and poems aloud.
>
> _____ Look at child's school work and let child explain it.
>
> _____ Tell child you know he or she is working hard and offer *praise*.
>
> _____ Visit child's reading class to see what your child is learning.
>
> _____ Talk with teacher regularly about child's reading progress.
>
> _____ Give child a place to work — to write letters that correspond to sounds and to look at books.
>
> _____ Play games that use simple reading.
>
> _____ Take child to different places — talk before the trip about what might be seen and after the trip about what was seen.
>
> _____ Let child help with household tasks — cooking, cleaning, gardening.
>
> _____ Explain in "child terms" when asked: "What does that mean?"

One third grade teacher sends home a weekly "Reading Newspaper," which tells what new skills are being taught, what is happening with the characters in the reading books, and timely ideas for supporting the children's reading growth. Parents are told of educational television shows, are given simple reading games to play, are told about the school's reading activities, and are informed about their child's reading matter.

Some parents will respond to an invitation for a night meeting to learn: "How should I ask my child questions about what he is reading?" "What do reading test scores mean?" "Comic books: good or bad?" Although not all parents will be interested in attending a parent education course or even a single meeting, those who do go are likely to tell other parents what they have learned.

> You are invited:
> Wednesday, 6 p.m., room 6,
> to learn about *Dynamite Dan.*
> See our reading diaries.
> Take home a reading game.

**How parents can make reading part of daily life**   In relating reading to daily living, parents can engage in hundreds of supportive reading activities. They can encourage children to read using telephone books, advertising flyers, television guides, food labels, menus, magazines, newspapers, the daily mail, recipes, how-to-make-things books, repair manuals, brand names, maps, signs, catalogs, and bulletin boards. When parents understand how important it is for children to apply reading in everyday life, they will let their children help with the shopping, learn to use a menu, and distribute the family mail. Older children can be encouraged to use maps, encyclopedias, newspapers, and magazines to plan trips, to decide upon purchases, and to affect other family decisions. Younger pupils might be asked to sort food items by label or find record albums by title. Even at the readiness stage, children can be led by parents to identify signs or the names of products using their knowledge of consonant sounds. Some pupils are able to read newspapers to their parents; most enjoy listening to their parents' reading.

**Helping parents communicate with children through reading**   One family encourages their child to read by leaving frequent notes. The messages start off simple, often with a picture attached, and then become more advanced according to the child's reading ability.

> I am in the garage.

> Sue,
> Choose one of these
> menus and make it for
> your lunch.
> Mom

We suggest that parents give books or magazines to each other and to their children for gifts, have a family reading time when all the members read and share what they learn, use the public library, and read school announcements out loud. Children who see and hear their parents reading often will be encouraged to use their reading skill in the same way. When asked the meaning of a word, a parent can look it up to demonstrate the value of a dictionary. Reading directions for household products out loud will indicate another purpose for reading, and sharing the Sunday comics will show that reading is for pleasure, too.

**How parents can relate reading to other communicative skills**  You should help parents understand that other skills, such as writing, spelling, listening, and speaking, also develop reading ability and help them create situations for practicing these skills. Writing thank you notes and letters to relatives, developing a critical analysis of a television program, and preparing a talk for a social club are cases in point. A very young child may be encouraged to form letters and make corresponding sounds: s s s s s s s s    s u z y

Later, the same child can be helped to write and read by (1) recording his or her "very own words" (concepts about which the child wants to talk) with a picture and caption; (2) dictating thoughts to a parent who writes them down to be read aloud by the child at a later time; and (3) recording pictorially and in writing while the parent helps with the spelling. For example:

cat                    My cat kills birds.

More advanced readers will pull together thoughts, ideas, and knowledge as they write. We suggest that parents listen to their children reading their writing aloud at each of these levels of achievement. Have children write letters regularly to friends or relatives and write their own party invitations, greeting cards, and other messages.

Listening and speaking activities strengthen phonics, vocabulary, and comprehension skills. Rhyming songs, word games, and "sound hunts" will help a very young child separate the speech sounds that must be distinguished to associate letters and sounds. Older children will improve their comprehension when they and their parents engage in vocabulary-building activities such as crossword puzzles and Scrabble. Parents can use television, radio, or phonograph records for teaching sequence, vocabulary, fact versus fiction, classification, categorization, propaganda analysis, and character development. For instance, parents can ask leading questions, explain unfamiliar terms, discuss situations, and encourage comments from the child about what he or she sees or hears in the media: "Is it a good title for a program? Why? Why not?" "What does this program teach you about the city? About food? About teachers, doctors, police, yourself?" "Does it make you sad? How? Glad? How? Mad? How? Scared? How?" or "What happened at the beginning?" (factual recall) "What did Tom's clenching teeth mean?" (interpretation) "How would you feel if you were in such a situation?" (empathy and appreciation).

Some libraries provide a telephone story. The child calls a special number and hears a story. When this service is available, parents can ask their child to explain the story heard on the phone. Parents of young children should also encourage them to use the phone to call for the time and to repeat it. Those with older children may let them place real orders over the phone. Tape recorders are useful for letting children hear how they sound while reading and for sharing their reading with others. Parents should make up stories with their children, tell familiar stories from memory, and play guessing games with different words. There is no end to the number and variety of enjoyable and helpful listening, speaking, writing, and spelling activities that parents can supply.

**Parents of retarded readers**   Parents of below-level or generally unsuccessful readers can do much to improve the achievement of their children. You must be especially concerned that parents of such children work closely with the school to help them develop a positive attitude toward reading. Although parents should be told (simply and clearly) what the child's reading needs or problems are, they should also be directed to praise the child's strengths. Notes, phone calls, and conferences must consistently include (1) what the child is working on, (2) what the parents can do to help, and (3) what successes the child is experiencing. For example:

---

Dear _____ ,
Joey is working on the 200 most-often-used sight words. He will have 10 new flashcards every Monday. Will you listen to him practice? He already knows 20 words!!
Mrs. F.

---

Parents of retarded readers need to recognize that their child is working extra hard at an important, exacting task. You can help these readers do this by arranging a classroom environment that encourages individual reading achievement. Success in the classroom carries over to success at home. Children share their feelings about reading at home. "Everyone else is in the big book and I'm not" gives parents little opportunity for positive reinforcement. "Listen to me read this story" or "I know all of these words" lets the parents and child celebrate success rather than failure.

At parent meetings, you can model ways of praising the child's work: "I'm proud of the way you work on reading. You said the sound for each of the initial letters in the words." Or "You are making progress every day. You now read three pages every morning instead of one."

**Keeping homework positive**   Homework should be a learning activity, not a punishment. To assign reading related work to children who have misbehaved or worked at a slower rate than others does not create motivation toward reading. Although the kind, amount, and frequency of assigned homework will depend on the reading level of the class or youngster, it is well to plan homework assignments that will let the child be successful in practicing a recently acquired skill. Do not upset the whole household. Children may ask parents or siblings for help, but vague or complicated directions, long-term assignments, and impossible challenges will result in more frustration than joy. Make assignments simple, fun, and meaningful.

Examples of homework for beginning readers are: "Cut out a word from a newspaper or magazine that begins with *s* and bring it to school tomorrow." Or "Write down the names of three kinds of food you have at home. Be ready to read them to me." As the children develop reading ability, the teacher might suggest that they: "Find out what a *gnu* is and how to pronounce it. Draw a picture of it." Or "How many restaurants are listed in the yellow pages? Which ones are closed on Monday?" More advanced readers may be assigned to: "Write down the information from five clothing labels and be prepared to tell what it means." Or "Read your creative writing story to one other person and write down any comments."

If homework is kept positive, youngsters will think up assignments spontaneously. It is a good idea to have word lists, phonics games, or simple questionnaires available for the eager reader to take home.

Daily reading assignments will help the children once they have developed their basic reading skills. Some schools encourage children to read aloud for fifteen minutes each night. If the child is able to choose reading material or to work in a familiar school book, this practice might help. To struggle over material that is too difficult will destroy the benefits of such a program.

Short-term research assignments, practice worksheets, flash cards, short stories, and simple investigative problems are all types of useful reading homework. Try to assign homework that recognizes individual need. One reason children whose parents help them with assignments learn so much more than other children is that the parents recognize what the child does not know and make an effort to overcome this lack.

**Volunteer parents and classroom aides: what to do with them**  Parents and aides in the classroom can be an effective means of meeting the individual needs of young readers. Positively, they provide more frequent practice sessions, added adult contact, assistance in creating materials, and help for managing a reading lesson. Negatively, they sometimes distract a child's attention away from reading work, give incorrect phonics instruction, criticize slower readers, and take over responsibilities that belong to the pupils. The teacher, in an effort to provide an efficient learning situation, must plan activities for the aide or volunteer that will enhance reading instruction, not conflict with it.

**Telling parents or aides what to do in the reading classroom**  The teacher who is attempting to provide reading instruction for thirty pupils cannot interrupt the lesson to tell a parent or aide what to do. Are they to sit and observe? Walk around and answer questions? Tell children words they do not know? What if a child asks for help and the parent does not know how to do the work? Some provision must be made for directing the volunteers without losing the continuity of the lesson. To answer this problem, some teachers leave detailed notes on a desk by the entrance with instructions for the day; others send letters home with a description of what the volunteers should and should not do. Directions should be kept simple, specific, and directed toward reading objectives. "Go work with Alice" does not give an aide the guidance of "Listen to Alice read. Write down the words she does not know and tell her what they are." Neither aides nor parents should be asked to do something for which they have not been prepared. You must assign activities that the volunteer can manage confidently and successfully. Adults should be reminded of what is expected of them, not to be boisterous, critical, or silly. At times, you will want to suggest that an adult work with a single youngster outside the classroom or in another supervised room or help by making games or flashcards at home.

Children, too, should be briefed regarding their roles in interacting with aides and parents in a classroom. One child may be responsible for directing visitors or showing a volunteer helper where to work. All children must learn that volunteers in the classroom are there to advance learning, not merely to observe and play.

Children that have difficulty staying with a task during the reading lesson gain motivation for their work if they see their own mother or father working on a reading activity. You should discuss the behavior you want the parents to model before this event takes place. You may want them to listen to their own child read or listen to other children reading, to read a story aloud to the class, to supervise a reading game, or to correct phonics worksheets. Parents must know ahead of time what the purpose of the assignment is if it is to be productive.

Long-term aides or parent volunteers will benefit from an adult education course or class that explains reading instruction strategies, defines reading terms, discusses the role of an aide in the classroom, and tells of school rules and procedures. If you expect to have a number of regular aides, you might prepare such a course, or even a series of meetings to instruct these people in what is expected of them.

The staff in some schools puts together an instructional booklet for aides that tells about school rules, gives directions for reading games, and advises the volunteer of jobs teachers would like to have done. This booklet includes references of materials for those interested in helping to teach reading and gives directions to the school reading resource library.

One teacher invites the parents of all her pupils to a reading materials workshop. There they learn the purpose of many reading games as well as how to make and use them. The parents use the games at home and also in the classroom when they come to visit.

**What parents, aides, and volunteers can do in the reading classroom** Persons who serve as extensions of the teacher in the classroom are not usually responsible for instructional planning. Rather they are reinforcers, motivators, models, and assistants. The responsibility for diagnosing the reading needs of youngsters, planning reading instruction, and maintaining an ongoing professional evaluation of reading growth belongs to the teacher. Aides, parents, and community volunteers can be a great boon to teachers in following up reading instruction, keeping records, listening, creating and organizing reading materials, and answering questions about reading.

Persons with talent or experience that can be related to reading should be encouraged to share this expertise with pupils. Special guests and speakers in the classroom can dramatize the importance of reading to the outside world and build the experiential base for reading comprehension. Members of one second-grade reading group had their story about monkeys brought to life when a parent introduced his pet chimpanzee. Local businesses, retirement homes, institutions, and cross-cultural neighborhoods are good places to look for specialized visitors. Ask the children if their families have special interests and try to relate reading in the classroom to those areas.

As listeners, other adults in the reading classroom are valuable. Some teachers post a notice telling the volunteer listener what to do when the child stumbles on a word.

When a child misses a word:

1.  Wait five seconds.

2.  Look for suffixes and prefixes.

3.  Ask the child the sounds of all vowels.

4.  Sound the word from beginning to end.

5.  Read the rest of the sentence.

6.  Read the word for the child.

7.  Have the child repeat the word three times.

Aides that listen to children read individually might instruct others in the group to read softly from their own books at the same time. This way the aide knows who is "on task." You must be careful that pupils working with an aide have review materials that do not require initial instruction. An aide or volunteer should handle a formal reading group primarily to give pupils practice.

Lunch or recess time is an excellent time for volunteers to work with individuals who need extra attention. In a relaxed atmosphere, often out of the classroom, the volunteer can flash vocabulary cards, help a child complete reading worksheets, or supervise silent reading for those who want to spend their free time this way.

School reading tours are guided by volunteers in one school. A volunteer takes one or two children at a time to visit reading classes to show what other readers, at levels above and below the tourists, are doing. Such an activity motivates children of different reading ability to work harder in their own classrooms and provides a kind of in-service training for the volunteers to see reading instruction techniques at all levels.

Aides contribute to learning by keeping records and correcting papers. You must be sure, however, that tests or inventories that indicate grade placement or reading ability are kept confidential. Single skill worksheets or records of books read are examples of records that volunteers can keep.

Parents, volunteers, and aides are excellent public relations people for a reading program. Not only will they share their positive feelings about a reading class with friends, they will also enlist community support if encouraged. One parent volunteered to make a videotape show to explain a new intermediate-level reading program to other parents and the Board of Trustees. Not only was the show a success, but the pupils who were filmed increased their reading ability and improved their attitudes toward reading.

Parents can organize book displays or book sales to make good literature available to the youngsters. Volunteers might collect magazines appropriate for young readers. Aides can organize a system for trading outgrown books. Helpers who extend the teacher's influence often do so by taking dictation or helping to spell the words for a young child's story and listening to the child read it back. They also do so by making reading materials or games for home practice, supervising reading centers, and operating audiovisual materials.

### Suggestions for Tutoring Programs to Meet Special Needs

Can you motivate children to work together for reading advancement? It is well known that children learn from one another. They show each other how to whistle, snap fingers, and make faces. They share schoolyard rhymes, riddles, and jokes. Without adult help, they teach each other new vocabulary words, the value of coins, and all kinds of theories about what happens in the next grade. Why not use this time-worn communication system to advance reading skills?

How is a tutoring program for young readers developed, monitored, and evaluated? Are there some children who should not be tutors? This section will prepare you to design a tutoring program to suit the individual needs of readers at any level. It will also describe techniques for training youngsters to be tutors, suggest methods for motivation, and indicate possible means for evaluating such a program.

**Tutoring versus mutual aid**    Tutoring and mutual aid are not the same. A tutor is a person who has acquired a specific skill and knows how to teach that skill to someone else. Two readers working together on a worksheet are not tutoring unless one of them has previously mastered the assignment and is distinctly responsible for instructing the other. Often a child who has successfully completed a particular reading book is assigned to listen to the reading of that book by another child who has not yet "passed" the material. This is not tutoring; it is helping or task minding. A tutor has specialized knowledge of how to teach others the skills he or she has already mastered.

Mutual aid is often found in the classroom, but it is not to be confused with tutoring. "Sam, you completed this phonics worksheet perfectly. Please go help Jim with it," is an example of one child being assigned to help another. "Sharon, you and Patty may work together in your readers" directs children to give each other mutual aid. To tutor, the child must have mastery of a specific skill and have mastery of the means by which that skill may be taught. However, mutual aid can be rendered without such specialized knowledge.

**Who should be a tutor? Who should be tutored?**   Primary teachers who want intermediate pupils to help their beginning readers tend to ask for responsible youngsters who have demonstrated high achievement in reading and some leadership ability. This usually provides a reward for the older child and easily managed practice or assistance for the younger child. Intermediate teachers, concerned with getting the reading skills of the total class up to par, will assign advanced readers to a primary class as helpers and work with the average- or low-level readers in their own classrooms. This is a very workable procedure as it provides for the practice of reading skills and an efficient means of classroom management for both classes. But it can be made even more workable and more productive in terms of reading growth.

Look at the situation more closely. Advanced intermediate readers, who are least needy in the areas of motivation or practice of basic reading skills, are being rewarded for their achievements by reviewing past challenges and receiving less instruction in advanced-reading skills. Low-level intermediate readers, most in need of motivation and practice, are denied the reward of showing off the reading skills they do have and the valuable review involved in teaching these skills to someone else. Primary-grade children benefit from the personal attention they receive from intermediate pupils, regardless of reading achievement, as long as the older children know something the younger ones do not.

More than one teacher has said, "I didn't really understand the rules for determining the antecedents of pronouns until I had to teach them." Why not give low- or average-level intermediate readers the opportunity to experience this clarification of knowledge by training them to be tutors? Might they not be particularly qualified to teach low-level primary readers? Certainly their empathy and understanding of how it feels to have to work extra hard in this area might give them added insight for helping the younger readers.

To provide purposeful reading instruction for all pupils, tutor and tutee should both be engaged in activities that support the learning of skills pertinent to their individual reading needs. If this criterion is met, any child may be selected to serve as an instructor of specific reading skills for another.

**How to train tutors**    Although individual pupils may be trained to be tutors, it is more economical to train groups of children together. Once the procedure for tutoring has been learned, any reading skill may be used. One school trains tutors by reading group, another according to grade level, and a third by room number.

When a group of tutors has been gathered, you must emphasize tutoring techniques first and reading skills second. Remember the purpose of this program is to motivate readers to practice their skills. The tutors must know how to act and what to say to stimulate the tutee's interest. Once they are confident in the tutoring situation, the tutors will be eager to learn the skill that will allow them to begin working with another child. Tutors are trained to look for answers to three questions as they work: (1) How does the tutee feel about reading? (2) What did I teach the tutee? (3) How does the tutee show what has been learned? Of course, you as the teacher will be asking these same questions about both tutor and tutee.

Step 1 is the *affective domain*. How do the tutors and tutees feel about reading?

1. Make tutors feel special. Tell them they were especially selected for this program.

2. Tell tutors they have important talents. They may be able to explain things to another child better than the teacher can. They know "kid talk."

3. Ask the tutors to try to remember how they felt when they could not read. Would they have liked help from another pupil?

4. Remind the tutors that the tutee really needs their help and wants this friendship. Practice thinking up friendly things to say when meeting the tutee.

5. What if the tutee has trouble doing the work? Practice thinking up encouraging statements like: "Good try!" "Not quite, but almost!" or "I had trouble with this, too."

6. Have the tutors make folders for their tutoring work. Give them a red pencil to use on the tutee's work.

7. Remind tutors to thank the tutees for working hard at the end of the lesson. They may shake hands or take the tutees for a drink of water if they worked very well.

8. Be serious. This is an important activity for the tutors' self-esteem. If they take their work seriously, it will be well done.

Step 2 is the *cognitive domain*. What will the tutor teach? Learn?

1. Choose a *single* reading skill for each lesson.

2. Begin with basic phonic skills or review vocabulary and advance to more difficult tasks.

3. Tell the tutors they must know the skill to teach it. Help the tutors learn the skill.

4. Plan "open-ended" lessons with some easy activities and some more challenging.

5. Prepare worksheets, task cards, books, and written assignments especially for tutoring. The skill may be familiar; the activity should be new.

6. Practice with the tutors: where to sit; what to do first, next; what to say; what to do when finished; where to put papers; and so on.

7. Give the tutors a chance to talk about their job. They will have many questions.

8. Reassure the tutors that they will have help while working with a tutee if they need it.

9. Have the tutors watch the tutees for work habits, effort, and skill achievement.

Step 3 is *psychomotor*. How do the tutors and tutees show what they have learned?

1. Plan some form of written work — underlining, circling, copying, tracing.

2. Have the pupils read out loud — sounds, words, sentences, stories.

3. Have the tutors practice saying sounds, reading words with the teacher before tutoring.

4. Move around the room during tutoring sessions. Are the tutors giving positive reinforcement? Can the tutors answer questions

put to them by the tutees? Do the tutoring teams begin work quickly? Do the tutors remember how to give directions? Do the activities flow comfortably? Do the tutors give their attention to the tutees, not each other? Is there enough work available to keep tutors and tutees "on task" for reading throughout the session?

**Evaluation**   The process of evaluation should enhance, not impede, tutoring activities. Tutoring is valuable only when tutors and tutees are motivated to work together on the assigned skills. To maintain that motivation, you must make sure that all youngsters participating in a tutoring session feel successful. This can be done by emphasizing effort and the following of procedures rather than reading skills. Praise the pupils often for being "on task," remembering directions, and working hard. Tell them you enjoy watching how well they work together. Discuss the difficulty of the task with them. "This is a very hard assignment. You are working well with it," or "Wow, I didn't think this would be so easy for you!" are statements that let the children know you know the work is difficult and appreciate their efforts.

Separate evaluation of the reading skill from evaluation of tutoring. Some skills will be more difficult than others for each tutor. You want the children to enjoy tutoring so much that they will tackle new reading challenges to participate in it. Let the tutors and tutees have a chance to evaluate the assignments separately from their performance. Ask "Was this worksheet too hard?" not "Did you have trouble with this worksheet?" Put the blame for nonachievement on the paper or book and give credit for hard work to the pupil.

One school has a report card for tutors to give tutees at the end of a session. Notice that evaluation of the child is separated from evaluation of the skill.

| | |
|---|---|
| *Tutee* David P. | *This skill was:* |
| *Tutor* John H. | Too easy |
| | OK |
| *Date* May 3 | Too hard |
| *Skill* | |
| Suffix "ing" | *We worked:* |
| | Super well |
| | Hard |

Eight steps should be followed when tutors are to handle a lesson. (A sample tutoring worksheet is presented.)

*Sample Tutoring Lesson*

1. Teacher meets with tutors to go over procedure.

2. Teacher presents skill to tutors and practices with them until they know it well enough to teach.

3. Teacher reminds tutors of procedure and makes sure they have materials.

4. Tutors meet with tutees under supervision of teacher.

5. Tutors present skill to tutee and practice an assignment.

6. Teams that complete assignment early use flashcards, games, or books that reinforce skill taught.

7. Teacher meets with tutors and tutees to evaluate lesson: (1) How do you feel about tutoring? (b) Was the work too hard, OK, too easy?

8. Teacher meets with tutors to plan next session and go over procedure.

*Sample Tutoring Worksheet*

Tutor _____  Tutee _____

ch

sh

th

wh

ph f

*Digraphs*

1. Please underline the *h* digraphs in these words.

2. Practice reading the digraphs only.

3. Try to read the words.

| | | |
|---|---|---|
| chair | thanks | reshape |
| thumb | thistle | threw |
| shoe | shoulder | sophisticated |
| what | catcher | telegraph |
| phone | pitcher | mother |
| rich | share | hush |
| swish | weather | sheet |
| with | birthday | shoot |
| telephone | phoney | graphics |
| phonics | gosh | thorn |
| whether | galoshes | thistle |
| moth | clothes | whistle |
| harness | think | chink |

How do you feel about this work?

Too easy _____

OK _____

Too hard _____

*Mystery word*

_____

# Tips for Working with Poor Readers

This section presents some techniques for helping poor readers. These techniques have worked for other teachers. You should use them as a guideline for developing your own ideas.

### Using Interesting, Unusual, or Sophisticated Artifacts

The technique of using interesting, unusual, or sophisticated artifacts "sugarcoats the medicine." The child who will not concentrate on a reader or worksheet may work persistently on a reading skill that is connected with a gadget, gimmick, or "grown-up" subject. Here are some items that require reading in an untypical form:

| | | | |
|---|---|---|---|
| passports | checkbooks | maps | globes |
| calendars | job | insurance | certificates |
| credentials; awards | applications | forms | blueprints |
| catalogs | stamps | *Who's Who* | advertisements |
| radio and TV | travel brochures | thesaurus | games |
| program guides | comic books | *Bartlett's* | Ripley's |
| *Guinness Book* | Chamber of | *Quotations* | *Believe It or* |
| *of Records* | Commerce | grave markers | *Not* |
| ingredient labels | publications | plays | make-it books |
| diaries | clothing labels | nature books | speeches |
| trial accounts | poems | weather | riddles, puns |
| baseball rules | animal books | reports | jokes |
| warranties | school notices | encyclopedias | stock market |
| | police reports | | reports |

### Attending to Perception Problems

You may have to arrange activities to deal with problems in perception. Difficulty in learning through one or more of the senses constitutes a perceptual problem. Children who have this difficulty sometimes display poor coordination, a tendency to reverse or invert letters or words, difficulty in shifting from one activity to another, messy work, frequent confusion between left and right, a tendency to ignore verbal directions, frequent misunderstandings or forgetfulness, mumbling while working, and a host of other responses conflicting with the learning activity. We recommend that teachers use multisensory teaching techniques and simplify the mode of response expected from the perceptually handicapped youngster. Kinesthetic or movement activities may help the pupil learn a reading skill, and tactile or touch assignments may be of help, too. Some suggested activities are to have children:

Read many books on the same level before advancing.

Read "below-level" books frequently.

Use color cues for visual discrimination difficulties.

Do framing, tracing, underlining, and copying activities.

Do crossword puzzles for discrimination of words.

Match words with the correct number of boxes:

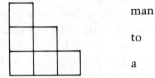

man

to

a

Write words with yarn or string.

Use sewing cards for writing words.

Use a rope to spell out a word and walk along it and say the word.

Read poems with rhyming out loud.

Use language masters, tape recorders, records, film strips, films, and so on.

Build stories with other children, each child adding a sentence.

Work in pairs or teams.

Use a magnifying glass for reading assignments.

Play charades with vocabulary words.

Use a typewriter, tapewriter, or rubber stamp for spelling responses.

Make letters or words in clay, in sand, with alphabet noodles, and so on.

Cut out words and letters and glue to another paper.

Write simple codes; for example, B = □      My dad's name is □ill.

Accentuate punctuation marks with color or size.

Feel letter shapes and label.

Play license plate games for visual memory.

Use simple sign language.

Listen to music with earphones while reading.

Use chalk, large crayons, fat pencils, or marking pens.

Participate in matching activities.

Use thermometers, scales, binoculars, stop watches, and compasses.

Play card games that require noticing details or matching; for example, Old Maid, Go Fish, Solitaire, Hearts, Slap Jack.

Telephone for information or the weather.

## Overteaching Pupils Who Have Difficulty with Phonics

Some pupils who have trouble with phonics may need additional practice. Intermediate and upper elementary grade pupils are often classified *remedial* because they cannot successfully respond to ordinary phonics lessons. These youngsters must be trained to differentiate words that will have the same or different speech sounds in initial, medial, and final positions. They may need primary reading materials and continual repetition and review, but these materials must not be insulting and this added practice must be kept interesting. Some possible activities are to:

Use musical instruments to train pupils to listen for beat.

Use a tachistoscope for practice reading short sentences and longer sentences.

Plan choral reading activities.

Have pupils read poems, songs, and tongue twisters.

Plan interesting alphabetizing activities (first names of teachers in the school).

Repeat license numbers and have pupils write them down.

Let pupils spell new vocabulary words out loud.

Let pupils take dictation from other youngsters by typewriter.

Play anagram-type spelling games.

Play games with names of things (cars, foods, tools, dogs).

Use dictionaries frequently.

Make up rhymes, poems, jingles, and limericks.

Use definitions to distinguish like words (hop, pop, mop): to jump on one foot.

Let pupils mark words diacritically (memory).

Use flip cards to teach blending; for example,

Let the deficient pupil give spelling tests to other pupils.

Limit vocabulary lists to the child's ability.

Play rhyming games with names — Ann's fans: Gary, Larry, Barry.

Give directions that rhyme: "It's time for lunch, let's eat a bunch."

## Giving Opportunities for Language Development

The ability to understand and use language is crucial to the pupil's reading process at any age, grade, or achievement level. The youngster who can decode words may be an unresponsive learner due to inability to perceive the meanings and concepts of the language used. Some possible means of closing language gaps are to:

Have children complete functional sentences (Knives are for cutting; pencils are for _____).

Play charades or perform familiar pantomimes.

Use role-play activities to depict point of view, characterization, and job descriptions.

Make address books, phone directories, and birthday calendars of class members.

Make word collections before assigning writing activities (words about dogs, scary words, and so on).

Have children illustrate nursery rhymes and riddles.

Have pupils rewrite newspaper articles with different endings.

Maintain regular class correspondence.

Let pupils proofread each other's work.

Plan time for partnership reading. One pupil questions the other on what is read.

Write memos to individual pupils or groups.

> Joe and Jim,
> Go to the library
> today at 2:00.
> Miss L.

Encourage pupils to write notes to you and each other.

Help pupils relay information about their experiences; for example,

Last Saturday I _____ .

I ate _____ .

I saw _____ .

Play "Mad Libs." I went to town and saw a _____ .

Duplicate pupils' writings and distribute for others to read.

Scramble sentences and let pupils rearrange; for example,
dog   over   there   is   my.

Teach youngsters to use their senses when describing something.

Let pupils act out familiar or recently read stories.

Have pupils dictate stories to each other.

Have youngsters write songs.

Give practice writing telegrams.

Play Scrabble, word-building, and sentence-building games.

Have pupils practice punctuating unpunctuated texts.

Give simple dictation to the class, increasing the difficulty.

Go on information hunts around the school. Compile and organize results. (How far is it from the office to the drinking fountain?

How many trees are in the yard? And so forth.)

Let pupils write about pictures.

Have pupils record what was said during Show and Tell.

Have pupils write directions for playing a game, cooking a meal, and so on.

Use short plays or melodramas.

Show pupils how to write or speak using stream of consciousness.

Read several stories with the same or similar theme — compare them.

Teach pupils how to debate.

## Using Children's Literature

Children's literature may be used to create interest in reading, to develop comprehension skills, to advance imaginative thinking, or to serve as a form of emotional social therapy. Much of the motivation for learning to read comes from the desire to read "real books," and pupils who experience joy in reading are well on their way to becoming lifetime readers. A leading specialist in the teaching of reading through literature recommends a variety of ways to use literature in a reading program: reading aloud to children to give them a sense of story and to introduce them to quality literature that may exceed their decoding ability but not their comprehension levels; giving opportunities for all children to read books of their own choosing and for their own purposes, to share impressions of books read, and to go more deeply into the meaning of what they have read through activities such as identifying stories with surprise endings, dramatizing tales, writing further adventures of principal characters, making wall hangings of scenes from favorite tales, making puppets of favorite story characters, and creating a game based on a story or group of stories.[3]

**Selecting interesting literature**   Regardless of the purpose for having the pupil read, interesting material will have a dynamic effect on achievement. Young children who struggle with conventional primers often respond quite differently when they encounter the characters of the Dr. Seuss books. Older children may not be particularly excited over their social studies text, but they may become animated when reading the true story of Harriet Tubman or Amos Fortune.

How do you know what will be interesting to the pupils? Some teachers answer this question through a class survey, observations, questionnaires, individual interviews, or group discussion about interests. However, teachers who read aloud to their classes regularly from samples of poetry, the classics, modern novels, plays, humorous stories, mysteries, and historical fiction will give youngsters the chance to create interests as well as to build upon those already present.

Interesting literary materials for children are reported in newspaper book reviews. Often there is a special review of children's literature in the fall or spring during National Library Week. Librarians are excellent sources of advice regarding current literature, and many book clubs or paperback book companies annotate their offerings.

Awards given for children's literature serve as guidelines for books

---

[3] Charlotte S. Huck, "Literature as the Content of Reading," *Theory into Practice* 16, no. 5 (December 1977): 363–371.

that are likely to appeal to children. The Newbery Medal, for example, is granted to one book each year determined to be the best American book for children. The Caldecott Medal is given once a year to the best American picture book. This award is primarily concerned with illustrations, but the quality of the writing must also be high. Pictures are an excellent interest stimulant for children of all ages. Other awards are varied in purpose and standards of evaluation. Some awards for books are determined by children, publishing houses, book clubs, religious groups, and youth institutions.

The reading interests of boys have been observed, indicating that most boys prefer exciting, suspense-filled dramatic stories with emotionally charged vocabulary rather than books about "ordinary" things such as pets and families. We should not, however, infer that girls prefer stories only about home life and common events. Any sexist generalizations about literature should be carefully tempered with consideration of boys and girls as individuals. In recent years, there have been increasing numbers of girls who enjoy sports stories and boys who like stories dealing with social conflict.

**Applying elements of literary criticism to children's literature**  In selecting literature for children, in helping youngsters evaluate what they read, look for the basic elements found in all lasting material:

*Character.* Does the material contain well-developed characters? For children, authors frequently use animals or make-believe creatures as human representatives. Whatever or whoever the characters are, they should be personalities with whom the child can relate.

*Plot.* Is there sufficient conflict or suspense? Older pupils will respond well to learning the author's tricks of foreshadowing and hints of inevitability.

*Setting.* For younger children, the setting may serve as a backdrop for events, such as the woods in *Goldilocks* or *Little Red Riding Hood.* As the youngsters mature, settings may be essentially related to the plot. Children who learn how the setting of a story may determine its events are usually intrigued by adventure or nature stories.

*Theme.* This is the idea that holds the whole story together. It may be explicitly stated, as in *Escape from Warsaw,* where the reader knows all along that escape is the theme that ties the book together. Or it may be implied as in *Charlotte's Web,* where the correspondence of life and death is illustrated but never stated. Select books that have themes that mean something to the youngsters and provide variety. Children who read comic books depicting continuous power struggles between the strong and the weak, the good and the bad characters are limiting their experiences of ideas. It may help to tell the pupils what the theme of a story is before they read it and draw their attention to that idea as they progress.

*Point of view.* Children are not always aware of the point of view of a story. Their limited experience makes it difficult for them to develop inferences about characters and events when seen through someone else's eyes. Help pupils understand point of view through the use of role play or acting out scenes.

*Style.* The words an author uses to say something may cause a youngster to be bored or interested in the story. This is especially true of outdated language. Although the stories of Charles Dickens might appeal greatly to a youngster of today, many of the phrases, figures of speech, and images will require instruction to be understood.

*Tone.* How the character of the author feels about the reader is indicated by the tone of the literature. Do not select books that are condescending to the reader or subject. Older pupils who have been or are below level in reading are especially sensitive to this element. A twelve-year-old may be reading at the second-grade level and need practice reading books at that level, but a "baby book" is insulting and the child will usually decide not to read at all. It is for the child such as this that literature has recently been gathered under the heading "high interest-low vocabulary" or "reluctant reader" books.

**Relating literature to the child's experience**   We recommend that you dramatize the stories, plays, poems, and songs the pupils read. The youngster who takes part in role play to demonstrate the character of Long John Silver will gain valuable perception of characterization. The use of charades or pantomimes can help the child retain key elements of stories or poems. The sequences of *Alice in Wonderland* or *The Mouse and the Motorcycle* may be dramatically expressed without a spoken word. Choral reading has been used to create interest in reading songs or poetry. Alternate voice parts between groups with unison reading, tape recorded for playback later, is a good activity. This technique is also useful for teaching about style in literature. With the power of many voices behind the words, children can hear clearly the differences and effects of each author's choice of words.

The techniques of readers' theater are helpful at any grade level. One teacher, using an overhead projector, marked the words *trip-trap* all through the story of *The Three Billy Goats Gruff.* Then she read the story, pausing before the marked words to give a child the chance to read. With older children, two-part plays may be purchased or written by a teacher and the pupils may perform them at a tape-recording center. Puppets may "act out" the play as the recording is played back.

In using drama to clarify literature, emphasize the story, poem, or song content rather than the acting ability. In this way, the children come to understand themselves and other people through the study of literature; literature is not incidental to life.

Young children often ask to hear the same story over and over again. In so doing, they are relating the events of the story to their own lives. *Curious George* may be a monkey, but he acts out events, feelings, and situations that have meaning for young girls and boys. Older children will understand Laura's feelings in *Little House in the Big Woods* or Tom's in *Adventures of Tom Sawyer* because these stories are dealing with human nature. Let pupils enjoy, study, and learn from these literary samples by making them as much a part of "real" life as possible. Acting out, writing down, discussing, reading aloud, reading alone, listening to someone else read, and retelling are all activities to use in meeting the special needs of pupils.

# Implications of Mainstreaming for the Teaching of Reading

The practice of mainstreaming is intended to help exceptional children regain more positive self-concepts, greater peer acceptance, and more positive expectancies from teachers and parents. Mainstreaming is the integration of handicapped children into regular classes on a part- or full-time basis. For these goals to be achieved in the reading class-rooms, handicapped children should be exposed to normalized reading role models as well as have the opportunity to show their own strengths — loyalty to persons and ideals, willingness to exert them-selves for a worthy cause, and personal goals and interests.

An exceptional child can be integrated into a regular classroom if the child is able to offer something to the class and the classroom is able to offer something to the child. However, if the child's needs are so specialized that the regular classroom teacher cannot adapt to meet them, the child should remain in a special class. There are children with severe physical, emotional, or intellectual impairments who may not be able to profit from reading instruction in the regular classroom. Some schools have highly developed resource rooms where children with special needs spend part of their time receiving particularized instruction, such as how to respond overtly, to attend, to order tasks, and to arrange given parts with wholes. Other schools arrange for tutors to work with exceptional children either in or out of class to give them particular help. In some cases, handicapped children spend up to

60 percent of their time in a special class and the remainder in a regular classroom.

When mainstreaming, each handicapped child will have an Individualized Education Program (IEP) prepared by the parents, the teacher, a specialist, and, perhaps, the child. The IEP could include (1) a description of the child's present level of functioning, (2) short- and long-term educational goals, (3) specific services to be provided and the time required, (4) starting time and expected duration of services, and (5) evaluation criteria to be used in determining whether objectives are being achieved. The IEP offers flexibility in programming. For example, a child may remain in a regular classroom for areas of reading in which the child has strength and, at other hours of the day, receive remedial instruction in a special setting for areas of weakness.

Often a technological approach is used in mainstreamed classrooms. This approach calls for matching a child's instruction to a specific objective, thus referencing instruction to the child rather than to the norm of the classroom. However, not all of the reading experience should be individualized. The child should have the opportunity to participate with others in listening to stories and discussing and giving opinions regarding what has been read. Isolating the exceptional child within the regular classroom defeats the purposes of mainstreaming. You must design and guide positive interactions between children based on clear common interests and common reading experiences.

We believe that mainstreaming will succeed if you can take advantage of varied organizational plans, including both (1) group activity, where all children work together to develop social skills and meet emotional needs, and (2) ability grouping, whereby children are taught at their own instructional level. The group activity might be a project in which children seek to resolve an issue or to complete some action that will improve a situation. In the process, questions are posed, committees are formed to seek the answers, resources are gathered, and pupils report their findings or take written action. One teacher organized a language arts activity around the topic of food — its origin, preservation, use, and so on. Children read to find answers to their questions, observed supermarkets in tracing food sources and determining how food is preserved, and collected labels to use in making maps depicting origins of food. They read and sang food songs and wrote letters to food companies in gathering materials. They learned how to evaluate food advertising and prices and how to read recipes, maps, etiquette books, and other materials. Noteworthy in this kind of activity is that children contribute to the project to the best of their ability — the variety of jobs and activities allows for freedom of choice.

At times ability grouping can be used to avoid forcing slow learners and holding back brighter pupils. There is some evidence that children who are at the lower end of ability do as well when placed in high ability groups as low ability pupils placed only with low-ability pupils. However, children in the medium and high ability levels may learn less in heterogeneous classes than in homogeneous classes.[4] In ability grouping, the data from diagnostic tests determine the level of instruction to be provided. Those children with particular abilities are grouped together; for example,

1.   A high achievement group might engage in independent reading research, supported, of course, by your observation and consultation.

2.   A slow reading group might compose a story for reading in which each member will read a part. Word study might follow, and when you move to another group, these children might read easy books for pleasure.

3.   An average group might work on an assignment and focused task, such as finding main ideas in stories.

4.   A remedial group might read a story silently and then later read aloud to each other under the direction of a tutor, coached by you in providing help with unknown words.

Ability grouping within a single teacher classroom allows you to work intensively with one group, check on each of the other groups, and help individuals. We reiterate, however, that grouping by ability should not be the only organizational pattern nor should the assignments to groups be rigid. Children should not be locked into groups, and children should not be stigmatized by grouping. Indeed, it has been found that achievement in reading is higher when children are in classrooms where they have many friends — a child's sense of acceptance by peers is related to higher reading achievement.[5] Wide differences in each group will need individual attention. Hence, interest grouping, individualized instruction, total class activity, and small, flexible grouping for projects are needed in mainstreaming.

The methods and activities presented in previous chapters can be used with exceptional, slow learners, although they may have to be

    [4] Rebecca Barr and Robert Dreeben, "Instruction in Classrooms," *Review of Research in Education,* American Educational Research Association, vol. 5 (Itasca, Ill.: Peacock Publishers, 1978), pp. 89–163.
    [5] Kenneth Zeichner, "Group Membership in the Elementary School Classroom," *Journal of Educational Psychology* 70, no. 4 (August 1978): 554–564.

adapted. That is, your pace of instruction may be slower. You might present fewer words, patterns, and principles to be learned at one time; you might give more examples before expecting the child to make generalizations; you might give more specific instructions and be more careful in specifying the behavior you are rewarding. Some teachers have found that retarded children make more progress in learning to read when the emphasis is on sight-word recognition rather than on decoding principles, although there is no clear and convincing evidence that learning disabled children as a group need any different techniques than those that are appropriate for other children.

Teaching skills for implementing a mainstreaming program include the following: ability to talk to children about handicaps, ability to work with special educators in planning for children, ability to support parents of exceptional children, and familiarity with the children's handicaps and with the therapy or other treatment the child is receiving elsewhere.

One's own feelings about differences, deviance, and handicaps are the most important factor in mainstreaming. Through a simulated reading activity with teachers, James Chalfant and Georgiana Foster helped teachers experience the problem that learning disabled pupils sometimes experience. The results of this activity (the feelings reported by the teachers after they assumed the roles of special pupils) constitute a negative lesson:

*Attitudes about Fellow Pupils*

1. "My neighbor at the table made the rest of us feel stupid."

2. "I felt competition from others and pressure to learn before everyone left me behind."

3. "I didn't want to seem dumb in front of everyone, so I faked it and repeated what everyone else said."

*Comments about the Teacher*

1. "You didn't care about me."

2. "You responded only to those who got the word right."

3. "Why should I try? You never knew if I knew the word or not."

4. "Every time you looked my way I smiled so you would think I was okay and you wouldn't call on me. . . ."

5. "You made me feel stupid by reminding me how simple it was and how many other people knew it."

*Comments about the Teaching Method*

1. "You went too fast for me to learn."

2. "You should have given us some time to practice or work together in small groups."

3. "We could have used peer tutors."

4. "You tried to teach us too much, too fast."[6]

A final, positive suggestion for mainstreaming emphasizes the importance of all children participating. Examples of activities to this end and to successful reading include:

*Show and tell* periods, where children present their new work (book, object, experience, and so on)

*Free play*, where children make up their own lines and roles to fit a given situation

*Pantomime*, whereby children play charades or dramatize favorite characters

*Script reading*, where children write their own scripts or use those in textbooks

*Role playing*, where children show what it is like to be someone else

*Talking books*, which are a variation of making a scroll movie. Children make a tape recording that serves as the "talking" part of the book. Once the tape is made, children illustrate their oral contribution. Pictures are fastened into sequence in book form. Each page is turned as the tape plays.

*Shadow plays*, in which stories and plays are used in connection with a shadow play for purposes of teaching dialogues, vocabulary, oral reading, logical sequence, and other reading skills. Paragraphs are numbered and each child is given a corresponding number. The teacher tactfully assigns parts and helps individuals rehearse parts before being asked to read or speak the part before others. The children practice reading the parts together. When comfortable

---

[6] James C. Chalfant and Georgiana E. Foster, "Helping Teachers Understand the Needs of Learning Disabled Children," *Journal of Learning Disabilities* 10, no. 2 (February 1977): 79–85. Used with permission of the Professional Press, Inc., Chicago, Illinois.

with their reading and dialogue parts, the presentation is taped, with or without musical background. Silhouettes for each scene can be made from thin pieces of wrapping paper cut to the size of an overhead projector. These silhouettes are focused on a sheet as background to the scenes the children are acting out.

## Summary

In this chapter, we tried to offer practical techniques on how to teach children with academic problems in the regular classroom. Suggestions were of three types: first, we introduced a heuristic by which you can generate your own instructional solutions to problems of individual differences; second, we recognized that teachers' efforts to meet the wide range of individual needs in a regular classroom are likely to be frustrating because of the finite time they can spend on an almost infinite number of needs with so many pupils. Hence, we showed how you can multiply the results of your own instructional expenditures many times over by designing and managing the resources and efforts of others — adults and pupil assistants. Our suggestions for involving parents, aides, and tutors will enable you to implement the individualized instruction required for meeting special needs. Third, we presented specific techniques, activities, and principles that experienced teachers have employed successfully in the direct instruction of learning disabled and mildly handicapped children in regular classrooms. The importance of these suggestions, as well as additional recommendations, were emphasized in connection with our concluding view of mainstreaming.

## Self-instructional Exercises

### Exercise 1. Matching Solutions with Problems of Poor Readers

Select the best answer to each problem.

1. Children are resistant to reading instruction, viewing it as bookish and unrelated to daily living.
    a. _____ Teach sequence skills through fairy tales.
    b. _____ Teach the drawing of conclusions through a basal reader.
    c. _____ Teach classification skills through the Sears catalog.

2. Children have difficulty decoding new words using phonics principles.

    a. \_\_\_\_ Provide spelling activities.

    b. \_\_\_\_ Provide speaking activities.

    c. \_\_\_\_ Provide writing activities.

3. Children read "was" for "saw."

    a. \_\_\_\_ Play a visual game in which the child matches different shapes — triangles, circles, squares.

    b. \_\_\_\_ Play an auditory game in which the child says words that begin like other spoken words.

    c. \_\_\_\_ Play a card game in which the child names *saw* and *was* when they appear on turned cards.

4. Children mumble, do not listen to directions, and draw beautiful pictures.

    a. \_\_\_\_ Refer the child for a test of hearing.

    b. \_\_\_\_ Have the child listen to tape recordings of recipes and other step-by-step materials.

    c. \_\_\_\_ Teach the child to use a balance beam and skip.

5. Children have difficulty attending to what words look like.

    a. \_\_\_\_ Have the child type words.

    b. \_\_\_\_ Have the child draw pictures depicting referents of words.

    c. \_\_\_\_ Have the child vocalize when viewing sight words.

6. Children are slow learners because of limited intellectual ability.

    a. \_\_\_\_ Give the child an opportunity to make appropriate responses to a particular set of circumstances, for example, to read familiar sentences only.

    b. \_\_\_\_ Give the child an opportunity to generalize from a specific conditioned circumstance to a similar circumstance, for example, to read unfamiliar sentences composed of familiar words.

    c. \_\_\_\_ Give the child an opportunity to apply the reading skill before mastering it.

**ANSWERS TO EXERCISE 1**

1c. A Sears or other merchandising catalog can be used to teach most of the skills of learning to read. The children will see such material as part of daily life, not school.

2a. Spelling activities show decoding from a different perspective. A child with a learning disability may respond well to spelling because it is reciprocal to reading.

3c. There are two theories to account for reversals. One theory is that the child has a perceptual problem and is visually and spatially confused; the other says the child perceives similar words but cannot remember their names. The suggested solution gives an opportunity for both perception and labeling.

4a. This child most likely has a hearing disability. If the screening reveals nothing and the child is physically coordinated but the problem persists, ask for speech screening and continue to use a lot of visual instruction.

5a. A typewriter is good for aiding word perception and for motivating. Asking pupils to visualize the meaning of what they read is excellent for developing comprehension. Vocalization will help learners learn to remember words that have been presented as sight words.

6b. Learning is not a process limited to making responses that have been conditioned to a particular stimulus. The slow child should learn to generate from a specific conditional stimulus to a similar but novel stimulus. When skill proficiency has been achieved at the practice level, the child is ready to apply the skill in a novel context.

## Exercise 2. Recognizing Activities That Teach Literary Elements

Match the activity with the literary element it best illustrates.

1. Plot

2. Character

3. Theme

4. Style

5. Point of view

6. Tone

a. Sixth graders read Edgar Allan Poe's "The Bells."

b. Third graders put on the play *Andy and the Lion.*

c. Choral readers perform using a textbook story.

d. First graders write an experience story after hearing and discussing *The Snowy Day.*

e. A fourth grader writes a story about falling off his bicycle after reading about a daredevil motorcycle rider.

f. A second grader wants to know where Dr. Doolittle really lives.

**ANSWERS TO EXERCISE 2**

1b. *Plot* is best illustrated through the activity of acting out *Andy and the Lion.* As the youngsters dramatize the story, they must be aware of the conflict and suspense that make this tale interesting.

2f. *Character* has been fully developed when a child considers fictional characters real. Dr. Doolittle exists for this youngster.

3d. These first graders have learned that weather or a particular kind of weather may be the *theme* of a story.

4c. The words chosen for this choral reading are those of a textbook *style.* The teacher should direct pupils in the choral reading of a poem and a short story so they may appreciate the differences in writing styles.

5e. The youngster has understood the author's *point of view* and is comparing it with his own.

6a. Although this poem repeats many vocabulary words, it does so very dramatically. Youngsters reading this selection could not miss Poe's expert use of *tone* to relay a very human message.

## Exercise 3. Responding to Individual Differences

Put a mark by the teaching practice that best goes with the learner described.

1. A superior reader has difficulty talking about personal problems.
   a. _____ Encourage the child to follow the textbook assignment given to other children in the class.
   b. _____ Encourage the child to read widely in a number of subjects and types of literature.
   c. _____ Encourage the child to read books that deal with the child's concerns.

2. A distractible reader has some strength in sight word recognition.
   a. _____ Begin by teaching the child word attack skills.
   b. _____ Begin by having the child read emotionally loaded sentences.
   c. _____ Begin by letting the child compete in learning sight words.

3. An antagonistic seven-year-old retarded reader thinks stories are irrelevant.
   a. _____ Introduce the child to stories where adults are shown to be foolish and the children are the heroes.
   b. _____ Give the child controversial books about animals.
   c. _____ Have the child finish all books started.

4. A slow reader in the first grade greatly needs success in reading.
   a. _____ Place more emphasis on verbal explanation of the reading skills.
   b. _____ Reinforce reading skills through motor movement — writing letters in the air and moving the body in time with the rhythm of what is being read.

c. _____ Give reading assignments that demand silent rather than oral reading or pointing at words.

5. A fourth-grade child has second-grade reading skills.

   a. _____ Give the child extra worksheets and practice exercises.

   b. _____ Give the child skill development exercises rather than recreational and information-getting reading experiences.

   c. _____ Give the child materials at lower than the fourth-grade level of difficulty.

6. A child has difficulty applying a reading skill when given unfamiliar reading materials.

   a. _____ Arrange instructional sequences of an isolated drill on the skill, followed by practice in using the skill in more complex situations, and finally application of the skill.

   b. _____ Offer the child many opportunities to make overt or active responses so the teacher can make a complete analysis of the child's errors and insure that the child is working.

   c. _____ Provide the child with immediate correction and feedback to enhance the child's learning.

**ANSWERS TO EXERCISE 3**

1c. Books often bring to light problems that children cannot bring themselves to talk about and with which they can make wholesome identification. It is true that a balanced program is likely to give a superior reader opportunities to satisfy many personal and social needs through reading.

2c. Relative strength is a good place to start in a teaching plan for a disabled learner. Being able to decide for oneself the rate with which to learn words is valuable in motivating a reader and preventing distractibility.

3a. Children prefer stories where the child is the important person, not the adult. Children find both fun and truth in stories where adults are somewhat foolish because that is how they sometimes look to children.

4b. Motor-skill programs further sensory reinforcement and aid learning. They are also usually success experiences that encourage the desire to participate in reading activities.

5c. Materials must be at an instructional level for the child; yet the reading program must have balance. Reading for information and pleasure is as important as a progression of skill exercises.

6a. Often children move too rapidly to application without adequate preparation at the drill (simple) and practice (more complex) levels. The teacher should be careful to arrange sequences of drills, practice, and application in small units so the learner will move through the complete cycle. The principles of overt responding and knowledge of results are important during drill and practice activities.

# Selected Readings

Bar-Tal, Daniel. "Attributional Analysis of Achievement-Related Behavior," *Review of Educational Research* 48, no. 2 (Spring 1978): 259–271.

This paper reviews studies showing that individuals with a high need for achievement attribute their successes to their ability and effort and their failures to lack of effort or external factors. Individuals low in achievement needs tend to perceive themselves as low in ability and to ascribe their failures to themselves. Those with high achievement needs experience more pride and reward for their successful performances. These highly motivated learners both persist longer in difficult learning situations and choose appropriate learning tasks.

The author suggests that pupils who perceive lack of ability as the cause of their failures expect failure, avoid achievement activities, and fail to reach their potential. Ways teachers can help pupils to establish realistic perceptions of self-ability and to value effort are presented. For instance, children experiencing reading difficulties are taught to attribute failure to lack of effort, with the result that they develop more reading persistence. The point is made about the desirability of emphasizing ability with effort as the cause of success.

Coles, Gerald S. "The Learning-Disabilities Test Battery: Empirical and Social Issues," *Harvard Educational Review* 48, no. 3 (August 1978): 313–340.

Coles reviews validation studies of the ten most frequently recommended tests for diagnosing learning disabilities, such as the Wepman Auditory Discrimination Test, the Illinois Test of Psycholinguistic Abilities, and the Frostig Developmental Test of Visual Perception. He finds that these tests lack a sound empirical base and predicts they will be discarded because the evidence against them is mounting. Coles then explores why children continue to be diagnosed and labeled as learning disabled. He concludes that specialists in the field have resorted to biological explanations such as "blaming the victim" for the failure of the schools, communities, and other institutions to rectify the problem, citing the fact that 60 percent of slum area children and only 2 percent of suburban children are severe reading disability cases.

Dunn, Rita, and Dunn, Kenneth. "Learning Styles — Practical Applications of the Research," *Practical Applications of Research* 1, no. 3 (March 1979): 2–3.

The authors claim that the teacher's accommodating each pupil's learning style will improve the child's self-image and retention, increase enthusiasm for learning, and raise test scores. Items such as alertness during the time of day, noise tolerance, self-directedness, media preference, preference for learning activities, need for structure or flexibility, and persistency are identified as related to learning style. The authors recommend, for example, that pupils who require food while they concentrate be permitted to eat nutritious snacks; that mobile youngsters have opportunities for moving built into their schedule — five minutes with the teacher, fifteen minutes in the reading center, ten minutes at the media corner.

Johns, Jerry L. "Is Reading Sensible to Children?," *Resources in Education* 14, no. 1 (January 1979): 45.

The author classified children's definitions of reading into categories, such as: reading is of educational value, reading is a classroom procedure, reading is decoding, and reading is meaning or understanding. The majority saw reading as a procedure and as decoding. Few children associated reading with meaning. On the basis of his findings, Johns recommended that teachers help children see meaning in reading.

Klausmeier, Herbert J., et al., *Individually Guided Motivation*. 3rd ed. Madison, Wisc.: University of Wisconsin, Wisconsin Research and Development Center for Cognitive Learning, 1975.

This book contains a chapter that summarizes theories of motivation — associative, cognitive, humanistic, and psychoanalytic: Skinner and his key motivational variables of *deprivation* and *reinforcement*; White and the concepts of the *competence* motive and *effectance*; Miller, Galanter, and Pribam's explanations of what gives direction to a person's actions and what helps to determine the plans one carries out; Atkinson's view of the achievement motive contrasting the behavior of those motivated by success and those motivated by fear-of-failure; Maslow's hierarchical system of needs; Rogers's emphasis upon persons being able to experience and trust their own feelings; and Freud's differentiation between *conscious* and *unconscious* motives.

Other chapters explain and illustrate instructional practices that are consistent with many of the motivational theories and principles. For instance, there are descriptions, exercises, and resources for learning the procedures necessary for developing self-direction, including ways to motivate children to read independently and set realistic reading goals.

Ripley, William H., and Blair, Timothy R. "Mainstreaming and Reading Instruction," *Reading Teacher* 36, no. 6 (March 1979): 762–765.

The authors summarize research on mainstreaming and describe model programs and training procedures. Attention is drawn to how the accommodation of children with more diverse needs increased emphasis on diagnostic-prescriptive teaching, heterogeneous grouping, differentiated staffing, paraprofessionals, self-concepts, and recreational reading.

Williams, Arnold L. "Beginning Reading: Are We Doing Only Half the Job?" *Kappa Delta Pi Record* 15, no. 4 (April 1979): 124–126.

The thesis in this article is that children who are primarily right-hemisphere learners have more success in learning to read if the teacher offers more right-hemisphere learning opportunities. Accordingly, the teacher should encourage (1) divergent thinking and open-ended questions which require synthesizing and for which no one answer is correct; (2) approaches such as USSR (uninterrupted, sustained, silent reading); reading centers where children select and read books in a relaxed environment, listening centers where children listen to poetry, plays, and stories read with expression; and (3) first-hand experiences involving field trips, resource people who come to the classroom, regalia, dioramas, pictures, pantomimes, dramatizations, and the like. The author recommends allowing children to spend at least as much class time in reading as they spend in the mechanics of reading.

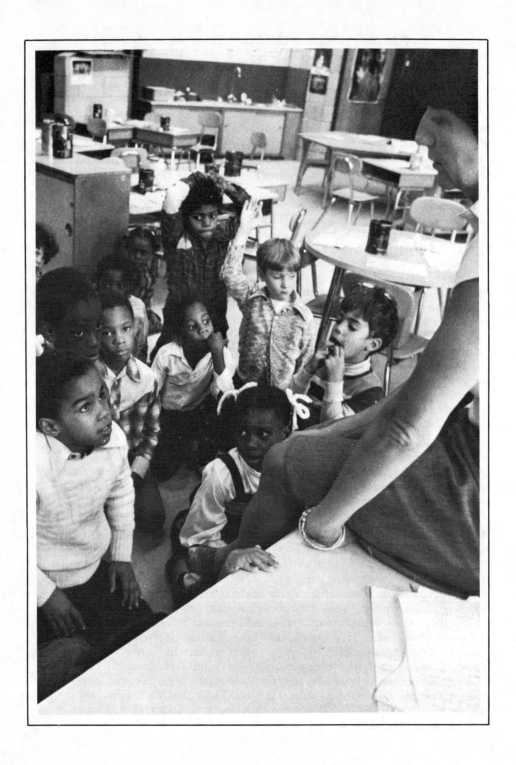

# 10
# Teaching Reading in a Multicultural Context

The many unanswered questions about teaching reading in a multicultural context point to the complexity of this problem. For instance, with respect to instructing those who speak black English, there is a question whether this dialect interferes with the entire reading process and, if so, which methods are best for minimizing that interference. For Spanish-speaking children, there is the issue of whether their first language should be used only until they acquire an ability in English or whether the school should provide for the continual development of their native language as well as English.

We realize how complex the problem is and, therefore, offer a range of educational considerations that should be taken into account in planning reading programs for black-dialect speakers, Spanish-speaking children, and children from other minority cultures.

## Teaching Reading to the Black-dialect Speaker

### Contrast between Standard English and Black Dialect

Although there are more similarities than differences between the black dialect called black English (BE) and standard English (SE), distinct linguistic features between the two influence the way reading is taught to black English-speaking pupils. One major difference between standard English and black dialect is the verb inflection in the present tense. Unlike standard English, black dialect requires no inflection in any syntactic construction in the present tense with the exception of *be,* which has a different pattern, nonexistent in standard English.

This contrast can be seen in the following:

| Standard English | Black Dialect |
| --- | --- |
| He does | He do |
| He doesn't | He don't |
| He hasn't | He haven't |
| He runs | He run |
| She doesn't run | She don't run |

In standard English, one would say, "The horse has spirit, and she runs the track in record time. She really does!" In black dialect, one might say, "The horse have spirit, and she run the track in record time. She really do!"

Syntactic differences occur, too. For example, some conditional clauses in black dialect require an inversion in word order similar to the question patterns in standard English.

| Standard English | Black Dialect |
| --- | --- |
| Mary doesn't know if she can go with us. | Mary don't know can she go with us. |

Other grammatical variations among black dialects are:

| Standard English | Black Dialect | Change |
| --- | --- | --- |
| He is going. | He goin. | (linking verbs) |
| Tom's cousin | Tom cousin | (possessive marker) |
| I have five cents. | I got five cent. | (plural marker) |
| Last night I walked home. | Last night I walk home. | (past marker) |
| An apple | A apple | (indefinite article) |

Variations among black-dialect speakers occur through a number of changes:

| Standard English | Black Dialect | Change |
| --- | --- | --- |
| We have to do it. | Us got to do it. | (pronoun form) |
| She is over at my house. | She over to my house. | (preposition) |
| He is sick all the time. | He be sick. | (*be* as indicator of time duration) |

The black-dialect speaker may not pronounce final consonants such as *d, t, l,* and *z.* Hence there are grammatical changes in pronunciation:

| Standard English | Black Dialect |
| --- | --- |
| Timed | Time |
| Passed | Pass |
| Grazed | Graze |
| He'll | He |

Word changes, too, occur because of phonological differences in the language:

| Standard English | Black Dialect |
| --- | --- |
| Three | Tree |
| Find | Fond |
| Help | Hep |
| Asked | Axed |
| Door | Dough (final sound of *r* is often left off) |

Sociolinguists believe that no language form is inherently superior to another as a mechanism for communication and that there is no absolute standard in language. Research by linguists, sociologists, and psycholinguists has shown that language of black-dialect, inner-city children is different but linguistically as highly structured and rule-governed as standard American English.[1] Further, black-dialect children receive a great deal of verbal stimulation and participate fully in a highly verbal culture. However, the fact that many teachers are biased against nonstandard dialect raises the question whether that bias may lower teacher expectations for achievement in reading and thereby inhibit learning to read.

Two assumptions underlie instructional suggestions for teaching black-dialect-speaking children. One assumption is that it is disruptive of learning to try to change children's dialects and to reject the way they think about the world (acceptance assumption). Another assumption is that there is a mismatch between black-dialect and conventional reading materials and methods (mismatch assumption).

**Instructional implications of the acceptance assumption** School efforts to change language dialect have not been very successful and indeed are questionable on the grounds of discrimination. Barbara

---

[1] Joan C. Baratz and Roger W. Shuy, eds., *Teaching Black Children to Read* (Washington, D.C.: Center for Applied Linguistics, 1969). W. A. Wolfram, "Sociolinguistic Alternatives in Teaching Reading to Non-Standard Speakers," *Reading Research Quarterly* 6 (1970): 9–33.

Hagerman and Terry Saario have provided an experiment for helping teachers understand what it is like to change one's dialect.[2] You may want to try it. Merely record yourself on tape, describing the activities of someone and following these directions:

1. Use in your own speech a very simple rule of black dialect; namely, do not inflect any verb in the present tense except with *be*. For example, "She have the book right now."

2. Construct one sentence without using an inflection on the third-person singular; for example, "He see the bird."

3. Record yourself in the endeavor for a three-minute period of connected speech.

4. Listen to the tape and count hesitations, corrections, and verbs that are inflected according to standard English.

5. Tell how you feel as you spoke on the tape.

Standard-English-speaking teachers who try this experiment find that they consciously edit their native dialect before being able to utter correct nonstandard verbs. The editing appears on the tape as a pause. Most must make a real effort to sustain speech that requires only one inflection difference. The conflict between the two dialects produces anxiety, editing, hesitation, and the inability to speak naturally. One implication for the teaching of reading is that you reduce anxiety by accepting children's dialects rather than pressuring them to attend simultaneously to the task of acquiring a second dialect while learning to read.

Kenneth Goodman and Catherine Buck have been helpful in showing that oral language dialects create no linguistic barriers to comprehending what is read.[3] Children who vary the text of what they are reading by substituting their own words appropriately and pronouncing written words in their own dialects are not making reading errors. Accordingly, you as a teacher must be able to distinguish between a difference in dialect and a reading error that requires remediation. You might look at black-dialect substitutions as signs that the child is comprehending and identifying with what is being read — something to be applauded.

---

[2] Barbara Hagerman and Terry Saario, "Non-Standard Dialect Interference in Reading," *Sign and Significance,* Claremont Reading Conference, 33rd Yearbook (Claremont, Calif.: Claremont Graduate School, 1969), pp. 158–162.

[3] Kenneth Goodman and Catherine Buck, "Dialect Barriers to Reading Comprehension Revisited," *The Reading Teacher* 27, no. 1 (October 1973): 6–12.

**Instructional implications of the mismatch assumption** Sociolinguists in the late 1960s thought that a mismatch between dialect and reading textbooks resulted in lower reading achievement.[4] Young black-dialect speakers come to school to find that their books "don't sound ri." The mismatch assumption is associated with the idea of *dialect interference* — a conflict of two dialects in the mind of the reader that causes one to use parts of the native dialect while trying to function in the second dialect. It occurs when the rules of pronunciation and meaning learned in the early years at home conflict with the rules for pronunciation and meaning found in the reading material of the school. Early suggestions for minimizing the interference of black English called for using the child's dialect when beginning to learn to read. The following are illustrative:

**Creating original material** A few teachers create reading material written in the black dialect that parallels the child's own speech. They argue that such material eases initial reading development, gives recognition to another language system, and supplements conventional writing. Dialect-based materials are followed by transition materials before introducing standard English. W. A. Stewart has illustrated the stages:[5]

> In Stage 1, black English is used — "Darryl and Kevin, dey runnin."
>
> In Stage 2, the most important features of standard English are introduced — "Darryl and Kevin, dey are runnin."
>
> In Stage 3, standard English is used — "Darryl and Kevin are running."

With few exceptions, such as the *Chicago Psycholinguistic Reading Series*, which was published by the Board of Education in Chicago, little effort has been made to produce dialect materials for national distribution. Community leaders often resist the idea, believing that black-dialect materials are less prestigious. Several linguists, too, oppose the practice on a number of grounds: difficulty of finding a suitable orthography for an unwritten dialect and the possibility that the use of dialect-based materials will not be appropriate for the wide language variability among black children.[6]

---

[4] Baratz and Shuy, *Teaching Black Children to Read.*

[5] W. A. Stewart, "On the Use of Negro Dialect in the Teaching of Reading," *Teaching Black Children to Read*, ed. Joan C. Baratz and Roger Shuy (Washington, D.C.: Center for Applied Linguistics, 1969), pp. 156–219.

[6] S. A. Cohen and Thelma Cooper, "Seven Fallacies: Reading Retardation and the

**Using the language experience approach**   The language experience approach, whereby children dictate, listen, speak, read, and write in their natural language, allows for a good match between the children's own language and what they read. Following this alternative, you would begin reading instruction by using the children's basic sentences and later develop patterns of standard English.

Stories are written in the children's dialect the first few times and then children are led to see that there is another way to write the story. Walter Loban has cautioned, however, that the teacher must not show disappointment with the child's language, but help the child recognize the idea of a "school language" and a "home language."[7]

**Providing prerequisites for reading standard English**   You may anticipate problems the black-dialect-speaking child is likely to encounter in reading standard English. This means, for example, that you (1) contrast the forms of the two dialects by writing examples on the board and having the pupils discuss the different rules that govern the conflicting language systems, (2) preface reading activity with pattern drills featuring the particular patterns of sentences and paragraphs to be met in the reading selection, (3) practice reading some anticipated difficult expressions whereby children look at the standard-English expressions and then say what they mean in their own words, and (4) provide background experiences for each unfamiliar concept that will appear in the reading selection.

Challenges have been made to the assumption that black dialect interferes with either oral reading or reading comprehension. Black-dialect speakers comprehend passages written in standard English as well as rewritten ones. Susanna Pflaum-Connor, for instance, reviewed the research literature and found no direct inference between black dialect and poor reading. She questions, therefore, the need for special materials to modify a mismatch between oral dialect and written prose.[8] However, she recognizes one specific teaching direction that is necessary when teaching generalizations about sound-symbol correspondence to black English-speaking pupils: *Do not ask these children to make distinctions in sounds that they do not hear.* If phonics instruction is incomprehensible to pupils, they are unlikely to look for

Urban Disadvantaged Beginning Reader," *Reading Teacher* 26 (October 1972): 38–45. R. L. Verresk, "Non-Standard Language and Reading," *Elementary English* 47 (1970): 334–341.

[7] Walter Loban, "Teaching Children Who Speak Social Class Dialects," *Elementary English* 45 (1968): 592–599, 618.

[8] Susanna Pflaum-Connor, "Language and Reading Acquisition for the English-Speaking Minority Student," *Aspects of Reading Instruction* (Berkeley, Calif.: McCutchan, 1978), pp. 154–173.

reliable spelling patterns to help in pronouncing words. You will recall that many black-dialect speakers do not differentiate the critical sounds for some final consonants and some short vowel features. Hence, you must either give practice in hearing and producing these sounds in words before engaging in phonics instruction or not use these sounds when developing phonic generalizations.

## Ethical Considerations in Teaching Black-dialect Children

Reading reform in response to pluralism has taken two directions. On the one hand, black-dialect-speaking children are asked to read materials that are thought to commit them to their subgroup. According to a few pluralists, materials should interpret events from the black point of view, reflect black aspirations, and stress reading skills that are thought to be related to increased political and economic power. On the other hand, most pluralists have an assimilationist bent.[9] They believe that the reading curriculum should reflect both black culture *and* the common culture. Black attainments should be respected and used in positive ways, but the major goal should be to help the individual function effectively within the common culture, black culture, and other ethnic cultures.

These two orientations are seen in the following continuum suggested by James Deslonde:[10]

> Separatism: Reading within the separatist situation emphasizes the learning of critical reading and reading in the content fields, has a racial identity thrust, focuses on inequality in the United States, and matches the content of reading to the community life-style.

> Segregation: Under segregation, remedial, compensatory, and enrichment reading instruction is given to minority pupils who are separated from pupils in the dominant culture.

> Desegregation: Federal and court guidelines require reassignments of pupils and teachers. Teachers are asked to be sensitive to minority children and their cultures.

> Postdesegregation: Reading programs include black literature and

---

[9] James A. Banks, "The Implications of Ethnicity for Curriculum Reform," *Educational Leadership* 33, no. 3 (December 1975): 168–172. Mary Boesnahan, "Selecting Sensitive and Sensible Books About Blacks," *The Reading Teacher* 30, no. 1 (October 1976): 16–20.

[10] James Deslonde, "Assessment of Needs for Achieving a Culturally Pluralistic Environment," *School Desegregation and Cultural Pluralism Stride* (San Francisco: Far West Laboratory for Educational Research and Development, 1976).

black special skill development, criterion-referenced tests, and a heavy emphasis on diagnosing and assessing reading skill levels of children.

Integration: Problems of low performance by low socioeconomic blacks are tackled by introducing more culture-fair and objective-based testing and more school-community cooperation in reading instruction. Some nontraditional content is introduced to reflect black culture and new teaching strategies are tried. There are more learning centers and alternative organizational patterns.

Cultural pluralism: The black achievement problem is no longer acute. Revised evaluation techniques to reduce cultural bias are operative; new reading materials that attend to the concerns of many subgroups and community cultural resources are used. There is much community involvement in reading programs, and cultural differences are emphasized.

Current multicultural literature uses the language of *rights* instead of the more familiar language of *needs*. The former language is adversarial in that it implies that teachers ought to champion the rights of pupils rather than claim to act in the best interests of people who are socially subordinate and dependent. Dean Asa Hillard of San Francisco State University sometimes mentions rights for black pupils. We think these rights imply practices for teachers of reading. For example, the right to:

A caring teacher. The teacher listens to what children say about the reading lessons.

Self-knowledge — truth and power. Reading content and method provide for a varied diet. Lessons illuminate the human situation, instruct, and give pleasure.

Role models. Teachers, resource persons, peers, autobiographers, and characters in books inspire children to follow desirable directions.

Real experiences — not necessarily ideal ones. Children read about life as it *is*, not just as it *should* be. Further, they are encouraged to better situations because of what they have read.

A school that one can call one's own. In addition to spending free time in the classroom and liking it, children invite their friends to visit.

Increasing liberation. Children grow in their ability to make choices about what they want to read.

Equal access to talent and resources. Children are not segregated by a reading organizational plan that groups them by ability and competence levels, denying them access to shared-reading experiences.

Expression. There is not a single right response to every book. Children freely relate the meanings they perceive in reading.

Defense against propaganda and exploitation. Children have practice in recognizing corruption and exploitation in print.

Cultural tradition and values. In reading literature, children apply the standards of literature; in reading factual pieces, they apply standards appropriate to the subject; and in all instances, they are sensitive to the values of minority groups.

# Teaching Reading to Spanish-speaking Children

Spanish-speaking pupils are entering the schools in increasing numbers. Ideas about how to teach these children are conflicting. Those who would use Spanish as the medium of instruction and teach these children first to read in Spanish may create a disadvantage for some Spanish-speaking students while eliminating a disadvantage for other Spanish speakers. This is so because not all Spanish speakers have the same proficiencies in Spanish or in English. Further, the environment in which a child lives — Spanish or English speaking — bears upon the decision of how best to teach that child. The Spanish-speaking child in an all-English-speaking neighborhood, for example, requires a different program from the Spanish-speaking child in a Spanish-speaking neighborhood. In the following section, we describe options for teaching Spanish-speaking children to read and then indicate how to decide which option to exercise in given circumstances.

### English as a Second Language (ESL)

The approach of accepting English as a second language provides for supplementary instruction in English. Children typically are "pulled out" of class for special English-language-skills training. Instruction time varies from several hours a week to one hour a day, depending on the availability of resources. Often ESL replaces work in art, music, or physical education. Training consists of learning the English phonological system (sounds), morphological system (words — vocabulary), syntactical system (grammar), and suprasegmental patterns (intonation, tones, pitch) that can be predicted. For example, pupils hear a word or phrase spoken by a native English speaker and then repeat it until they say it well. Next, pupils learn to respond to questions and to substitute new words in the pattern, such as the following:

| Teacher | Child |
| --- | --- |
| This is a pen. | This is a pen. |
| This is a pencil. | This is a pencil. |
| This is a chair. | This is a chair. |
| It is a pen. | It is a pen. |
| It is a pencil. | It is a pencil. |
| It is a chair. | It is a chair. |
| What is this? | It is a pen. |
| What is this? | It is a pencil. |
| What is this? | It is a chair. |

After the oral drill, the teacher writes the phrases and pupils listen, speak, read, and write the patterns. This oral-aural approach is built on systematic repetition. By drawing attention to the rules and patterns and by providing imitation and reinforcement, the teacher helps the child avoid trial and error in acquiring English. Also formal ESL training focuses on the elements of English that cause Spanish speakers the most difficulty. For example, many Spanish speakers need assistance in using English prepositions. They may say "in the table" when they mean "on the table" because the word *en* means both *in* and *on* in Spanish.

Training often varies for children of different ages. Young children especially are stimulated to use the language in real situations through nature walks, singing, dancing, rhymes, and dramatizations. They receive less instruction in cognitive awareness of rules and patterns. Unlike most foreign language instruction, ESL is designed to meet the immediate communication needs of children by providing the skills necessary for communicating with teachers and peers and for receiving instruction in English. Ideally, the ESL program is correlated with the child's work in the regular program.

## Spanish Adjunct Lessons (Programmed Learning)

Spanish adjunct lessons are one answer to the criticism made of ESL, namely, that children fall behind in what is being taught in the regular classroom because they are elsewhere learning English. A Spanish adjunct consists of self-instructional material that parallels in Spanish the instruction that the child will receive in the regular English-speaking classroom.[11] The purpose of an adjunct is to make sure that Spanish-speaking children know what their English-speaking teacher is asking them to do and that they have the ability to make the correct responses in English. Thus, children are given instruction in Spanish via tape and accompanying workbook. The children know what they are being asked in Spanish and learn how to respond before hearing other taped instructions in English. Transition from Spanish to English is made by gradually substituting English for Spanish. Taped instructions in English are given immediately following successful performance in response to Spanish instruction. In this way, the children learn the English directions for the task that they can already perform. For example, to teach the preschool or kindergarten child the concept of matching to sample in both Spanish and English, the lesson sequence would be as follows:

Mira está serie de dibujos. Estoy poniendo el dedo debajo del pájaro que está en la caja. ¿Ves otro pájaro? Pon el dedo tuyo debajo del otro. . . . Estos dos pájaros son iguales.

Pon el dedo debajo del coche que está en la caja. . . . Ahora pon el dedo debajo del otro coche.

Marca una línea del dibujo que es igual al dibujo que está en la caja, etc. Ahora vamos a hablar en ingles. Put your finger under the "key picture." (Pon el dedo debajo del dibujo que está en la caja.) Draw a line under the picture that is the same. (Marca una linea debajo del dibujo que es igual.) Put your finger under the key picture. . . . Put a line under the pictures that are the same.

Implementation of the program is simple. You merely select the tape and worksheet that corresponds to a forthcoming lesson. These materials are administered to the child or children by an aide, tutor, or are self-administered by the child. After completing the taped lesson, the child is ready to participate in the regular reading lesson with English-speaking children. Indeed the Spanish-speaking child is likely to do as well or better than the native English speakers in the lesson because of the focused instruction and practice available through the adjunct.

---

[11] John D. McNeil, "Adapting a Beginning Reading Program for Spanish-speaking Children," *Experiments in Kindergarten Reading* (Los Alamitos, Calif.: Southwest Regional Laboratory for Educational Research and Development, 1968).

### Bilingual-Bicultural Approach

The bilingual-bicultural approach is comprehensive in that it involves the teaching of reading skills in English and Spanish as well as the development of cultural awareness. A philosophy of cultural pluralism emphasizes the development and maintenance of the native language as well as English. With this approach, reading is taught first in the Spanish language. However, once the Spanish-speaking children have learned to speak English, they are taught to read it. In some programs, instruction in learning to read Spanish continues after the children are competent in English. The inclusion of the child's historical, literary, and cultural traditions is thought to strengthen identity and self-concept.

Many reasons are given for teaching the Spanish-speaking child to read Spanish first. The decoding skills are easier to learn in Spanish than in English because the written code is more consistent with the oral language. Also, the fact that Spanish-speaking children already have subconsciously learned most of the rules for syntax governing the use of their language is a great advantage. This knowledge aids them in decoding Spanish and in reconstructing meaning. Children should be allowed to use and develop the language they know best when acquiring the complex skills of reading. Further, once children have learned to read in their native language, learning to read English as a second language is easier because many of the basic reading skills are transferable.

### Variations in Bilingual Approaches

**The concurrent method**   With this method, instruction is given in both languages to the same group of pupils. Sometimes two teachers, one English dominant and one Spanish dominant, alternately present portions of the lesson in their respective language and ask pupils questions that may be answered in either of the languages. Other times a single teacher explains a concept in both languages, taking care not to resort to direct translation but to explain each concept only in terms of the language being used. In classrooms where there are both English and Spanish speakers, the children may learn each other's language, although the purpose of this method is not to teach a second language but to facilitate learning; that is, to avoid having the pupil not learning because of language difference.

**Alternate days variation**   By this variation, pupils receive instruction one day in English and the other day in Spanish.

**Immersion**   Immersion is placing a child to learn a second language in a setting where the second language is the only vehicle of instruction. Often this is an effective method after the child has had some ESL or adjunct training. In the Culver City, California, Spanish Immersion Program (SIP), however, English- and Spanish-speaking kindergartners are encouraged to speak as much Spanish as possible. (The program is primarily for native English speakers.) Most children in the SIP kindergarten learn to speak words and phrases in Spanish. In the first grade, the children are expected to speak more Spanish and by the time they are in the second grade they are speaking, reading, and writing Spanish and use no English except during English language arts classes. In second grade, the children are well founded in encoding and decoding skills in Spanish and then begin one hour a day reading English. Pupils get instruction on the difference between English and Spanish pronunciation, but otherwise they transfer easily to English reading.[12] These children become bilingual, developing their English skills through the influence of the home and the larger society, even though Spanish is the medium of instruction in school.

**Vernacular method**   With the vernacular method, Spanish-speaking children are taught to read in their native language while *separately* learning to speak English as a second language via aural-oral activities.

Decoding and comprehending the second language are taught as follows:

1.   The teacher arranges oral preparation for what is going to be read.

2.   The children participate in oral discussion followed by chart reading, with modeling by the teacher.

3.   The children individually read the expression modeled.

4.   Using pocket charts, the teacher constructs different sets of sentences quickly for additional practice by the children.

5.   After adequate preparation, the children read from printed books.

### Issues of Transition and Maintenance in Language Instruction

A major difficulty in teaching limited- or non-English-speaking children to read in English is that they cannot anticipate the meanings of words in a sentence because of their lack of knowledge of the syntax of

---

[12]   Karen Joseph Shender, "Bilingual Education — How American Can You Get?" *Learning* 5, no. 2 (October 1976): 32–41.

English. Hence some persons prefer to delay the teaching of reading in English until oral English skills are mastered and, meanwhile, to teach non-English-speaking children how to read their native language.

Conversely, there are those who oppose delaying the teaching of reading until fluency in English has been achieved. They believe that the learning of some English skills or vocabulary can occur immediately and that there is no need to delay English reading instruction until the child has mastered the language. Proponents of this latter position encourage the non-English-speaking child to read English words, phrases, and sentences just as soon as these expressions are in the child's oral repertoire.

A second issue concerns how long to maintain bilingual programs. Some school districts offer instruction in reading Spanish only for the first year or two — until the child has acquired enough English skills to profit from instruction in English. Other school districts prize the Spanish-speaking culture, including its language, and want the children to develop their knowledge of Spanish and to extend the literacy and cultural heritage of the Spanish-speaking peoples as ends in themselves. School districts such as Dade County Public Schools maintain instruction in reading Spanish and English beyond initial instruction to reading in the content fields at all grade levels.[13]

## Decision Rules for Determining Which Approach to Adopt

You should consider three factors before deciding whether to place a child in a *concurrent* or *vernacular* program: linguistic realities, parent-community expectations, and external factors.

**Linguistic realities**    Not all Spanish-speaking children have the same ability in Spanish or English. These differences must be considered in placement. A common way to differentiate among pupils is on the basis of whether the child understands (1) only Spanish (Spanish monolingual); (2) spoken Spanish much better than English (Spanish dominant); (3) Spanish and English equally well (equivalent); (4) English a little better than Spanish (English dominant); (5) English much better than Spanish (English dominant); and (6) only English (English monolingual). Spanish monolingual children and Spanish-dominant children are given a vernacular program offering reading instruction in Spanish while separately learning to speak English before being asked to read it.

---

[13] Marta M. Bequer, "A Look at Bilingual Programs in Dade County: Gateway to the Latin World," *Educational Leadership* 35, no. 8 (May 1978): 644–649.

To determine the linguistic reality for an individual, you can use the following techniques:

1. Interviewing. Ask pupils and parents about the relative use of languages in the home.

2. Indirect measures. Ask the child to name favorite television programs or channels. If the community has a Spanish-speaking channel and the child names it, you have indirect evidence that the child is Spanish dominant or equivalent. Similarly, the language used by the child with friends is an indirect measure of the child's own linguistic ability.

3. Parallel testing. Give the child a Spanish and English variation of a test measuring the same objective. Performance differences will indicate language capacity. Science Research Associates (SRA), for example, publishes parallel versions of criterion-referenced tests of reading skills in both English and Spanish.[14]

4. Rating scales. You can observe and rate the child's relative use of Spanish in arranged situations. For example, you can place seven items on a table and ask the child to name them. The labels given will indicate language preference in the situation. It is desirable to break down the child's language ability into categories, such as aural competence and oral fluency. Assessing only pronunciation on vocabulary does not indicate the child's total second language ability.

**Parent-community expectations**  Some parents and communities want Spanish-speaking children to enter the dominant culture as quickly as possible, even if it means losing minority values. Other parents and communities want to maintain and strengthen minority values while acquiring the ability to read English. These two attitudes should be taken into account when deciding on a program.

**External factors**  Geographic location and percent of Spanish-speaking persons within the community bear upon your decision whether to keep the two languages separate or to encourage using both languages within the same situation. Concurrent methods are popular in border communities that typically use both languages simultaneously. On the other hand, Spanish-speaking children living away from the frontier often get much exposure to English outside of school. Such children find the ESL approach useful and learn to function as native speakers in a relatively short time. Spanish-speaking pupils whose major exposure

---

[14] *Sober-Espanol, System for Objective-Based Evaluation of Reading Spanish* (Chicago: Science Research Associates, 1975).

to language is the Spanish of their barrios have little difficulty in maintaining their native language but need intensive instruction in learning to read English.

### Bilingual-Bicultural Materials

Basal reader, language experience, individualized reading, and technological approaches to the teaching of reading are all used in teaching Spanish speakers. The Educational Products Information Exchange (EPIE) issues reports describing and analyzing just about every available Spanish instructional material produced in the United States and other countries (see appendix). The number of materials reviewed in these reports by many educators, all fluent in English and Spanish, is more than twelve hundred. They evaluate the different bilingual reading programs on the basis of validity of goals, content, methodology, and means of assessing learner progress.

*Bidialectism* is a special problem in getting commercial material that will serve all populations. The Spanish language has many different dialects and local communities want materials that reflect their own. The teacher trying to elicit a particular response from a picture of a kite, for example, may get: "papalote," "cometa," "pandorga," "barrilete," or something else depending on the dialect of the community.

Answers to this problem are to use the language experience approach, to create materials based on the dialect, to rewrite the standard material, to teach the child to speak the standard dialect before reading it, or to let the child read the standard material in his or her own dialect.

### Teaching Beginning Reading in Spanish

Just as one can learn to decode English, one can learn to decode Spanish by analytic or synthetic methods. You will recall from Chapter 4 that analysis is the decomposing of words into their different elements. For instance, the familiar word *Mama* is presented and analyzed to reveal first the syllables *Ma* and *ma* and then the letter-sound correspondence m – a.

Afterward the analyzed elements are recombined:

M a (Ma)

m a (má)

Ma ma (Mamá)

**Auditory discrimination**   The following are illustrations of analytic techniques for the teaching of Spanish vowels:

1.   Select a word that begins with a vowel such as *hijo*.

2.   Pronounce clearly the word *hijo*.

3.   Pronounce *hijo* in a way to exaggerate the first syllable /e/ — i i i i jo.

4.   Pronounce the word separating the syllables i — jo.

5.   Ask pupils what they *hear* first.

6.   Ask pupils to supply other words that begin with the sound /e/.

   *Letter-Vowel Sound Correspondence*
   "Aquí esta la *a*
   la trajo mamá
   y aquí esta la *e*
   vino con bebé
   mira esa es la *u*
   es igual a la cuerda
   que saltas tú
   y viene la *o*
   de cara redonda
   diciendo no no
   pero esta la *i*
   con su punto arriba
   que dice sí sí."

**Método onomatopeyico**   This is an old but still popular method for teaching letter-sound correspondence. It calls for the child to associate sounds with letters through prompting by pictures of animals and objects from the environment that make sounds similar to the sound values of particular letters ("nature talks"). The letter *i*, for example, might be shown with a picture of a mouse and then you would complete these steps:

1.   Tell a short story in which a mouse squeeks /e/ "i i i".

2.   Elicit choral and individual oral responses of the sound for the

letter. You might elicit these responses by presenting a series of words with the desired sound value: *I*nez, *i*glesia, *i*gual, *I*rene.

3. Ask children to read new words composed of familiar patterns and the new letter *i*.

4. Ask children to write the letter.

In brief, children are expected to hear, pronounce, see, and write each letter.

As in teaching children to read English, *synthesis* as a method in teaching children to read Spanish requires recomposing words by reuniting their elements. After pupils can write the five vowels and are learning beginning consonants, you might have them complete exercises such as this one:

1. You write on the chalkboard the initial consonant just learned followed by the five vowels, *a, e, i, o, u*.

2. Have the children pronounce the syllables formed by joining the consonant with the vowels, for example: *as, es, is, os, us, sa, se, si, so, su*.

3. Have the children combine vowels and syllables to form words such as: *eso, osa, uso, soso*.

A syllabic method, *Método Silábico,* is appropriate for teaching reading in Spanish and Portuguese because these are highly syllabic languages. Consequently syllables are introduced, often in the form of a syllabary (a table of syllables), practiced and then combined into words and sentences.

Beginning reading in Spanish is sometimes taught by *El Método Natural.* This method is similar to the phrase, sentence, and story methods for teaching beginning English. It is based on the idea that a complete phrase is the critical element in reading, not separate letters, syllables, or words. Procedures for carrying out this method are as follows:

1. Write phrases or sentences from children's conversation on the chalkboard, usually phrases with one-syllable words are selected for beginning sessions.

2. Have the children read the written phrases exactly as they were spoken.

3. Have the children write the phrases.

4.   Print the phrases on cards and distribute the cards to the children for subsequent practice.

Weekly activities for teaching the *El Método Natural* are:

*Monday*   — Assigning stories or activities to elicit the phrases, writing and reading the phrases, making the printed copy, and using configuration clues to improve visualization of the phrases.

*Tuesday*   — Review stories, visualize the phrases, discuss the phrases, and compare the phrases written in lowercase and uppercase letters. Individuals and groups read the phrases and then all children write the phrases in their notebooks.

*Wednesday* — Review the prior day's work. Cut up the phrases in the presence of the children, dividing the phrases into words.

*Thursday*   — Cut up the words, dividing them into syllables. Children complete dictation exercises and write the words on the chalkboard.

*Friday*   — Provide a general review. Children write the phrases with seeds, straws, and sand. They may reverse the order of the phrases and form new sentences with the words previously learned:

Eso es el oso.

Lalo sale solo.

El dedo de Dimas.

might become

Ese oso es de Lalo.

**Método ecléctico**   This method makes use of both analysis and synthesis. Children apply analysis by first associating a printed word with the concept for which it stands — *libro* is associated with a book. Next, they identify the syllables of the word — *li-bro*. The syllables are further divided into their fundamental elements — *li* becomes *l* and *i; bro* becomes *b r o*. Children then apply synthesis by combining the *l* in *libro* with the five vowels to form syllables — *la, le, li, lo, lu*. The syllable *bro* can also be modified by substituting vowels to form *bra, bre, bri,* and *bru*. These syllables are combined with other vowels to form words like *lado* and *bravo*. These new words are then used in sentences and simple stories.

### Differences between Spanish and English: Teaching Spanish Speakers to Read English

The fact that the same letters in English have a different sound value than in Spanish (phonological differences) accounts for how a Spanish-speaking child may pronounce words read in English. We have already pointed out that English pronunciation is not per se the responsibility of the reading teacher but that you must distinguish between the children's reading in their own dialects and failing to associate the meaning of what is read. For example, it is not unusual for Spanish speakers to pronounce some words in a distinctive way: /i/ as /iy/ *hit=heet;* /u/ as /uw/ *full=fool;* /sh/ as /ch/ *shoe=chew;* /ch/ as /sh/ *chain=shain;* /m/ (final) as /n/ *comb=cone;* /w/ as /gw/ *way=guay;* /z/ as /s/ *zoo=soo;* /j/ as /y/ *jello=yello.*

Differences in syntax may present English-comprehension problems for some Spanish speakers.[15] Illustrated contrasts are as follows:

|  | English | Spanish |
|---|---|---|
| Verb-subject-predicate | The boys run. | The boys runs. |
|  | The boy runs. | The boy run. |
| *Be* | I am ten years old. | I have ten years. |
| *Negation* | He isn't here. | He no is here. |
|  | I don't want anything. | I don't want nothing. |
|  | Don't go. | No go. |
| *Word order* | The black cat is pretty. | The cat black is pretty. |
|  | Where am I? | Where I am? |
| *Possession* | The dog's head | The head of the dog |

To help the child with difficulties in reading unusual syntax, you might give activities that apply patterns, whereby semantic content is held constant, while grammar and lexicon vary. Listening while

---

[15] A complete cross-language description of the language correspondences that create difficulties for the Spanish-speaking learner of English is found in Rose Nash, *Comparing English and Spanish Patterns in Phonology and Orthography* (New York: Regents Publishing Company, 1977).

looking is another device to employ — the child listens while you read the selection aloud, indicating correct phrasing, stress patterns, and stress-signaled associations.

## Teaching the Spanish-speaking Child

The critical factor in teaching Spanish-speaking children is in the quality of the relationship that exists between you and the child. We should not stereotype Spanish-speaking children when describing their characteristics. There are many individual differences. Yet it seems that successful teachers act upon some generalizations about Spanish-speaking children; for example, that these children respond better when the reading material has human content and is characterized by fantasy and humor — where it is less abstract and more personal. Successful teachers accept the children's colloquial language; communicate with the children in Spanish; relate instruction to roles and activities of the community; use dances, songs, games, and other resources of the community; and make parents welcome in the classroom. These teachers use parents as incentives. Instead of asking children to read for the teacher or for their personal profit, they ask children to read for their mothers and fathers. Further, pupil cooperation rather than competition tends to prevail in the higher achieving Spanish-speaking classrooms.

## Teaching Reading to Other Minority Cultures

American Indian — Navajo, Hopi, Sioux, and others; Korean, Vietnamese, Tagalog; Chinese — Mandarin and Cantonese; Samoan, and many other cultural groups are represented by pupils in classrooms. The Los Angeles schools, for example, must consider eighty-two different languages within its student population. In teaching limited English-speaking children from whatever culture to read English, you can follow the guidelines given previously for teaching those who speak black dialects and Spanish: (1) become familiar with the home life and economics of the particular minority community; (2) compare the children's native language with English to identify and ease the special language difficulties that these children are likely to have in learning to read English; (3) identify the value system operating in the minority culture and take these values into account, both in the selection of content and in the conduct of lessons; (4) use aspects of the minority pupils' culture in the teaching of reading to enhance self-development; and (5) participate with minority parents in designing and carrying out reading activities.

# Summary

Many forces account for the advance of bilingual and cross-cultural education: the presence of about five million pupils whose home languages are other than English; appreciation of black dialect and the importance of using children's own language and cultural background in teaching them to read; national bilingual acts; legislative and judicial decisions encouraging the creation of bilingual programs; and the growing belief that, although there must be shared values and common outlooks, the nation is richer because of the cultural diversity of its people.

This chapter gave attention to unresolved issues concerning the teaching of reading in a multicultural context — for instance, the value of teaching children to read in their native language — but the major emphasis was on planning reading programs for children whose home language is black English, Spanish, or another language.

We began with the topic of teaching reading to the black-dialect child, showing the practical applications of the differences in black and standard English and examining the range of thinking about the issue of interference of black English in learning to read. The reading rights of the black-dialect-speaking child were illustrated. Next, we considered the teaching of reading to Spanish-speaking children describing the different approaches used and giving guidelines for determining which approach to adopt. Methods for teaching beginning reading Spanish were presented in some detail. Throughout the chapter, we stressed the need for teachers to differentiate between reading errors and differences in dialects. We concluded with general principles for teaching reading to children from minority cultures.

# Self-instructional Exercises

### Exercise 1. Differentiating between Reading Errors and Spanish Dialect

Put a mark by each departure from standard-English oral reading that is a dialect characteristic of Spanish speakers and *not* a true reading error.

1. The child says:
    a. _____ "yes" when reading *Jess*
    b. _____ "was" when reading *saw*

2. The child says:

a. _____ "television" when reading *telephone*

b. _____ "taught" when reading *thought*

3. The child says:

a. _____ "exit" when reading *extra*

b. _____ "estep" when reading *step*

4. The child says:

a. _____ "cut" when reading *caught*

b. _____ "first" when reading *fast*

5. The child says:

a. _____ "sings" when reading *sing*

b. _____ "feets" when reading *feet*

**ANSWERS TO EXERCISE 1**

1a. Spanish speakers often substitute /y/ for /j/ — pronouncing *yam* for *jam*; *yet* for *jet*; *Yon* for *John*; and so on. Calling *saw* "was" is a reversal common to native English speakers who are beginning to read.

2b. Spanish speakers often substitute /d/, /f/, or /t/ for the voiceless *th* as in *them* and substitute /z/, /v/, or /d/ for the voiced *th* as in *thin*.

3b. There is a tendency for Spanish speakers to carry over from their native language the addition of /e/ before words beginning with *sp*, *st*, and *sc*.

4a. When learning to read English, Spanish speakers often pronounce /au/ and /ou/ with the short /u/ sound.

5b. Spanish speakers often try to apply the more common way for forming plurals, having had little experience with irregular inflectional forms like goose-geese, mouse-mice, and man-men.

## Exercise 2. Differentiating between Reading Errors and Black Dialect

Put a mark by the response in each pair that is a dialect characteristic of the black speaker and *not* a true reading error.

1. The child says:

a. _____ "away" when reading *among*

b. _____ "a apple" when reading *an apple*

2. The child says:

   a. \_\_\_\_ "walk" when reading *walked*

   b. \_\_\_\_ "weak" when reading *walk*

3. The child says:

   a. \_\_\_\_ "men" when reading *meant*

   b. \_\_\_\_ "me" when reading *met*

4. The child says:

   a. \_\_\_\_ "do" when reading *go*

   b. \_\_\_\_ "run" when reading *runs*

5. The child says:

   a. \_\_\_\_ "wif" when reading *with*

   b. \_\_\_\_ "so" when reading *too*

**ANSWERS TO EXERCISE 2**

1b. The indefinite article in black dialect is often *a* even before nouns beginning with a vowel.

2a. A syntactical difference between black and standard English is found in frequent omission of the past marker in the black dialect.

3a. The black-dialect speaker frequently omits the last consonant sounds in words ending in consonant clusters; for example, hold-hoe, past-pas, disk-dis.

4b. Unlike standard English, black dialect does not inflect the third-person singular; for example, he has — he have; he does — he do; he runs — he run.

5a. When in the terminal position, *th* is often pronounced as /f/ in black dialect; for example, mouth=mouf.

## Exercise 3. Responding to Cultural Differences

Put a mark by the most appropriate action in light of the information presented.

1. If you want to teach non-English-speaking children to read English, the first element to stress would be:

   a. \_\_\_\_ Phonic skills

   b. \_\_\_\_ Oral language facility

   c. \_\_\_\_ Ability to follow directions

2. Children are more fluent in Spanish than English, so you should select a reading program that:

   a. _____ Stresses decoding rather than comprehension

   b. _____ Aims at correcting learners' accents and pronunciation in English

   c. _____ Gives emphasis to English language patterns

3. When reading aloud, children do not pronounce words in standard English but instead use a dialect so the best solution is to:

   a. _____ Have children compose their own materials and read them.

   b. _____ Use standard-English material but help children with unfamiliar syntax.

   c. _____ Teach children to speak standard English through oral drills and basic dialogues.

4. Children who are learning English as a second language need to read and understand English word structure, so a good activity is:

   a. _____ Matching words that have the same vowel sound as a sample word

   b. _____ Writing spelling words from dictation

   c. _____ Selecting from a list of words all of those words with the prefix *not*

5. Black-dialect-speaking children often do not pronounce /ed/ in words such as *passed, climbed,* and *laughed;* neither do they have the concept of *ed* as a tense marker, often considering the *ed* as a meaningless set of silent letters. So you should teach the children:

   a. _____ The phonological rules for pronouncing *ed*

   b. _____ The grammatical rule that *ed* signals the past tense

   c. _____ To ignore both grammatical and phonological functions of inflections that have no function in the child's dialect

**ANSWERS TO EXERCISE 3**

1b. Language comprehension is fundamental to reading.

2c. Competency in English requires the ability to generate and understand novel but grammatical sentences.

3b. The teacher who accepts the dialect of children realizes that the children's language is part of their culture. Children should be permitted, even encouraged, to read the way they speak. Although the practice suggested in answer (a) is very appropriate as a supplementary activity, it is not enough that children learn to read materials written only in their own dialect.

4c. The activity given in (c) is related to structural analysis. The other activities are associated with letter-sound correspondence.

5c. The failure to distinguish grammatical signals of tense may affect the child's comprehension. Such loss of understanding is more important in reading than the absence of phonological clues that affect pronunciation but not comprehension.

## Selected Readings

Feldman, Doris. "A Special Reading System for Second Language Learners," *TESOL Quarterly* 12, no. 4 (December 1978): 415–424.

An account of an ESL teacher's effort to design and carry out during a four-year period a "pullout" program for teaching reading in English to children who were not native learners of English. The program has four phases: a *readiness phase*, where children learn to recognize that reading is a message written down, to recognize phonetic contrasts, to compare and read words composed of a few initial consonants and regular vowel patterns, to read small stories composed of a few sight words and words composed of familiar consonant and vowel patterns; an *application phase*, where children expand their knowledge of phonetic elements and learn to read for fun; a *reading written language phase*, where pupils learn to generate their own rules, such as one governing the final *e*, to read with intonation sentences in context, and to develop the vocabulary for what they will say and read; and a *reading for learning phase*, where films, trade books, and other resources are used for understanding the culture about them.

Other features of the program include giving the children opportunities to follow along with the reading groups in the regular classroom (though they may not always be able to understand what is read) and to apply what they are learning in the ESL class to the reading materials of the regular classroom. Success of the program is indicated by the facts that all those in the program for at least one year learn to read and those in the program for three years are generally found in the top quarter of the English-speaking classroom.

Fletcher, Barbara P., et al. *A Guide to Assessment Instruments for Limited English Speaking Students.* New York: Santilliana Publishing Co., 1979.

This is a guide to tests that are appropriate for limited English-speaking children of elementary school age whose first language is Chinese, French, Italian, Navajo, Portuguese, Spanish, or Tagalog.

Lee, Grace E. "Reading for Asian Students," *Resources in Education* 14, no. 2 (February 1979): 44. ERIC Ed. 159 585.

The author claims that Asians can best learn to read English as a second language by receiving strong oral language experiences and opportunities to experience the culture and geography of America. These pupils are more motivated to learn to read English when they like Americans and sense positiveness, sensitivity, and support from the teacher. Linguistic difficulties center on beginning consonants, certain final sounds, digraphs such as "th" and "gh", changing pronunciation of the same vowel combination, and syntactical rules.

Perez, Samuel A. "How to Effectively Teach Spanish-speaking Children Even If You're Not Bilingual," *Language Arts* 56, no. 2 (February 1979): 159–162.

The author recommends that teachers (1) show approval of each child's language, (2) learn enough of the child's native language to demonstrate to pupils that knowing two languages is more useful than knowing only one, (3) team teach with a bilingual teacher or a Spanish-speaking aide, (4) involve Spanish-speaking parents in the classroom work, and (5) introduce peer teaching because it helps both tutee and tutor learn skills, gain self-esteem, and have better interpersonal relationships.

*Reading Teacher* 32, no. 6 (March 1979).

This issue features nine articles, each treating an aspect of teaching in a multicultural context. Suggestions are offered for *what* and *how* to teach bilingual pupils. For instance, one author addresses the question of when a child with limited English should begin the transition from reading in the home language to beginning reading in English. Another describes how the language experience approach can be successful with bilingual children who are reading below their potential. Still another indicates the advantages of using discussion to link what minority children already know to what they will be reading in the basal reader.

Swain, Merrill, and Cummins, James. "Bilingualism, Cognitive Functioning and Education," *Language Teaching and Linguistics: Abstracts* 12, no. 1 (January 1979): 4–18.

A review of recent studies treating the relationship between bilingualism and cognitive functioning. Negatively, the studies indicated that bilinguals suffered from a language handicap when measured by tests of academic achievement. Positively, a variety of cognitive advantages are reported for bilinguals. Higher levels of linguistic skills, divergent thinking, and analytical orientation are among the advantages found.

Several educational implications are drawn. For instance, when the home language is different from the school language and the home language tends to be denigrated by others and selves, it is better to begin initial instruction in the child's first language, switching at a later stage to instruction in the school language. On the other hand, when the home language is a majority language valued by the community and where literacy is encouraged by the home, it is better to provide initial instruction in the second language.

# 11
# Evaluating and Selecting Reading Materials

Teachers as a group have primary responsibility for selecting the materials to use in reading classrooms. That selection may be made by an individual teacher for a particular classroom or by a committee of teachers making a decision for the school or the district. You as a reading teacher will probably, a number of times in your career, participate in the process of evaluating and choosing reading materials.

Moreover, evaluating the strengths and weaknesses, the adequacies and deficiencies, of instructional materials already in use is an activity required of any conscientious teacher. Dolores Durkin reported observations of reading instruction in classrooms in which the unquestioned use of various reading instruction materials led teachers to commit grievous errors.[1] In some instances, blind use of instructional materials may lead to practices totally inappropriate for a specific situation. In other cases, the materials may be incompatible with the instructional goals or with the teacher's philosophy of learning. Finally, outdated materials still in use may simply be incorrect. It is clear that the teacher who is a potential user of reading materials must make *regular* and ongoing evaluations of those materials.

In this chapter, we suggest a number of general criteria to use in evaluating reading instruction materials. Following this, each of the four reading approaches is examined in terms of which criteria to apply

---

[1] Dolores Durkin, "Some Questions about Questionable Instructional Materials," *Reading Teacher* 28 (1974): 13–17.

355

in analyzing materials and what additional factors must be taken into account. Since the language experience and individualized approaches rely on books, articles, and literature, in a concluding section we discuss procedures to use in selecting literature for the classroom.

# General Criteria for Evaluating Instructional Materials

Five general criteria to be used in evaluating instructional materials are (1) consistency with reading approach, (2) adequacy of objectives, (3) instructional content, (4) instructional methodology, and (5) validation. These criteria are especially useful in reviewing instructional materials that employ a basal or technological approach. To a lesser extent, the criteria are also applicable to the language experience and individualized approaches.

### Consistency with Reading Approach

An overarching question that arises in the evaluation of all instructional materials is whether the reading materials are consistent with your desired reading approach. To answer this question, you must first clarify your own views about the way reading should be taught. In general, it is best for a beginning teacher to start with a single approach that is well understood and to use it efficiently. In Chapter 2, we described the four basic approaches to reading and identified suitable materials for each of them. It might be timely for you to review that chapter now and on future occasions when you actually review reading materials.

### Adequacy of Objectives

Another area to consider in the evaluation of reading instruction materials is the objectives. The objectives emphasized within a set of reading materials are not always specified, and you may need to examine the materials carefully to determine which ones are emphasized the most. In addition, several other issues need to be considered. First you should ask whether the objectives appear appropriate to you. Do you believe the right skills have been stressed? Do the objectives correspond to the objectives advocated by the school or school district? In some cases, districts explicitly advocate certain objectives through district-developed, grade-level curriculum frameworks or guidelines. In other instances, the district acceptance of objectives is much more implicit. For example, when a specific test of reading is employed widely throughout the district and school administrators pay attention to the results, there is, in essence, an assumption of the importance of the objectives implied within the test. The objectives of most tests are not explicit, and you must therefore examine the tests carefully to determine the objectives.

## Content of Materials

In studying the content of instructional materials, you should bear in mind (1) the organization of the materials, (2) their scope, and (3) their suitability for your students. You should decide whether the organizational schema is a reasonable one. Second, does the scope of the materials, or the extent of the coverage, reflect your concept of reading? Is it based on research to determine how much material to use? Third, are the content and level of difficulty appropriate for the maturity and interests of most of your pupils? Often in reviewing instructional materials, it is helpful to call on your own experience about what kinds of content are of interest to children. Alternatively, it is sometimes possible to involve your pupils in the process of selection by letting them help determine which materials are particularly interesting to them.

## Instructional Methodology

One aspect of the materials, then, is the content; another is the instructional methodology suggested for the teacher. Is this methodology based on research or accepted learning theories? Although your own philosophical preferences about the modes of interaction with students are relevant in the consideration of materials, there is now some well-defined evidence relating instructional procedures to high levels of student achievement. Drawing on literature on the psychology of learning and the technology of instruction, Edys Quellmalz and others have identified a number of characteristics of instructional material that are known to facilitate learning: teacher-directed instruction, written instruction, supervised practice, independent practice, knowledge of results, testing, and remediation.[2]

## Validation

Every set of instructional materials should be tried out and its effectiveness shown before it is foisted upon the classroom teacher. American schooling suffers because validation data is frequently not avail-

[2] Edys Quellmalz, Nancy Snidman, and Joan Herman, "Toward Competency-Based Reading Systems (Paper presented at the annual meeting of the American Educational Research Association, Chicago, March 1977).

able for reading materials. We urge you to consider product validation information and ask publishers to provide it.

## Evaluating a Basal Series

The characteristics of basal reading materials in large part determine which criteria to use in their evaluation. The objectives of a basal series are important criteria to employ in the selection process. Are the objectives stated for the basal series? Do they match your view of what is to be taught at the grade level? Are they internally consistent?

Most teachers prefer that objectives be stated rather than be implicit. One reason is the belief that when objectives are explicit, the designers of the material have been more systematic in their preparation because the stated objectives have served as a guideline for what is to be accomplished. When the objectives are only implicit, you can try to intuit them by a careful examination of the materials, but this is an onerous task and you are advised to stay with basal series in which objectives are well stated.

Finally, you should decide whether the objectives are internally consistent. For any grade level, can they be accomplished without conflicting with each other? Considering the range of potential objectives — cognitive and affective — it is conceivable that seeking the attainment of one objective will impede the attainment of others.

You need to analyze the *content* of the materials to see if the selections are suitable for the interests and maturity of your children. Also you need to evaluate the sequence of materials to determine whether more difficult materials might precede those that are less difficult. Another issue is whether the scope of one basal reader is adequate for an indicated period; for example, one-half of the school year.

Another factor of significance is the *methodology*. Simply presenting reading selections without providing a plan for using them in some systematic way does not constitute a good basal reader series. Thus, you must question whether the teachers' manuals offer suggestions for teaching the required skills. A basal series should have explicit instructional cues to use in the presentation of material. It is especially relevant to examine how well the model lessons cover the full range of reading skill areas, including literal and inferential comprehension, and are not restricted to phonics analysis, word meaning, and word structure.

An instructional element that has increased in prominence in more recent basal reader series is the use of *independent practice*. How well do the materials designed for independent practice relate to the full range of reading skills, including the areas of phonics, word meaning, and location study skills and literal comprehension? Research studies indicate that feedback to the learner about whether a response is correct and, if not, what it takes to make it correct is useful in the facilitation of learning.[3] You should check how much feedback is provided to students in independent practice materials.

Most modern basal readers have available as supplements a variety of *assessment materials*. These might include skills tests of various types, mastery tests, or end-of-year summary tests. You will need to know: Are evaluation materials available and usable? Are these materials compatible with the objectives of a particular year's basal reader series?

A final factor of importance in evaluating a basal series is the adequacy of the *teacher's manual* or guidebook. You should find out whether the instructions are sufficient for you to make full use of the system from the first day of lessons. Furthermore, you might want to see if there are specific reminders for the experienced teacher and suggestions for improving the instruction of the new teacher.

## Rating a Basal Series

A mini rating form can be employed to evaluate a basal series. To rate each series on the listed criteria, use the following scale:

> 4 = strongly agree
>
> 3 = agree
>
> 2 = disagree
>
> 1 = strongly disagree

The scores for each series can then be tallied and compared to see which one obtained the highest rating, or you may decide to weigh some items as more important than others and thus reach a different conclusion. Figure 11.1, a mini rating form, shows nineteen specific criteria within four major headings. We have provided the ratings for one hypothetical basal series, but a number of series could be comparatively evaluated by completing the rating for each.

---

[3] R. H. Gagné and L. J. Briggs, *Principles of Instructional Design* (New York: Holt, Rinehart and Winston, 1974).

Rating Basal Materials: A Mini Form

| Criteria | Basal 1 Name: *Living + Growing* | Basal 2 Name: | Basal 3 Name: |
|---|---|---|---|
| A. Objectives | | | |
| 1. The objectives of the program are well stated. | 4 | | |
| 2. The objectives are consistent with your view of what is to be taught at each grade level. | 3 | | |
| 3. The objectives are internally consistent. | 3 | | |
| B. Materials — content | | | |
| 1. The content is well organized. | 4 | | |
| 2. The content is appropriate for the interests and maturity level of your students. | 3 | | |
| 3. The content is appropriately sequenced. | 4 | | |
| 4. The scope is appropriate for the indicated time period. | 2 | | |
| C. Materials — methodology | | | |
| 1. Instructional methodology corresponds with your preferred method of instruction. | 3 | | |
| 2. Methodology incorporates: | | | |
| a. Teacher-directed instruction | 4 | | |
| b. Written instruction | 2 | | |
| c. Supervised practice | 2 | | |
| d. Independent practice | 3 | | |
| e. Testing | 3 | | |
| f. Knowledge of results | 2 | | |
| g. Provisions for remediation | 3 | | |
| D. Other considerations | | | |
| 1. Sufficient evaluation materials are available. | 3 | | |
| 2. Evaluation materials are compatible with the objectives of the series. | 4 | | |
| 3. Teacher's manual provides adequate instructions and valuable suggestions. | 4 | | |
| 4. The effectiveness of the materials has been validated. | 2 | | |

# Selecting Technological Materials

To evaluate competing sets of instructional materials consistent with the technological approach, you must first judge the adequacy of each of the components: a set of well-stated instructional objectives, procedures for assessing those objectives, a management system, and instructional materials that relate to those objectives. From these components are derived the criteria to use in their evaluation.

One important issue is the specificity of the objectives. If the number of objectives is few, the question of the degree to which the objectives are precisely teachable is raised. On the other hand, if there are many objectives, perhaps even hundreds, an enormous amount of testing time will be consumed in determining how well each of the minutely stated objectives has in fact been attained by students. You must decide how many objectives are appropriate for each set of technological materials.

The nature of the *assessment procedures* used within the instructional system constitutes a second dimension on which technology-based reading instruction materials are evaluated. Many technical questions could be considered but they would not be in keeping with the test sophistication, interest, or time of classroom teachers. The kinds of issues that might be considered by the classroom teacher are the validity of the test items, the number of items per objective, and the definition of mastery (satisfactory attainment). With respect to the first of these issues, validity can be thought of simply as how well the items measure the objectives. Do they ask students to demonstrate the same kinds of skills that are stated within the objective? Without much technical experience, teachers can easily use as a first screening device their own good judgment about the validity of test items. The question they would want to ask is whether on the face of it (by reading the items), the test items appear to measure the same thing as the objectives.

A final point related to the assessment materials in a technology based reading instruction system is the definition of mastery that is employed. By *mastery* we mean the standard to be established for determining whether a pupil has or has not attained the specified objective. Typically we advocate that 80 or 90 percent attainment of the items is a good rule, for example, eight out of ten or seven out of eight correct responses.

Another major component of technologically based instruction is a management system; that is, the method of recording student data on

◀ FIGURE 11.1   Rating basal materials: A mini form.

the mastery of specific objectives. The first question is whether the management procedures are specific enough to measure the progress of each pupil. Management systems range from systems that require teachers to code data on individual pupil profile cards, to systems that are completely computer-based and computer-maintained. The questions of concern to you are: Is this management system understandable and feasible? How much time will it take? Which of the competing systems do you believe is "workable"?

Some technological systems include objectives-related materials available for self-instruction by students. Alternatively, the materials might be made available in sets (like reference materials) to be used by the teacher or provided to the pupil on the basis of diagnosed pupil needs. You need to decide which configuration of instruction material fits your needs.

A chief criterion for the evaluation of technology-based reading instruction materials is the evidence of validation. Materials of this type rely on specific procedures that are employed by the teachers and that are expected to be highly reproducible. Thus evidence that the procedure is effective is essential. Although one might make a case that instructional materials of all types should present evidence of their effectiveness, this is especially true for technology-based reading instruction materials in which the reliance on the materials themselves is so great.[4]

The validation report should provide information on the extent to which the materials have been field tested using precisely the instructional procedures, testing system, management system, and so on that are available in the package being considered by the teacher. The report should indicate the extent to which the success pattern varied among students with different characteristics.[5] A determination of *cost* is part of the process of evaluating instructional materials within each of the four approaches, but it is even more important in analyzing technology-based reading materials. Both the initial cost and the operating costs of materials of this type vary enormously. Computer-based materials or those that can be used only once are often expensive; for other materials, costs might be more modest.

Technologically based reading instruction materials, when first introduced in a school, require staff training. These materials require

[4] Marvin C. Alkin and Arlene Fink, "Education Product Reports: A User Orientation." In *Educational Product Evaluation*, ed. G. D. Borich (Englewood Cliffs, N.J.: Educational Technology Press, 1974).

[5] Teachers might also examine published documents that provide validation ratings for various instructional materials. A number of reports prepared by the EPIE Institute provide data of this type. For example, see: *Selectors Guide for Elementary School Reading Programs*, vol. 2, EPIE Report no. 83 (New York: EPIE Institute, 1978).

that the teacher will act in specific, preestablished ways. Thus the extensiveness of the materials available for training teachers in the use of the system is certainly a key factor in the selection of competing instructional systems.

## Rating of Technology-based Materials

As a summary of criteria that might be used in judging technological reading materials, we show in Figure 11.2 a mini rating form for evaluating such systems. As with the basal rating form, the teacher would rate each set of materials on the listed criteria using the following scale:

4 = strongly agree

3 = agree

2 = disagree

1 = strongly disagree

In Figure 11.2, we have filled out the rating form for a hypothetical technology-based series — "The Reading System." You might use this form for appraising other systems, too. As suggested in our discussion on the basal series mini form, scores here might also be tabulated by adding the ratings, or you might want to place greater importance on one or more criteria.

## Evaluating Materials for an Individualized Reading Approach

In the individualized reading approach, reading materials are chosen by children to meet their own needs, interests, and abilities. The teacher not only must help children learn procedures to use in selecting materials, he or she must determine which materials will be made available for the children to pick from. On what basis are the decisions to be made about which magazines, literary books, or trade books will be offered?

In Chapter 2 we indicated that commercially packaged individualized reading systems generally consisted of a number of trade books packaged in units, along with procedures to assist the teacher in managing the individualized reading. When a teacher must choose

*Rating Technological Materials: A Mini Form*

| Criteria | System 1 Name: *The Reading System* | System 2 Name: | System 3 Name: |
|---|---|---|---|
| A. *Objectives* | | | |
| 1. The objectives correspond to your view of appropriate objectives. | 3 | | |
| 2. The objectives correspond to your school's view of appropriate objectives. | 3 | | |
| 3. There is sufficient objective specificity. | 4 | | |
| B. *Assessment* | | | |
| 1. The test items satisfactorily measure the objectives. | 3 | | |
| 2. There are an adequate number of test items per objectives. | 3 | | |
| 3. An appropriate definition of mastery is used. | 3 | | |
| C. *Management system* | | | |
| 1. The management procedures provide sufficient specificity to assure awareness of the progress of each student. | 3 | | |
| 2. There is an adequate record-keeping system. | 4 | | |
| D. *Instructional materials* (applicable when objective-related materials are included within the system) 1. Sufficient material is provided to teach each objective adequately. | 3 | | |
| E. *Additional considerations* 1. Adequate staff training is provided or available. | 2 | | |
| 2. A validation report attesting to the effectiveness of the materials is provided. | 2 | | |
| 3. The cost is appropriate, given the nature of the system. | 2 | | |

**FIGURE 11.2** Rating technological materials: A mini form.

from commercially packaged individualized systems, the major criterion to use is the completeness and appropriateness of the materials.

The alternative to using a packaged system is to select from a variety of materials in an effort to build your own individualized system. You would thus be making your own choices from available books, magazines, and other literature. The criteria for evaluation in this case are the same as those that would be employed in appraising literature.

# Evaluating Materials for the Language Experience Approach

Because the language experience approach relies heavily on the generation of material by the children themselves, very little is available in the way of instructional materials. However, to motivate pupils to the full extent of their capacity, supplementary materials are used in conjunction with the self-generated materials.

According to Roach Van Allen, a leading proponent of the language experience approach, it is important for the teacher to read an excerpt from children's literature every day.[6] Therefore it is essential that you become familiar with good literature. You might use a number of sources to review new books for children. The "Children's Books" section of *The Booklist*, a monthly publication, comprises a summary of theme and content, a recommendation about grade level, and a notation if the book is superior in quality. *The Horn Book Magazine*, another monthly publication, is devoted entirely to children's reviews. *Adventuring with Books* is a reference source intending to reflect the best of current children's literature.[7] It contains an annotated booklist of more than twenty-five hundred titles, with descriptions of each book's content, commending characteristics, and suggested age level. In addition, many of the procedures and suggestions related to evaluating literature presented in the following section would also be applicable here.

---

[6] Roach Van Allen, "How a Language Experience Program Works," in *A Decade of Innovations: Approaches to Beginning Reading, Proceedings of the Twelfth Annual Convention of the International Reading Association*, vol. 12, pt. 3 (Newark, Del., 1968), pp. 1–8.

[7] J. P. Cianciolo, *Adventuring with Books* (Urbana, Ill.: National Council of Teachers of English, 1977).

# Criteria for Evaluating Literature

Literature forms the basis of the individualized reading approach and is an important component of the language experience approach. In evaluating literature, you must consider (1) the readability of the materials, (2) the literary quality, and (3) the lack of bias.

## Readability

The major purpose in assessing readability is to match students with materials that are written on appropriate reading levels. Three ways of determining readability are through the use of cloze tests, informal reading tests, and readability formulas. In Chapter 8, a portion of the discussion dealt with diagnostic tests used in materials-referenced evaluation. In that section, the cloze test and the informal reading inventory were described. The tests were presented from the point of view of deciding the placement of individual students according to a set of instructional materials already available — such as a basal reader series. Presumably materials had already been determined and the cloze test and informal reading assessment were presented as diagnostic instruments to be used in making a materials selection for an individual student. The present chapter is intended to guide the choice of reading materials for *classroom* availability.

It is possible to determine the general readability of material by preparing cloze-test passages from the set of materials under consideration and then allowing a number of students to read the tests to obtain a measure of the readability. However, this procedure is probably a more difficult means of obtaining a general measure of grade-level readability than using one of the readability formulas. Assessment of materials for readability is not a new concept. Research has been conducted for over half a century to determine an accurate method of measuring the difficulty of material. Irving Lorge devised a formula to cover grades 3 through 12;[8] then Edgar Dale and Jeanne Chall developed a formula in 1948 designed primarily for adult materials.[9] In the same year Rudolf Flesch came out with new formulas reflecting his belief that the relationship between words and their abstractness contributed to reading difficulty.[10] The Spache formula (1953) was devised

---

[8] Irving Lorge, "Predicting Reading Difficulty of Selections for Children," *Elementary English Review* 16 (1939): 229–233.

[9] Edgar Dale and Jeanne S. Chall, "A Formula for Predicting Readability: Instructions," *Education Research Bulletin* 27 (1948): 45–54.

[10] Rudolf Flesch, "A New Readability Yardstick," *Journal of Applied Psychology* 32 (1948): 221–233.

for children's materials from grades 1 through 3;[11] finally, a time-saving model, the Fry Readability Graph, was published in 1968.[12]

Basically readability formulas consist of selected linguistic components inserted into a mathematical equation to predict the reading difficulty, sometimes measured as grade placement. Among the attributes thought to be indications of readability are the (1) number of syllables in a word, (2) familiarity of words as determined by word lists, (3) sentence length, (4) grammatical complexity, (5) concept load and difficulty, and (6) abstractness and multiple meanings of words. Obviously it would not be practical or desirable to use all of these variables to derive a formula. For the classroom teacher, little is gained from the choice of a highly complex readability formula. We recommend that you consider the use of the Fry readability formula. To help you understand its use, we apply it to one sample passage of one hundred words. Directions for syllable and sentence counts and a diagram of the Fry Readability Graph are found in Figure 11.3.

> Susie Jones ran home from school as fast as she was able. Tonight was the last evening to make something for the art show. Every day Susie had worked on a new project. She did not like her drawing. Even the clay doll was not pretty enough.
>
> She sat down to dinner with a frown on her face. Her father asked her what was wrong. Susie told him about her problem. Father smiled and picked up his paper napkin. He folded it many ways. The worried look changed to a grin. Susie loved the bird her father had made.

The sentence count for the above passage is 12 and the total number of syllables is 127. (If you are in doubt about the number of syllables in a given word, refer to a good dictionary or count the syllables as they would normally be read aloud.) Plotting syllable count and the sentence count of the passage on the graph, you will observe that the readability of this sample material is at a level between the second and third grades. (Note the dot plotted on the graph.) When choosing materials for students, a teacher should also consider pupil background and interest along with readability.[13]

---

[11] George Spache, "A New Readability Formula for Primary Grade Reading Materials," *Elementary School Journal* 53 (1953): 410–413.

[12] Edward B. Fry, "A Readability Formula That Saves Time," *Journal of Reading* 11 (1968): 513–516, 575–578.

[13] Timothy C. Standal, "Readability Formulas: What's Out, What's In," *Reading Teacher* 31 (1978): 642–646.

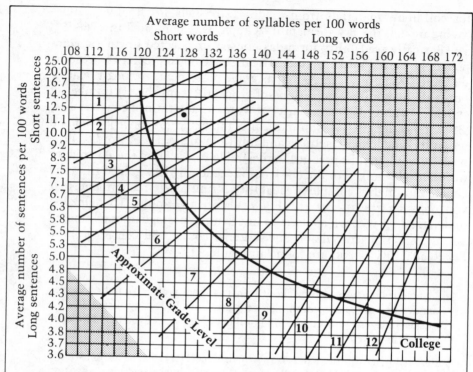

DIRECTIONS:
Randomly select three 100-word passages from a book or an article. Plot average number of syllables and average number of sentences per 100 words on graph to determine the grade level of the material. Choose more passages per book if great variability is observed and conclude that the book has uneven readability. Few books will fall into the gray area, but when they do grade level scores are invalid.

ADDITIONAL DIRECTIONS FOR WORKING READABILITY GRAPH

1. Randomly select three sample passages and count exactly 100 words beginning with a beginning of a sentence. Don't count numbers. Do count proper nouns.

2. Count the number of sentences in the hundred words, estimating length of the fraction of the last sentence to the nearest 1/10th.

3. Count the total number of syllables in the 100-word passage. If you don't have a hand counter available, an easy way is to simply put a mark above every syllable over one in each word, then, when you get to the end of the passage, count the number of marks and add 100.

4. Enter graph with average sentence length and number of syllables; plot dot where the two lines intersect. Area where dot is plotted will give you the approximate grade level.

5. If a great deal of variability is found, putting more sample counts into the average is desirable.

**FIGURE 11.3**   Using the Fry Readability Graph.

Source: From *Elementary Reading Instruction* by Edward B. Fry. Copyright © 1977. Used with permission of McGraw-Hill Book Company.

## Literary Quality

Quality in children's literature is defined in much the same way as it would be in adult literature, except that the subject matter and its handling are geared to the young audience. Aside from making decisions about literary quality, you must determine appropriateness for students. Do children enjoy what they are reading? Literature has little value if a child is unable to understand the content or finds it boring, even though it is rated as a children's classic.

Criteria for judging literature vary for different kinds of literature. However, since the story constitutes a basic form of literature and one that children are familiar with, we set forth the major criteria used in judging stories: theme, plot, characterization, archetypal imagery, tone, texture, form and unity, and style.[14]

The theme and the plot of a story are important elements to consider. The theme constitutes the idea of the story and must be strong enough to support a plot with action, suspense, and a clear-cut conclusion; a good theme teaches children a personal philosophy based on the ideals by which men strive to live, or it deals with basic needs such as achievement, need for physical well-being, and intellectual and emotional security. Young readers require plots that are simple enough to follow, yet exciting enough to maintain interest. The developing mind relates to obvious heroes who overcome obstacles and settle conflicts to attain difficult goals. A positive outcome builds faith in the child's ability to succeed through hard work, planning, and persistence.

The characters presented and the models portrayed can be important factors in determining literary quality. If the child is to develop a critical appreciation of literature and to learn to apply problem solutions to his or her own life, characters must be unique and convincingly drawn. Good literature is replete with archetypes and exposes children to imagery that taps a child's imagination and encourages creativity. Such models are to be found not only in characterization but in descriptions, plot patterns, and so on.

Additional characteristics of literary quality are the tone, texture, and style of the writing. The tone is reflected in the author's attitudes toward the subject matter, the characters, and the audience. The textural quality is represented by choice of words that add dimension and depth to the work. Style, the sound and sensory characteristics of the author's written expression, adds another dimension to the story, one that is essential to good literature.

---

[14] M. H. Arbuthnot, *Children and Books* (Chicago: Scott, Foresman, 1964), pp. 193–195.

Finally, you should consider the form and unity of the story. Form is the structure of thought in a work. In good literature, form should relate to content perfectly. The work should be unified; all the parts should seem to interrelate to create a cohesive whole.

Although stories may take the form of myths, epics, folk tales, or drama, these criteria apply. However, emphasis shifts according to the requirement of the type of reading material. For instance, the pattern of the folk tale is clear-cut and definite, with very little preamble; themes often involve conflict. Criteria used in reviewing poetry are different from those used in analyzing stories. Emphasis is placed on style: there is an interrelationship between form and imagery.

### Lack of bias

A final basis for the selection of materials to use in individualized reading instruction is lack of bias. Materials should be free of both sex and ethnic bias.

**Sex bias**  Beginning readers are at a crucial stage in their sex-role education. Even if young children have been indoctrinated by their families to perceive rigid sex roles for themselves, introducing them to non-sex-typed literature can do much to change their perceptions of how they fit into sex roles. Obviously, the material must meet certain criteria: the work must be good literature; and it must replace male dominance not by female dominance, but by a varied picture of sex roles.

Since children look to adults throughout their development, books about the family are commonplace. And family stories are a major source of sex-stereotyped behavior. Women are almost always confined to the house where they function as servants who care for their husbands and children; the woman is the helpmate and observer of male activities and the husband and father is cast in a role of power and prestige; in essence, the woman is shown in relation to the man.

With regard to the homemaking role, you as the teacher should consider whether the woman's duties are portrayed as difficult or challenging. You should ask whether the woman participates in decision-making processes at home and outside. If she has a job, does she function in a nurturing and supporting role such as nurse, teacher, sales clerk, or secretary?

When women in children's stories are portrayed in a professional capacity, attention is often centered exclusively on their job-related activities. Therefore to inculcate in the minds of young readers the idea that women, as well as men, can lead interesting and full lives, it is necessary to present literature that portrays both grown-ups and children who cross sex-role boundaries.

**Ethnic bias**   Another kind of bias to be avoided in reading materials is ethnic bias. One criterion for judging ethnic bias in literature is *language*; the range of that language is broad — it varies from the choice of descriptive words to the type of English employed. Regional vernacular is acceptable in a story about an ethnic group when it adds texture by means of an easy rhythmic pattern of speech, but dialect should be used with care. It is important that descriptions are not used in ways that demean any ethnic group.

Another criterion for judging ethnic bias is *theme*. The idea that success depends on the assimilation of white, middle-class behavior is inexcusable. As you review literature for ethnic bias, you must ask the question, Does the white middle-class child dominate the story? In other words, is the story's conflict resolved by a white benefactor, thus placing the white child in a superior position, or is the conflict resolved by joint effort.[15] Further, are the characters presented stereotypically?[16]

*Illustrations* are often an interesting addition to literature for children, and several questions should be asked about them: for instance, do they include black or ethnic children, and if so, are the children portrayed positively?

Above all, literature should be chosen that makes children from ethnic backgrounds proud of their own history, language, and literature at the same time that they are acquiring competence in standard English and the history and literature of the majority.

# Summary

Teachers do, in some way, have an effect on the evaluation and selection of reading materials. Instructional materials are used by nearly all teachers, and it is essential that teachers know the strengths and weaknesses of the material.

A number of criteria are used in reviewing sets of reading instruction materials. The most important question to answer is whether the materials are consistent with the teacher's desired approach. Given the variety of approaches — basal reading, technological, language experience, and individualized — it is best for a beginning teacher to become

---

[15] Elaine Wunderlich, "Black American in Children's Books," *Reading Teacher* 28 (1974): 282–285.
[16] Holly O'Donnell, "ERIC/RCS Report: Cultural Bias: A Many-Headed Monster," *Elementary English* 51 (1974): 181–184, 214.

familiar with one approach before attempting to use a combination. So the basic issue is which one you plan to use and whether the materials fit it. Within each approach, you will find applicable evaluation criteria and considerations.

In selecting instructional materials for a basal series, several concerns must be borne in mind. Are the objectives stated in the basal series? Do they match your view of what is to be taught at the grade level? Are they internally consistent? In looking at the materials themselves, you should note their organization, scope, and sequence. The methodology also must be examined to determine the range of instructional techniques prescribed and their appropriateness. Many basal readers have evaluation materials that should be reviewed. Also the teacher's manual should be reviewed. Finally, the field tests used to validate the series should be considered.

A technological approach consists of a number of components: a set of well-stated instructional objectives, procedures for assessing those objectives, a well-formulated management system, and a set of instructional materials. The objectives must correspond with those of the teacher, grade level, and school and district, and they must be specifically defined. Measurement procedures must be established to determine whether a student has attained the specific objectives. In the management system, the method of recording student data on the mastery of each objective must be defined. The cost and training requirements are critical concerns in the evaluation of technology-approach reading materials. Perhaps of greatest concern in appraising this type of material is the evidence that children have achieved the stated objectives.

Although the individualized reading approach emphasizes selection by students themselves of books to be read, the teacher must decide which books should be made available. When choosing literature, the three major factors are readability, literary quality, and lack of bias. The Fry Readability Graph offers a formula to measure readability. The literary quality is determined by the same criteria used in assessing all forms of literature: theme, plot, characterization, archetypal imagery, tone, texture, form and unity, and style. Finally, materials should be free of sex bias and ethnic bias.

In the language experience approach, little instructional material is available since this approach relies mostly on materials generated by the children. However, the reading of literature is important in stimulating children to produce materials of their own. Hence, the same factors that govern the selection of materials for individualized reading apply to the language experience approach.

# Self-instructional Exercises

## Exercise 1. Evaluating Different Reading Series

Read the *Barber Valley Unified School District Reading Evaluation Form* and then answer the following questions. You may need to refer back through the chapter discussions to complete some of the questions.

1. The form has twelve rating dimensions or scales. Are these ratings related to the category of objectives listed in the basal reading sections of this chapter? If so, which ones, and indicate the adequacy of the rating category(ies).

2. Are any rating scales related to the category of materials content? If so, how many, and what is the extent of coverage of the rating scales?

3. Which rating dimensions apply to testing and remediation in the materials methodology category?

4. Under the heading of "Other considerations" and related to the teacher's guidebook, you will note that no rating dimension attempts to evaluate creativity and self-expression. Therefore frame a rating-scale question that would adequately evaluate this area.

### CONFIRMATION FOR EXERCISE 1

1. Rating scale no. 1 is related to the question "Do the objectives match your view of what is to be taught at the grade level?" and precisely defines the area to be measured. Rating scale no. 1 is also related to the question of internal consistency to the degree that the objectives should not conflict to be clearly stated.

2. Rating scale no. 4 relates to the sequence and organization of comprehension materials, and rating scale no. 8 relates to the scope of materials for specific grade levels. Therefore questions 4 and 8 provide good coverage for the categories of scope, organization, and sequence, although question 4 should be expanded to include other areas besides comprehension to afford full coverage.

3. Rating scale no. 6 adequately covers remediating, since, by their very nature, testing and remediation imply that different individuals attain different standards and require different levels of instruction. Rating scale no. 11 is somewhat related to the testing and remediation categories, since assessment is the purpose of testing.

4. You might make the statement: "Instructions to the teacher that include suggestions for changing various components of the story so the child must

*Barber Valley Unified School District Reading Evaluation Form*
Please compile one evaluation form for each publisher:

_____ American Book Co.
_____ The Economy Co.
_____ Ginn                            _____ Houghton Mifflin
_____ Harcourt Brace Jovanovich       _____ Macmillan
_____ Harper & Row                    _____ Scott, Foresman
                                      _____ Other

1. The objectives of the program are clearly stated and are related to the instructional materials and learning opportunities.

| Strongly Agree | Agree | Uncertain | Disagree | Strongly Disagree |
|---|---|---|---|---|
| 5 | 4 | 3 | 2 | 1 |
|  |  |  |  |  |

2. The instructional materials and objectives are compatible with the district objectives continuum.

| Strongly Agree | Agree | Uncertain | Disagree | Strongly Disagree |
|---|---|---|---|---|
| 5 | 4 | 3 | 2 | 1 |
|  |  |  |  |  |

3. The decoding component is sequential and complete.

| Strongly Agree | Agree | Uncertain | Disagree | Strongly Disagree |
|---|---|---|---|---|
| 5 | 4 | 3 | 2 | 1 |
|  |  |  |  |  |

4. The comprehension development is logical, hierarchical, and obvious.

| Strongly Agree | Agree | Uncertain | Disagree | Strongly Disagree |
|---|---|---|---|---|
| 5 | 4 | 3 | 2 | 1 |
|  |  |  |  |  |

5. Material is designed to develop critical reading and thinking skills.

| Strongly Agree | Agree | Uncertain | Disagree | Strongly Disagree |
|---|---|---|---|---|
| 5 | 4 | 3 | 2 | 1 |
|  |  |  |  |  |

6. The materials clearly provide for individual differences and flexibility of instruction.

| Strongly Agree | Agree | Uncertain | Disagree | Strongly Disagree |
|---|---|---|---|---|
| 5 | 4 | 3 | 2 | 1 |
|  |  |  |  |  |

Barber Valley Unified School District Reading Evaluation Form

7. The instructional materials and teachers guide can be effectively used
   without in-service training.

   | Strongly Agree | Agree | Uncertain | Disagree | Strongly Disagree |
   |:---:|:---:|:---:|:---:|:---:|
   | 5 | 4 | 3 | 2 | 1 |
   |   |   |   |   |   |

8. The series is appropriate for children at specified grade levels. Consider
   vocabulary, concepts, activities, *content areas*, personal experiences, etc.

   | Strongly Agree | Agree | Uncertain | Disagree | Strongly Disagree |
   |:---:|:---:|:---:|:---:|:---:|
   | 5 | 4 | 3 | 2 | 1 |
   |   |   |   |   |   |

9. The materials are attractive in design and appealing to children.

   | Strongly Agree | Agree | Uncertain | Disagree | Strongly Disagree |
   |:---:|:---:|:---:|:---:|:---:|
   | 5 | 4 | 3 | 2 | 1 |
   |   |   |   |   |   |

10. The literature is interesting and includes representation of various literary
    types, such as realistic, fanciful, myth, legend, fable, poetic pattern, etc.

    | Strongly Agree | Agree | Uncertain | Disagree | Strongly Disagree |
    |:---:|:---:|:---:|:---:|:---:|
    | 5 | 4 | 3 | 2 | 1 |
    |   |   |   |   |   |

11. The evaluation materials (management systems) provide clear procedures
    for both ongoing and final assessment based on the objectives.

    | Strongly Agree | Agree | Uncertain | Disagree | Strongly Disagree |
    |:---:|:---:|:---:|:---:|:---:|
    | 5 | 4 | 3 | 2 | 1 |
    |   |   |   |   |   |

12. If you were asked to use this series, rate it on a scale of one to ten (ten
    being the highest): _____

13. Comments.




Signature: _____

School: _____

Grade: _____

create a new story conclusion are sufficient incentive to encourage creativity and self-expression.''

## Exercise 2. Determining Readability

Recalling the Fry Readability Graph illustrated in Figure 11.3, and using the following passage, determine the reading ease according to Fry's formula:

Steve climbed through a hole in the fence, dragging the mud-caked shovel behind him. He followed his usual path through the brush. At the ravine, he turned left and scrambled over rough terrain until he came to an area of rising ground. The boulders were as smooth as a bald man's head. He knew that this was the area where he would find the first sign. The sun was scorching the back of his neck. Instinctively he made for a shady tunnel between two rocks. There on the ground, unmistakably, was the marker he had been searching for.

**CONFIRMATION FOR EXERCISE 2**

There are 129 syllables and eight complete sentences in the passage. Plotting the figures 8 and 129 on the Fry Readability Graph shown here,

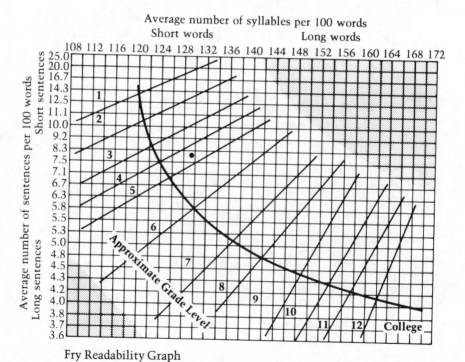

Fry Readability Graph

you will note that the passage is appropriate for children between the fourth and fifth grades.

## Exercise 3. Determining Ethnic and Sex Bias in Literature

With reference to our discussion of ethnic and sex bias in the section Ethnic Bias, pick out all the statements that could be construed as biased in the following passage.

Jose and Cindy decided to go on a picnic the following Saturday. They asked all of their neighborhood friends to go, and Cindy's mother agreed to pack a lunch.

On the day of the picnic, Cindy helped her mother fry chicken and make potato salad. Cindy's father, who usually worked at a lumber yard on Saturdays, offered to drive the children to the park.

Cindy waited excitedly as the other children assembled at her house. It was already past two o'clock, and Jose had not arrived yet. She was worried because he had never been late before, even though he often had to work for his father — a farm laborer.

Just as the children were about to leave, Jose's father phoned to say that Jose's sister had been insulted by a gang, and that Jose and his Mexican friends had gone out to track down the culprits.

### CONFIRMATION FOR EXERCISE 3

You undoubtedly noticed that a number of items fall into the categories of sex and ethnic stereotyping:

1. Cindy's mother is portrayed as a housewife and cook — a female role.

2. Cindy is cast in the role of junior housewife because she is portrayed as helping her mother with household duties.

3. Cindy's father is engaged in a typical male occupation as a lumber worker.

4. Jose's father is involved in a stereotyped Mexican occupation as a farm laborer.

5. Jose is portrayed as a Mexican stereotype because his ties to his family are very strong, and he is involved in a gang war.

# Selected Readings

Jackson, Shirley A. "The Quest for Reading Programs That Work," *Educational Leadership* 36, no. 3 (December 1978): 168–171.
   This article lists reading programs assessed by a national panel as having met

the following criteria: effected a change that was consistent and statistically significant; could be implemented in another location with a reasonable expectation of comparable impact; and the observed effects came from the intervention.

Among the characteristics of programs that met the criteria were these:

1. There is a structured hierarchy of objectives with instructional activities, materials, and tests keyed to the objectives.
2. The program is individualized to accommodate specific skill needs and varied learning patterns with a heavy focus on direct teaching of decoding skills.
3. There is a trained support staff, such as reading specialists and parent volunteers, who work well with the regular teacher.
4. There are multiple methods for grouping pupils.
5. There is the expectation that pupils can achieve and that the school is responsible for assuring achievement. Varied strategies are used to involve parents.
6. There is varied, positive, and immediate reinforcement of instruction as well as frequent repetition strategies.
7. There is a cumulative, consistent, and varied testing program as well as frequent monitoring of pupil progress.
8. Reading is interrelated with other basic skills.
9. A literature reading and enjoyment component is part of the program.
10. Varied approaches to teaching reading are used with emphasis on diagnostic teaching.
11. At least 30 to 45 minutes a day is spent on teaching reading.
12. Staff development is directly related to instructional program planning, implementation and evaluation.

Problems in assessing programs are also mentioned, including those related to defining an acceptable level of success, the need to adapt a program in different settings, and the failure to assess the affective consequences that follow a given program.

Kamm, Karlyn. "A Five Year Study of the Effects of a Skill Centered Approach to the Teaching of Reading," *Journal of Educational Research* 72, no. 2 (December 1978): 104–113.

This article is important in light of controversies over approaches for teaching children to read. Results from this five-year study reflect favorably on the skill-centered program with gains in both general reading comprehension and specific reading skills.

The program focuses instruction on all pupils instead of on the middle population of pupils (a former practice in the district). Improvements in the program are currently being tried: continued teaching of word attack skills in the upper grades, increased concentration of study skills and comprehension, and more attention in helping children apply the reading skills in their daily lives.

Lehr, Fran. "Textbook Evaluation," *Reading Teacher* 32, no. 7 (April 1979): 886–890.
Documents that can assist educators in evaluating reading textbooks are described. An overview of materials issued by the Association of American Publishers and the National Education Association is one such document. This publication places evaluation of materials in the context of recent social and educational developments. Other documents reviewed include those that present guidelines for determining reading skills, content, readability, physical features, values, teaching aids, and teachability; documents that help teachers understand the elements of instructional design; documents reporting on the effectiveness of educational materials; and documents treating sex and racial bias in textbooks.

Rutherford, William L. "Criterion-Referenced Programmes: The Missing Element," *Journal of Curriculum Studies* 11, no. 1 (1979): 47–52.
A report of an extensive project aimed at answering the question of why some criterion-referenced programs fall short of the schools' expectations. Partial answers suggest that the programs do not develop the necessary support system. Included in such a system are provisions for teaching teachers how to organize and manage all the components of the program, and to allow them time to develop a pattern of effective use, which may require two or more years.

Strange, Michael C. "Considerations for Evaluating Reading Instruction," *Educational Leadership* 36, no. 3 (December 1978): 178–181.
A description of elements that reading experts endorse as part of a sound instructional program. These elements include provision for individualizing, diagnosing, prescribing, placing children in materials of appropriate level of difficulty, relating isolated skills to reading, modifying basal readers to needs of pupils, keeping track of what pupils have learned and what they have yet to learn, and direct teaching of children.

# Appendix

Besides the references in the footnotes and bibliography, this appendix presents a partial listing of further sources of information for reading teachers. Sources of ideas, suggestions, and activities for teaching will enable the individual to broaden areas of personal interest, explore specific topics in greater depth, and become familiar with the array of materials and programs that are available. The appendix categories are arranged as follows:

1. The Teaching of Reading
   Basal Reading Approach
   Technological Approach
   Language Experience Approach
   Individualized Reading Approach

2. Professional Journals

3. Trade Books

4. Learning Centers

5. Test Evaluation

6. Bilingual Resources

## 1.  The Teaching of Reading

*Basal Reading Approach*

Basal readers offer reading programs for grades K–6 or K–8. In addition to textbooks and teacher's manuals, publishers of basal reading series offer supplementary materials, such as study books, duplicating masters, manipulatives, records and sound filmstrips, posters, and independent reading books. Indeed, with the growing interest in competency-based education, publishers of basal readers have started to issue optional management systems to accompany the basal series. These technological approaches consist of criterion exercises, mastery tests, reteaching components, and record sheets or reading progress cards.

Some differentiation among the most widely used series can be noted in the intended learners and elements featured in decoding.

*Allyn and Bacon Reading Program 1978* (470 Atlantic Avenue, Boston, Mass. 02210)

intended for preschool–grade 6 learners

Decoding lessons emphasize recognition of initial and final consonants and frequently found phonograms (grapheme bases).

*American Book Reading Program 1977* (135 West 50th Street, New York, N.Y. 10020)

intended for K–grade 6 learners

Decoding lessons are based upon frequently occurring spelling patterns, structural analysis, and language experience.

*The Economy Company "Keys to Reading" 1975* (P.O. Box 25308, Oklahoma City, Okla. 73125)

intended for K–grade 8 learners

Unlike many reading series which either utilize sight words as the basis for development of phonic generalizations or develop the meaning of words before asking children to decode them, this reading series focuses upon the teaching of phonic skills followed by applying the word discriminate skills in reading new material.

*Ginn and Company "Reading 720" 1976* (Xerox Education Group, 191 Spring Street, Lexington, Mass. 02173)

intended for K–grade 8 learners

The introduction of decoding skills is focused upon consonant clusters and various vowel sounds represented by the letter *o*, along with the sound of /u/ in *bus*. Decoding through structural analysis, whereby pupils decode words containing phonograms or grapheme bases such as *ing, ung, any*, is emphasized in addition to phoneme analysis.

*Harcourt, Brace, Jovanovich "The Bookmark Reading Program" second edition 1974* (757 Third Avenue, New York, N.Y. 10017)

intended for K–grade 6 learners

Decoding is taught through sound-letter correspondence and context clues. Consonant sounds and vowel sounds (short vowel sounds first) are taught followed by teaching word parts for structural analysis.

*Harper and Row "Reading Basics Plus" 1977* (10 East 53rd Street, New York, N.Y. 10022)

intended for K–grade 8 learners

Decoding is taught through sound and letter relations: initial and final consonants, initial clusters, and final clusters.

*The Holt Basic Reading System 1977* (Holt, Rinehart and Winston, Inc., 383 Madison Avenue, New York, N.Y. 10017)

intended for K–grade 8 learners

Decoding is taught from sound symbol relations, word parts, and context.

*Houghton Mifflin Reading Series 1976* (One Beacon Street, Boston, Mass. 02107)

intended for K–grade 6 learners although more advanced material may be used with pupils in the "upper grades"

Decoding is taught first through recognition of consonant letter-sound relations; then by introducing high frequency sight words and other letter-sound associations; and finally vowel sounds and common phonograms, such as *ot, ame* and affixes such as *ful.*

*D. C. Heath and Company "Reading Beginnings, Patterns, Explorations" 1974* (125 Spring Street, Lexington, Mass. 02173)

intended for K–grade 3 learners

Decoding is taught through spelling patterns.

Note: These descriptions are meant to give a general impression of some of the programs that are available from publishers of basal readers. Since these series are often revised, we suggest writing to the publishers for later information.

Other publishers of basal reader series include: Scott, Foresman and Company (1900 Eastlake Avenue, Glenview, Ill. 60025); The Macmillan Company (866 Third Avenue, New York, N.Y. 10022); and J.B. Lippincott Company (East Washington Square, Philadelphia, Penn. 19105).

*Technological Approach*

Among the most widely used materials within the technological approach are

*Croft Inservice Reading Program: A Systems Approach to Word Attack Skills.* New London, Conn.: Croft Educational Services.

*Croft Inservice Reading Program: Reading Comprehension Skills.* New London, Conn.: Croft Educational Services.

*Developmental Reading Program.* St. Paul, Minn.: Paul S. Amidon and Associates, Inc.

*Distar Reading.* Chicago, Ill.: Science Research Associates, Inc.

*Fountain Valley Teacher Support System.* Huntington Beach, Calif.: Richard L. Zweig Associates, Inc.

*Prescriptive Reading Inventory.* Monterey, Calif.: CTB/McGraw Hill.

*Programmed Reading.* St. Louis: Sullivan Associates, Webster Division, McGraw-Hill.

*Read On.* New York: Random House School Division.

*Wisconsin Design for Reading Skill Development.* Minneapolis, Minn.: National Computer Systems.

*Language Experience Approach*

Useful sources include:

Allen, Roach V., and Allen, Claryce. *Language Experience in Reading, Teacher's Resource Book,* Level I, II, III. Chicago: Encyclopaedia Britannica Education Corporation.

King, Joyce, and Katzman, Carol. *Imagine* יוצל. Pacific Palisades, Calif.: Goodyear.

*Learning Readiness and Language Experience Kit.* Menlo Park, Calif.: Addison-Wesley.

Moffett, James. *A Student Centered Language Arts Curriculum* — Grades K–6. Boston: Houghton Mifflin.

*Self.* Morristown, N.J.: Silver Burdett Company, General Learning Corporation.

*Individualized Reading Approach*

Commercial materials to assist teachers who want to try the individualized approach but are concerned about materials, procedure, and time include: *House of Books,* a multilevel individualized reading program (Westchester, Ill.: Benefic Press); *Individualized Reading,* six graded units, each consisting of one hundred different paperbacks and other components (Englewood Cliffs, N.J.: Scholastic Book Services); *Individualized Reading Program,* four classroom libraries for elementary grades (Evanston, Ill.: Harper and Row); *PAL Kits,* four easy reading, high-interest paperbacks kits for grades 5–12. The reading level of the kits ranges from primer to grade 5. (Columbus, Ohio: Xerox). In addition to providing a wide variety of titles at different grade levels, most commercial individualized reading programs include such components as summaries of each book (to aid the teacher in conferences with pupils), record sheets, discussion cards, and other activities and suggestions.

## 2. Major Professional Journals

*The Reading Teacher* is an indispensable resource for teachers in elementary schools. Regularly, it features accounts of successful classroom practices, notices of courses and conferences, critiques of new instructional materials, book reviews, and summaries of research reports. Published nine times a year, a subscription is included with membership in the International Reading Association, and membership is available to anyone concerned with the improvement of reading.

*Reading Horizons* is devoted to reading at all levels of education. It provides teachers with reports on movements and important changes in the field of reading. Articles announce methods and approaches which are the result of experiment; describe developments in tests, teaching strategies, theory, and teacher preparation; provide reviews, information, and bibliographies; and suggest solutions to special problems.

*Language Arts* is published by the National Council of Teachers of English. It contains original contributions on all facets of language arts teaching and learning but is primarily of interest to teachers in the preschool through middle school years. Viewpoints appear from a variety of fields — linguistics, psychology — that have implications for the language arts. Language-related products for children, children's literature, and a number of theme issues appear regularly. Research summaries, editorials, book reviews are among other features of this excellent publication.

*Journal of Reading,* an International Reading Association publication, contains material of special interest to the teacher of reading at the secondary school, college, and adult levels. However, elementary teachers will find many articles of interest to them. Reading in the content areas, study skills, development of reading interests, and suggestions for meeting special needs are topics frequently reported on. The journal is also rich in suggestions for improving vocabulary, competencies, speed reading, and other reading aspects. Book reviews, viewpoints, and research summaries are regular features.

*Journal of Reading Behavior* is published by the National Reading Conference. It provides original experimental and theoretical articles concerned with reading. Both instructional issues and studies of cognitive processes in learning through reading are presented. Although the journal is characterized by well-conceived research articles, it also offers interesting editorials on the status of reading instruction, book reviews, and comments on ideas and materials of interest to reading people.

*Reading Research Quarterly,* published four times a year by the International Reading Association, is characterized by articles reporting reading research studies in considerable depth; usually three or four articles appear in an issue. The advancement of research in the field of reading is a central purpose for this quarterly.

### 3. Trade Books

Professional journals, such as the *Reading Teacher, Language Arts,* and *Horn Book Magazine,* carry articles describing new trade books. Also, two ERIC documents facilitate choosing trade books: *New Books for Young Readers,* compiled by Norine Odland, provides annotations of new trade books, indicating selections from age 3 to adulthood; and *Good Reading for Poor Readers* by George Spache contains a chapter that lists trade books for poor readers.

*Childrens' Books,* prepared by the Library of Congress (No. 007F, U.S. Government Printing Office, 1978), contains a descriptive listing of selected books for children from preschool through junior high school age. *Books for Children* by Bonnie Bacon and Sara Hadley (Washington, D. C.: Association for Childhood International, 1977) is another excellent source to build a library to use with individualized reading.

### 4. Learning Centers

Ideas for learning centers are found in such books as:

Blackburn, Jack E., and Powell, W. Conrad. *One at a Time All at Once.* Santa Monica, Calif.: Goodyear, 1976.

Davidson, Tom, et al. *The Learning Center Book.* Santa Monica, Calif.: Goodyear, 1976.

Fish, Lois, and Lindgren, Henry. *Learning Centers.* Glen Ridge, N.J.: Exceptional Press, 1974.

Forgan, Harry W. *The Reading Corner.* Santa Monica, Calif.: Goodyear, 1977.

Commercially prepared centers are also available; see, for example,

*Instructo.* Paoli, Penn.: McGraw-Hill Book Company.

*Learning Center Materials.* Chicago: Science Research Associates.

### 5. Test Evaluation

Evaluation of many of the currently available criterion-referenced and norm-referenced tests can be found in the following:

Buros, Oscar K. *Seventh Mental Measurements Yearbook.* Highland Park, N.J.: Gryphon Press, 1972.

—————. *Reading Tests and Reviews II.* Highland Park, N.J.: Gryphon Press, 1975.

*CSE-ECRC Preschool Kindergarten Test Evaluations.* Los Angeles: University of California, Center for the Study of Evaluation and the Early Childhood Research Center, 1971.

*CSE Secondary School Test Evaluations: Grades 7 and 8.* Los Angeles: University of California, Center for the Study of Evaluation, 1974.

*CSE Elementary Test Evaluations.* Los Angeles: University of California, Center for the Study of Evaluation, 1976.

Tuinan, J. Jaap, ed. *Review of Diagnostic Reading Tests.* Newark, Del.: International Reading Association, 1976.

Walker, Clinton B., et al. *CSE Criterion-Referenced Test Handbook.* Los Angeles: University of California, Center for the Study of Evaluation, 1979.

## 6. Bilingual Resources

EPIE Report: *Selectors Guide for Bilingual Education Materials.* Spanish Language Arts. New York: EPIE Institute, 1979.

EPIE Report: *Selectors Guide to Bilingual Education.* Spanish "Branch" Program. New York: EPIE Institute, 1979.

Information concerning other multicultural materials for the teaching of reading can be obtained from one of these bilingual-multicultural dissemination and assessment centers: Massachusetts Dissemination and Assessment Center, Fall River Public Schools, Fall River, Mass.; Dissemination and Assessment Center for Bilingual Education, Austin, Texas; and Los Angeles Dissemination and Assessment Center, California State University Los Angeles, Los Angeles, California.

The Institute for Cultural Pluralism, San Diego State University, San Diego, California, has information on evaluating instructional materials for bilingual-multicultural education.

# Bibliography

## Chapter 1

Fisher, Donald. *Functional Literacy and the Schools.* Washington, D.C.: National Institute of Education, 1978.

Gibson, James M., and Hall, James C., Jr. *Damn Reading!* New York: Vantage Press, 1969.

Karlin, Robert, ed. *Reading for all.* Proceedings of the Fourth IRA World Congress on Reading. Newark, Del.: International Reading Association, 1972.

Sebesta, Sam L., and Wallen, Carl J., eds. *The First R: Readings on Teaching Reading.* Chicago: Science Research Associates, 1972.

Smith, Nila Banton. *American Reading Instruction.* New York: Silver, Burdett, 1934.

Sullivan, George. *A Reason to Read: A Report on an International Symposium on the Promotion of the Reading Habit.* New York: Academy for Educational Development, 1976.

Walcut, Charles Child, et al. "Reading Today," In *Teaching Reading.* New York: Macmillan, 1974, pp. 3–9.

Waples, Douglas, et al. *What Reading Does to People.* Chicago: University of Chicago Press, 1940.

## Chapter 2

Fry, Edward. "Basals: Reading Systems and Individualized Reading." In *Elementary Reading Instruction.* New York: McGraw-Hill, 1977, pp. 134–154.

Hall, Mary Anne. *Teaching Reading as a Language Experience.* 2nd ed. Columbus, Ohio: Charles E. Merrill, 1976.

Jacobs, Leland. "Individualized Reading Is Not a Thing." In *Individualizing Reading Practice – Practical Suggestions for Teaching,* no. 14, ed. Alice Miel. New York: Columbia University, Teachers College, Bureau of Publications, 1958.

Johnson, Dale D., and Pearson, P. David. "Skill Management Systems: A Critique." *Reading Teacher* 28, no. 8 (May 1975): 757–765.

Otto, Wayne, and Chester, Robert D. *Objective-Based Reading.* New York: Addison-Wesley, 1976.

Ransom, Grayce A. "Curriculum Approaches to Reading." In *Preparing to Teach Reading.* Boston: Little, Brown, 1978, pp. 71–92.

Stauffer, Russell. *The Language Experience Approach to the Teaching of Reading.* New York: Harper and Row, 1970.

Van Allen, Roach, and Van Allen, Claryce. *Language Experience Activities.* Boston: Houghton Mifflin, 1976.

Veatch, Jeannette, et al. *Key Words to Reading: The Language Experience Approach Begins.* 2nd ed. Columbus, Ohio: Charles E. Merrill, 1979.


## Chapter 3

Barr, Rebecca. "How Children Are Taught to Read: Grouping and Pacing." *School Review* 83, no. 3 (May 1975): 479–498.

————. "Instructional Pace Differences and Their Effect on Reading Acquisition." *Reading Research Quarterly* 9, no. 4 (1974): 526–554.

Dahloff, Urban S. *Ability Grouping, Content Validity and Curriculum Process Analysis.* New York: Teachers College Press, 1971

Duffy, Gerald G., and Sherman, George B. "Improving Achievement Through Differentiated Instruction." In *Reading in the Middle School,* ed. Gerald G. Duffy. Newark, Del.: International Reading Association, 1974, pp. 117–129.

Durkin, Dolores. "The Little Things That Make a Difference." *Reading Teacher* 28, no. 5 (February 1975): 473–477.

Esposito, Dominick. "Homogeneous and Heterogeneous Ability Grouping — Principal Findings and Implications for Evaluating and Designing More Effective Educational Environments." *Review of Educational Research* 43, no. 3 (Spring 1973): 163–179.

Guthrie, John. "Grouping for Reading." *Reading Teacher,* 32, no. 4 (January 1979): 500–506.

Helton, George B., Morrow, Henry W., and Yates, James K. "Grouping for Instruction 1965, 1975, 1985." *Reading Teacher* 31 (October 1977): 28–33.

Martin, Lyn S., and Pavan, Barbara A. "Current Research on Open Space, Non-Grading, Vertical Grouping, and Team Teaching." *Phi Delta Kappan* 57, no. 5 (January 1976): 310–315.

Otto, Wayne, et al. "Organizing Learning Situations for Individual Differences." In *Focused Reading Instruction*. Reading, Mass.: Addison-Wesley, 1974, pp. 223–256.

Sartain, Harry W. "Organizational Patterns of Schools and Classrooms for Reading Instruction." In *Innovation and Change in Reading Instruction*. NSSE Yearbook 1967, ed. Helen M. Robinson. Chicago: University of Chicago Press, 1968, pp. 195–236.

Smith, James A. *Classroom Organization for the Language Arts*. Itasca, Ill.: Peacock Publishers, 1977.

Smith, Susan J. "DOGS — Designs for Organizing 'Gobs' of Students." Ed. 140249. *ERIC Resources in Education* 12, no. 11 (November 1977), p. 56.

## Chapter 4

Cordts, Anna D. *Phonics For the Reading Teacher*. New York: Holt, Rinehart and Winston, 1965.

Dechant, Emerald. *Linguistics, Phonics, and the Teaching of Reading*. Springfield, Ill.: Charles C. Thomas, 1969.

Durkin, Dolores. *Phonics, Linguistics, and Reading*. New York: Columbia University, Teachers College, Bureau of Publications, 1972.

Fries, Charles. *Linguistics and Reading*. New York: Holt, Rinehart and Winston, 1962.

Heilman, Arthur W. *Phonics in Proper Perspective*, 3rd ed. Columbus, Ohio: Charles E. Merrill, 1976.

Hull, Marion A. *Phonics for the Teacher of Reading*, 2nd ed. Columbus, Ohio: Charles E. Merrill, 1976.

Lamb, Pose. *Linguistics in Proper Perspective*, 2nd ed. Columbus, Ohio: Charles E. Merrill, 1977.

Lefevre, Carl A. *Linguistics and the Teaching of Reading*. New York: McGraw-Hill, 1964.

Wylie, Richard E., and Durrell, Donald D. "Teaching Vowels Through Phonograms." *Elementary English* 47 (October 1970): 787–791.

## Chapter 5

Anderson, Richard C., et al. "Frameworks for Comprehending Discourse." *American Educational Research Journal* 14, no. 4 (Fall 1977): 367–381.

Barnitz, John. "Toward Understanding Syntax in Reading Comprehension: Review of Resources." *Studies in Language Learning* 1, no. 1 (Fall 1975), Urbana, University of Illinois.

Golinkoff, Roberta Michnick. "Comparison of Reading Comprehension Process in Good and Poor Comprehenders." *Reading Research Quarterly* XI/I, no. 44 (1975–76): 635–659.

Guthrie, J. T. "Reading Comprehension and Syntactic Responses in Good and Poor Readers." *Journal of Educational Psychology* 65 (1973): 294–299.

Haviland, S. E., and Clark, H. H. "What's New? Acquiring New Information as a Process in Comprehension." *Journal of Verbal Learning and Verbal Behavior* 13 (1974): 515–521.

Jund, Suzanne, ed. "Focus on Comprehension." *Wisconsin State Reading Association Journal* 22, no. 1 (March 1978): 2–76.

Kamil, Michael. "Models of Reading: What Are the Implications for Instruction in Comprehension?" In *Aspects of Reading Education.* Berkeley, Calif.: McCutchan, 1978, pp. 63–88.

Paris, Scott G., and Brooks, Penelope. *Cognitive Factors in Children's Listening and Reading Comprehension.* Nashville, Tenn.: George Peabody College for Teachers, February 1977.


## Chapter 6

*Study Skills*

Atwood, Beth S. *Building Independent Learning Skills.* Palo Alto, Calif.: Learning Handbooks, 1974.

Feeman, George F. "Reading and Mathematics." *Arithmetic Teacher* (November 1973): 523–529.

Lees, F. "Mathematics and Reading." *Journal of Reading* 19 (May 1976): 621–626.

Robinson, H. A. *Teaching Reading and Study Strategies: The Content Areas.* Boston: Allyn and Bacon, 1975.

Snoddy, James E. "Improving Study Skills: A Review of Selected Research." In *Views on Elementary Reading,* ed. Thomas C. Barrett. Newark, Del.: International Reading Association, 1973, pp. 81–87.

Walker, James E. "Techniques for Developing Study Skills." In *Reading in the Middle School,* ed. Gerald G. Duffy. Newark, Del.: International Reading Association, 1974, pp. 175–182.

*Reading in Content Areas*

Dunlin, Kenneth. "Teaching and Evaluating Reading in the Content Areas." In *Views on Elementary Reading Instruction,* ed. Thomas C. Barrett. Newark, Del.: International Reading Association, 1972, pp. 73–80.

Herber, Harold L. *Teaching Reading in Content Areas.* Englewood Cliffs, N.J.: Prentice-Hall, 1970.

Laffey, J. L., ed. *Reading in Content Areas.* Newark, Del.: International Reading Association, 1972.

Lunstrum, John P., ed. "Improving Reading Skills." *Social Education* 42, no. 1 (January 1978).

Palmer, W. W. "Teaching Reading in Content Areas." *Journal of Reading* 19 (October 1975): 43–51.

Shepherd, D. C. *Effective Reading in Science.* New York: Harper and Row, 1960.

Stanchfield, J. M. "Teaching Content-Area Reading: Readiness, Motivation, and Questioning Techniques." *Educational Horizons* 55 (Spring 1977): 119–123.

Thomas, E. L., and Robinson, H. A. *Improving Reading in Every Class: A Sourcebook for Teachers.* Boston: Allyn and Bacon, 1972.

*Critical Reading*

Clary, Linda Mixon. "How Well Do You Teach Critical Reading?" *Reading Teacher* 31, no. 2 (November 1977): 142–146.

Duquette, Raymond. "Critical Reading — Can It Be Taught?" *Elementary English* 50 (1973): 925–928.

Flower, F. D. *Reading to Learn: An Approach to Critical Reading.* Cambridge, England: National Extension College, British Broadcasting Corporation, 1970.

King, Martha L., Ellinger, Bernice, and Wolf, Willavene. *Critical Reading: A Book of Readings.* Philadelphia: Lippincott, 1967.

Larter, S. J., and Taylor, P. A. "A Study of Aspects of Critical Thinking" *Manitoba Journal of Education* 5 (1969): 35–53.

Schnell, Thomas R. "Identifying the Basic Elements of Critical Reading" *Reading Horizons* 19, no. 1 (Fall 1978): 34–39.

## Chapter 7

*Readiness Instruction*

Calfee, R., Chapman, R., and Venezky, R. "How a Child Needs to Think to Learn to Read." In *Cognition in Learning and Memory,* ed. Lee W. Gregg. New York: Wiley, 1972.

Gibson, E., and Levin, H. "The Development of Prereading Skills." In *Psychology of Reading.* Cambridge, Mass.: MIT Press, 1975, pp. 227–261.

Hoskisson, K. "Reading Readiness: Three Viewpoints — Maturational, Behavioristic, Cognitive Psycholinguistic. *Elementary School Journal* 78 (September 1977): 44–52.

McDonell, G. M., and Osburn, E. B. "New Thoughts About Reading Readiness." *Language Arts* 56, no. 1 (January 1978): 26–29.

Ollila, L. "Reading: Preparing the Child." In *Reading: Foundations and Instructional Strategies,* ed. P. Lamb and R. Arnold. Belmont, Calif.: Wadsworth, 1976, pp. 272–320.

*Methods in Primary Reading*

Anderson, I. I., and Dearborn, W. F. *The Psychology of Teaching Reading.* New York: Ronald Press, 1952.

Arnold, R., and Miller, J. "Reading: Word Recognition Skills." In *Reading Foundations and Instructional Strategies,* ed. P. Lamb and R. Arnold. Belmont, Calif.: Wadsworth, 1976, pp. 321–360.

Ashton-Warner, S. *Teacher.* New York: Simon and Schuster, 1963.

Biemiller, A. "The Development of the Use of Graphic and Contextual Information as Children Learn to Read." *Reading Research Quarterly* 6 (1970): 75–96.

Chall, J. S. *Learning to Read: The Great Debate.* New York: McGraw-Hill, 1967.

Downing, J. "Alternative Teaching Methods in I.T.A." *Elementary English* 45 (1968): 942–951.

Gleitman, L. R., and Rozin, P. "Teaching Reading by Use of a Syllabary." *Reading Research Quarterly* 8, no. 4 (Summer 1973): 447–484.

Kavale, K., and Schreiner, R. "Psycholinguistic Implications for Beginning Reading Instruction." *Language Arts* 55, no. 1 (January 1978): 34–40.

Kevfoot, J., ed. *First Grade Reading Programs. Perspectives in Reading,* no. 5. Newark, Del.: International Reading Association, 1965.

Mason, G., McDaniel, H., and Callaway, B. "Relating Reading and Spelling: A Comparison of Methods." *Elementary School Journal* 74, no. 6 (1974): 381–386.

*Teaching Reading Comprehension in the Middle Grades*

Aull, M. W. "Relating Reading Comprehension and Writing Competency." *Language Arts* 52 (1975): 808–812.

Blackowicz, C. L. Z. "Semantic Constructivity in Children's Comprehension." *Reading Research Quarterly* 8, no. 2 (1977–78): 188–199.

Cox, J. "Comprehension Revisited." *English Journal* 66, no. 7 (October 1977): 66–82.

Doctorow, M., Wittrock, M. C., and Marks, C. "Generative Processes in Reading Comprehension." *Journal of Educational Psychology* 70 (April 1978): 109–118.

Flood, J., and Lapp, D. "Inferential Comprehension: A Grand Illusion." *Language Arts* 55, no. 2 (February 1978): 188–191.

Guszak, F. "Teachers' Questions and Levels of Reading Comprehension." In *The Evaluation of Childrens' Reading Achievement. Perspectives in Reading,* no. 8. Newark, Del.: International Reading Association, 1967, pp. 97–110.

Jenkins, J. R., and Pany, D. "Teaching Reading Comprehsnsion in the Middle Grades." ERIC No. Ed. 151 756 (January 1978).

Lanier, R. J., and Davis, A. P. "Developing Comprehension Through Teacher-made Questions." *Reading Teacher* 26 (1972): 153–157.

Manzo, A. V. "Guided Reading Procedures." *Journal of Reading* 18 (1975): 287–291.

Olshavsky, J. E. "Reading as Problem Solving: An Investigation of Strategies." *Reading Research Quarterly* 12, no. 4 (1976–77): 654–675.

Schell, L. M. "Promising Possibilities for Improving Comprehension." *Journal of Reading* 15 (1972): 415–424.

Smith, F. *Understanding Reading.* 2nd ed. New York: Holt, Rinehart and Winston, 1978.

*Teaching Study Skills and Critical Reading*

Berg, P. C., and Rental, V. M. "Improving Study Skills." *Journal of Reading* 9 (1966): 343–348.

Eller, W., and Wolf, J. G. "Developing Critical Reading Abilities." *Journal of Reading* 10, no. 3 (December 1966): 192–199.

Herber, H. C. "Study Skills: Reading to Develop, Remember and Use Ideas." In *Reading in the Content Areas.* Syracuse, N.Y.: Syracuse University, 1969, pp. 13–21.

Piercey, D. *Reading Activities in Content Areas: An Idea Book.* Abridged edition. Boston: Allyn and Bacon, 1976.

Robinson, H. A. *Teaching Reading and Study Strategies: The Content Areas.* 2nd ed. Boston: Allyn and Bacon, 1978.

Stauffer, R. G., ed. *Dimensions of Critical Reading: Proceedings of the Annual Education and Reading Conference.* Vol. 11. Newark, Del.: University of Delaware, 1964.

Vacca, R. T. "Readiness to Read Content Area Assignments." *Journal of Reading* 20, no. 5 (February 1977): 387–392.

Wagener, E. H. "Recipe for Reading Comprehension." *Journal of Reading* 20, no. 6 (March 1977): 498–502.

## Chapter 8

Barrett, T. "Predicting Reading Achievement Through Readiness Tests." In *Measurement and Evaluation Readings,* ed. R. Farr. New York: Harcourt, Brace and World, 1970.

Bormuth, J. R. "Factor Validity of Cloze Tests as Measures of Reading Comprehension." *Reading Research Quarterly* 4 (1969): 358–365.

Burnett, R. W. "The Diagnostic Proficiency of Teachers of Reading." In *Measurement and Evaluation Readings,* ed. R. Farr. New York: Harcourt, Brace and World, 1970.

Buros, O. K., ed. *Reading Tests and Reviews.* Highland Park, N.J.: Gryphon Press, 1968.

Buros, O. K. *Seventh Mental Measurements Yearbook.* Highland Park, N.J.: Gryphon Press, 1972.

Chall, J. S. *Reading 1967–1977: A Decade of Change and Promise.* Bloomington, Ind.: Phi Delta Kappa Educational Foundation, 1977.

Cheyney, F. R. "The Informal Reading Inventory: How to Construct It, How to Use It." In *Readings on Teaching Reading,* ed. S. L. Sebesta and C. J. Wallen. Chicago, Ill.: Science Research Associates, 1972.

Goodman, K. S., ed. *Miscue Analysis.* Urbana Ill.: ERIC/RCS and National Council of Teachers of English, 1973.

Goodman, K. S., and Goodman, Y. M. "Learning about Psycholinguistic Processes by Analyzing Oral Reading." *Harvard Educational Review* 47 (1977): 317–333.

Guszak, F. J. *Diagnostic Reading Instruction in the Elementary School.* New York: Harper and Row, 1972.

Johnson, D. D., and Pearson, P. D. "The Weakness of Skills Management Systems." *Reading Teacher* 28 (1975): 757–764.

Johnson, M. S. "Reading Inventories for Classroom Use." In *Measurement and Evaluation Readings.*, ed. R. Farr. New York: Harcourt, Brace and World, 1970.

King, M. "Evaluating Reading." *Theory Into Practice* 16 (1977): 417–418.

McCracken, R. A. "The Informal Reading Inventory as a Means of Improving Instruction." In *The Evaluation of Children's Reading Achievement,* ed T. C. Barrett. Newark, Del.: International Reading Association, 1967.

Ransom, G. A. *Preparing to Teach Reading.* Boston: Little, Brown, 1978.

Tuinan, J. J., ed. *Review of Diagnostic Reading Tests.* Newark, Del.: International Reading Association, 1976.

Zutel, J. B. "Teacher Informed Response to Reader Miscue." *Theory Into Practice* 16 (1977): 384–391.

## Chapter 9

Allen, K. Eileen. "The Least Restrictive Environment: Implications for Early Childhood Education." *Educational Horizons* 56, no. 1 (Fall 1977): 34–41.

Bateman, Barbara. "Teaching Reading to Learning Disabled Children." In *Theory and Practice of Early Readers.* Hillsdale, N.J.: Lawrence Erlbaum Associates, 1978.

Becker, W. C. *Parents Are Teachers.* Champaign, Ill.: Research Press, 1971.

Bettleheim, Bruno. *The Uses of Enchantment.* New York: Vintage Books, 1976.

Blumenfield, S. L. *The New Illiterates — and How to Keep Your Child from Becoming One.* New Rochelle, N.Y.: Arlington House, 1974.

Bruiniks, Virginia L. "Designing Instructional Activities for Students with Language Learning Disabilities." *Language Arts* 55, no. 2 (February 1978): 154–160.

Canney, George. "Reading Problems — Prevention Rather than Cure." *Reading Horizons* 18, no. 1 (Fall 1977): 7–13.

Coles, Gerald S. "The Learning-Disabilities Test Battery: Empirical and Social Issues." *Harvard Educational Review* 48, no. 3 (August 1978): 313–340.

Fehl, Shirley. "Reading That Makes a Difference." In *Classroom Practice in Reading,* ed. Richard A. Earle. Newark, Del.: International Reading Association, 1977, pp. 57–64.

Gilford, Valerie. "Paraprofessionals in Reading Programs: A Survey." *Paraprofessional Today,* vol. 1, *Education,* ed. Alan Gartner, Frank Riesmann, and Vivian Carter Jackson. New York: Human Sciences Press, 1977.

Haring, Norris G., and Bateman, Barbara. *Teaching the Learning Disabled Child.* Englewood Cliffs, N.J.: Prentice-Hall, 1977.

Haring, Norris G., and Schiefelbush, R. L., eds. *Teaching Special Children.* New York: McGraw-Hill, 1976.

Harris, A. J. "Practical Applications of Reading Research." *Reading Teacher* 29, no. 6 (1976): 559–565.

Hewett, Frank M., and Taylor, Frank D. *Emotionally Disturbed Learners in the Schools.* Boston: Allyn and Bacon, 1979.

Lerner, J. W. *Children with Learning Disabilities,* 2nd ed. Boston: Houghton Mifflin, 1976.

Otto, Wayne, Peters, Nathaniel A., and Peters, Charles W. *Reading Problems: A Multidisciplinary Perspective.* Reading, Mass.: Addison-Wesley, 1977.

Piper, Terrence, and Power, Rosemary Hahn. "Motivating the Slow Reader." *Academic Therapy* 12, no. 3 (Spring 1977): 357–361.

Richardson, Carmen C. "Rediscovering the Center in Children's Literature." *Language Arts* 55, no. 2 (February 1978): 138–145.

Richek, Margaret Ann. "Learning Disabilities and Remedial Reading." In *Aspects of Reading,* ed. Susanna Pflaum-Connor. Berkeley, Calif.: McCutchan, 1978, pp. 188–217.

Traver, Sara G., and Dawson, Margaret M. "Modality Preferences and the Teaching of Reading: A Review." *Journal of Learning Disabilities* 11, no. 1 (January 1978): 5–17.

Van Etten, Glen, Van Etten, Carlene, and Watson, Bill. "Reading Comprehension: An Overview of the Concept and a Review of Materials." *Journal of Learning Disabilities* 11, no. 1 (January 1978): 30–39.

Vernon, Magdalen D. "Varieties of Deficiency in the Reading Process." *Harvard Educational Review* 47, no. 3 (August 1977): 396–410.

## Chapter 10

Baratz, J. C. "The Relationship of Black English to Reading: A Review of Research." In *Language Differences: Do They Interfere?* ed. J. Laffey and R. Shuy. Newark, Del.: International Reading Association, 1973.

Cornejo, Ricardo. "Reading in the Bilingual Classroom: Methods, Approaches, Techniques, and the Transfer of Knowledge." In *Reading — The Teaching Learning Process,* 39th Yearbook. Claremont, Calif.: Claremont Reading Conference, 1975, pp. 107–113.

De Stefano, J. S., ed. *Language, Society, and Education: A Profile of Black English.* Belmont, Calif.: Wadsworth, 1973.

Dixon, Carol N. "Teaching Strategies for the Mexican-American Child." *Reading Teacher* 30, no. 2 (November 1976): 141–146.

Foerster, Leona M. "Teaching Reading in Our Pluralistic Classrooms." *Reading Teacher* 30, no. 2 (November 1976): 146–150.

Harber, Jean R. *Black English: Its Relationship to Reading: An Annotated Bibliography.* Baltimore: University of Maryland, 1976. ERIC Ed. 132865.

Harber, Jean R., and Bryen, Diane N. "Black English and the Task of Reading." *Review of Educational Research* 46, no. 3 (Summer 1976): 387–405.

Lamberg, Walter J., and McCaleb, Joseph L. "Performance by Prospective Teachers in Distinguishing Dialect Features and Miscues Unrelated to Dialect." *Journal of Reading* 20, no. 7 (April 1977): 581–585.

Nava, Alfonso, R., and Sancho, Anthony R. "Bilingual Education: Una Hierba Buena." In *Reading: The Teaching Learning Process*, 39th Yearbook. Claremont, Calif.: Claremont Reading Conference, 1975, pp. 113–119.

Olsen, Bruce H. "Teaching Reading to Bilingual Students." *Journal of Reading* 20, no. 4 (January 1977): 346–349.

Onativia, Oscar, and Donaso, Maria Alejandra Reyes. "Basic Issues in Establishing a Bilingual Method." *Reading Teacher* 30, no. 7 (April 1977): 727–735.

Rigg, Pat. "Dialect and (in) for Reading." *Language Arts* 55, no. 3 (March 1978): 285–290.

Rodriguez, Norma. *Materials for Teaching Reading in Spanish.* West Hartford, Conn.: Hartford University College of Education, 1974. ERIC Ed. 106252.

————. *Methods for Teaching Reading in Spanish.* West Hartford, Conn.: Hartford University College of Education, 1974. ERIC Ed. 106251.

Valdes, Maria Elena. "Non-English Speaking Children and Literacy." In *Aspects of Reading Education.* Berkeley, Calif.: McCutchan, 1978, pp. 173–188.

## Chapter 11

Baker, A. "The Changing Image of the Black in Children's Literature." *Horn Book Magazine* 2 (1975): 79–88.

Botel, M., and Granowsky, A. "A Formula for Measuring Syntactic Complexity: A Directional Effort." *Elementary English* 49 (1972): 513–516.

Dykstra, R. "Selecting Basal Texts: Some Criteria to Avoid." *Educational Product Report* 2 (1969): 14–17.

*Educational Evaluation: Theory and Practice.* Vol. 2. New York: The Educational Products Information Exchange (EPIE) Institute, 1969.

Fry, E. "The Readability Principle." *Language Arts* 52 (1975): 847–851.

Holman, H. C. *A Handbook to Literature,* 3rd ed. Indianapolis, Ind.: Bobbs-Merrill, 1972.

Huck, C. S. "Literature as the Content of Reading." *Theory Into Practice* 16 (1977): 363–369.

Klare, G. R., "Assessing Readability." *Reading Research Quarterly* 10 (1974–1975): 62–102.

Ladevich, L. "ERIC/RCS Report: Determining Literary Quality in Children's Literature." *Elementary English* 51 (1974): 983–989.

"McGraw-Hill Book Company Guidelines for Equal Treatment of the Sexes." *Elementary English* 52 (1974): 725–733.

*Selectors Guide for Elementary School Reading Programs.* Vol. 1, EPIE Report No. 82m. New York: The Educational Products Information Exchange (EPIE) Institute, 1977.

Stephens, E. C. "Guidelines for Evaluation: An Instructional Reading System." *Journal of Reading* 18 (1975): 528–530.

Tibbets, S. "Sex Differences in Children's Reading Preferences." *Reading Teacher* 28 (1974): 279–381.

Tyler, Louise L., Klein, Frances M., and Associates. *Evaluating and Choosing Curriculum and Instructional Materials.* Los Angeles, Calif.: Educational Resource Associates, 1976.

Wood, P. A. "Judging the Value of a Reading Program." *Journal of Reading* 19 (1976): 618–620.

# Index